THE GATHERING,

PERFECTION AND REDEMPTION OF ISRAEL

The True Believers in Messiah/Christ

Norman L. Heap
Virginia T. Heap

FIRST EDITION

Published by Family History Publications
5205 High Point Road
Greensboro, North Carolina 27407

Manufactured in the United States of America
ISBN: 0-945905-08-4

Dedication

To our children: David, Elisabeth, Paul, Glenn and Janet, and to our grandchildren: Carrie, Melissa, Michele, Matthew, Nathaniel, Adam, Natalie, Emily, Veronica, Savannah and Lucas.

We are pleased that all of our posterity, to date, have been born in the covenant. We express our confidence in them, that they will remember the Lord's blessings, and will remember and keep the promises they have made, or will make, with the Lord.

Acknowledgments

Translations of the Holy Scriptures are generally in the public domain. Nonetheless, the authors acknowledge The Church of Jesus Christ of Latter-day Saints, and The Reorganized Church of Jesus Christ of Latter Day Saints for quotations used from their respective scriptures.

Much help has been received from near life-time friend, church leader, and confidant, Richard Taylor, and from Alan Johnson, distinguished professor, former mission president and premier patriarch of the Bay area. They, and our son David, have read through portions, or all, of the manuscript, have suggested re-phrasing of some thoughts to improve clarity, and have recast others for our review and use. To all we are most grateful.

Abbreviations

Standard abbreviations for the books of the Bible and for Book of Mormon sources were used where warranted. Less well known abbreviations used include:

AEN - Adam, Enoch and Noah
AIJ - Abraham, Isaac and Jacob
HC - History of the Church
JSH - Joseph Smith History in the Pearl of Great Price.
JST - Joseph Smith Translation, Appendix in 1979 Bible edition.
MAJ - Moses, Aaron and Joshua
ROI - Redeemer of Israel
TSI - The Twelve Sons of Israel
PGP -Pearl of Great Price
D&C - Doctrine and Covenants
BD - Bible Dictionary, contained in the 1979 edition of The
       Church of Jesus Christ of Latter-day Saints publication of
       the King James Version of the Bible.
TPJS - Teachings of the Prophet Joseph Smith

THE GATHERING,

PERFECTION AND REDEMPTION OF ISRAEL,

The True Believers In Messiah/Christ

Chapter Titles and Pages

INTRODUCTION

The Gathering, Perfection and Redemption of Israel is the seventh volume of a seven book series about the Lord's covenant people beginning with Adam and Eve. Their choice to eat the fruit of the tree of knowledge of good and evil set in motion a series of events which were anticipated by God, the Eternal Father, and which established the need for a Redeemer or Savior of mankind, who was prepared for that role before the foundation of the world. Hopefully, this series of books will help readers to see more clearly the patterns Heavenly Father has established for teaching His children and the rewards or consequences that are associated with their individual choices of obedience or disobedience.

In the main, the books of this series focus on the testimonies of the leaders, and the people they led, of seven dispensations: Adam, Enoch, Noah, Abraham, Moses, Jesus Christ, who functioned as prophet of the dispensation of the Meridian of Time, during His earth life, and functions as Redeemer of mankind after His resurrection; and the seventh such leader, Joseph Smith, prophet of the dispensation of the Fullness of Time, the period in which we now live. In total, these seven books provide the reader with a comprehensive insight into a kind Father's dealings with His children in all dispensations of time with love, mercy and equity.

While the seven books are linked with seven dispensations, the titles differ somewhat to reflect an expanded view of what was going on during that time period. In hindsight, one can often see the "golden thread" of a singular message the Lord is teaching. In one's own life such clarity is not always apparent, because so many other things are going on. Similarly, the titles of the seven books take a more expanded view of the time period and the people involved.

Titles of the seven books may appear different from this focus in some cases because special emphasis is placed on Israel, the name given to Jacob and to the Lord's covenant people over the centuries,

i

following the covenant God established with men through Abraham, Isaac and Jacob/Israel.

Three of the books are entitled: **ADAM, ENOCH AND NOAH; ABRAHAM, ISAAC, AND JACOB** and **MOSES, AARON AND JOSHUA.** The remaining four are entitled: **THE SCATTERING OF ISRAEL; THE REDEEMER OF ISRAEL,** and **THE GATHERING, PERFECTION AND REDEMPTION OF ISRAEL, The True Believers in Messiah/Christ.** At this date, all have been published except **THE SCATTERING OF ISRAEL,** which is still in the process of development.

Picking up the story after the life, death, resurrection and ascension of the Savior, **THE GATHERING ...** foreshadows the need for a sixth restoration of the Gospel of Jesus Christ, and its seventh introduction to the world's people, the first introduction being through the prophet Adam. After setting forth the need for this final restoration, the elements essential to it are briefly described and discussed. Not intended as a comprehensive or authoritative book on the restoration, it hopefully does set the stage for a discussion of Israel as the Lord's covenant people, who are currently being gathered spiritually, and to some extent geographically, that the Lord might redeem all those who choose to enter a covenant with Him and keep its provisions.

For a more comprehensive treatment of the restoration, readers are referred to the many books on that subject published by The Church of Jesus Christ of Latter-day Saints, Deseret Book, Bookcraft, the Brigham Young University, its Foundations, and many other publishers.

The patterns of Heavenly Father's dealings with mankind are clear. He deals with His children through prophets and the making of covenants. Prophets of every era since Adam have prophesied about the last days, the restoration during that period, and the gathering of Israel. Doesn't it make sense that He, God, would follow the same pattern as in the past, and would call a prophet and put those who accept His words under covenant in this the last dispensation?

Not only does God, the Eternal Father, have a plan for each individual who comes to earth, which, if followed, will exalt him/her, He has a plan for His covenant people as a whole, called Israel; and it is the people of Israel who help carry out God's plan to share the Gospel with every nation, kindred, tongue and people, who help perfect the Saints or members of the covenant, and who help redeem the dead in an organized way.

The more we can know and understand about the way God deals with His children, the more we can be helped by the patterns established over time, and apply them beneficially to our lives.

Richard Taylor, near lifetime friend and confidant of the authors, and fellow Church member, suggests at least six patterns to which the authors have added a seventh: **(1) the cyclical pattern,** as seen among the children of Israel, of **obedience and disobedience;** of worshiping the true God and worshiping false God's or idols; **(2) the teaching pattern,** contained in the faith, repentance, baptism, and Holy Ghost sequence. We must recognize, accept, align ourselves, make a commitment or covenant, keep its provisions, and then we get the promises, blessings and knowledge from God.

Brother Taylor believes and the authors concur, the Lord requires us to follow **(3) a discovery pattern,** to prepare us for the "line upon line, precept upon precept" expansion of our knowledge. As the prophets have said, we must work out our own salvation. Yes, resurrection or physical atonement is an unconditional gift to all, but spiritual atonement is only for those who discover it, embrace it, and receive it. Heavenly Father has not sent His children down to earth for a mortal experience without signs and guides, that give them the opportunity if they will recognize it, to find the way home.

(4) The pattern of calling prophets to provide navigational insights for God's children who are looking for landmarks and headings to chart their course. For example, there is a clear pattern among Old Testament prophets of having personal experiences with the Lord to initiate their ministry. This serves as an ongoing reminder that God has the power, the capability and the desire to provide guidance to His children. It signals to us in all ages that God will establish an ensign through His prophets for us to follow.

Hence prophets are called by Deity to re-establish the truth, the priesthood or power to act for Him, and the ordinances necessary for His children to enter the covenants of salvation and eternal life. From the current missionary discussions we learn that God chooses witnesses called prophets, who teach the plan of salvation and testify of Christ's role in that plan. The Holy Ghost confirms the truth of what is being taught and the hearer is invited to obey.

(5) The pattern of limited acceptance. Unfortunately, the true Gospel of Jesus Christ, as spoken by the prophets, is mostly ignored or rejected by the people. Along with each restoration, prophets were called, but in most cases, they were not overly popular with the masses. These prophets delivered messages that most did not want to hear, and yet, they were true to their callings throughout their lives. The masses have traditionally not accepted the Gospel. They have opted for more convenient and self-serving belief systems.

Whatever the choices others may make however, the charge to Israel, the true believers in Messiah/Christ who have voluntarily entered a covenant with the Lord and to whom He refers to as His covenant people, remains constant: to help preach the Gospel to every nation, kindred, tongue and people, to help perfect the Saints or members, and to help redeem the dead, that all may have the opportunity for salvation, exaltation and eternal life.

(6) The pattern of choices or two voices. In the Garden of Eden, Adam walked and talked with God. He was taught the Gospel by its author. He understood the plan included a mortal experience requiring personal choices. If we are to return to Father in Heaven, at the conclusion of mortality, we will need to have demonstrated our desire to inherit all He has, by making choices and living a life that is consistent with the desires, characteristics and attributes that will be required of us to live in the presence of God. Just as Adam had, each of us have at least two voices that give us choices.

Unfortunately, the closer we get to the last days, the more closely the counterfeit choices the adversary presents, look like those from Heavenly Father's plan, but nevertheless, we must choose which voice we will listen to. Our reward depends on it.

(7) The pattern of revelation from God to man, through His servants the prophets, evident in all dispensations. The prophets foreshadowed God's work and glory, the preeminence of agency or choice in the lives of each person made in the express image of God, the role His Only Begotten Son, yet to be born in the future, would play in bringing to pass an atonement or reconciliation; revelation, foreshadowing major future events, including the personal sojourn of God's Only Begotten Son on earth, twice, for finite periods of time, first in His humble birth, life, example, teachings, death on the cross, resurrection and ascension, and second: His return to earth in glory and majesty, when He shall redeem all mankind who have repented, have entered a covenant with Him and have kept its provisions.

Messiah/Christ, as Son of God the Father, will personally reign on earth for a thousand years, after the earth and its people have been cleansed, upgraded, improved and made worthy of His presence. Prophets in all dispensations have known and prophesied concerning these things. Past prophets were, and current prophets are, aware that a final upgrade of planet earth is necessary for it to become a celestial abode, a place worthy of the presence of both the Father and the Son, with whom those made in His express image have been judged worthy to dwell.

ALL THE FAMILIES OF THE EARTH TO BE BLESSED

From Adam to Abraham, Heavenly Father dealt with His children through the "fathers" the patriarchs, holding the priesthood or power to act for Him. These rights were passed from father to son. All were blessed through their family association starting with Abraham. As the children of men became more numerous, Heavenly Father numbered His children by their covenants with Him. Abraham is considered to the father of the faithful, or the one through whom the covenant with God was established by which all mankind would be blessed. This covenant continued through Isaac, then through Jacob, who later was called Israel. Through the house of Israel, or the twelve tribes, named after his sons, will all the faithful be blessed. Hence, through the seed of Abraham will God bless all of His children.

Because of the righteousness of Abraham and Sarah they were promised that through them all the families of the earth would be blessed. In the initial stages therefore, the descendants of Abraham and Sarah were those through whom the messages of the Gospel were spread throughout Abraham's world, but even then there were souls they had won who helped do the same. And so it was during and following Jacob/Israel 's days. Israel's twelve sons and their posterity, as members of Lord's people in the covenant, were given assignments in the form of blessings throughout the ages and have carried some of them out since.

The posterity of Israel and others entering a new and everlasting covenant with God in these last days, will continue to play a key role in assisting the Savior in redeeming all mankind. Chosen from those entering this new and everlasting covenant will be 144,000 high priests, 12,000 from each of the twelve tribes of Israel whose roles have not yet been revealed.

The first steps toward redemption are taken by exercising faith in the Lord Jesus Christ sufficient to bring about the desire to repent, followed by actual repentance; by entering the covenant through baptism, and by receiving the gift of the Holy Ghost, each ordinance having been performed by those having authority.

This pattern is important- we accept, we align, we enter the covenant and we receive help and assistance from God. We have to do something before God will give us more information. The choice is ours. This pattern is not new. The children of Israel followed a similar pattern in that they had to sanctify themselves before they could receive the blessings of the Lord or perform ordinances in His behalf. In this case, faith and repentance fill the same role as the sanctification process did for the children of Israel in Moses' day. Hence we see God dealing with His children in all periods of time with similarity and consistency.

The process of gathering Israel includes presenting the Gospel message and testifying of its truth, first, to the literal descendants of Jacob/Israel, generally, because Abraham, Isaac and Jacob/Israel and their wives obeyed the voice of God. Its presentation to the rest of the world follows in an organized way, the Lord's way.

Once a person not of Israel's lineage enters the covenant, he/she acquires that lineage by adoption and becomes the seed of Abraham and Israel. They, then, have like responsibilities to help take the message to every nation, kindred, tongue and people; to help perfect members in the covenant and to help redeem their and other kindred dead.

Interestingly, the unfolding of God's plan through this final restoration when the messages are to be spread throughout the earth, the technology, travel and communications capabilities necessary to complete this charge have been provided. During no other dispensation has man had the capability to do the things the ancient prophets foretold.

Gathering, perfecting and redeeming Israel will continue through the Millennium and the literal and adopted posterity of the tribes of Israel will have particular roles to play just before and immediately after the Savior comes a second and final time to recover His covenant people. This process has been foretold by all the major prophets since Adam and Eve. Regardless of the disobedience of man, God has regularly, in His patience and long suffering, restored the Gospel and allowed the operation of agency. This book is about the final restoration during the mortal probation of mankind, and the final gathering of God's covenant people Israel. It is also about the fulfillment of His plan to bless His children and prepare them to inherit all that He has.

As in all previous ages, God takes an active part in teaching, guiding, and directing His children without preempting individual agency or right to choose. Revelation is an ongoing pattern evidenced in every dispensation and should not be a surprise for this final dispensation.

The Gathering, Perfection and Redemption of Israel is inextricably connected to the restoration of the Gospel this final time and with the ushering in of the dispensation of the Fullness of Time, brought about by the gift and power of God through Joseph Smith.

A substantial portion of this book, therefore, is related to the restoration, and Joseph Smith's role in that restoration, his introduction of the gathering of Israel for and in behalf of God, his writings on the subject and the prophecies related to the roles gathered Israel, as the Lord's covenant people, will play just prior to the ushering in of the Millennium and shortly after.

Many scriptural references to the gathering, perfection and redemption of Israel are extant. Old and New Testament and Book of Mormon prophets knew and understood the scattering and eventual gathering of Israel would take place, including Abraham, Moses Isaiah, Jeremiah, Ezekiel, Nephi, Jacob, Paul and others. They will be cited and discussed in the pages ahead. Emphasized is the gathering, perfection and redemption of Israel through the sacrificial work of Jesus Christ, who delivered us from sin and redeemed us with His blood on condition of our repentance and His forgiveness. (Acts 20:28; Eph. 1:7; Col. 1:14; Heb. 9: 11-15; 1 Pet 1:18-19, 3:18; Rev.5:9; BD p. 360)

A FEW DEFINITIONS

ISRAEL

Israel is the name used to denote Jacob, son of Isaac, son of Abraham, through whom the covenant with Abraham was continued. The name Israel was given by the Lord to Jacob at Penuel (Gen 32:38) and again at Bethel (Gen. 35:10). Later, the name applied to Jacob's descendants and to their kingdom. (2 Sam 1:24, 23:3)

As the larger part, after the division of the kingdom, the northern tribes retained the name Israel, while the southern kingdom was called Judah. However, today, the land of Canaan where Abraham originally settled, is called Israel, where the Jews are still gathering. As explained by Paul (Rom. 10:1, 11:7; Gal. 6:16; Eph. 2:12), Israel means the true believer in Christ, regardless of lineage or geographical location.

GATHERED ISRAEL

When used to describe gathered Israel, the name Israel hereafter, is defined as those who are descendants of Abraham and Isaac through Jacob/Israel, as well as those adopted into the family of Abraham by entering the new and everlasting covenant set forth by Jesus Christ, of which portions of the original Abrahamic Covenant are still a part. (See Chapter 4, this book and BD p. 708)

Gathered Israel, in essence, is synonymous with Christ's true Church, whose members have entered a covenant with God, led by apostles and prophets under the direction of Jesus Christ, its chief cornerstone.

THE SCATTERING OF ISRAEL

Through the allegory of the olive tree, Book of Mormon

prophet Zenos teaches us the principle of the scattering and gathering of Israel. We are taught that they are not random events, but carefully planned by the master of the vineyard, with the outcome in mind. While most likely explained in logical terms by the observers of the world, the faithful will be able to recognize the hand of the Lord in action as He brings His marvelous work and a wonder to pass.

The Scattering of Israel means the scattering of Israel's descendants throughout the world, and it is the title of a book with that name which discusses that subject extensively. As a reminder, to set the stage for this topic, because of disobedience and idol worship, substantial numbers of the covenant people brought to their promised land Canaan, were scattered throughout the earth. Others were separated from the main body to protect them and their records from being polluted. Regardless of the reason for being scattered, the covenant blood has been mingled with essentially all nations, tongues and peoples.

THE GATHERING OF ISRAEL

Now, as we move to the gathering, essentially all can lay claim to the blood of Abraham and the covenant blessings of Israel. By entering the new and everlasting covenant, the literal and adopted seed of Abraham and of Israel, are candidates for God's blessings through faith in the Lord Jesus Christ, repentance, baptism by immersion and by receiving the Holy Ghost.

The Gathering of Israel in the last days refers to the gathering of Israel's literal descendants and other true believers in Messiah/Christ who have entered the new and everlasting covenant of salvation.

Just as Moses gathered the children of Israel out of Egypt, led them to Mount Sinai, placed them under covenant with God to live His laws, statutes and teachings, and ready them for entry into the promised land; so is scattered Israel of the last days to be gathered

x

into stakes of Zion throughout the world and placed under the covenant of salvation with God to live His higher laws as exemplified in the Sermon of the Mount. Living the provisions of the covenant will perfect His people prior to His coming and ushering in the Millennium, when the earth, as the promised land of Zion, will first be upgraded to a state worthy of the presence of the resurrected Son of God, a place akin to the Garden of Eden before the Fall. This upgrade is to be followed by another upgrade of the earth to a celestial glory, worthy of both God the Father and His Messiah-Son's presence.

Who then, could the Lord more appropriately send than Moses, to commence the gathering of Israel in the last days?

After the Lord appeared in glory to accept the Kirtland Temple as His house, He declared: "I am the first and the last, I am he who liveth, I am he who was slain: I am your advocate with the Father. After this vision closed, the heavens were again opened to us [said Joseph Smith] and Moses appeared before us, and committed unto us the keys of the gathering of Israel from the four parts of the earth, and the leading of the ten tribes from the land of the north." (D&C 110:4,11)

RESTORATION

Just as the term Israel has more than one related meaning, so does the term restoration. It can be used on several levels. When used in reference to an individual soul, "it means a return of the individual to the presence of God, and includes the reuniting of the physical body with the spirit."

When used in reference to the Lord's covenant people, Israel, "it means a re-establishment of the gospel of Jesus Christ on the earth in the last days with the powers, ordinances, doctrines, offices and all things as they existed in former ages", and "a return to something once present, but which was taken away or lost. It involves, for example, the renewal of the earth to its paradisiacal glory as it was before the fall of Adam."(A of F 10;c D&C 133;23-24 with Gen. 10:25; BD p. 761)

Restoration also means, "a gathering together of the house of Israel [the Lord's covenant people] from its scattered condition, thus it is frequently spoken of as the restitution [or restoration] of all things, as in Acts 3:19-21. The time in which all these things are accomplished is called the Dispensation of the Fullness of Times. (Eph.1:10;D&C 27:6,13)" BD p.761.

Whether gathering Israel from its scattered condition, the re-establishment of the gospel of Jesus Christ on the earth in the last days, or the renewal of the earth to its paradisiacal glory as it was before the Fall, the aim of each is to uplift individual souls and assist them to comply voluntarily with the requirements of the gospel which will return him or her to the presence of God.

ASSUMPTIONS AND HYPOTHESES

The fundamental assumptions and hypotheses of this book are:

1. That God's purpose, or work and glory, is to bring to pass the immortality and eternal life of all men and women;

2. That God raised up prophets, seers and revelators in all dispensations for the purpose of gathering the true believers in Messiah/Christ, perfecting them; redeeming them through Christ's atonement and eventually returning them to the presence of God in a perfected, exalted state;

3. That the Church, or Zion in the last days, its Temples and its scriptures, the Pearl of Great Price, the Book of Mormon, the Doctrine and Covenants, are the works and word of God. The Old and New Testaments are also the word of God as far as they are translated correctly. Revelation comes to the world through prophets, seers and revelators. They and living apostles, as testators, facilitate

the gathering of Israel, the true believers in Messiah/Christ, into the covenant; helping the gathered to perfect their lives as they live the covenant's provisions, preparing them and their dead, for redemption through the atonement of Christ. Eventually, the perfected and exalted will return to the presence of God in an organized way;

4. That the role of members in the covenant individually and collectively is to let their lights so shine before men and women that their good works, or lights may be seen by others, that they too, may glorify their Father in Heaven. Stakes of Zion are to arise and put on their beautiful garments, that others may be attracted to the covenant.

The authors assume full responsibility for the contents of this book, for the paraphrases of various words and works, for the order of direct quotations from scripture and other sources, and for any errors.

Norman L. and Virginia T. Heap
December 25, 1998

CHAPTER I

WHY ANOTHER RESTORATION?

Why was another restoration needed in the nineteenth century, since there had already been five restorations of the Gospel following the days of Adam and Eve?

Answers are multifaceted and lie in the nature of God, His work and glory, His relationship to His children and other creations, and in His plan of salvation intended for all. Though He has unconditional love for His children, He consistently has been no respecter of persons, judging each one entirely on the basis of his or her personal righteousness in the light of the totality of his or her circumstances. He will not preempt any individual's agency or right to choose, regardless of the dispensation into which they were born and lived or may live.

As in previous dispensations, the choices made by their forebears, resulted in the loss of the essential parts of Heavenly Father's plan of salvation for all; a loss which came through rebellion, disobedience and sin. With an established pattern of restoring the Gospel when His children lost it, why wouldn't the Lord provide the same opportunities to His children in this last dispensation when Israel is to be gathered and redeemed, as He did with His children in earlier dispensations? Even though He will not preempt the agency of His children, He will make sure they have an opportunity to choose for themselves. Thus all have an equal chance under Heavenly Father's plan, whether in this life or in the next.

Answers also lie in the need for the process of gathering and redeeming Israel to be based on a foundation of apostles and prophets, and upon the only true God and Jesus Christ whom He sent. The gospel ordinances required for salvation cannot be properly exercised without this authority.

From Paul we learn the primitive church was built upon a foundation of apostles and prophets with Jesus Christ as its chief cornerstone. (Eph. 2:19-21) However, by 325 A.D. this foundation of apostles and prophets with Jesus Christ as its chief cornerstone crumbled and disintegrated. As the first set of apostles and prophets died, or were killed by oppressors, the remaining decision-makers within the Primitive Church did not replace them, even though a pattern had been set for such a procedure at the time Matthias was called to replace Judas Iscariot. Succeeding primitive church organizations bore the names of many early Christians, but failed to bear the name of Jesus Christ, its original and only chief cornerstone.

This was a time when men in not knowing the answers, met in Nicea to decide without the benefit of God's input. By design or neglect they had already rejected apostles and prophets as the governing body of the Church. Historically, God has always communicated His nature, His attributes, plans, purposes, His work and glory through prophets, and during and after His earthly ministry, through apostles and especial witnesses. Without the apostles and prophets and the authority they received directly from Jesus Christ the Church collapsed into a state of apostasy. And when they took away the foundation of apostles and prophets and divine authority, replacing its chief cornerstone, Jesus Christ with the names of men for the Church, it became a church of a man, or of men, rather than the Church of Jesus Christ.

The restored Church had to be based on a foundation of apostles and prophets before the rest of the organization could be fitly framed and made ready to perform its functions, which includes readying the world for the Second Coming of Jesus Christ and assisting Him in the Gathering Perfection and Redemption of Israel, preparatory to ushering in His Millennial Reign.

Throughout time, God has chosen leaders and given them the guidance and authority they needed to choose others to participate in His work. During His personal ministry on earth He identified twelve special witnesses, called apostles, and said unto them: "Ye have not chosen me, but I have chosen you and ordained you..." (John 15:16) Jesus gave the apostles commandments by revelation through the Holy Ghost after His resurrection as we see in Acts 1: 1-3. He also gave them power to make replacements as needed.

With the death of Judas Iscariot, who hanged himself, the vacancy in the Twelve was yet to be filled, and with the departure and

2

ascension of Jesus Christ, the Holy Ghost was yet to fall upon them. To reiterate, Jesus continued to communicate with His Apostles even after His resurrection (Acts 1: 1-3), and among His last words to them before His ascension nearly two thousand years ago were: "But ye shall receive power, after that the Holy Ghost is come upon you: and ye shall be witnesses unto me both in Jerusalem, and in all Judaea, and in Samaria, and unto the uttermost parts of the earth." (Acts 1:8)

Through the process of revelation the vacancy in the Twelve was filled: "Beginning from the baptism of John unto that same day that he was taken up from us' (said Peter) must one be ordained to be a witness with us of his resurrection. And they appointed two, Joseph called Barsabas, who was surnamed Justus, and Matthias. And they prayed, and said, Thou Lord, which knowest the hearts of all men, Shew whither of these two thou hast chosen, That he may take part of this ministry and apostleship, from which Judas by transgression fell, that he might go to his own place. And they gave forth lots; and the lot fell on Matthias; and he was numbered with the eleven apostles." (Acts 1:22-26)

Shortly after, on the day of Pentecost the Holy Ghost fell upon them as promised. "And when the day of Pentecost was fully come, they were all with one accord in one place. And suddenly there came a sound from heaven as of a rushing mighty wind, and it filled all the house where they were sitting. And there appeared unto them cloven tongues like as of fire, and it sat upon each of them. And they were filled with the Holy Ghost, and began to speak with other tongues, as the Spirit gave them utterance..." Following these events Peter bore witness of the resurrection and many were converted

"...But Peter, standing up with the eleven, lifted up his voice, and said unto them ... Ye men of Israel hear these words: Jesus of Nazareth, a man approved of God among you by miracles and wonders and signs, which God did by him in the midst of you, as ye yourselves also know: Him, being delivered by the determinate counsel and foreknowledge of God, ye have taken, and by wicked hands have crucified and slain: Whom God hath raised up, having loosed the pains of death: because it was not possible that he should be holden of it... This Jesus hath God raised up, whereof we are all

3

witnesses. Therefore being on the right hand of God exalted, and having received of the Father the promise of the Holy Ghost, he hath shed forth this, which ye now see and hear ... Therefore let all the house of Israel know assuredly, that God hath made this same Jesus, whom ye have crucified, both Lord and Christ.

"Now when they heard this, they were pricked in their heart, and said unto Peter, and the rest of the apostles, Men and brethren, what shall we do? Then Peter said unto them, Repent and be baptized every one of you in the name of Jesus Christ for the remission of sins, and ye shall receive the Holy Ghost ... Then they that gladly received his word were baptized: and the same day there were added unto them about three thousand souls. "(Acts 2:1-41)

Shortly afterwards the mission and organization of the Primitive Church began to take shape founded on these apostles and prophets, and the fledgling church was off to a good start. After Paul was converted he would say there was one Lord, one faith and one baptism, (Eph. 4:5) and that He, Jesus "...gave some apostles, and some prophets; and some evangelists; and some pastors; and teachers; For the perfecting of the Saints, for the work of the ministry, for the edifying of the body of Christ ... That we henceforth be no more children tossed to and fro, and carried about with every wind of doctrine, by the sleight of men, and cunning craftiness, whereby they lie in wait to deceive; But speaking the truth in love, may grow up into him in all things, which is the head, even Christ." (Eph. 4:11-15)

While often misunderstood, Jesus gave the apostles, through Peter, the key to maintaining the Church in its intended state. He told Peter that the rock of revelation was the method for receiving guidance on choices and or changes in the Church. This was the same process that Peter was able to respond to the Lord's query, "Whom say ye that I am?"

The essential nature of revelation was also reinforced as the mechanism for knowing God's will in the conversion of Saul/Paul. Well after His ascension Jesus spoke to Paul and instructed him in what to do, (Acts 9:1-22) just as He did with Moses...(Exodus 4:6-10, see also Acts 1: 13, and Heb 5:4) One must also observe that the resurrected Lord did not answer all of Saul/Paul's questions. He was

4

sent to a local believer, Ananias. The same is true for each of us. The Lord will not solve all of our problems or meet all of our needs, but He will direct us and then we must seek more information and apply it to our life.

God revealed His will through His apostles and prophets, including Paul through his writings, and it soon became evident that preaching the Gospel to all the world, perfecting the Saints or members, and redeeming the dead were all part of the developing Church's mission. The Savior's charge to His apostles before His departure and ascension made clear the "work of the ministry" was to include preaching the Gospel to the uttermost parts of the earth, that is, to every nation, kindred, tongue and people. Through the Apostle Paul, Jesus made clear He had called leaders for the perfecting of the Saints, for the work of the ministry, and for the edifying of the body of Christ.

All who believed in Christ, repented and followed His example of entering the covenant through baptism were now under charge to become perfect as their Father in Heaven is perfect. This was the same charge that Abraham received, to become perfect. This they could only do this through Jesus Christ, who is the way, the truth, and the light, and no man cometh unto the Father except by Him (John 14:6) and through the mechanisms He put in place to bring perfection about. That is why the Church is important. It helps us learn of Jesus, make covenants with Him, practice His teachings, and mold our lives after the pattern of perfection, that we might be one, even as Jesus is one with His Father. Members of His church (those who have entered the covenant) are also under charge to participate in the work of the ministry, which includes preaching the Gospel to all the world, baptizing with authority in the name of the Father, and of the Son and of the Holy Ghost, and to edify the body of Christ through unity in thought, purpose and action, with Christ being Lord and God.

Essential to perfection is repentance. Again, our salvation is through Jesus Christ, to whom we are beholden and who has the power to remit and forgive our sins. Each person who continues in sin offends God, making it impossible to dwell in His presence. Because

5

such individuals are denied the presence of God, they are classified as spiritually dead. Paul wrote to the Romans that, "the wages of sin is death; but the gift of God is eternal life through Jesus Christ our Lord," and of course, to take advantage of the atonement brought through Jesus Christ, repentance is an essential ingredient to receiving forgiveness and mercy.

As each disciple repents and perfects his or her life, step by step, principle by principle, sin and error are reduced and eventually eliminated, and one becomes eligible for eternal life, as judged by the Savior, who paid the price for all of mankind's sins through His sacrifice. It is He who sets the standards which qualify individuals for eternal life. Each person who conquers sin conquers spiritual death, through Christ's atonement and this conquest gives meaning to Isaiah's words that he "will swallow up death in victory, and the Lord God will wipe away tears off from all faces" (Isa. 25:18).

Conquering sin requires more than lip service. To become perfect one must make and keep covenants with the Lord. Salvation is not a one step process. Becoming perfect requires us to align ourselves perfectly with the Savior. Repentance, baptism and receipt of the Holy Ghost start us on the covenant path back to God. These covenants and ordinances open the gate as Book of Mormon prophets Lehi and Nephi, said, and then we must stay on the straight and narrow path. Temple covenants allow us to increase our knowledge and improve ourselves through the endowment, a gift of knowledge, which we need to endure the trials of life. We must do more than bear our crosses in mortality. We must do many good things of our free will and choice through initiative, commitment and endurance.

Conquering sin also gives meaning to the Apostle Paul's words when he quoted Isaiah: "So when this corruptible shall have put on incorruption, and this mortal shall put on immortality, then shall be brought to pass the saying that is written, Death is swallowed up in victory. 0 death where is thy sting, 0 grave, where is thy victory? The sting of death is sin; and the strength of sin is the law. But thanks be to God, which giveth us the victory through our Lord Jesus Christ," (I Cor. 15:54-56), and thanks be to God it makes possible re-entrance into His presence. Sin which brings spiritual death was and is one of two major enemies of Israel and all the world. The Messiah or Savior did not come to save the house of Israel generally and the tribe of Judah specifically from their political and territorial enemies. Rather, He came to save them from their long term enemies: death and sin. But conquering sin requires effort and compliance on the part of every individual, and the help of a higher power, even the Savior. The other enemy is physical death.

In reviewing his own conversion, and while testifying as to the reality of the resurrection, Paul said in part: "If in this life only we have hope in Christ, we are of all men most miserable. But now is Christ risen from the dead, and become the first fruits of them that slept. For since by man came death, by man also came the resurrection of the dead. For as in Adam all die, even so in Christ shall all be made alive. But every man is his own order. Christ the first-fruits, afterwards they that are Christ's at his (second) coming. Then cometh the end, when he shall have delivered up the kingdom to God, even the Father, when he shall have put down all rule and all authority and power. For he must reign until he hath put all enemies under his feet. The last enemy that shall be destroyed is death." (Redeemer of Israel p 212-3, 1 Cor 15:19-26)

Physical death, as an enemy, has already been destroyed by Jesus Christ, who was the first-fruits of them that slept, and for many others whose graves were opened at the time of His resurrection. Resurrection is to be universal, entirely a gift from God's Son to mankind. However, the order in which each person is called from the grave, as well as the glory with which he or she is resurrected depends on his or her progress in perfecting his or her life, as judged by the Lord. Those who have made little or no progress in this perfection will be the last to be resurrected, hence Paul's comment, the last enemy that shall be destroyed is death. This is why a series of covenants have been provided. As we progress in our efforts to live the provisions of each covenant completely we increase our capacity to accept the effects of the atonement. Covenants help us to become '"perfect" so we can eventually receive all that God has. It can be easily suggested that covenants are the rungs of the ladder the angels

7

used to ascend and descend from heaven in the Jacob's ladder account by that ancient prophet.

The scriptures confirm that the Fall of Adam and the need for a Redeemer were part of an eternal plan anticipated by the Father, not a mistake or twist of fate for which another plan had to be developed. As part of the plan, to overcome spiritual death, the other enemy, one must meet the standards set by the Lord, which includes, first, faith in the Lord Jesus Christ, second, repentance, third, entrance into the covenant of salvation through baptism by immersion for the remission of sin, and fourth, the laying on of hands for the gift of the Holy Ghost. Then one can be timely resurrected to the glory s/he has earned through obedience and initiative.

A major portion of the work of the ministry, therefore, is to proclaim these four principles and ordinances: faith in the Lord Jesus Christ, repentance, baptism by immersion for the remission of sins, and the laying on of hands for the gift of the Holy Ghost, as essential prerequisites for returning, with Christ to the presence of God. Those accepting them and do what is required of them after baptism are "no more strangers and foreigners, but fellow citizens with the Saints, and of the household of God, And are built upon the foundation of apostles and prophets, Jesus Christ himself being the chief cornerstone;" (Eph 2:19) as Paul said, whose lives could now be perfected, and through that perfection each could overcome spiritual and physical death, and receive immortality and eternal life, through the atonement of Jesus Christ.

Just as God sought to get the children of Israel back into His presence long-ago by preparing them for that experience at the foot of Mount Sinai, so does He want to do the same for us by readying us for the return to His presence, as the time of His second coming approaches. We cannot be ready if we are in a sinful state. We are dependent on the Savior to take us back into God the Eternal Father's presence. To be ready for that experience we must be sanctified, just as Jehovah was attempting to sanctify the children of Israel at Mount Sinai at the time of Moses. Covenants, especially in the Temple, help sanctify us and prepare us to enter the presence of God.

It then becomes the responsibility of all who enter these

8

covenants with the Lord that they do all they can to help others receive the same promises and blessings including eternal life. Those entering the covenant become partners and joint heirs with Jesus in redeeming mankind as they help lead God's children into His presence. In the process the Gospel is be preached to the uttermost parts of the earth. All of God's children are to have the opportunity for themselves, whether in this life or in the next, for He is no respecter of persons.

Toward the end of His mortal ministry Jesus expressed concern for others who had not heard His messages, some who were living in far away lands, and those who had died without hearing His messages. In metaphor, He referred to Himself as the good shepherd, stating that the good shepherd giveth his life for the sheep, and that he had other sheep which were not of the Palestinian fold, "them also I must bring, and they shall hear my voice, and there shall be one fold and one shepherd." (John 10: 11- 16)

Jehovah as the pre-mortal Christ had previously made clear that there are more nations than one, that He had created all men and women and remembers them all, that He brought forth His word unto the children of men, even upon all nations of the earth, that he had caused His words to be written by the Jews, and by the Nephites, and that others throughout the world had also written it. (2 Nephi 29: 7-14) Disciples of Christ entering the covenant become the children of Israel and, as such, shoulder themselves with the yoke of a shepherd, helping Jesus redeem as many of His children as will respond. This is the role of Israel: for the faithful to participate in the great work of redemption.

From the Nephite account we read that Jesus indeed visited some of His sheep not of the Palestinian fold, and ministered unto them. Nephite forebears had been led from Jerusalem by the hand of the Lord some six hundred years before the Savior's mortal ministry, under the stewardship of Lehi, a prophet contemporary with Jeremiah, Ezekiel and Daniel. Lehi and his family brought with them their scriptures which included the five books of Moses and the writings of the prophets up through Isaiah, and some of Jeremiah's words. Later God would declare that His glory is intelligence and that man cannot be saved in ignorance. Knowing this from the beginning, God instructed Lehi to bring these records so that this prophet's posterity could know how God deals mercifully with His children, and that all His promises will be fulfilled for the faithful. Under command of God the posterity of Lehi added to these records, which included many prophecies of the coming of Christ, His death on the cross and His subsequent resurrection. These records also included an account of the Savior's appearances in the western hemisphere after His crucifixion and resurrection, some of which are reported here in abbreviated form:

"And it came to pass in the thirty and fourth year, in the first month on the fourth day of the month, there arose a great storm, such an one as never had been known in the land. And there was also a great and terrible tempest; and there was terrible thunder, insomuch that it did shake the whole earth as if it was about to divide asunder. And there were exceeding sharp lightnings, such as never had been known in the land... And there was great and terrible destruction in the land southward. But behold, there was a more great and terrible destruction in the land northward; for behold, the whole face of the land was changed.... and the highways were broken up, and the level roads were spoiled and many smooth places became rough. And many great and notable cities were sunk, and many were burned, and many were shaken till the buildings thereof had fallen to the earth ... And thus the face of the whole earth became deformed.

"...... when the quaking of the earth did cease, (after about three hours) ... then behold there was darkness upon the face of the land ... thick darkness ... inhabitants ... could feel the vapor of darkness ... there could be no light ... neither candles ... (nor) fire kindled ... And there was not any light seen. neither fire, nor glimmer, neither the sun, nor the moon, nor the stars it did last for the space of three days that there was no light seen; and there was great mourning and howling and weeping among the people continually ... they were heard to cry and mourn saying: 0 that we had repented before this great and terrible day, and had not killed and stoned the prophets and cast them out; then would our mothers and our fair daughters and our children have been spared.

[This is a pattern to look for at His Second Coming –sun shall be darkened, moon turned to blood, stars lose their shining. Then after the cleansing comes the Savior, the light and life of the world. The most wicked have already lost their lives, the more righteous spared]

"... And it came to pass there was a voice heard ... crying, Wo, wo, wo unto this people; wo unto the inhabitants of the whole earth except they shall repent ... because of their iniquity and abominations they are fallen! ... 0 all ye that are spared because ye are more righteous than they, will ye not now return unto me, and repent of your sins and be converted, that I may heal you? Yea, Verily, I say unto you, if ye will come unto me ye shall have eternal life. Behold, mine arm of mercy is extended towards you, and whosoever will come, him will I receive; and blessed are those who come unto me.

"Behold, I am Jesus Christ, the Son of God, I created the heavens and earth, and all things that in them are. I was with the Father from the beginning. I am in the Father, and the Father in me; and in me hath the Father glorified his name. I came unto my own, and my own received me not. And the scriptures concerning my coming are fulfilled. And as many as have received me, to them have I given to become the sons of God; and even so will I do to as many as shall believe on my name, for behold, by me redemption cometh, and in me is the law of Moses fulfilled. I am the light and life of the world. I am Alpha and Omega, the beginning and the end.

"And ye shall offer up unto me no more shedding of blood; yea your sacrifices and your burnt offerings shall be done away, for I will accept none of your sacrifices and your burnt offerings. And ye shall offer for a sacrifice unto me a broken heart and a contrite spirit. And whoso cometh unto me with a broken heart and a contrite spirit, him will I baptize with fire and with the Holy Ghost ... Behold, I have come unto the world to bring redemption unto the world, to save the world from sin. Therefore, whoso repenteth and cometh unto me as a little child, him will I receive, for as such is the kingdom of God. Behold, for such have I laid down my life, and have taken it up again; therefore repent, and come unto me ye ends of the earth and be saved." (3 Nephi 8:5-25, 9:1-22)

11

"And it came to pass that thus did the three days pass away. And it was in the morning and the darkness dispersed from off the face of the land, and the earth did cease to tremble, and the rocks did cease to rend, and the dreadful groanings did cease, and all the tumultuous noises did pass away. And the earth did cleave together again, that it stood; and the mourning and the weeping and the wailing of the people who were spared alive did cease; and their mourning was turned to joy, and their lamentations into praise and thanksgiving unto the Lord Jesus Christ, their Redeemer. And thus far were the scriptures fulfilled which had been spoken by the prophets. ... And it came to pass ... after the ascension of Jesus Christ into heaven he did truly manifest himself unto them- Showing his body unto them, and ministering unto them; and an account of his ministry shall be given hereafter..." (3 Nephi 10:9-19)

Heavenly Father testified of His Beloved Son about six weeks after the Son's resurrection, when a great multitude gathered together of the people of Nephi, round about the temple which was in the land Bountiful. The wicked of the land had been destroyed and the remaining righteous "were also conversing about this Jesus Christ of whom the sign had been given concerning his death ... while they thus were conversing, they heard a voice as if it came out of heaven ... it was not a harsh voice, neither was it a loud voice, -notwithstanding it being a small voice it did pierce them that did hear to the very center... it did pierce them to the very soul and it did cause their hearts to burn ... They heard the voice, and they understood it not ... And behold, the third time they did understand the voice which they heard; and it said unto them: Behold my Beloved Son, in whom I am well pleased, in whom I have glorified my name- hear ye Him ... as they understood they cast their eyes up towards heaven and behold, they saw a Man descending out of heaven; and he was clothed in a white robe; and he came down and stood in the midst of them ... he stretched forth his hand saying: Behold, I am Jesus Christ, whom the prophets testified shall come into the world.

"And behold, I am the light and life of the world, and I have drunk of that bitter cup which the Father hath given me, and have glorified the Father in taking upon me the sins of the world, in the which I have suffered the will of the Father in all things from the beginning.

"... the whole multitude fell to the earth, for they remembered it had been prophesied among them that Christ should show himself unto them after his ascension into heaven. And it came to pass that the Lord spake unto them saying: Arise and come forth unto me, that ye may thrust your hands into my side, and also that ye may feel the prints of the nails in my hands and in my feet; that ye may know that I am the God of Israel, and the God of the whole earth, and have been slain for the sins of the world.

"And it came to pass that the multitude went forth, and thrust their hands into his side, and did feel the prints of the nails in his hands and in his feet; and this they did do, going forth one by one until they had all gone forth, and did see with their eyes and did feel with their hands, and did know of a surety and did bear record, that it was he, of whom it was written by the prophets, that should come. And when they had all gone forth and had witnessed for themselves, they did cry with one accord, saying: Hosanna! Blessed is the name of the Most High God! And they did all fall down at the feet of Jesus, and did worship him. " (3 Nephi 11: 1- 17)

Following these experiences Jesus used the same pattern as before. He called leaders. He gave them authority and power. He instructed them to teach the four basic principles and ordinances to the people: faith, repentance, baptism, and the gift of the Holy Ghost. He prepared them so the Church could continue after He, as Savior, departed. In so doing He called forth a western hemisphere leader, instructed him and the multitude in doctrine, gave them power, authority and a charge to go forth among the people and declare His messages unto them.

" ... he (Jesus) spake unto Nephi and commanded him that he should come forth ... And the Lord said unto him: I give unto you power that ye shall baptize this people when I am again ascended into heaven. And again, the Lord called others and said unto them likewise ... And he said unto them: On this wise shall ye baptize, ... Behold, ye shall go down and stand in the water, and in my name, shall ye baptize them ... these are the words which ye shall say,

13

calling them by name, saying: Having authority given me of Jesus Christ, I baptize you in the name of the Father, and of the Son and of the Holy Ghost, Amen. And then shall ye immerse them in the water, and come forth again out of the water." (3 Nephi 11: 18-26) ...

"And this is my doctrine and it is the doctrine which the Father hath given me; and I bear record of the Father, and the Father beareth record of me, and the Holy Ghost beareth record of the Father and me; and I bear record that the Father commandeth all men everywhere, to repent and believe in me. And whosoever believeth in me, and is baptized, the same shall be saved; and are they who shall inherit the kingdom of God. And whoso believeth not in me, and is not baptized, shall be damned." (3 Nephi 11:32-34)

All those who follow the Savior are free to progress. Obedience is an eternal principle of freedom. Those who reject the Savior's and Father's plan are damned, or stopped in the ability to return to the presence of God.

Continuing, the Savior said:

"Verily, verily, I say unto you, that this is my doctrine, and I bear record of it from the Father; and whoso believeth in me believeth in the Father also; and unto him will the Father bear record of me, for he will visit him with fire and with the Holy Ghost. And thus will the Father bear record of me, and the Holy Ghost will bear record unto him of the Father and me; for the Father, and I, and the Holy Ghost are one", confirming they are three separate personages , but are of one mind, heart and purpose .

"And again I say unto you, ye must repent, and become as a little child, and be baptized in my name, or ye can in no wise receive these things. And again I say unto you, ye must repent, and be baptized in my name, and become as a little child, or ye can in no wise inherit the kingdom of God. Verily, verily, I say unto you this is my doctrine, and whoso buildeth upon this buildeth upon my rock, and the gates of hell shall not prevail against them." [We must rid ourselves of pride and arrogance to demonstrate our dependence upon the Savior for our redemption. We cannot do it ourselves.]

"And whoso shall declare more or less than this, and establish it for my doctrine, the same cometh of evil, and is not built upon my rock, but he buildeth upon a sandy foundation, and the gates of hell stand open to receive such when the floods come and the winds beat upon them. Therefore, go forth unto this people and declare the words I have spoken unto the ends of the earth." (3 Nephi 11:34-41)

After this Jesus called forth the twelve who received power and authority to baptize, spake unto Nephi and commanded him, the twelve and the multitude: ...

"Blessed are ye if ye shall give heed unto the words of these twelve whom I have chosen from among you to minister unto you, and to be your servants; and unto them I have given power that they may baptize with water, and after that ye are baptized with water, behold, I will baptize you with fire and with the Holy Ghost; therefore, blessed are ye if ye shall believe in me and be baptized, after that ye have seen me and know that I am.

" And again, more blessed are they who shall believe in your words because that ye shall testify that ye have seen me, and that ye know that I am. Yea, blessed are they who shall believe in your words, and come down into the depths of humility and be baptized, for they shall be visited with the Holy Ghost, and shall receive a remission of their sins." (3 Nephi 12:1-3)

Note the importance the Savior placed on faith and obedience. Those who would believe in the testimony of the Apostles would receive the Holy Ghost. He indicated that those who would believe without seeing would be more blessed than those who required proof or evidence.

Following these messages Jesus delivered a sermon nearly identical to the Sermon on the Mount given in Galilee during His mortal ministry with a few differences. Among the most notable were:

"Therefore those things which were of old time, which were under law, in me are all fulfilled. Old things are done away, and all things have become new. Therefore I would that ye should be perfect even as 1, or your Father who is in heaven is perfect." (3 Nephi 12:46-48)

Now that He was resurrected. and glorified by the Father, with His work completely accepted by Deity, Jesus Christ was offered as a role model for all people to pattern their lives after, along side the Father. In another visit to these western hemisphere people, a short time later, it was made clear that He, Jesus Christ, sets the standards for judgment, and that people everywhere should strive to become like Him. He said: "And know ye that ye shall be judges of this people according to the judgment which I shall give unto you, which shall be just. Therefore, what manner of men ought ye to be? Verily, I say unto you, even as I am." (3 Nephi 27:27)

Jesus established His life as the exemplar. If we will do as He has done, we will be rewarded even as He will be rewarded, with all that the Father has. Centuries earlier Jehovah, as the pre-mortal Christ, said unto Abraham when he was ninety and nine years old: "I, the Almighty God, give unto thee a commandment that thou shalt walk uprightly before me and be perfect." (JST Genesis 17: 1) This command was part of the covenant Abraham made with Jehovah then, and has continued as part of the covenant each disciple of Christ makes when he or she is baptized and receives the Holy Ghost. To achieve a state of perfection meeting the Lord's standards, a higher law than the Law of Moses was needed for His disciples and/or for members of His Church. The higher law is exemplified in the Sermon on the Mount given in Galilee and reiterated to His covenant people in the western hemisphere after His ascension.

In living the higher law the Lord's disciples who have entered the covenant were and are expected to replace selfishness, pride, envy, jealousy, licentiousness, haughtiness, anger, self aggrandizement, and compulsion with selflessness, humility, love, generosity, compassion, patience, chastity, self control, personal righteousness and persuasion. To walk uprightly before the Lord and be perfect, and to become as He is, as challenged, means lives were and are to be upgraded and improved, and to be ones of sacrifice, service, and consecration of self to a higher cause. Such goals and the achievement of them demonstrate worthiness to receive God's blessings, leads to true happiness, eternal life and being able to dwell in the presence of God.

Many more rich and enlightening things did Christ teach His covenant people in the western hemisphere about the gathering of

Israel and of His second coming yet in the future. Some of them will be reported in the chapters ahead.

Writing to the Galatians the Apostle Paul declared: "for ye are all one in Christ Jesus. And if ye be Christ's then ye are Abraham's seed and heirs to the promise ... Wherefore thou art no more a servant but a son; and if a son, then an heir of God through Christ." And to the Romans: " The Spirit itself beareth witness with our spirit, that we are the children of God. And if children, then heirs, and joint heirs with Christ; if it so be that we suffer with him, that we may be glorified together." (Gal 3:28-29, Romans 8:16-17) In other words, those who enter this covenant with the Lord and keep its provisions, become heirs and joint heirs with Jesus Christ and will inherit the many mansions prepared for them as He promised when He said: "In my Father's house are many mansions: if it were not so I would have told you. I go to prepare a place for you." (John 14:2)

Even so, we seem caught in a paradox. We must be like Jesus. We must seek to be perfect. We must adhere to the higher law, and yet we cannot achieve our goal of perfection ourselves without the grace of God through the infinite atonement that paid for our sins. After we have done all we can do we fall short of perfection. The difference is made up by His grace, if and when He finds us ready and worthy of exaltation and eternal life.

Not all who are made alive again through Jesus Christ will inherit these mansions. Inheritors of these mansions are heirs and joint heirs with their brother, Jesus Christ. Only those who choose to follow Jesus' teachings in word and deed, and perfect theirs lives to His satisfaction, inherit all that the Father hath, even eternal life.

REDEMPTION OF THE DEAD

For those already dead, faith in the Lord Jesus Christ and repentance in the spirit world is possible, but baptism for them has to be done on earth vicariously, as Paul alluded to when he said to those who understood the Gospel: " Else what shall they do which are baptized for the dead, if the dead rise not at all? Why are they then baptized for the dead?" (I Cor 15:29)

During His mortal ministry Jesus expressed concern for those who had died in sin or who had died without a knowledge of the Gospel, and He promised to take the Gospel to the dead in these words: "Verily, Verily, I say unto you, The hour is coming, and now is, when the dead shall hear the voice of the Son of God: and they that hear shall live. For as the Father hath life in himself, so hath he given the Son to have life in himself; And hath given him authority to execute judgment also, because he is the Son of man. Marvel not at this: for the hour is coming, in the which all that are in the graves shall hear his voice, And shall come forth, they that have done good, unto the resurrection of life; and they that have done evil, unto the resurrection of damnation." (John 5:25-29)

Though His body lay in the tomb three days, His spirit ministered among those in the spirit world who had laid their bodies down, as we see from the words of Peter:

"For Christ also hath suffered for sin, the just for the unjust, that he might bring us to God, being put to death in the flesh, but quickened by the Spirit: By which also he went and preached unto the spirits in prison; Which sometime were disobedient, when once the ark was a preparing, wherein few, that is, eight souls were saved by water."(1 Peter 3:18-20) "For, for this cause was the gospel preached also to them that are dead, that they might be judged according to men in the flesh, but live according to God in the spirit." (I Peter 4:6) Again we are taught the pattern. The plan is eternal and gives all of God's children an opportunity to exercise their agency. The dead, as we call them, are not dead to God. They are merely at a different stage preparatory for immortality and eternal life.

The Lord's work and glory, which is to bring to pass the immortality and eternal life of man, therefore, is intended to cover all the physically dead as well as the living. This means each candidate must receive the Gospel through the baptismal covenant, which is the covenant of salvation: salvation meaning being placed beyond the power of death and sin: and accept the ordinances and covenants of the higher or Melchizedek Priesthood, which were conferred upon Abraham by Melchizedek, and must enter into celestial marriage, which is the covenant of exaltation and eternal increase. This is God's plan for man, (Moses 1:39) as it was established before the world was created. In mortality, even though the gospel, priesthood and ordinances have been lost several periods over the eons of time through sin, in mercy to fulfill His plan, God has orchestrated restorations so all of His children can be judged by the same standards. These same principles apply to the dead [a mortal term], they too will have the opportunity to accept or reject God's plan to make sure all are treated fairly.

Vicarious work for the redemption of the dead was part of the Primitive Church's mission, but the major portion of this work was and is to be done in the Dispensation of the Fullness of Time, just prior to the Millennium, and the work will continue to be done during that thousand year period after the Savior comes a second time. From Malachi we read that Elijah the prophet, who held the keys of the sealing power, would play a key role in restoring that work to the earth when he declared: "Behold, I will send you Elijah the prophet before the coming of the great and dreadful day of the Lord: And he shall turn the heart of the fathers to the children, and the heart of the children to the fathers lest I come and smite the earth with a curse." (Malachi 4:5-6)

Though vicarious work for the redemption of the dead was introduced and practiced for a time in the Primitive Church, its purpose and practice was obscured and eventually lost after the apostles and priesthood were driven from the earth, and in its place appeared numerous theories and dogmas of men, many of which are utterly incomprehensible in their inconsistency and mysticism. (Articles of Faith, Talmadge p. 53)

The Gospel plan is the ultimate expression of love by our Heavenly Father. He has offered us everything. He has made certain that His message has been restored at least once each dispensation, and each time He allows us to choose. All of His children have the same opportunity to choose their inheritance, because God is no respecter of persons.

A TIME OF REFRESHING TO COME IS PROPHESIED

As the Savior ascended into heaven two men in white apparel stood by testifying: "Ye men of Galilee, why stand ye gazing up into heaven? this same Jesus, which is taken up from you into heaven, shall so come in like manner as ye have seen him go into heaven." (Acts 1: 11)

Some believed Christ's second coming would take place very soon, but many prophets and apostles knew otherwise and so prophesied. They knew a falling away and apostasy would occur prior to the Lord's second coming, and that a final restoration or time of refreshing would also precede it. They also knew this falling away was not a first, to be followed by a time of refreshing. From the days of Adam and Eve this cycle repeated itself several times. The Gospel was introduced to Adam and Eve, and through them to their posterity, but as their posterity grew numerous and spread over the land, and as Adam aged, many of the Lord s covenant people descended from Seth fell away.

The Lord restored the truth through Enoch. He successfully put together a city whose people lived a higher law, and the Lord rewarded them by elevating the whole city to a terrestrial state akin to the Garden of Eden before the Fall. However, those who were left behind, were, in the main, far from righteous. After several hundred years another restoration was required. Noah was the Lord's anointed this time. He preached the true Gospel and called the people to repentance, but only eight souls responded well enough to warrant their being saved from the Flood. After the Flood, Noah's family lived in righteousness for several generations and multiplied rapidly. As Noah grew very old and neared death, however, his posterity, in the main, turned to the worship of idols. Among the idol worshipers was Abraham's father Terah. Once again the Lord restored His true Gospel, this time through Abraham, who was put under a covenant which included a promise that his posterity would become numerous, would spread over the earth, and that through his seed all the families of the earth would be blessed in the latter days. If Abraham and

Sarah's posterity kept the covenant many blessings would also come to them. The covenant was extended to Isaac and his seed through Jacob, and to Jacob or Israel and his seed, and through Joseph and his brethren being the twelve sons of Israel and their seed. After Joseph's actions saved Israel and his family from the famine of bread, he invited them to live in Goshen, part of Egypt, with the Pharaoh's approval.

After Joseph's death and the deaths of his brethren, the children of Israel fell into physical and spiritual bondage in Egypt, beholden to their false gods or idols. Egyptian taskmasters enslaved the children of Israel physically and during the intervening years the God of Abraham, Isaac and Jacob/Israel took a back seat to Egyptian gods of wood and stone that could not speak, hear or deliver. By Moses' day the children of Israel were so beholden to the Egyptians and their idols, they had clearly fallen away from the Gospel Abraham, Isaac, and Israel and their twelve sons once knew; that another time of refreshing or restoration of the truth was needed. Moses was raised up to restore the truth, free the children of Israel from physical and spiritual bondage, and reintroduce them to the Abrahamic covenant.

If they lived the covenant, they would receive permanent protection and freedom from their long term enemies of death and sin. through Messiah/Christ. Messiah/Christ's delivery of Israel from the bondage of death and sin through an atonement was foreshadowed by Moses, who, with Deity's help, delivered the children of Israel from their physical and spiritual bondage in Egypt.

But they were not ready to live the higher law of the Abrahamic covenant, so a lesser law, the law of Moses or the law of carnal commandments took its place, of which the Ten Commandments are a part. This was the operable law until the ministry of Jesus Christ.

The pattern of men continues. The mercy of God continues. The gospel, priesthood authority and ordinances are introduced over and over. Man continues to worship false gods and moves from righteousness to physical and spiritual bondage. Regardless of the long suffering of God, the pattern of many men and women is repeated- pride, selfishness, greed, false gods, then bondage.

Jesus re-introduced the higher law during His ministry and restored His Gospel during His life, prior to His death and resurrection. After His resurrection and ascension, Jesus announced the Law of Moses had been fulfilled in His coming, that by Him redemption cometh, that there was to be no more shedding of blood of sacrifices, that he would accept no more sacrifices or burnt offerings, but in their place each person in the covenant should offer a broken heart and a contrite spirit, as each seeks to perfect his or her life, being under charge to become perfect, even as God the Father or Jesus Christ is perfect. The covenant observance changed from a public offering to a very private, even sacred and secret promise, evidenced only by how the individual conducts his life and treats others. Public offerings seem limited to participation in gospel ordinances such as baptism, confirmation and renewal of covenants at sacrament service etc.

It becomes clear that Jesus is the role model for all to pattern their lives after, but after His ascension the Savior would continue to need prophets and apostles on earth to help keep the people on track and through whom He would communicate His word and works: men holding the higher priesthood like Peter, James and John, and Paul who left many valuable messages orally and in writing. In other words, vacancies in the twelve would need to be filled on the death of the then existing council of twelve apostles, just like they did by appointing Matthias to take Judas' place, in order to keep the foundation of the Church in place and His Church fitly framed.

He also promised to return to the earth a second time, and again, through His prophets, foretold a final falling away, and a final time of refreshing or restoration, to take place before His second coming. Neither restoration or refreshment would have been necessary had many plain and precious truths and priesthood authority not have been lost through apostasy. At His second coming He will usher in His Millennial reign, and great numbers of people will be resurrected, as Ezekiel saw in his vision of the valley of dry bones, where these bones came together, were enveloped in flesh, covered with skin and the breath of life was once again breathed into them.(Ez. 37:1-12)

Great calamities are to precede His second coming. The earth is to be in commotion and the tares will be gathered and burned and the righteous still living will be caught up to meet Him. But before that day, a falling away from the truth established by the Savior Himself while on earth was foreshadowed, as was the time of refreshing and restoration, one last time. A comprehensive account of this falling away, or apostasy in and of the primitive Church entitled: **The Great Apostasy Considered In The Light Of Scriptural And Secular History**, by James E. Talmage, sets forth the interrelated causes for it. Only a few highlights of Talmage's work are paraphrased here.

External and internal causes contributed to the apostasy or falling away. Included in the disintegrating forces bearing down on the Primitive Church from the outside was the persistent persecution of the Saints connected with both Judaistic and pagan opposition.

Under this pressure many who professed membership deserted the Church. This defection of individuals resulted in a wide spread apostasy from the Church. [It should be noted that the gospel has always been embraced by a relative few, rather than many. Adhering to the gospel requires on-going choices, opposition and obedience. Even among those who have embraced the gospel, some have departed through the ages, because of the personal sacrifices that are required. Participating in the things of the world is usually more appealing and popular.]

Even more serious was internal dissension, schism and disruption which led to an absolute apostasy of the Church itself from the way and word of God. Christianity's earliest oppressor was Judaism, and Judaism's oppression instigated and abetted succeeding pagan atrocities and persecution. Those who dared to profess the name of Christ were subjected to inhumane cruelty and savage barbarity during these centuries of heathen domination. Such acts are accepted now as a matter of history.

A radical change was inaugurated in the attitude of the state toward the Church after Constantine the Great came to the throne about 325 A.D. Christianity of his time was made the religion of his realm. Zealous devotion to the Church was the surest way to get ahead under Constantine. Any remaining vestiges of genuine Christianity which had survived to this date were buried under the abuses that resulted from the elevation of the churchly organization to secular favor. The emperor Constantine made himself the head of the Church even though he was not yet baptized, making a mockery of the Savior's declaration: "Except a man be born of water and of the spirit he cannot enter the kingdom of heaven." (John 3:5) The internal causes of the apostasy by the Primitive Church included the corrupting of the simple doctrines of the Gospel of Jesus Christ by admixture with philosophic systems. unauthorized additions to the prescribed rites of the Church and the introduction of alterations in essential ordinances, and unauthorized changes in Church organization and government. These were the most important causes of the Primitive Church's apostasy. (Jesus The Christ pps. 745-757)

Demonstrated by the accepted records of divine dealing with man is that three individual personages physically distinct from each other comprise the presiding council of the universe. They are: God the Eternal Father, His Son Jesus Christ and the personage of the Holy Ghost. The plain and precious truths revealing the character and attributes of God taught by Christ and His apostles were lost after the apostles and their priesthood were driven from the earth, by persecutors, by councils appointed by the emperor, or who appointed themselves. Plain and precious truths which were part of the Primitive Church's teachings and practices were replaced with numerous theories and dogmas, many being incomprehensible; not the least of which is the Church of England's orthodox view of God-which is:

"There is but one living and true God, everlasting, without body, parts, or passions; of infinite power, wisdom and goodness."

The immateriality of God implicit in this and other declarations of sectarian faith are entirely at variance with the scriptures and are clearly contradicted by the revelations of God's person and attributes contained therein. If there is but one living and true God then that God cannot be Jesus Christ, because He repeatedly referred to Himself as the Son of God. On the other hand, if Jesus Christ is the one living and true God then He could not have a Father who is also God, because that would mean there is more than one true and living God. Contradictions of the only one and true living God theory espoused by the Church of England, other sectarian faiths and by the Roman Catholic Church derived from the Nicene and Athanasian Creeds are found in the scriptures themselves. For example:

Jesus Christ cried out,"My God, my God, why hast thou forsaken me", while on the cross. Are we to believe Jesus was talking to Himself? In the garden of Gethsemane, Jesus prayed three times, asking:"Father if thou be willing, remove this cup from me; nevertheless, not my will, but thine be done". Are we to believe Jesus was praying to Himself, and that He didn't want to do it, but would drink of the cup if He wanted Himself to? When Jesus prayed: "Father, the hour is come, glorify thy Son", was He asking Himself to glorify Himself? Jesus said: "The Father is greater than I? Are we to believe Jesus was greater than Himself? On the Mount of Transfiguration a voice from heaven declared: "This is My Beloved Son in whom I am well pleased." Are we to believe Jesus spoke from heaven declaring he was the Beloved Son of Himself? Many more examples could be cited.

With reference to the physical attributes of the resurrected Christ, when He appeared to His disciples they were affrighted thinking they had seen a spirit, but Jesus said unto them: "Why are ye troubled? and why do thoughts arise in your hearts? Behold my hands and my feet, that it is I myself: handle me, and see; for a spirit hath not flesh and bones, as ye see me have. And when he had thus spoken, he shewed them his hands and his feet. And while they yet believed not for joy, and wondered, he said unto them, Have ye here any meat? And they gave him a piece of a broiled fish, and of an honeycomb. And he took it, and did eat before them." (Luke 24:38-43) Are we to believe that the resurrected Christ is without body, parts, or passions, when this passage of scripture clearly indicates that He, the Christ, has a physical body with hands and with feet and that He has internal organs demonstrated as He ate the broiled fish while they watched? The Epistle to the Hebrews also clearly states that Jesus Christ the Son of Man and the Son of God is in the express image of His Eternal Father, and implied that God, the Eternal Father also has a body of flesh and bone as tangible as man's, as attested to by latter-day scripture.(D&C 130:22)

It becomes clear from these scriptures and from latter-day revelation that these three, the Father, the Son and the Holy Ghost, are three separate and distinct personages who function together as one in purpose and effort, but such clarity was clouded and made incomprehensible by those who wrote the Nicene Creed and its successor the Athanasian Creed from which many Churches have drawn to make their own incomprehensible conclusions about the nature of God and the Godhead of three personages.

The Nicene creed reads: "We worship one God in Trinity, and Trinity and Unity, neither confounding the persons, nor dividing the substance. For there is one person of the Father, another of the Son, and another of the Holy Ghost. But the Godhead of the Father, Son and Holy Ghost, is all one; the glory equal, the majesty co-eternal. Such is the Father, such is the Son, and such is the Holy Ghost. The Father uncreate, the Son uncreate, and the Holy Ghost uncreate. The Father incomprehensible, the Son incomprehensible, the Holy Ghost incomprehensible. The Father eternal, the Son eternal, the Holy Ghost eternal. And yet there are not three eternals, but one eternal. As also there is not three incomprehensibles, nor three uncreated; but one uncreated, and one incomprehensible. So likewise the Father is Almighty, the Son Almighty, and the Holy Ghost Almighty. So the Father is God, the Son is God and the Holy Ghost is God, and yet there are not three Gods but one God."(Articles of Faith, Talmage p. 43-44)

Without the priesthood authority and access to the guidance of the Holy Ghost, men do not have the same understanding of the things of God. (I Cor 10: 16) [Things of God are foolishness to them]

As Talmage declared: "It would be difficult to conceive of a greater number in inconsistencies and contradictions in words as few." {Ibid. p. 44) This version of the Trinity is certainly not taught in the Bible. It was introduced after the apostles were killed and the priesthood delegated to them had been driven from the earth. This creed and all those who embraced it were major contributors to the long night of apostasy and to the dark ages which lasted about 1,500 years.

This long night of apostasy followed by the dawning of brighter days was prophesied by Isaiah, Amos, Matthew, Luke, Paul's letters to the Corinthians, Galatians, Thessalonians, and by Peter and others. Both were to precede the Lord's second coming.

The Apostle Paul seeking to encourage the Saints, referred to the second coming of Christ, saying, he would be revealed from heaven with his mighty angels, that he would take vengeance on them that know not God and obey not his Gospel. Paul also said he prayed always for them, and that God would count them worthy of their callings, and that he may be glorified in them. However, he said there would be a falling away first, in these words: "Now we beseech you brethren, by the coming of our Lord, Jesus Christ, and by our gathering together unto him, That ye may not soon be shaken in mind, or be troubled, neither by spirit, nor by word, nor by letter, as from us, as that day of Christ is at hand. Let no man deceive you by any means; for that day shall not come, except there come a falling away first.' (2 Thess 2:1-3) Amos foreshadowed this period with the words: "... the Lord God ... will send a famine in the land, not a famine of bread, nor a thirst of water, but of hearing the words of the Lord." (Amos 8:11)

Peter referred to the time following the famine of hearing the words of the Lord as a time of refreshing and of the restitution of all things, prior to His second coming. (Acts 3:19-26) Making reference to this final restoration the Lord through Isaiah said in part: "Therefore, behold, I will proceed to do a marvelous work and a wonder, for the wisdom of their wise men shall perish and the understanding of their prudent men shall be hid."(Isaiah 29:13-14)

Once again, the Lord was required to intervene, as He had done so often in the past, to overcome the rebellion of men.

It is this marvelous work and a wonder which the Lord is performing in the last days, when the keys of the dispensation of the Fullness of Time have been delegated to His authorized servants again, and when scattered Israel is being gathered, perfected and redeemed by the Lord Jesus Christ, that is the main focus of this book. It is during this final period that the Redeemer of Israel's gift of immortality to all mankind is becoming apparent, that the opportunity to obtain eternal life is being extended to all mankind, both the living and the dead, if they will follow Him, that the promise of God that all the families of the earth shall be blessed through the seed of Abraham is being fully realized, and that the earth is being made ready for the Savior's Millennial Reign.

A common thread running through the Plan of Salvation and Exaltation, from the days of Adam, intended for all of mankind, is God's work and glory, which is to bring to pass the immortality and eternal life of men and women. Implicit in the covenant the Lord God made with His people through each of their leaders: Adam, Enoch, Noah, Abraham, Moses, and Jesus Christ, over time, is that there are things one must know which motivates one to do what must be done, in order to be, or to become perfect as He is, and thereby obtain immortality and eternal life.

Rather than be like those referred to by the Apostle Paul, who are "ever learning and never able to come to a knowledge of the truth," (11 Tim 3:7) Jesus' disciples entering the covenant should come to know the truth and accept His words offered to His Father in prayer: "And this is life eternal, that they might know thee the only true God, and Jesus Christ whom thou hast sent," (John 17:3) and when He declared: "except a man be born of water and of the spirit he cannot enter the kingdom of God." (John 3:5)

With reference to the doing, Jesus said, "it is not everyone that saith unto me, Lord, Lord, shall enter the kingdom of heaven, but he that doeth the will of my Father which is in heaven." (Matt 7:21) After the Savior's resurrection Peter responded to the question: "Men and brethren, what shall we do," by saying, "Repent and be baptized every one of you, in the name of Jesus Christ for the remission of sins, and ye shall receive the gift of the Holy Ghost." (Acts 2:37-38) In the Epistle of James we read: "Be ye doers of the word and not hearers only." (James 1:22) The doing includes charitable acts modeled after the Savior, as exemplified during His earthly ministry, described by Paul, James and Moroni, underpinned by the notion that when you are in the service of your fellow beings you are only in the service of your God. (I Cor 13:1-13, 1 Jn 1:22-27, Mor 7:44-48, Mos 2:17)

As Jesus' disciples enter the covenant they become part of His chosen people Israel embarking on a path to knowing, doing and becoming, perfecting their lives step by step, principle by principle, until they eventually become as the Savior is. When that happens they become heirs and joint heirs with Jesus Christ, inherit mansions of the Father, and are given all that the Father hath, even eternal life. However, this can only be done when men and women voluntarily elect to be "even as I am".

To know, to do, and to be or become as the Father and the Son are: that is Jesus Christ's challenge to all of mankind.

Many questions are left unanswered. Some may ask: is immortality a reality for all? What must one do to obtain it? What does it mean to be heirs and joint heirs with Jesus Christ; The many mansions in our Father's house being prepared for Jesus' disciples who have entered the covenant; are they the same for all, or are there gradations is size and quality based on performance? Little has been written here about the ordinances and covenants of the higher or Melchizedek Priesthood and entrance into celestial marriage, which is the covenant of exaltation and eternal increase. By what authority are they performed? Who performs them? Where are such ordinances performed? What is the difference, if any, between salvation and exaltation? What does it mean to have eternal increase? Just how and where is the work done that redeems the dead, alluded to by the Savior and by the Apostle Paul?

These questions and an array of others will be answered in the chapters ahead, based on revelation from God to the prophet Joseph Smith. However, elements essential to the restoration of God's plan for mankind which preceded its restoration will first be discussed.

Just as the Lord God set the time for a restoration of His Gospel and chose the person and place through whom He would work to organize and implement that restoration, as in the case of Enoch, Noah, Abraham, and Moses in the past, so did He select the time, place, and person through whom He would work to organize and implement the final restoration just prior to the Millennium.

29

Over time, following the dispensations of Enoch, Noah, Abraham, Moses and the Savior's however, populations continued to grow and the posterity of Abraham, Isaac and Israel through whom God had promised all the families of the earth would be blessed, were scattered across the earth and mixed among nations. Daniel had envisioned the gospel restoration as a "stone cut without hands" that would overcome the political powers of the world and would eventually encompass the whole earth preparatory to Christ's Millennial Reign.

However, circumstances had to be right for the restoration of His Gospel to take root and grow without being permanently uprooted or suppressed, before it could be spread across the earth. Right of agency, or choice, is paramount in God's plan, and those rights from political, economic and religious perspectives would have to be secured before the actual restoration could take place this final time.

Individual rights and freedom to choose under governments were essentially non-existent in most of the world until the Greek civilization began to rise. These rights for selected individuals were adopted by the Romans before their civilization fell. Eventually protections for individual rights of citizens flowed from the expansion of rights for them brought about first, by providing rights for the aristocracy, and by limiting the king' powers, written into the Magna Charta of England. But these rights did not flower until later in the United States Constitution, which set the stage for the final restoration of the Gospel in all of its fullness in North America just prior to the Millennium.

CHAPTER 11

ELEMENTS ESSENTIAL TO THE   RESTORATION
OF GOD'S PLAN FOR   MANKIND
WHICH PRECEDED ITS RESTORATION

Full accountability to God for choices made pre-supposes individuals are free to choose. Essential to the Lord's plan of salvation and exaltation for all mankind is the principle of agency, the right to choose, or the right of self-determination. No man or woman can be held fully accountable for choices made between good and evil, unless she/he is able to know good and evil for her/himself, is able to identify which is which, and is free from political, economic and religious perspectives to do so. For this reason, the choices made by Adam and Eve which brought about the Fall were essential for mankind to experience mortality with agency and progress.

In the days of Abraham the state, under the power of Nimrod, mandated the worship of idols and blind obedience to its leaders. Failure to comply with the wishes of the state and its leaders was punishable by death. When Abraham sought the blessings of the fathers and the right to administer the same, having been a follower of righteousness, desiring to be a greater follower of righteousness, and desiring greater knowledge, concluded that in order to do so, he needed to obtain another place of residence.(Abraham 1: 1-3) Though unstated in his record, it is clear that Abraham could not worship God according to the dictates of his own conscience in Chaldea without incurring the wrath of the state and reprisals from its leaders, including his own father Terah, who had sought to take Abraham's life. (Abraham 1:30)

Having made known his heart's desire to the Lord God in prayer previously, Abraham, when about to be offered up as a sacrifice to Chaldean idols, appealed to the living God for deliverance. The Lord hearkened and heard. He filled Abraham with a vision of the Almighty, an angel unloosed his bands, and the Lord addressed Abraham personally, saying, "Abraham, Abraham, behold my name is Jehovah, and I have heard thee, and have come down to deliver thee, and to take thee away from thy father's house and from all thy kinsfolk, into a strange land which thou knowest not of." (Abraham 1: 15-16) Thus the Lord placed Abraham and his family in an environment where they were able to worship God according to the dictates of their respective consciences, where there was little or no political, economic or religious interference. There the Lord's covenant people began to flower: first under Abraham, then Isaac, and then Jacob-Israel.

Moving from the land of Canaan to Egypt at the invitation of the Pharaoh, after Joseph had saved the children of Israel from a famine of bread, Israel's people lived apart from the Egyptians and lived their covenants with God for a few generations. However, as the children of Israel grew in number, and interacted more frequently with Egypt's people, they eventually broke their covenants with God and began worshiping Egyptian idols of wood and stone. Later they fell, or were tricked, into bondage to the Egyptians and lost their political, economic and religious independence and freedoms altogether, along with any right of self-determination. (Exodus chapters 1- 13, Moses, Aaron, and Joshua chapters VIII- XIII)

When Moses was called of God to lead the children of Israel out of Egypt to the promised land in Canaan, while speaking for the Lord, he declared again and again, "Let my people go". But the children of Israel, though mighty in number, were not free to go, nor were they able to worship God according to the dictates of their respective consciences. The Lord inflicted ten plagues of increasing severity on Egypt, but it was only after the tenth plague which took the firstborn of Egypt, that Pharaoh let the children of Israel go. Finally, the miracles of the parting of the sea, the safe passage of Israel on dry ground, and the closing of the sea upon the pursuing Egyptian army completely freed Israel so that her people could once again enter a covenant with God in the wilderness preparatory to entering the promised land. (Exodus chapters 7-40)

From this story we learn several things about how God deals with His children: 1) He uses the wicked to punish the wicked. When the children of Israel broke the covenant and worshiped idols, He used the idol worshiping Egyptians to punish them. 2) He will not take away the agency of the righteous or the wicked. The righteous suffered at the hands of the wicked as a consequence of their sin. The wicked suffered the plagues as a consequence of their failure to obey the warnings. 3) He will be merciful when His children decide to obey.

After their arrival in the promised land, had the children of Israel been completely obedient to their part of the covenant they would have been completely free to worship God according to the dictates of their respective consciences. Failure to drive all idol worshipers out of Canaan with its competing religion inhibited the Israelites to freely worship the God of Abraham, Isaac and Jacob, or not worship anything if they so chose. Failure also to destroy all their idols led to resurgence of idol worship in Israel, the breaking of the covenant once again, and the corresponding loss of political, economic and religious freedoms.

Once again the pattern of men continued through the children of Israel is repeated. The gospel, priesthood authority and ordinances are introduced over and over. Man returns to the worship of false gods, disobeys God, moves from righteousness and succumbs to physical and spiritual bondage with its corresponding loss of political, economic and religious freedoms. Regardless of the long suffering of God, the children of Israel repeated the pattern: pride, disobedience, selfishness, greed, false gods, then political, economic and religious bondage. (Moses, Aaron and Joshua chapters I-XXXVI)

By the time Jesus was born, the united Kingdom under David and Solomon had long since been broken into two main divisions, the northern Kingdom of Israel and the southern Kingdom of Judah, each of which later broke the covenant with God, was led into captivity and scattered across the earth. The Kingdom of Israel was overrun by the Assyrians who depopulated the area and moved the people to other lands where they lost their identity. Though some of the people of Judah did return to Jerusalem after seventy years of Babylonian captivity, the major portion of the people of the Kingdom of Judah were scattered across the earth. Over the intervening years those in Jerusalem and environs fell into a state of apostasy and were far from the righteousness expected of those the Lord had wanted to enter the

Abrahamic Covenant and its successor the new and everlasting covenant introduced by the Savior, which was a higher law than the law of Moses.

At the birth of Jesus Christ, Jerusalem was subordinated to Roman rule, not politically independent, nor were they in control of their economic condition. They did have a measure of religious freedom and ability to worship God, but the Savior Himself was severely criticized for having religious views at variance with the ruling Jewish hiarchy. Jesus came to restore some of the provisions of the Abrahamic Covenant which would be continued as part of the new and everlasting covenant, a higher law once lived by Enoch's people, exemplified by the Sermon on the Mount (Matthew chapters 5-7), and to save the world from their real enemies of death and sin.

Those entering the covenant during and following Jesus' ministry kept its provisions for awhile, but due to political, economic and religious interference it proved too much for future generations and they fell into apostasy. After the original twelve apostles were gone, self appointed councils selected what they thought should be classified as scripture and what should not. These councils systematically rejected many sacred writings of a revelatory nature.

They tried to exclude any such writing which supported the testimony of past prophets that the Lord's covenant people would always include prophets, seers and revelators, as it had from the very beginning, and would continue to have in all dispensations, even after the resurrection and ascension of the Savior of mankind.

Old and New Testament prophets foretold there would be one more falling away after the resurrection and ascension of the Savior of mankind. That falling away would include a breaking of the covenant by the Lord's people, and a fall into apostasy. These conditions would require a final restoration of the Gospel before the Lord' s second coming to usher in the Millennium.

Put another away, a long night of apostasy would precede the dawning of brighter days which would set the stage for the final restoration. The breaking of the covenant did, in fact, lead to political, economic and religious bondage. The rights of self-determination from these perspectives would have to be restored before a restoration of the Lord's Gospel in all of its fullness could be made, and these rights would need to be protected by law, otherwise the restoration might be quashed. The prophecy of Daniel would come to pass. The political and economic conditions and religious protections were to be such that the Kingdom of God would be restored and following restoration would roll forth as a stone cut without hands to consume the whole earth.

The rights of self-determination, implied in participatory democracy have roots in the Greek civilization, where selected individuals had some degree of self-determination, but participatory democracy soon became unwieldy and was replaced with a limited representative democracy picked up by the Romans. Not until the Magna Charta was written did individual rights and freedoms for the ordinary citizen receive much attention or official recognition. The Magna Charta contained the seeds for expanding rights for ordinary citizens brought about by first providing rights to the aristocracy and by limiting the king's powers.

A synergism or inner harmony seemed to develop during the middle and upper-teens centuries involving the renaissance in science, art, and literature, its people, the early religious reformers such as Luther, Calvin, and Knox, and the stirring of groups like the Puritans and Pilgrims who chafed under state appointed religions. This synergism seemed to propel governments in the direction of political, economic and religious freedoms for their citizenry. Some of these reformers, including explorers, musicians, and framers of constitutions affirmed they were moved upon by the Holy Ghost in their work. The United States Constitution in particular, Joseph Smith declared, is divinely inspired.

Within a fifteen year period after the Declaration of Independence was signed July 4, 1776 and subsequently defended, a United States Constitution was created which clearly set forth individual citizens have certain inalienable rights, and attached to that constitution is a Bill of Rights with protections for citizens to exercise their agency and self--determination from political, economic, and religious perspectives. There are provisions for the election of officials to represent the electorate by vote of the people, implicit in rights of self determination. Set forth also are provisions for the government to look after the general welfare of its citizens, protecting them from internal and external harm, giving citizens rights to hold property, to bear arms, protects them from illegal searches and seizures, reaffirms the concept a person's home is his/her castle, and most importantly, gives every man and woman the right to worship God [a power higher than the state] according to the dictates of his/her own conscience by forbidding the establishment of a state religion or church.

As the Constitution and Bill of Rights took hold in the newly born United States of America the stage was now set for the restoration of the Gospel one last time. The time the Lord chose for this event to take place was in the early nineteenth century and the place, the United States of America. Without these protections for individual citizens the restored Gospel of Jesus Christ in all of its fullness, probably could not have endured its early persecutors, and the slings and arrows of its critics who wanted it destroyed. Though political, economic and religious forces combined to destroy the fledgling group of the Lord's covenant people, the protections necessary for its survival held, the Gospel of Jesus Christ took root once again in these latter days, and the principle of agency essential to accountability before God for choices made remains intact, at least in the United States of America. Foundation footings for the restored Gospel of Jesus Christ were now laid.

CHAPTER III

THE DAWNING OF BRIGHTER DAYS
THE RESTORATION BEGINS

Given the agency of man is a pillar principle of God's plan for salvation and eternal life for His people, a principle He will not preempt, it is unlikely the restoration could have taken place as well in the nineteenth century in Europe, Asia, Africa, Middle East, Central or South America or any of their countries or cities.

Only in North America in general, and the United States of America and territory soon to become part of the United States in particular, were the conditions right, there was space enough for the Lord's people to grow and move about, and the protections were in place for the organization to take root and flourish. But where in the United States would the restoration take place? Boston, New York, Philadelphia? And a person of what background would the Lord choose to lead this great and grand effort?

Would he be a well known philosopher, a scientist, a musician, an artist, a poet, a writer of great prose, a lawyer or physician, a theologian or teacher of great renown? Would He choose a young man like Enoch, an old man like Noah, a middle aged man like Abraham when he was called out of Ur, an elderly man like Moses when he was called to serve by a voice coming out of a burning bush; or someone in the prime of life like Jesus when he began his ministry at age thirty? What place would soon become hallowed, sacred and known for this astonishing event?

THE RESTORATION - A SUMMARY

The amazing story in the chapters ahead includes the story of the restoration of the Gospel of Jesus Christ in all of its fullness in this the final dispensation before the Millennium is ushered in. It is inextricably connected to the Gathering, Perfection and Redemption of Israel, and all the world, people who elect to enter a covenant with God and keep its provisions.

37

Summarizing the major events of the restoration, it began in the early spring of 1820 with an over-arching visit of God the Eternal Father, and His Son, Jesus Christ in answer to a humble prayer offered in the privacy of a grove of trees in upper New York State. The restored Gospel includes: (a) the restoration of the temporal and spiritual Priesthoods and the reestablishment of the ordinances and covenants of those Priesthoods essential to salvation and exaltation in the Kingdom of God; (b) the coming forth of the Book of Mormon, another Testament of Jesus Christ; (c) the reestablishment of Christ's Church in 1830 with six members; (d) the laying down of a foundation of apostles and prophets, with Jesus Christ being the chief cornerstone, and other ecclesiastical leaders for the edifying of the body of Christ, for the work of the ministry, and for the perfecting of the Saints; (e) the Church's westward movement to Ohio, where a Temple was built and accepted by the Lord; (f) the heavenly manifestations surrounding that event, and the appearance of several heavenly messengers, angels, and beings, including the appearance of the head of the church, even Jesus Christ, personally. Elias appeared and committed the dispensation of the Gospel of Abraham, saying, that in us [apostles, prophets and righteous members of the Church], and our seed, all generations after us should be blessed. Moses appeared and committed the keys of the gathering of Israel from the four parts of the earth, and the leading of the ten tribes from the land of the North. Elijah appeared in fulfillment of Malachi's prophecy testifying that he (Elijah) should be sent to turn the hearts of the father's to the children and the children to the fathers .... thus committing all the priesthood keys necessary for the church's continuation on earth, to the prophets and apostles of this dispensation. (D&C 110)

The restoration also included (g) additions to scripture which came through translation of holy writ long buried in the dust, such as the Book of Mormon, and the Book of Abraham, and by direct revelation to Joseph Smith, God's words for this dispensation now called the Doctrine and Covenants. Further reported is (h) the Church's move to Independence and environs where the members were harassed, robbed, beaten, ravaged, some murdered, and the rest driven out of Missouri; (i) the Church's taking root in Nauvoo the beautiful in Illinois, where another Temple was built, the fledgling Church more fully established and its earthly leader was martyred; (j) uprooted once again due to intolerance and persecution, the Saints take refuge in Salt Lake valley where they put down roots to stay, and there they make the desert blossom as a rose; (k) once again the Lord's covenant people sent forth missionaries to all the world to gather Israel and all those interested in entering a covenant with God, in fulfillment of Daniel's prophecy that a stone would be cut out of a mountain without hands, and shall roll forth until it filled the whole earth. (Daniel 2:34-45, D & C 45:2)

But through whom would the Lord work to get the stone in motion, and would he be of a particular lineage? Worthy of note is that Joseph of old when he saved the family of Israel from famine by moving them to Egypt was a type and shadow of the role of Joseph's posterity in the last days. He, Joseph, personally saved the covenant people Israel physically from the famine of bread. Similarly it is Joseph's posterity, through Ephraim and Manasseh, that will save the Lord's covenant people Israel, and all the world who enter the covenant, from a famine of hearing the words of the Lord, that is, a spiritual famine, through a record they kept and hid up to come forth in the last days: the Book of Mormon, another Testament of Jesus Christ; and through leaders called to lead the Lord's work in the last days, who initially were from the lineage of Ephraim, of that tribe that received the greater blessing, and from the lineage of Manasseh. (D & C 133:34, Jer 31:9, Gen 48:19) From I Chronicles we learn Reuben lost the birthright blessings through sin and it "was given unto the sons of Joseph, the son of Israel." (I Chr 5: 1) From the Book of Mormon we learn that Joseph Smith Jr. is the fulfillment of the prophecy of Joseph, the son of Israel, and that the latter day prophet was and is a descendent of Ephraim, son of Joseph, son of Israel.

Look for the well established pattern of restoration in the past to be repeated this final time: through revelation a prophet is called, many of the people will reject what the prophet says, because his messages from God are not what they want to hear, but those who choose to have faith and repent, will receive the Holy Ghost, and all the teachings of the final restoration will be consistent with previously revealed truth.

Before discussing the major aspects of the restoration in greater detail, however, a discussion of what is meant by the Lord's covenant people in general, and the Abrahamic Covenant in particular, may prove helpful.

CHAPTER IV

THE ABRAHAMIC COVENANT
ITS PROMISES AND BLESSINGS

ORIGINS OF THE LORD'S COVENANT PEOPLE

To accomplish His purposes the Lord works through His authorized agents and servants. Taken collectively, they are a people willing to enter a covenant with Him, and as such, form His Church. He reminds us in latter-day scripture that when we enter a covenant with Him we are to take upon us the name of Christ, and endure to the end, and we shall be saved at the last day... "therefore ye shall call the church in my name... For if a church be called in Moses' name then it be Moses' church, or if it be called in the name of a man then it be the church of a man; but if it be called in my name then it is my church, if it so be that they are built upon my gospel." (3 Nephi 27:7-8)

Hence the church in these latter days is called The Church of JESUS CHRIST of Latter-day Saints.

Historically, who were the people willing to enter a covenant with God in former times? The Lord has always worked through covenant people and has done so from the beginning of mankind's sojourn on earth, originating with Adam, followed by the people led by Enoch, then Noah. After the Flood, the Lord's covenant people came into fruition in the days of Abraham, Isaac and Jacob. As their numbers increased, it became clear that those who honor their commitments to the covenant are to receive innumerable and marvelous blessings. People committed to those portions of the Abrahamic Covenant, still operable, and who enter the new and everlasting covenant were, and are, to play a central role in the Lord's plan of salvation and exaltation for all who qualify. It matters not whether they lived during antediluvian times, in the days of Abraham, Isaac and Jacob, Joseph, or Moses, in the Meridian of Time, when the Savior walked the earth in the flesh, or in the last days, just prior to the Millennium, sometimes called the dispensation of the Fullness of Time.

While a covenant is sometimes denoted as an agreement between persons, more often between God and man, or mankind, it is important to remember the two parties to this kind of a covenant do not stand in the relation of independent and equal contractors. God, in His good pleasure selects the parties, and fixes the terms which man accepts. (BD p. 651) In like manner, God invited Abraham to enter a covenant with him. The covenant placed Abraham under strong obligation and responsibility to honor the commitments he made as part of the covenant. But if he demonstrated to the Lord's satisfaction his determination to live his life within the terms of the covenant, no matter what the future brought him, great blessings would flow to him, his family and posterity forever. (BD p. 601-2)

THE ABRAHAMIC COVENANT

The covenant Abraham entered with God as the other party became known as the Abrahamic Covenant and includes provisions lost to the world for many centuries, but which were restored through revelation in this the Dispensation of the Fullness of Time. These restorations came by way of additional scripture, long buried in the dust. They were translated by Joseph Smith. (BD p. 601-2, Book of Abraham.)

The Abrahamic Covenant was introduced to help people, bound by that covenant, to understand the importance of sacrifices, and what was required of them to obtain immortality and eternal life. Before the time of Christ, the sacrifices offered were made in similitude of the sacrifice God's Only Begotten Son would make sometime in the future. He, the Savior, would also bring about the resurrection of the dead. Implicit in the covenant is the commitment to offer sacrifice. In Abraham's and Moses' day it included offering the best of lambs, of birds and of grains. In our day that kind of sacrifice has been replaced with an offering of our time, energy, talents and resources, each offered in humility for the purpose of building the Kingdom of God on earth. (3 Nephi 4:17-20)

After the atonement of Jesus Christ the sacrifices required

were a broken heart and a contrite spirit, following the pattern of faith, repentance, baptism and receipt of the Holy Ghost. Ongoing obedience and endurance to the end, leads one back to the presence of God.

As announced to Moses on the top of a high mountain, after his experience with the burning bush and before his encounters with the Egyptian Pharaoh, God's work and glory is to bring to pass the immortality and eternal life of man.(Book of Moses 1:39, Moses, Aaron and Joshua Chapter 7)

The first part, immortality is entirely a gift from God's Son, and therefore the full provisions of the Abrahamic Covenant are not required for mankind to achieve it. According to scripture, all will be resurrected and through resurrection achieve immortality. (I Cor 15:22)

Eternal life, the second part, cannot be achieved without work, obedience and effort on the part of the recipient and the approval of the Lord. Eternal life can only be achieved by embracing the provisions of the Abrahamic Covenant still operable, and the Lord's plan of salvation and exaltation within the new and everlasting covenant. It includes (1) receiving the Gospel through the baptismal covenant, which is the covenant of salvation: salvation meaning being placed beyond the power of death and sin: (2) acceptance of the ordinances and covenants of the higher or Melchizedek Priesthood, which were conferred upon Abraham by Melchizedek, and (3) entrance into celestial marriage, which is the covenant of exaltation and eternal increase. (BD p. 602)

Hence, through Jesus Christ, the true enemies of Israel, and mankind, were defeated. The enemy of death was overcome with the resurrection, which will result in the universal resurrection of all mankind - automatic immortality. The other enemy, sin, is not as easy for mankind to overcome. The question remains as to the level, or quality of immortality one will receive. At Calvary, the Savior paid for the sins of all mankind. Those sins will be remitted for all who choose to accept the Savior and that sacrifice. [mercy] For those who choose not to accept the Savior, they must pay for their own sins. [justice] And thus we see that the quality of our immortality will be

43

determined by our individual choices. If we choose to accept Jesus and live a life that will qualify us to live in the presence of God, by our obedience, we will have eternal life. If our choices are lesser, our rewards will be lesser.

Abraham received a promise from the Lord that all these blessings would be offered to all of his mortal posterity. Included in the divine promises to Abraham were assurances that Christ would come through his lineage, and that Abraham's posterity would receive certain lands as an eternal inheritance. These promises taken together are called the Abrahamic Covenant. This covenant was renewed with Isaac, and again with Jacob or Israel. The portions of the covenant that pertain to personal salvation and eternal increase are renewed with each individual who receives the ordinance of celestial marriage. (BD p. 602)

The gift of eternal life is bestowed only upon those who meet the Lord God's standard of perfection through repentance, work, effort and righteous living. It is God who does the judging to see who passes His tests and enters into eternal life. The full provisions of the plan of salvation and exaltation implicit in the new and everlasting covenant, re-introduced by Jesus during His ministry, including portions of the Abrahamic Covenant still operable, patterned after those given to Enoch and his city, are required for those who aspire to eternal life.

In our day the Lord has challenged His covenant people to go and do the works of Abraham, and has also declared He will try them, His covenant people, even as Abraham. (D&C 101:4)

The tests and trials God put Abraham through were of no small moment. After trying Abraham with a series of tests over many years, God put Abraham through the severest test of all. With great faith, nothing wavering, Abraham was willing to sacrifice Isaac, his long awaited and only son born in the covenant, that son upon whom the fullness of Abraham's and Sarah's future blessings depended. He would do so, if need be, "notwithstanding it was written, thou shalt not kill, Abraham, however, did not refuse, and it was accounted unto him for righteousness." (D&C 132:36)

An angel of the Lord had said unto Abraham: "Lay not thine

hand upon the lad: neither do thou anything to him: For now I know that thou fearest God, seeing thou hast not withheld thy son, thine only [covenant] son from me ... By myself have I sworn, saith the Lord, for because thou hast done this thing, and hast not withheld thy son; thine only [covenant] son: That in blessing, I will bless thee, and in multiplying I will multiply thy seed as the stars of the heaven, and as the sand of the seashore; and thy seed shall possess the gate of his enemies; and in thy seed shall all the nations of the earth be blessed because thou hast obeyed my voice." (Genesis 22:12-18)

PROMISES AND BLESSINGS OF THE ABRAHAMIC COVENANT

By this period in his life, Abraham had demonstrated to the Lord's satisfaction, that he, Abraham, would live His laws of obedience and sacrifice, live the laws of His Gospel, and consecrate all he had to the Lord. Also by now, Abraham had performed his part of the covenant, and therefore, some of God's promises could not be annulled, because an operable law of God is, "when ye do what I say I am bound", (D&C 82: 10) and that "there is a law irrevocably decreed in heaven before the foundation of the world upon which all blessings are predicated, and when we obtain any blessing from God, it is by obedience to that law upon which it is predicated." (D&C 130:20-21)

Implicit in the Abrahamic Covenant is the Patriarchal Priesthood which includes both temporal and spiritual blessings related to birth, kings and priesthood, all of which Abraham, Isaac, and Israel held, and these blessings were to continue in Israel's posterity as long as they kept the covenant's provisions. However, once the covenant was broken, some of the blessings ceased until evidence surfaced that the children of Israel had once again, faith in the Lord, repentance was evident, and their re-entrance into the covenant was approved and accepted by the Lord, should He choose to restore them.

In Abraham's day the Patriarchal Priesthood was passed from father to son, as were the temporal and spiritual blessings related to birth, kings and priesthood, all held by Abraham, Isaac, and Jacob /Israel. After Israel's day these blessings were divided up, the birthright blessing went to Joseph, the right of kings to Judah, and the right of the temporal priesthood to Levi. The birthright blessing continued through Joseph's sons Ephraim and Manessah, the right of kings continued through Judah's posterity, and the right of the temporal priesthood through Levi's posterity, including Aaron and his posterity until the time of Christ.

There never was a lineal requirement for holding the Melchizedek Priesthood which administers the ecclesiastical organization of the Lord's covenant people as a whole.

This leadership role was held variously by Moses, a descendant of Levi, by Joshua, a descendant of Ephraim, and by Jesus during His ministry, a descendant of Judah. Through disobedience, rebellion and sin the rights connected with these blessings were lost temporarily, as the united kingdom under Solomon was broken into the kingdom of Israel and kingdom of Judah. These two kingdoms fell, and the once covenant people were scattered across the earth. As the posterity of scattered Israel accept the covenant through the servants of the Lord in these last days, and are obedient to its provisions, the blessings of the covenant, that is, salvation and eternal life will be theirs. During or after that time the blessings of the Patriarchal Priesthood will again hold sway, especially during the Millennium.

Just as immortality is a pure gift through the atonement of Christ to the recipient, and the recipient does not have to do any earthly deed to be resurrected, so are some of the blessings of the Abrahamic Covenant a pure gift of God to his posterity, because Abraham obeyed the voice of God.

And just as eternal life cannot be achieved without work, effort, obedience and approval of the Lord, other blessings for Abraham's posterity are likewise conditional on the performance of his literal and adopted posterity. This new and everlasting covenant still contains portions of the old Abrahamic Covenant.

What were and are some of the blessings promised Abraham and his posterity, some of which the Lord is bound to fulfill because

Abraham kept his covenants with God, and others of which their fulfillment is conditional on the personal righteousness and obedience of each individual among his posterity? In some instances the Lord speaks of blessings unspecified and in other instances He is specific in identifying blessings which come through meeting conditions set or in complying with His commands.

For the purposes of this presentation, some of the blessings and promises of God to Abraham and his posterity are put in three categories: a) a multitudinous, notable and distinguished posterity, b) lands of promise, wealth and resources for Abraham and his future posterity, and c) through Abraham's priesthood power received from Melchizedek and that of his righteous posterity [both literal and adopted] all the families of the earth were and are to be blessed, and through that priesthood power shall all of his righteous posterity [both literal and adopted] be protected from their enemies.

These promises and blessings of God to Abraham and his posterity were made long before Abraham and Sarah's covenant son Isaac and covenant grandson Israel were born, some 3,600 or more years ago. By our day their fulfillment is clearly evident as we shall see. However, before Abraham had proven himself to the Lord's satisfaction, these promises and blessings were all made conditional on Abraham's willingness and demonstrated action in living the laws of obedience and sacrifice, the laws of the Gospel, and the law of consecration.

Nevertheless, if Abraham and Sarah were obedient to the laws upon which these blessings are predicated they were bound to receive them, and so were their posterity within the limits of God's judgment of their respective use of individual agency. Given that God has power to control the order in which pre-mortal spirits receive physical bodies and appear on earth, and the selection of earthly parents at or shortly after conception takes place, it follows that Abraham and Sarah's covenant posterity could become multitudinous, notable and distinguished without preempting each individual's right to make choices while on earth.

THE BLESSINGS OF MULTITUDINOUS, NOTABLE AND DISTINGUISHED POSTERITY

To Abram God said: "Get thee out of thy country and from thy kindred, and from thy father's house unto a land that I will shew thee," [the conditions or commands], "And I will make of thee a great nation, and bless thee, and I will make thy name great, and thou shalt be a blessing ... and in thee shall all the families of the earth be blessed. " [the promises and blessings if conditions are met and or commands obeyed] (Gen 12:1-3)

Attempting to comply with the conditions or commands, Abram, Sarai and Lot their nephew, and others moved to a place they called Haran, named after Lot's deceased father; but the Lord wanted them in Canaan. Again the Lord commands, Abram obeys, and moves his family to Canaan. After Abram returned from Egypt where they had gone because of famine, and after Lot was separated from him, the Lord said to Abram, "And I will make thy seed as the dust of the earth: so that if a man can number the dust of the earth, then shall thy seed also be numbered." [the number of Abram's posterity now seems limitless, but none have thus far been born.] (Gen 13:16)

Time passes, and still the eighty-five year old Abram and seventy-five year old Sarai have no offspring. They desire fulfillment of the previously promised blessings. Again the Lord reaffirms the promises and blessings in these words: 'And he [the Lord) brought him [Abram] forth abroad and said, Look now toward heaven, and tell the stars, if thou be able to number them: and he said unto him, So shall thy seed be. And he believed in the Lord; and he counted it unto him for righteousness." (Gen 15:5-6)

Observe this important lesson: Often, God will provide foreknowledge, as he did with Joseph, Moses and others. Once given, we must be faithful, for God's purposes will be brought to pass, even though it may not look possible through our mortal eyes and limited understanding. Looking back, we can see that all the promises made to Abraham and Sarah have been very literally fulfilled.

"And when Abram was ninety years and nine, the Lord appeared to Abram, and said unto him, I am the Almighty God; walk [uprightly JST] before me, and be thou perfect." [the conditions or commands] "And I will make my covenant between me and thee, and will multiply thee exceedingly." [the promises and blessings] (Gen 17:1-2) "And it came to pass that Abram fell on his face, and called upon the name of the Lord.... and God talked with him, saying, As for me, behold my covenant is with thee, and thou shalt be a father of many nations." (Gen 17:3-4) "And this covenant I make, that thy children may be known among all nations. " [the blessings are now being extended to Abram's posterity](Gen JST 17:9) Continuing the Lord said to Abram: "Neither shall thy name any more be called Abram, but thy name shall be Abraham; for a father of many nations have I made thee. And I will make thee exceeding fruitful, and I will make nations of thee, and kings shall come out of thee." [more extensive promises and blessings are made if Abraham lives a higher law requiring perfection to the Lord's satisfaction] (Gen 17:5-6)

At ninety-nine, it would have been very easy for Abraham to give up hope and lose his promise. Regardless of the sacrifice required we must each be faithful to the knowledge we are given and endure to the end.

"...As for Sarai thy wife, thou shalt not call her name Sarai, but Sarah shall her name be, And I will bless her, and give thee a son also of her: yea, I will bless her and she shall be a mother of nations; and kings of people shall be of her." [Sarah too, shall be blessed as Abraham, and rejoice in their joint posterity and blessings.] (Gen 17:15-16)

Note the pattern the Lord used with Abraham and Sarah. He gave them a command to leave Ur with their family and go to Canaan with a promised blessing that of Abraham, he would make a great nation and eventually all the families of the earth would be blessed if Abraham obeyed. Abraham obeyed, and the Lord added another blessing: That Abraham's seed or posterity would be for number as the dust of the earth or the stars in the sky. Abraham's faith in the Lord was counted unto him for righteousness. The Lord then invited Abraham to enter a higher covenant with Him and promises him he will become a father not just of one nation, but of many nations, and that his children or posterity would be known among all nations.

49

Later the Lord was even more specific in blessings: not only would Abraham be the father of many nations, but that his posterity would include kings [and queens]. These promised blessings were to come through Sarah who was to be the mother of nations and kings of people would come through her also. In short, obedience to God's commands and meeting His conditions brings the promised blessings.

Additional or more extensive blessings are not specified until after the first commands are followed and first conditions met. Obedience to the first commands and compliance with first conditions indicates a readiness to live a higher law with higher and greater blessings, which are subsequently spelled out.

Note the blessings of eternal life must be won with individual choices and a life that endures to the end in obedience. Hence the ecclesiastical order following Israel's [son of Isaac] days was established to 1) accomplish the purposes of the Lord through the scattering, giving all a claim to the blood of Abraham/Israel, and 2) putting the burden on the individual, rather than heredity to establish their lot in the eternities.

At this point in Abraham's and Sarah's lives they had demonstrated their readiness, willingness, and worthiness to enter into additional covenants with the Lord, which they did. They became candidates for exaltation and eternal life, and were given new names by the Lord in the process. No doubt they had previously received the ordinance of baptism, which is the ordinance of salvation, for the Lord explained to them that the ordinance of baptism, once operable, had been abandoned by their forebears and needed to be restored. Their new names related to the covenant and ordinances of exaltation and eternal increase which they entered with the Lord.

With reference to the ordinance and covenant of baptism which the Lord said Abraham's forebears had abandoned, the Lord declared: "My people have gone astray from my precepts, and have not kept mine ordinance which I gave unto their fathers; and they have not observed mine anointing, and the burial, or baptism wherewith I commanded them; But have turned from the commandment, and taken unto themselves the washing of children, and the blood of sprinkling: And have said that the blood of the righteous Abel was shed for sins; and have not known wherein they are accountable before me." (JST Gen 17:4-7)

"... And I will establish a covenant of circumcision with thee, and it shall be my covenant between me and thee, and thy seed after thee, in their generations that thou mayest know forever that children are not accountable before me until they are eight years old. And thou shalt observe to keep all my covenants wherein I covenanted with thy fathers; and thou shalt keep the commandments which I have given thee with mine own mouth, and I will be a God unto thee and thy seed after thee." (JST Gen 17:11-12)

Note the promises and blessings have now been extended to Abraham's posterity if they meet the conditions set by the Lord, i.e. they are baptized at the age of accountability or older. Note also that circumcision at eight days old was to be a reminder that baptism was to be performed when children are eight years or older, as well as men and women who have arrived at the years of accountability. (D& C 18:42)

Children who die before the years of accountability are saved in the celestial kingdom of heaven. (D&C 137: 10) Children under age eight cannot sin because Satan has no power to tempt them until they begin to become accountable before the Lord which is at eight years of age. (D&C 29-:46-47)

If men, women and children who have arrived at the age of accountability are to be baptized, why then were men given the token or reminder, by submitting to the ordinance of circumcision, why were male babies circumcised at eight days old? One reason may be to be obedient to God's commands. Another possible explanation is that males were given the authority to act for God, or the priesthood, and it is that power that is used to baptize others, such as the power and authority John the Baptist used to baptize Jesus. Abraham was acting under the authority of the Patriarchal Priesthood, in which every father has the responsibility to see that his children are taught the doctrine of repentance, faith in the Lord Jesus Christ and of baptism and the gift of the Holy Ghost by the laying on of the hands, when eight years old. (D&C 68:25)

Acting under the authority of those holding priesthood keys

every father holding the appropriate priesthood, not only may, but has a duty to baptize his children. Circumcision of all males born to parents within the covenant, eight days of age or older, all being potential fathers, would indeed be a reminder to teach and baptize their children by the time they had reached eight years, an age when children begin to become accountable before the Lord.

Many generations later the Lord declared he had fulfilled His part of the covenant with Abraham, that circumcision as a token of that agreement was done away, as was sacrifice of grains, birds and animals, following the birth, death, resurrection and atonement of God's only Begotten Son, Jesus Christ. They were replaced with a new and everlasting covenant which retained some provisions of the Abrahamic Covenant. (Moroni 8:8) The complete provisions of the new and everlasting covenant will be discussed later.

That these promises and blessings relating to Abraham's posterity were extended to Isaac is confirmed in these words the Lord spoke to him. "And I will make thy seed to multiply as the stars of heaven... and in thy seed shall all the nations of the earth be blessed, Because that Abraham obeyed my voice, and kept my charge, my commandments, my statutes and my laws." (Gen 26:4-5)

And again to Isaac: "And the Lord appeared unto him the same night, and said, I am the God of Abraham, thy father, fear not for I am with thee and will bless thee and multiply thee for my servant Abraham's sake." (Gen 26:24) Thus Isaac received blessings because of what his father Abraham had done, just like we receive the blessings of the resurrection because of what Christ has been for us.

Multitudinous seed was promised Rebekah, Isaac's betrothed also. "And they blessed Rebekah and said unto her, Thou art our sister; be thou the mother of thousands of millions, and let thy seed possess the gates of those which hate them." (Gen 24:60)

That these promises and blessings were extended to Jacob-Israel, Isaac's and Rebekah's son, are confirmed in these words from the Lord when Israel had not yet any children. "And Isaac called Jacob and blessed him, [saying] And God Almighty bless thee, and make thee fruitful, and multiply thee, that thou mayest be a multitude of people; and give thee the blessing of Abraham to thee, and to thy seed with thee." (Gen 28:1-4)

En route to take a wife from the daughters of Laban, Israel was met by the Lord, who stood above a ladder, introduced himself as the God of Abraham and Isaac, and said to Israel: "...And thy seed shall be as the dust of the earth, and thou shalt spread abroad to the west, and to the east, and to the north, and to the south: and in thee and in thy seed shall all the families of the earth be blessed." (Gen 28:13-15)

More than twenty years later, after Jacob- Israel was married and had children, and after Jacob had been given a new name, Israel, and after he had returned to the land of his father Isaac, the Lord again reminded Jacob his name was now Israel and said unto him:

"I am God Almighty, be fruitful and multiply; a nation and a company of nations shall be of thee, and kings shall come out of thy loins." (Gen 35:11) It may be said that the symbolism of Jacob's ladder represents the covenants required for man to climb up the presence of God. Each rung in the ladder represents a covenant or part of one. As individuals are obedient to one rung, they can climb to the next, and eventually ascend into heaven through obedience.

Later, after Jacob-Israel had moved his family to Egypt, at the invitation of his son Joseph and the Pharaoh of Egypt, he retold the Lord's promises as he conversed with Joseph saying, the Lord had told him: "Behold, I will make thee fruitful and multiply thee, and I will make of thee a multitude of people. " (Gen 48:4)

In conversation with Joseph, shortly before Israel's death, Israel turned his attention to Joseph's two sons Ephraim and Manasseh, adopting them as his own and said: "And now of thy two sons, Ephraim and Manasseh, which were born unto thee in the land of Egypt, before I came unto thee into Egypt: behold, they are mine, and the God of thy fathers, shall bless them; even as Reuben and Simeon, they shall be blessed, for they are mine; wherefore they shall be called after my name. (Therefore, they were called Israel). And thy issue which thou begettest after them, shall be thine, and shall be called after the name of their brethren in their inheritance, in the tribes, therefore they are called the tribes of Manasseh and of Ephraim... Therefore, 0 my son, he hath blessed me in raising thee up

53

to be a servant unto me, in saving my house from death; In delivering my people, thy brethren, from famine which was sore in the land; wherefore the God of thy fathers shall bless thee, and the fruit of thy loins, that they shall be blessed above thy brethren, and above thy father's house. For thou hast prevailed, and thy father's house hath bowed down unto thee, even as it was shown unto thee, before thou wast sold into Egypt, by the hands of thy brethren; wherefore thy brethren shall bow down unto thee, from generation to generation, unto the fruit of thy loins forever." (JST Gen 48:5-10)

After Moses led the children of Israel out of Egypt the Lord chose to intermingle the posterity of Levi among the other tribes where they 'performed temporal priesthood functions and received their land inheritance. Ephraim's tribe took the place of Joseph in the house of Israel and Manasseh took Levi's place, giving Joseph's posterity a double portion as promised. Therefore, when the tribes entered the promised land, land inheritances went to the posterity of Asher, Zebulun, Naphtali, Issachor, Gad, Dan, Reuben, Simeon, Benjamin, Judah, Manasseh and Ephraim.

While all the tribes of Israel were to be fruitful, the tribes of Israel's grandson's Ephraim and Manasseh would clearly be the most fruitful. Israel had blessed Joseph and had blessed Ephraim and Manasseh affirming: "let my name (Israel) be named upon them, and the name of my fathers Abraham and Isaac: and let them grow into a multitude in the midst of the earth." (Gen 48:16) The company of nations promised Israel's seed was also referred to as a multitude of nations and this honor fell to the posterity of Joseph through Ephraim, as a blessing associated with the birthright. (Gen 48:19)

Notable and distinguished people, especially kings and queens were to come out of Judah, particularly the King of Kings and Lord of Lords, the Savior of mankind, as part of the right of kings conferred upon Judah by Israel. In blessing Manasseh and Ephraim Israel said: "... he [Manasseh] also shall become a people, and he shall also be great; but truly his younger brother [Ephraim] shall be greater than he, and his [Ephraim's] seed shall become a multitude of nations." (Gen. 48:19) Thus the blessing of multitudinous posterity was conferred upon Abraham, Isaac, Israel and Israel's twelve sons, especially Joseph, who had conferred upon him the birthright, and Ephraim also, had the birthright blessing conferred upon him. It is through the posterity of Ephraim the multitude or company of nations blessing was conferred.

Clarifying why Joseph and his posterity were blessed above his brethren, Israel said: "In delivering my people, thy brethren, from famine which was sore in the land, wherefore the God of thy fathers shall bless thee, and the fruit of thy loins, that they may be blessed above thy brethren, and above thy father's house; For thou hast prevailed, and thy father's house hath bowed down unto thee, even as it was shown unto thee, before thou wast sold into Egypt by the hands of thy brethren; wherefore thy brethren shall bow down unto thee, from generation to generation, unto the fruit of thy loins forever; For thou shalt be a light unto my people, to deliver them in the days of their captivity, from bondage; and to bring salvation unto them, when they are altogether bowed down under sin.". (JST Gen 48:5-11) From these scriptures we may conclude that the posterity of Joseph through Ephraim and Manasseh were and are to lead the effort to gather, perfect and redeem scattered Israel, under the leadership of the Redeemer of Israel, even Jesus Christ.

This is not to say that Joseph's posterity were more deserving in every way than the posterity of other tribes. Joseph's posterity was blessed with this role because of what Joseph had done. From other scripture we learn that 144,000 high priests will be called 12,000 from each of the tribes. These high priests and the people they lead will have assigned roles. The role of one tribe may be different from another to achieve the purposes of God during the millennium.

Once again, there are blessings that come to all because of what Jesus Christ did for mankind as a whole through His atonement, as a free gift saving all mankind from death, and individual souls do not have to do any earthly deed for it. There are also blessings that come to Abraham's seed, because Abraham obeyed the voice of God; such as a multitudinous posterity which was also conferred upon Isaac, then Israel, then Israel's twelve sons especially Joseph, and then upon Joseph's sons Ephraim and Manasseh and their posterity, because Abraham, Isaac, Israel and Joseph each obeyed the voice of

God, perfected their lives and lived a higher law. But the atonement of Jesus Christ will not save any person, even the lineage of Abraham, Isaac and Israel from his/her individual sins, without full and complete repentance, and the Lord God's forgiveness. Illustrious lineage traceable through any of Israel's sons to Isaac and to Abraham will not save him or her from sin. The law of repentance is equally operable for all, regardless of lineage. Nonetheless, multitudinous posterity came to Abraham, Isaac, Israel, to Israel's twelve sons and to Joseph's posterity as a blessing because of the lives each of these prophets lived.

With reference to Abraham's multitudinous posterity, some writers indicate Abraham is the father of more than forty nations.

With reference to Abraham's notable and distinguished posterity, they likely have come through all twelve tribes, but of particular note are those who have come through Judah as part of the right of kings blessing; and of course the most notable and distinguished of all is Jesus Christ, the Son of Man and the Son of God, the Savior of all mankind.

Through Judah have also come David, Solomon, Isaiah, Jeremiah, who was also of the lineage of Levi, Ezekiel, Daniel, Peter, James and John and others. Through Levi have come Moses, Aaron, Jeremiah, John the Baptist and others. Through Joseph have come Joshua, Lehi, Nephi, Mosiah, King Benjamin, Abinadi, Alma, Helaman, Samuel the Lamanite, Mormon, Moroni, Joseph Smith and Gorden B. Hinckley and a host of other latter-day religious leaders. Elijah is said to be of the tribe of Gad. Most of the kings and queens of Europe are descendants of Abraham, Isaac and Israel through Judah and Levi, according to Archibald F. Bennett, noted researcher. Many of the leaders of Islam are Abraham's descendants, as are distinguished scientists, political, social and commercial leaders of the nineteenth and twentieth centuries such as Einstein, Freud, Marx, Baruch etc. all through Judah. Because the seed of Abraham has spread across the earth, there are likely many distinguished and notable people of his lineage in many nations not normally associated with or identified as descendants of Abraham. The lineage of some of Judah's posterity is a matter of public record and is obtainable.

Lineage from other tribes can only be obtained by direct revelation at present, through those duly authorized to give patriarchal blessings.

THE BLESSINGS AND PROMISES
OF LANDS OF INHERITANCE, WEALTH
AND RESOURCES

After he complied with the conditions by entering Canaan, a strange land to him: "the Lord appeared unto Abram, and said, unto thy seed will I give this land: and there builded he an altar unto the Lord who appeared unto him". (Gen 12:7) Later ...

"the Lord said unto Abram after that Lot had separated from him, Lift up now thine eyes, and look from the place where thou art northward, and southward, and eastward, and westward: and remember the covenant which I make with thee; for it shall be an everlasting covenant and thou shalt remember the days of Enoch thy father. For all the land which thou seest to thee will I give it, and to thy seed forever. ... Arise, walk through the land in the length of it and in the breadth of it, for I will give it unto thee." (Gen 13:14,15,17; JST Gen 13:13)

From the Book of Abraham we learn that when Abram initially entered Canaan he recognized it as the place where the Lord wanted them to be and that he had built an altar and "offered sacrifice there in the plains of Moreh, and called upon the Lord devoutly, because we had already come into the land of this idolatrous nation. And the Lord appeared unto me in answer to my prayers, and said unto me: Unto thy seed will I give this land." (Abr 2:18-19)

Ten years later Abram and Sarai still had no children, so they sought reaffirmation of God's promises to them. The Lord reaffirmed His promises of posterity as the stars of the sky, and counted Abram's belief in the Lord for righteousness, and also reaffirmed His promise of land of inheritance: ..."And he (the Lord) said unto him, I am the Lord that brought thee out of Ur of the Chaldees, to give to thee this land to inherit it." (Gen 15:7)

The Lord expanded His blessings of multitudinous, notable

and distinguished posterity far beyond His initial promises to Abraham, as Abraham complied with the initial conditions and obeyed God's commands. So did He broaden and expand the size and shape of the land to be given as an inheritance to Abraham's posterity far beyond the original boundaries of Canaan. This was done after Abraham obeyed the initial commands and complied with the provisions. They are part of an additional covenant with eternal implications.

When Abram wondered how the Lord could give him this land after he, Abram, was dead, the Lord spoke to him of the resurrection, referring to it as a quickening, and said that in the resurrection Abram and his posterity would inherit the land promised.

" And Abram said, Lord God, how wilt thou give me this land for an everlasting inheritance? And the Lord said, Though thou wast dead, yet am I not able to give it to thee? And if thou shalt die, yet thou shalt possess it, for the day cometh, that the Son of Man shall live; but how can he live if he be not dead? he must first be quickened. And it came to pass, that Abram looked forth and saw the days of the Son of Man, and was glad, and his soul found rest, and he believed in the Lord, and the Lord counted it unto him for righteousness." (JST Gen 15:9-12)

As part of this experience which involved sacrifice of particular animals: a heifer, a goat, a ram, a turtledove and a pigeon, Abram fell into a deep sleep in which he saw his future posterity. They would be in bondage, but would return to the land where he now was with great substance, and on that same day in which he saw the future the Lord made a covenant with Abram saying: "Unto thy seed have I given this land, from the river of Egypt unto the great river, the river Euphrates: The Kenites, and the Kenizzites, and the Kadomites, And the Hittites, and the Perizzites, and the Rephaims, And the Amorites, and the Canaanites, and the Girgashites, and the Jebusites." (Gen 15:18-21)

At this juncture, the Lord promised He would give Abram and his seed the land of ten groups of people, the borders extending from the Nile on the west to the Euphrates on the east, from the Arabian desert on the south to what is now Turkey on the north, where the Hittites once lived, an area far beyond the original boundaries of Canaan.

It is important to remember that an earth life inheritance is quite different from an eternal life inheritance, the first being temporary and ends when earth life is over, while the latter is permanent and without end in duration. Apparently the Lord chose to use his promise of land for Abram's posterity to reaffirm the reality of a future resurrection for all of his posterity, when they would receive bodies that would never again die, and that this resurrection would be brought about through the Son of Man, also known as the Son of God. He would be born of Abram's future lineage, bringing about the resurrection through His atoning sacrifice, and the possibility of life eternal. Book of Mormon prophets, who lived before the time of Christ's ministry on earth, similarly testified that Moses, Abraham, and prophets after Abraham knew of the Father's plan and His Son's role in that plan.

From the Book of Mormon:

"... the words which he [Moses] hath spoken concerning the coming of the Messiah. Yea, did he not bear record that the Son of God should come? And as he lifted up the brazen serpent in the wilderness even so shall he be lifted up who should come. And as many as should look upon that serpent should live, even so as many as look upon the Son of God with faith, having a contrite spirit might live, even unto that life which is eternal. And now behold, Moses did not only testify of these things, but also all the holy prophets, even to the days of Abraham, Yea, and behold, Abraham saw of his coming, and was filled with gladness and did rejoice.". (Helaman 8:13-17)

To Isaac, Abraham's covenant son, the Lord said: "Sojourn in this land, and I will be with thee; for unto thee, and unto thy seed, I will give all these countries, and I will perform the oath which I sware unto thy father." (Gen 26:3) [Note the promised land was all these countries.]

To Jacob-Israel, Abraham's covenant grandson, after pronouncing that Israel's seed would be given the land whereupon he lieth and that they would be as the dust of the earth in number; said: "thou shalt spread abroad to the west, and to the east, and to the north,

59

and to the south." (Gen 28:14)

After promising Israel a nation and a company of nations would come out of him, the Lord again promised the land "which I gave Abraham and Isaac, to thee [Israel] I will give it, and to thy seed after thee." (Gen 35:12) Before Israel died, he reiterated these same promises while conversing with Joseph. (Gen 48:4)

Coupling this promise to Abraham's grandson Israel, with the promises made to Abraham directly, that he should be a father of many nations, (Gen 17:4), one may conclude that the lands of inheritance for Abraham's seed, literal and adopted, fill the earth. If one assumes that the Lord is talking about an earth life only inheritance, a far different meaning is obtained, than if one assumes He is talking about a permanent eternal life inheritance.

From latter-day scripture we learn that all those who enter the new and everlasting covenant, of which some of the provisions of the Abrahamic Covenant are still a part, -- that is his seed, who enter the covenant and those adopted into Abraham's family, are the seed of Abraham. (D&C 84) Ultimately, the earth is to be upgraded during the Millennium, when most of the world's people will be resurrected, to a terrestrial glory or state, and after the Millennium upgraded again to a celestial glory at the final judgment. At that time only those committed to the new and everlasting covenant including portions of the old Abrahamic Covenant and living the provisions of that covenant will be able to live on this earth in its celestialized state. Those resurrected persons who remain unwilling and unworthy of a celestial glory at judgment will not inherit any portion of planet earth. They will be removed to another place and live elsewhere in the universe, in or on a planet worthy of a terrestrial or telestial glory, or designated for such a glory.

One may also conclude the space needed for the house of Israel who have been scattered across the earth and who are to become as the dust of the earth in number will ultimately be the entire earth, which is to be inherited by those committed to the new and everlasting covenant. Even in our day, those nations and lands of which Abraham is considered to be the father, control much of the world's real estate, wealth and resources. As the stone cut out of the mountain without hands continues to roll forth and fills the earth, the literal and adopted posterity of Abraham, committed and living the new and everlasting covenant, will control more and more of the world's land, wealth and resources. This control will not be for selfish reasons but to enable the earth to be upgraded to a terrestrial glory, that glory akin to the city of Enoch, or Zion, where the pure in heart live. And where there is no poor among them, where more and more people consecrate all they have to building the kingdom of God on earth. When that kingdom is more fully built, the Savior will reign.

After all have been resurrected and judged, planet earth is to be upgraded again to a celestialized glory. This is a glory in which the laws of obedience, sacrifice, of the Gospel and of consecration are lived, after having been learned. These laws lead to perfection, and to a return to the presence of God the Father in an exalted state.

THROUGH ABRAHAM'S PRIESTHOOD POWER RECEIVED FROM MELCHIZEDEK, ALL THE FAMILIES OF THE EARTH WERE AND ARE TO BE BLESSED, AND THROUGH THAT PRIESTHOOD POWER, ALL OF ABRAHAM'S RIGHTEOUS POSTERITY (LITERAL AND ADOPTED) MAY BE PROTECTED FROM THEIR ENEMIES,

Abraham had sought the blessings of the Patriarchal Priesthood he knew some of his forebears held. He also knew the guiding principle in obtaining and using this priesthood power was and is personal righteousness. Hence, in seeking the blessings of his fathers and the right to be ordained to administer the same, he declared himself to be a follower of righteousness, with a desire to be a greater follower of righteousness. In desiring to possess great knowledge, and to be a father of nations and a prince of peace, he became a rightful heir, an High Priest, and this power was conferred upon him by Melchizedek, who was also known as a great high priest, and a prince of peace. (Abr 1: 14, D&C 84:14)

Abraham may have seen Melchizedek as his role model. Note also that Abraham also is a type and shadow of Adam and Eve, and indeed each, of us. Adam and Eve had to leave their heavenly home and sojourn in the wilderness, exercise agency, choose to obey God, enter into covenants, keep them, endure to the end and return home to God in a celestial unit, this is, as man and wife. Abraham was commanded to depart into the wilderness, and follow the same pattern. His blessings, just like Adam's, and ours, come from obedience. Through these examples we learn the pattern and requirements of "becoming perfect."

But others, by way of review, including his father Terah, wanted him to worship dumb idols. When Abraham refused they sought to sacrifice him to their idols. Abraham appealed to the living God for help. God intervened, saved Abraham, and destroyed those who tried to take his life. God also granted Abraham his desire for another place of residence by taking him out of his native environment into a strange land he didn't know. It was Abraham, himself, who wanted to move to a place where he could worship God according to the dictates of his own conscience. Though Canaan was a place where the people worshiped idols, they permitted Abraham to worship as he pleased and made little or no effort to control him politically or economically. (Abr 1: 1)

In the process of guiding Abraham to that land the Lord said:

"Behold, I will lead thee by my hand, and I will take thee, to put upon thee my name, even the Priesthood of thy father, and my power shall be over thee. As it was with Noah, so shall it be with thee, but through thy ministry my name shall be known in the earth forever, for I am thy God." (Abr 1: 18-19)

[Noah was commanded to go forth and declare the Lord's gospel unto the children of men as was Enoch] (Moses 8:19)

Abraham's immediate forebears, including his father Terah, had fallen into idolatry and were not worthy to bear the Patriarchal Priesthood, so he was chosen to receive it in their place.

To assist Abraham in his future roles and to bless the lives of others, the Lord saw to it that "the records of the fathers even the patriarchs, concerning the right of Priesthood, the Lord my God preserved in my own hands; and therefore a knowledge of the beginning of the creation, and also of the planets, and of the stars, as they were made known unto the fathers, have I kept unto this day, and I shall endeavor to write some of these things upon this record, for the benefit of my posterity that shall come after me." [a posterity not yet born to Abraham] (Abr 1: 31)

Also in his possession was an Urim and Thummim which the Lord God had given Abraham in the Ur of the Chaldees. Through these instruments Abraham learned about the sun, moon and stars. He learned of the eternal nature of spirits, of pre-earth life, of fore-ordination, the creation, the choosing of a Redeemer in the preexistence, and that earth life is a second estate for man.(Abr. Ch 3)

These concepts written by Abraham in his own hand, and embellished by revelation through the prophet Joseph Smith, are very much a part of the restored Gospel of Jesus Christ in all of its fullness.

One of the functions of the priesthood in the latter days is missionary work, fulfilling the leadership role of Joseph to save the house of Israel from a spiritual famine. Heavenly Father's eternal plan also requires that all of His children have a chance to exercise their agency to accept or reject His Gospel. It also was one of the functions of the priesthood in the days of Abraham as it was made clear to him in this message:

"Arise and take Lot with thee; for I have proposed to take thee out of Haran and to make thee a minister to bear my name in a strange land which I will give unto thy seed after thee for an everlasting possession when they hearken unto my voice." (Abr 2:6)

The Lord made clear Abraham's ministry and priesthood would be borne to all nations and that Abraham would be a blessing to his seed after him in these words:

"My name is Jehovah ... my hand shall be over thee, and I will make thy name great among all nations; and thou shalt be a blessing unto thy seed after thee; that in their hands they shall bear this ministry and Priesthood unto all nations; and I will bless them through thy name; for as many as receive this Gospel shall be called after thy name, and shall be accounted thy seed, and shall rise up and bless thee as their father; and I will bless them that bless thee ... and in thee (that is in thy Priesthood), and in thy seed (that is, thy

Priesthood) for I give unto thee a promise that this right shall continue in thee, and in thy seed after thee (that is to say, the literal seed or seed of the body) shall all the families of the earth be blessed, even with the blessings of the gospel, which are the blessings of salvation even of life eternal. (Abr 2:8-11)

In this the last dispensation, the Lord explained through Joseph Smith, that this greater priesthood, named after Melchizedek because he was such a great high priest and such a great example, administers the Gospel and holds the key of the mysteries of the Kingdom, even the key of the knowledge of God, and in the ordinances thereof the power of Godliness is manifest. (D&C 84:19-20)

Further, referring to both the priesthood of Aaron, and of Melchizedek, the Lord said those who receive these two Priesthoods through faithfulness and who magnify their callings become the sons of Moses and of Aaron, and the seed of Abraham, and the church and kingdom and the elect of God. (D&C 84:14-34)

Note that those who receive the Gospel, that is, those who enter the baptismal covenant, which is the covenant of salvation, salvation meaning being placed beyond the power of death and sin, are counted as Abraham's seed, entitling them to the blessings of Abraham's posterity, even though they may not be his literal descendants. In addition, males who accept these two priesthoods and magnify their callings and sanctify themselves bring upon themselves, with the Lord's approval, salvation, and the possibility of exaltation and eternal increase. They and their families who so qualify become the church and kingdom and the elect of God and inherit all that the Father hath.(D&C 84:33-38)

Grasping all this, euphoric Abraham responded to his encounter with the Lord God concerning the priesthood saying in his heart: "Thy servant has sought thee earnestly; now I have found thee ... and I will do well to hearken unto thy voice, therefore let thy servant rise up and depart in peace. " (Abr 2:12-13)

Departing Haran, Abram took Sarai whom he had married in Ur and Lot, his brother's son: "and all our substance that we had gathered, and the souls that we had won in Haran, and came forth in the way to the land of Canaan, and dwelt in tents as we came on our way; Therefore, eternity was our covering and our rock and our salvation, as we journeyed from Haran ... to the land of Canaan." (Abr 2:15) Though Abram and Sarai had no literal seed then, there were souls whom they had won, who were accounted as their seed.

The very fact the Lord had intervened in Abraham's life and appeared to him on various occasions in answer to his prayers is evidence of the protective power of Abraham's priesthood. Particular evidence of this surfaced when the Lord intervened and saved Abraham from those who would sacrifice him to dumb idols.

A very grievous famine in Canaan prompted Abram and Sarai to go down into Egypt to escape it. Early on, as they came near to Egypt, according to Abraham's own account, the Lord said to him:"Behold Sarai, thy wife is a very fair woman to look upon; Therefore it shall come to pass, when the Egyptians shall see her, they will say - she is his wife; and they will kill you, but they will save her alive; therefore see that ye do on this wise: Let her say unto the Egyptians, she is thy sister and thy soul shall live." (Abr 2:22-23)

By Abraham's own account we see it was the Lord who intervened again, spoke with Abraham and told him what he should do to save himself, his wife and future family. From Genesis we see that Sarah was the (grand) daughter of Abraham's father Terah, but not the daughter of Abraham's mother, who was Terah's second wife. This unusual truth that Sarah was Terah's grand daughter and Abraham was Terah's son, thereby making Sarah Abraham's sister, was used to save the lives of Abraham, Sarah, and their future covenant son Isaac, not yet born.

The Lord gave Abraham advance knowledge of what He would want them to do in the future. This advance knowledge helped him endure the trials and tribulations he would later face, and so it was with future prophets, including Joseph, son of Israel. The Lord explains through Isaiah that He will foretell the future, and the people will know it comes from Him and not a dumb idol. (Isa 13) Again, this is part of the pattern. If we are obedient to the knowledge we get, we become eligible for more. On the other hand, if we are not obedient, insights from God stop.

The Lord's promises and blessings to Abraham's and Sarah's posterity are numerous and great, and from them have come a multitudinous, notable and distinguished posterity, a posterity through whom all the families of the earth were and are to be blessed, especially through Jesus Christ, and by the examples of a host of prophets, seers and revelators such as Joseph, son of Israel, Moses, Aaron, Samuel, Elijah, Isaiah, Jeremiah, Ezekiel, Lehi, Nephi, Abinadi, Mosiah, King Benjamin, Alma, Helaman, Samuel the Lamanite, and many others of the pre-Christian era; as well as those of the period of Jesus' ministry, and shortly after, including John the Baptist, Peter, James, and John, and Paul, and prophets of the latter-days including Joseph Smith, all being literal descendants of Abraham and Sarah. These and other such descendants are a literal fulfillment of Abraham's blessing, that he would have a multitudinous, notable and distinguished posterity.

Summarizing, through the priesthood power of those so ordained to the higher priesthood of Melchizedek, all the families of the earth are being blessed, protected and saved from their real enemies of death and sin through repentance and the atonement of the greatest high priest of all, the Redeemer of Israel. Through Him all the world's people are saved from the effects of physical death and sin. Salvation from physical death for all is by His grace. Salvation from spiritual death, for repentant sinners is also by His atonement, and by each individual's living the laws of obedience, sacrifice, and the laws of the Gospel and of consecration. Permanent protection from death and sin comes to all who enter a new and everlasting covenant with God, and who keep its provisions. Through repentance and obedience we are protected by God's law of mercy, which is the essence of Christ's atonement. Without repentance for our disobedience, the law of mercy is inoperable, so we become subject to God's law of justice. Without repentance and Christ's atonement we are shut out from God's presence and are spiritually dead. The blessings of Christ's atonement come through living the law of the Gospel, of obedience, sacrifice, and consecration of self to a higher cause. We now return to the restoration story as the morning breaks.

CHAPTER V

THE MORNING BREAKS

When protections for individual agency founded on the principles of personal freedom from political, economic and religious perspectives were in place in the United States of America, undergirded by its Constitution and Bill of Rights; conditions were right for the Lord to choose a prophet, seer and revelator for this last dispensation, one like Enoch, Noah, Abraham and/or Moses. The stage was now carefully set in world events to allow the restoration early in the nineteenth century.

Making His selection, the Lord did not choose a big city person, a philosopher, scientist, musician, artist, poet, a writer of great prose, a professor, lawyer, physician, a politician, or a theologian or teacher of great renown. Instead, He chose a bright, intelligent, healthy, athletic, vigorous, but humble unschooled farm boy, younger than any of the prophets who headed previous dispensations, someone not yet fifteen years old at the time he was called, one who had a simple but transcendent question on his mind: -Which of all the churches is right, thought he, which of them shall I join?

Following a pattern, the Lord chose someone teachable, unschooled in the sophistry of the world, like "a little child", of great faith in his Father, similar to David, Samuel, Joseph, son of Israel, John the Baptist and others.

Like Abraham of old, this young man took the initiative and sought the help of the living God of heaven and earth, in whom he had complete faith; a God who would answer his prayer. Putting his question to God in the privacy of a grove of trees in rural, upper New York state, young Joseph, no doubt, was just as surprised with the answer, as were those about him, whom he later told, and the world has not been the same since. Upon answering Joseph's earnest prayer the Lord God through His Beloved Son, Jesus Christ has woven a tapestry unequaled anywhere, and has fulfilled scores of Old and New Testament prophesies in the process. Let us read from Joseph's personal record of his petition to God and the answer received.

67

After describing what he called a war of words and tumult of opinions among the various religious groups contending for members in frontier America, particularly where he lived, Joseph wrote:

" I often said to myself: what is to be done? Whom of all these parties are right, or, are they all wrong together? If any one of them is right, which is it, and how shall I know it? While I was laboring under the extreme difficulties caused by the contests of these parties of religionists, I was one day reading the Epistle of James, first chapter and fifth verse which read 'If any one of you lack wisdom, let him ask of God, that giveth to all men liberally, and upbraideth not and it shall be given him.'

"Never did any passage of scripture come with more power to the heart of man than this did at this time to mine. It seemed to enter with great force into every feeling of my heart. I reflected on it again and again, knowing that if any person needed wisdom from God, I did; for how to act I did not know, and unless I could get more wisdom than I then had, I would never know; for the teachers of religion of these different sects understood the same passage of scripture so differently as to destroy all confidence in settling the question by an appeal to the Bible.

"'At length I came to the conclusion that I must either remain in darkness and confusion, or else I must do as James directs, that is, ask of God. I at length came to the determination to ask of God, concluding that if he gave wisdom to them that lacked wisdom, and would give liberally, and not upbraid, I might venture. So in accordance with this, my determination to ask of God, I retired to the wood to make the attempt.

"'It was on the morning of a beautiful, clear day, in the spring of eighteen hundred and twenty. It was the first time in my life that I had made such an attempt, for amidst all my anxieties I had not as yet made the attempt to pray vocally. After I had retired to the place where I had previously designed to go, having looked around me, and finding myself alone, I kneeled down and began to offer up the desires of my heart to God.... [soon] ... I saw a pillar of light exactly over my head, above the brightness of the sun, which descended gradually until it fell upon me ... When the light rested upon me I saw two personages, whose brightness and glory defy all description, standing before me in the air. One of them spake unto me, calling me by name and said, pointing to the other -This is My Beloved Son, Hear Him.

"'My object in going to inquire of the Lord was to know which of all the sects was right, that I might know which to join. No sooner, therefore did I get possession of myself, so as to be able to speak, than I asked the Personages who stood above me in the light, which of all the sects was right (for at this time it never entered into my heart that all were wrong) - and which I should join.

"'I was answered that I must join none of them, for they were all wrong; and the Personage who addressed me said that all their creeds were an abomination in his sight; that those professors were all corrupt; that: they draw near to me with their lips, but their hearts are far from me, they teach for doctrines the commandments of men, having a form of godliness, but they deny the power thereof. He again forbade me to join with any of them, and many other things did he say unto me." (JSH 1: 10-20)

But many preachers and professors of religion in his community and elsewhere rejected Joseph's account of the First Vision. They called him a liar, and many other untrue and unkind names. Persecution was heaped upon him, but Joseph stood firm in his testimony as to what had happened to him, and the answer he received concerning which church to join. From his own account:

"It caused me serious reflection then, and often has since, how very strange it was that an obscure boy, of a little over fourteen years of age, and one, too, who was doomed to the necessity of obtaining a scanty maintenance by his daily labor, should be thought a character of sufficient importance to attract the attention of the great ones of the most popular sects of the day, and in a manner to create in them a spirit of the most bitter persecution and reviling. But strange or not, so it was, and it was often the cause of great sorrow to myself.

"However, it was nevertheless a fact that I had beheld a vision. I have thought since, that I felt much like Paul, when he made his defense before King Agrippa, and related the account of the vision he had when he saw a light, and heard a voice; but still there were few who believed him; some said he was dishonest, others said he was mad; and he was ridiculed and reviled. But all this did not destroy the reality of his vision. He had seen a vision, he knew he had, and all the persecution under heaven could not make it otherwise; and though they should persecute him unto death, yet he knew, and would know to his latest breath, that he had seen a light and heard a voice speaking to him, and all the world could not make him think or believe otherwise.

"So it was with me. I had actually seen a light, and in the midst of that light I saw two Personages, and they in reality did speak to me; and though I was hated and persecuted for saying I had seen a vision, yet it was true; and while they were persecuting me, reviling me, and speaking all manner of evil against me falsely for so saying, I was led to say in my heart; why persecute me for telling the truth? I had actually seen a vision; and who am I that I can withstand God, or why does the world think to make me deny what I have actually seen? For I had seen a vision; I knew it, and I knew that God knew it, and I could not deny it, neither dared I do it; at least I knew that by so doing I would offend God, and come under condemnation.

"I now had got my mind satisfied so far as the sectarian world was concerned - that it was not my duty to join with any of them, but to continue as I was until further directed. I had found the testimony of James to be true - that a man who lacked wisdom might ask God, and obtain, and not be upbraided." (JSH 1:23-26)

No doubt the Lord's answer that Joseph join none of the churches of his day because these sects drew near to God with their lips but their hearts were far from Him, both surprised and perplexed the young man. It surprised because that meant none of his family were in the right church, and perplexed him because ministers of the churches around him reacted to his experience with such anger and hatred. Many temptations came his way as he grew to manhood, and he confessed that he fell into many foolish errors and displayed at times the weaknesses of youth, and the foibles of human nature offensive in the sight of God. In making this confession Joseph said no one need suppose him guilty of any great or malignant sins, but that he was guilty of levity and sometimes associated with jovial company not consistent with that character which ought to be maintained by one who was called of God as he had been. But Joseph repented of these behaviors and while in this repentant state of mind, the Lord communicated with him again, this time through His angel and servant, Moroni. (JSH 1:28)

Three and a half years had passed before Joseph received more direction from God through this angel as to what to do, if anything, about his desire to join a church and worship God in a manner acceptable to Him. As Joseph, in a repentant state of mind, approached eighteen years of age, a heavenly messenger named Moroni sent from the presence of God appeared and told him God had a work for him to do. Moroni quoted many prophecies that were about to be fulfilled and gave Joseph instructions and commands to follow.

Joseph was obedient to these commands and followed the instructions given. Moroni, appeared to Joseph many times over the next four years, preparing him for the work ahead. Not until Joseph was over twenty-one years of age in the fall of 1827 was he given his full charge by God, at the age of full accountability. He was given the responsibility to restore the Gospel of Jesus Christ through gifts and powers of God delegated to him. Let us examine in greater detail these events and experiences of Joseph from age eighteen upward, as he was preparing to assume his role in the Gospel's restoration one last time.

CHAPTER VI

AND I SAW ANOTHER ANGEL FLY

"And I saw another angel fly in the midst of heaven, having the everlasting gospel to preach unto them that dwell on earth, and to every nation, kindred, tongue and people." (Rev 14:6)

Thus recorded John the Revelator foreshadowing the gospel's restoration in the latter days.

It was more than three years after he received an answer to his prayer concerning which church to join, and the marvelous experience of seeing God the Eternal Father and His Son Jesus Christ face to face, that Joseph Smith was visited by Moroni. Indeed, Moroni was the angel who came from the midst of heaven of whom John the Revelator spoke. After declaring that he was indeed a messenger sent from the presence of God, the Angel Moroni told Joseph Smith that God had a work for him to do; and that his name would be spoken of for both good and evil among all nations, kindred, tongues and people. He told Joseph about a book written on gold plates which contained the everlasting Gospel as delivered to the ancient inhabitants of America by the Savior, and described the Urim and Thummim deposited with the plates which would aid young Joseph in translating the Book of Mormon from reformed Egyptian into English.The Angel Moroni, a resurrected personage, then commenced quoting prophecies of the Old Testament, beginning with part of the third chapter of Malachi, followed by the fourth or last chapter of that same book with a little variation from the way it reads in the King James Version of the Bible. (JSH 1:33-36)

"For behold, the day cometh that shall burn as an oven, and all the proud, yea, all that do wickedly shall be as stubble; for they that come shall burn them, saith the Lord of Hosts, that it shall leave them neither root or branch ... Behold, I will reveal unto you the Priesthood, by the hand of Elijah the prophet, before the coming of the great and dreadful day of the Lord ... And he shall plant in the hearts of the children the promises made to the fathers, and the hearts of the children shall turn to their fathers. If it were not so, the whole earth would be utterly wasted at his coming." (JSH 1:37-39)

Of great significance is the realization the Lord chose Malachi's prophecy and Elijah's priesthood as His first reference to priesthood power in this last dispensation. From latter-day revelation we learn Elijah held the sealing power of the Melchizedek Priesthood and was the last prophet to do so before the time of Christ. A translated being, he appeared on the mount with Moses also translated, and conferred the keys of the Priesthood on Peter, James and John. (Matt 17:3) The sealing power is the power by which things bound or loosed on earth are bound or loosed in heaven. Thirteen years after Moroni's declaration Elijah the prophet did appear to Joseph Smith and Oliver Cowdery in the newly constructed Temple in Kirtland, Ohio, April 3, 1836 and conferred the same keys upon them. Thus the keys of this power are once again operative on earth and are used in performing some of the ordinances of the gospel for the living and all the ordinances the dead. (BD p 664) Through these sealing and other ordinances performed in Temples for the living and the dead, all the families of the earth are blessed through Abraham's literal and adopted seed. Keys to the Aaronic or the Levitical Priesthood and other keys of the Melchizedek Priesthood were conferred upon Joseph Smith and others during the intervening years of 1829 through 1836. These conferrals are reported in the pages ahead.

Moroni also quoted the eleventh chapter of Isaiah, as he continued to speak to Joseph Smith, in which Isaiah prophesied that the stem of Jesse (Christ) shall judge in righteousness and that the knowledge of God shall cover the earth in the Millennium; that that day was about to be fulfilled, and the gathering, perfection and redemption of Israel was about to begin. [Moroni's first appearance to Joseph was in 1823]

Isaiah's prophecy: ... "And it shall come to pass in that day, that the Lord shall set his hand a second time to recover the remnant of his people, which shall be left from Assyria, and from Egypt, and from Pathros, and from Cush, and from Elam, and from Shinar, and from Hamath, and from the isles of the sea. And he shall set up an ensign for the nations, and shall assemble the outcasts of Israel, and

74

gather together the dispersed of Judah from the four comers of the earth. The envy also of Ephraim shall depart, and the adversaries of Judah shall be cut off. Ephraim shall not envy Judah, and Judah shall not vex Ephraim ... they shall lay their hand upon Edom and Moab; and the children of Ammon shall obey them, and the Lord shall utterly destroy the tongue of the Egyptian sea; [facilitate the return, as in the days of Moses] and with his mighty wind shall he shake his hand over the river, and shall smite it in the seven streams, and make men go over dry shod. And there shall be an highway for the remnant of his people, which shall be left, from Assyria; like it was to Israel in the day that he came out of the land of Egypt. " (Isa 11: 1- 16)

True knowledge of God has not yet covered the earth, but an ensign for the nations has been set up, the gathering of Israel in general has begun and continues, the outcasts of Israel are being assembled, and the gathering of the dispersed of Judah from the four comers of the earth is well underway. The rest of Isaiah's prophecy appears to lie in the future. Those left from Assyria may refer to the lost tribes of Israel for which an highway is to be set up like unto the highway provided for the children of Israel when they departed Egypt. Whether that highway will be elevated above the water, or depressed below the surface as in the case of their forebears isn't known. Movement by airplane may also satisfy the highway metaphor, as in the case of the Berlin airlift when a veritable air highway saved the people of Berlin with food, clothing, medicines and fuel in 1948. Some forty plus years later Ethiopian Jews were airlifted to Israel from Ethiopia, by an air highway, as they became part of the gathering of the dispersed of Judah from the four comers of the earth. The highway might also be knowledge of the Gospel which will lead people to their appointed gathering places, as they seek the protection of the priesthood. (Joel 10)

During his initial appearance to Joseph Smith, which was repeated several times for emphasis, the Angel Moroni also quoted the twenty-second and twenty-third verses of the third chapter of Acts, precisely as contained in the King James Version of the New Testament:

"For Moses truly said unto the fathers, A prophet shall the

Lord your God raise up unto you of your brethren, like unto me, him shall ye hear in all things whatsoever he shall say unto you. And it shall come to pass, that every soul which will not hear that prophet, shall be destroyed from among the people." (Acts 3:22-23) Moroni said that prophet referred to here was Christ, but the day of destruction of those who would not hear him was not yet, but soon would come. (JSH 1:40)

Moroni also quoted the second chapter of Joel from the twenty-eighth verse to the last, indicating the Lord's spirit would soon be poured out upon all flesh and that the gifts of the spirit vested in mankind in times past were about to return.

From Joel: "And it shall come to pass afterward, that I will pour out my spirit upon all flesh; and your sons and your daughters shall prophesy, your old men shall dream dreams, your young men shall see visions; and also upon your servants and your handmaids in those days will I pour out my spirit. And I will shew wonders in the heavens, and in the earth, blood and fire, and pillars of smoke. The sun shall be turned into darkness, and the moon into blood, before the great and terrible day of the Lord come. And it shall come to pass, that whosoever shall call on the name of the Lord shall be delivered: for in Mount Zion and in Jerusalem shall be deliverance as the Lord said, and in the remnant whom the Lord shall call." (Joel 2:28-32)

It appears this reference in Joel is to two centers for the Lord's covenant people, one in Jerusalem, and the other in America, as we learn from prophets in the western hemisphere, variously named Mount Zion or the New Jerusalem. Deliverance would also come through the remnant of the house of Israel the Lord shall call, that is, the righteous posterity of Abraham, and of Israel, and his sons through whom all the families of the earth are to be blessed in the last days. Men and women of this lineage were foreordained to this work as was Jeremiah to whom the Lord declared: "Before I formed thee in the belly I knew thee; and before thou camest forth out of the womb I sanctified thee, and ordained thee a prophet unto the nations." (Jer 1:5)

From the Book of Abraham and from Alma, a Book of Mormon prophet, we learn that while the physical body of each human being comes into existence at conception, that person's spiritual self already existed and unites with the physical body for a season. Each person's spiritual self includes intelligence and the God given right to make choices. Having made the right choices in the pre-mortal world not only qualified them for the privilege of coming to earth, it qualified them for leadership roles in this life, as they continue to live in righteousness and in harmony with God's laws and commands here on earth, such as Jeremiah and others "having chosen good and exercising exceedingly great faith, are called with a holy calling, yea, with that holy calling, which was prepared with, and according to, a preparatory redemption for such." These were:

"called and prepared from the foundation of the world according to the foreknowledge of God, on account of their exceeding faith and good works." (Alma 13:1-3, Abr. 3:1-28) It is from these in the remnant of Israel the Lord called and in whom there is deliverance.

Joel's prophecy was soon to be fulfilled, said Moroni, and the Gentiles would soon hear the word of the Lord. Other scriptures were quoted and explained to Joseph Smith not reported in this account. (JSH 1:41)

The work the Lord had for the foreordained Joseph Smith to do ultimately included: restoring the Gospel of Jesus Christ to earth in all of its fullness, ushering in the dispensation of the fullness of time, receiving all the Priesthood keys necessary for administering the Gospel in the latter days, and beginning the gathering, perfection and redemption of Israel and of all the world, just prior to the Millennium. This work was not to be done by Joseph Smith alone, nor was it placed on his shoulders all at once. Other faithful, righteous men and women of good works were called and given assignments. It would take about twenty years for the foundation of the Church to be laid, all the keys of the Priesthood to be restored and a Temple built for and accepted by the Lord, where all the appropriate ordinances could be performed.

Let us now return to Joseph's own account of Moroni's messages from God, how and when Moroni appeared and to other aspects of his messages.

A little more than three years after receiving an answer to his prayer concerning which church to join, being commanded to join none of them, and realizing it was not his duty to join any of them, and after having endured much humiliation and persecution at the hands of many, Joseph realized he also was imperfect and subject to sin and folly. In humility, young Joseph said: "I betook myself to prayer and supplication to Almighty God for forgiveness of all my sins, and also for a manifestation to me, that I might know of my state and standing before him; for I had full confidence in obtaining a divine manifestation, as I previously had one. While I was thus in the act of calling upon God, I discovered a light appearing in my room, which continued to increase until the room was lighter than at noon day, when immediately a personage appeared at my bedside, standing in the air, for his feet did not touch the floor.

"He had on a loose robe of the most exquisite whiteness. It was a whiteness beyond anything earthly I had ever seen; nor do I believe that any earthly thing could be made to appear so exceedingly white and brilliant. His hands were naked, and his arms also, a little above the wrist; so, also, were his feet naked, as were his legs, a little above the ankles. His head and neck were also bare. I could discover that he had no other clothing on but this robe, as it was open, so that I could see into his bosom.

"Not only was his robe exceedingly white, but his whole person was glorious beyond description, and his countenance truly like lightning. The room was exceedingly light, but not so very bright as immediately around his person. When I first looked upon him, I was afraid, but the fear soon left me. He called me by name, and said unto me that his name was Moroni; that God had a work for me to do,..." (JSH 1:29-33)

The Angel Moroni said that there was a book written on gold plates giving an account of ancient inhabitants of the American continent and the source from which they sprang, and that a Urim and Thummim was deposited with them which would aid in the translation of the book. While the Bible says little about a Urim and Thumimm, its description, purpose or function; related writings including latter-day scripture have more to say. Joseph Smith's description: "there were two stones in silver bows - and these stones, fastened to a breastplate, constituted what is called the Urim and Thummim, deposited with the plates; the possession and use of these stones were what constituted 'seers' in ancient or former times; and that God had prepared them for the purpose of translating the book." (JSH 1:35)

Abraham also had a Urim and Thummim, which he said: "the Lord my God had given me, in the Ur of Chaldees. " (Abr 3: 1) As previously mentioned, through the Urim and Thummim, Abraham learned of pre-earth life, of foreordination, of the creation, of the choosing of a Redeemer, and the second estate of man; all important doctrines which are part of the restored Gospel of Jesus Christ.

"Using a Urim and Thummim is the special prerogative of a seer, and it would seem reasonable that such instruments were used from the time of Adam. However, the earliest mention is in connection with the brother of Jared. (Eth 3:21-28) Abraham used a Urim and Thummim (Abr 3:14), as did the priests of Israel, and also the prophets among the Nephites." (Omni 1:20-21, Mosiah 8:13-19, 21:26-28, 28: 11-20, Eth 4:1-7,BD p 787)

" There is more than one Urim and Thummim, but we are informed Joseph Smith had the one used by the brother of Jared (Eth 3:22-28, D&C 10:1, 17:1). Joseph Smith used it in translating the Book of Mormon and in obtaining other revelations." (BD p 787)

Urim and Thummim is an Hebrew term which means lights and perfection, and in the Greek means revelation and truth. They were used to reveal the will of God after a perfect manner to His people Israel, but they would not work if the high priest were not worthy. The Legends and Antiquities of the Jews say the Urim and Thummim   the children of Israel had, quit working and ceased to give oracular sentences after the death of the last good high priests and prophets, after the reign of David and before the destruction of the Jerusalem temple by the Babylonians. (MAJ p 124-29)

Following Moroni's announcement concerning a Urim and Thummim being deposited with the plates, he quoted the Malachi, Isaiah, and Joel prophecies and Paul's prophecy in Acts as reported. After placing him under strict command not to show the Book of

Mormon plates to anyone except those so commanded to see them, lest he be destroyed, young Joseph saw in vision the place where the golden, metallic plates were deposited, in a hill not far from his father's farm house. After completing his messages Moroni left, but returned two other times during the night, repeating his messages verbatim. Moroni's visits had consumed the night. Joseph had had no sleep, and while attempting to work in the fields the next day his strength faltered. His father sent Joseph to the farm house, but his strength failed again as he attempted to cross a fence. While on the ground looking skyward Joseph saw Moroni, the messenger of the night before, who appeared and repeated his messages a fourth time; and told him to tell his father Joseph Smith Senior. Father Joseph, upon hearing his sons account, declared the messenger and the messages were of God, and advised his son to go and do as commanded.

Obeying God's messenger young Joseph went to the place seen in vision where the plates were deposited. Convenient to the village of Manchester, Ontario, New York, there stood a hill of considerable size. On the west side not far from the top, under a stone of substantial size, lay a stone box. With a stick or limb for a lever Joseph raised the lid, removed it and there beheld the plates, the Urim and Thummirn and the breastplate reported by the messenger.

Joseph's attempts to take the plates out of the stone box were forbidden by Moroni, who appeared this time on site. He declared the time for them to come forth was not yet, and the plates must remain in the box for a period. Joseph was to visit the site each year where God's messenger would meet and instruct him. Accordingly, seventeen year old Joseph did as commanded, received intelligence and instruction from Moroni each year respecting what the Lord was going to do, how and in what manner his kingdom was to be conducted in the last days.

Four years later, at age twenty-one, an age accepted in the country when a male is legally considered to be a man, Joseph was ready. This same heavenly messenger, Moroni, delivered up the plates to Joseph Smith Jr. on the 22nd day of September 1827, and Joseph began to copy and examine some of the characters engraved on the plates in the months following.

Wanting those who knew about his efforts to see what the characters looked like, although he was forbidden to show them the plates directly, Joseph copied some of the characters down to test whether they were true characters. He showed them to selected individuals, including Martin Harris. Initially, his wife Emma, whom Joseph had married the previous January, served as scribe, but by April, 1829, Oliver Cowdery was serving in that role. In the meantime Martin Harris of Palmyra, in Wayne County, New York, had befriended Joseph and Emma by giving them fifty dollars, which they sorely needed to make the trip from Palmyra to Susquehanna County, Pennsylvania where Emma's parents lived.

Joseph sought to escape the harassment and persecution his testimony of God the Eternal Father's and His Son Jesus Christ's visits and the visits of the Angel Moroni had engendered in the Palmyra area, and to locate where he could continue the work of translation free from interference. (JSH 1:55-61)

From Joseph's account: "By this timely aid [from Martin Harris] was I enabled to reach the place of my destination in Pennsylvania: and immediately after my arrival there I commenced copying the characters off the plates. I copied a considerable number of them, and by means of the Urim and Thummim, I translated some of them, which I did between the time I arrived at the house of my wife's father, in the month of December (1828) and the February following. Sometime in this month of February, the aforementioned Mr. Martin Harris came to our place, got the characters which I had drawn off the plates, and started with them to the city of New York. For what took place relative to him and the characters, I refer to his own account of the circumstances, as he related them to me after his return, which was as follow: Martin Harris reported: "' I went to the city of New York, and presented the characters which had been translated, with the translation thereof, to Professor Charles Anton, a gentleman celebrated for his literary attainments. Professor Anton stated that the translation was correct, more so than any he had before seen translated from the Egyptian. I then showed him those which were not translated, and he said that they were Egyptian, Chaldaic,

Assyriac and Arabian; and he said that were true characters. He gave me a certificate, certifying to the people of Palmyra that they were true characters, and the translation of such of them as had been translated was also correct. I took the certificate and put it into my pocket, and was just leaving the house, when Mr. Anton called me back, and asked how the young man found out there were gold plates in the place where he found them. I answered that an angel of God had revealed it unto him.

"' He then said to me, Let me see that certificate. I accordingly took it out of my pocket and gave it to him, when he took it and tore it to pieces, saying that there was no such thing now as ministering angels, and that if I would bring the plates to him he would translate them. I informed him that part of the plates were sealed, and that I was forbidden to bring them. He replied, I cannot read a sealed book. I left him and went to Dr. Mitchell, who sanctioned what Professor Anton had said respecting both the characters and the translation.'" (JSH 1:62-65)

Thus was another prophecy of Isaiah fulfilled: for he declared the Lord had closed the eyes of the people and covered their understanding of prophets, rulers and seers, because the people had fallen away from the Lord; but future people's understanding would be restored through a "book that is sealed which men deliver to one that is learned, saying, Read this, I pray thee: and he saith, I can not; for it is sealed; And the book is delivered to him that is not learned, saying, Read this, I pray thee: and he saith I am not learned. " (Isaiah 29:10-12)

Professor Anton is believed to be the learned man in this prophecy, and the unlearned man is Joseph Smith. However, the Lord would show the unlearned man how he could read a sealed book through the gift and power of God, and with the aid of the Urim and Thummim provided for that purpose. The Lord closely paraphrased Isaiah's words in His very first visit with Joseph. From Isaiah:

"Wherefore the Lord said, For as much as this people draw near me with their mouth, and with their lips do honor me, but have removed their heart far from me, and their fear toward me is taught by the precept of men: Therefore, behold, I will proceed to do a marvelous work and a wonder, for the wisdom of their wise men shall perish, and the understanding of their prudent men shall be hid." (Isaiah 29:13-14)

Unlearned as he was, the young man soon learned some valuable and painful lessons along the way. Following the Anton episode fulfilling Isaiah's prophecy Joseph Smith accommodated himself to Martin Harris' desire to show the first one hundred sixteen pages translated from the Book of Mormon plates to Harris' wife and friends. Perhaps Joseph felt obliged to Martin Harris because Martin had helped him financially during a very difficult period. Whether Joseph was obligated to Martin Harris or not, the Lord quickly let him know he had done the wrong thing, and he should not have feared man more than God, because the one hundred sixteen pages disappeared. The event is the subject of Sections two and ten of the Doctrine and Covenants, given in the summer of 1828.

The Lord withdrew his power from Joseph Smith for a season and explained to him why. He could not translate any more characters from the plates, or receive any additional revelations until the Lord restored these powers to him several months later. (D&C 2 and 10) When these gifts and powers were returned the unlearned man would translate the remaining 500 plus pages of the entire book in about sixty days. While in the process of translating the plates, the Lord bestowed upon him and his companion Oliver Cowdery, the Levitical or Aaronic Priesthood held by Levi, son of Israel, and selected members of his family, including Aaron, the priests of Israel and John the Baptist. Who other than John the Baptist could the Lord send to act for Him? Shortly thereafter the Melchizedek Priesthood held by the great prophets of the past, including Adam, Enoch, Noah, Abraham, Elijah, Peter, James and John, was bestowed upon them, at or near the end of the process of translating the plates, and who better could the Lord send than Peter, James and John to confer this power upon them? A review of these two priesthoods, descriptions of their purposes and functions and their respective restorations follow.

CHAPTER VII

THE RESTORATION OF THE TEMPORAL AND SPIRITUAL PRIESTHOODS AND THE REESTABLISHMENT OF THE RELATED ORDINANCES

Nine years had passed since Joseph Smith sought the help of the living God to find out which of the churches of his day was true and which of them he should join, by putting the promise in the Epistle of James to the test. He found James's testimony to be true: that if any man lacks wisdom let him ask of God, who giveth to all men liberally, and it shall be given him. God the Eternal Father and His Son, Jesus Christ, responded to Joseph's prayer with a personal appearance and answer, which was, to join none of the churches of his day. Three years later, following this astonishing experience, another heavenly messenger by the name of Moroni appeared to Joseph Smith, again in answer to prayer, when he sought forgiveness of his sins, imperfections and weaknesses, and to know his status before God. Moroni answered in behalf of God, implying Joseph was acceptable before Deity, and that God had a work for him to do, and part of that work was to translate the Book of Mormon into English through the gift and power of God.

Now characteristic of Joseph was his appeal to God whenever he felt he lacked wisdom or needed answers to perplexing questions. This often happened when he was in the process of translating the Book of Mormon. As scribe, Joseph's friend Oliver Cowdery had been writing down in English what Joseph had been translating from reformed Egyptian since April 7, 1829. During translation they found references to baptism among the Lord's covenant people in America. The mode of baptism referred to in the Book of Mormon was different from baptisms he had witnessed in the churches of his day, Joseph Smith and friend Oliver Cowdery, prayed about it in the privacy of woods near the banks of the Susquehanna River in Pennsylvania close to the farm house of his father-in-law. Thus on May 15, 1829, another heavenly messenger appeared.

85

THE RESTORATION OF THE AARONIC PRIESTHOOD

From Joseph's account: "We still continued the work of translation, when, in the ensuing month (May, 1829) we went on a certain day into the woods to pray and enquire of the Lord respecting baptism for the remission of sins, that we found mentioned in the translation of the plates. While we were thus employed, praying and calling upon the Lord, a messenger from heaven descended in a cloud of light, and having laid his hands upon us, he ordained us, saying, Upon you my fellow servants, in the name of Messiah, I confer the Priesthood of Aaron, which holds the keys of the ministering of angels, and of the gospel of repentance, and of baptism by immersion for the remission of sins; and this shall never be taken again from the earth until the sons of Levi do offer again an offering unto the Lord in righteousness.

"He said this Aaronic Priesthood had not the power of laying on hands for the gift of the Holy Ghost, but that this should be conferred on us hereafter; and he commanded us to go and be baptized, and gave us directions that I should baptize Oliver Cowdery, and afterwards he should baptize me. Accordingly, we went and were baptized. I baptized him first, and afterwards he baptized me - after which I laid my hands upon his head and ordained him to the Aaronic Priesthood, and afterwards he laid his hands upon me and ordained me to the same Priesthood, for we were so commanded.

"The messenger who visited us on this occasion and conferred the Priesthood upon us, said that his name was John, the same that is called John the Baptist in the New Testament, and that he acted under the direction of Peter, James and John, who held the keys of the Priesthood of Melchizedek, which Priesthood said he, would in due time be conferred on us, and that I should be called the first Elder in the Church, and he (Oliver Cowdery) the second. It was on the fifteenth day of May, 1829, that we were ordained under the hand of this messenger and baptized." (JSH 1:68-72)

Following the appearance of God the Eternal Father and His

Son Jesus Christ to personally answer Joseph's question concerning which church to join, observe that they sent Moroni, a resurrected personage, who had stewardship over the Book of Mormon records, which contained another testament or witness of Jesus Christ's mission, work, glory and doctrine related to the fulness of His Gospel. Following Moroni's visits, the next heavenly messenger sent to help implement the Restoration, was John the Baptist, another resurrected personage, who had authority to baptize the Son of God Himself, even Jesus Christ, which he had done some nineteen centuries previously. Observe that John the Baptist said he was acting under the direction of Peter, James and John, who held the keys to the Melchizedek Priesthood, which John the Baptist foreshadowed would soon be conferred upon Joseph and Oliver, enabling them to confer upon each other and others, the gift of the Holy Ghost.

With reference to the Aaronic Priesthood, its purposes, functions and previous usages, and John the Baptist's role in that priesthood, the Baptist had conferred upon Joseph and Oliver a number of duties, privileges and responsibilities, indicating the Aaronic Priesthood holds the keys of the ministry of angels, of the gospel of repentance, and of baptism by immersion for the remission of sins, but has not the authority to confer the gift of the Holy Ghost. Not surprising then, is the emphasis in the four gospel' s Matthew, Mark, Luke and John's on repentance and baptism for the remission of sins, particularly in reporting John the Baptist's role in preparing the way of the Lord and in baptizing Jesus Christ to fulfill all righteousness.

Historically, the rights of the temporal priesthood held by Abraham, Isaac and Israel were conferred upon Levi, by his father Israel after his eldest son defiled his father's bed. Reuben also forfeited the right of kings which was conferred upon Judah, and the birthright blessings which were conferred upon Joseph and later his sons Ephraim and Manasseh, also by father Israel. After the children of Israel moved to Egypt from Canaan to escape the famine, at the invitation of both Joseph and the Pharaoh, "there went a man of the house of Levi and took to wife a daughter of Levi." (Ex 2: 1) The man was Amram, son of Kohath, son of Levi. He married his Aunt

Jochobed, daughter of Levi. Amram's and Jochobed's children included Miriam, Aaron, the first son, and Moses. (Moses, Aaron and Joshua p 14-19)

Because he was called to lead the children of Israel out of Egypt, and had seen God face to face, Moses functioned "under the power of the non-lineal Melchizedek Priesthood, which was conferred upon him by his father in-law Jethro. (D&C 84:6) This priesthood must be present and functioning whenever the kingdom of God is upon the earth in its fullness." (BD p 730) Initially, the Lord desired the children of Israel to live a higher law as exemplified by some of the provisions of the Abrahamic Covenant, and by the Sermon of the Mount, but they failed to live the law administered by Moses under the authority of the Melchizedek Priesthood. (BD p 599) So the Lord gave an additional law of performances and ordinances and "confirmed a priesthood also upon Aaron, and his seed, throughout all their generations" (D&C 84 :18) to administer it.

Of lesser power and authority than the Melchizedek Priesthood, this priesthood was used to administer the outward ordinances in the ceremonies of the law of Moses. Sometimes referred to as the Aaronic and sometimes referred to as the Levitical Priesthood, there are differences between the two. This lesser priest hood was conferred only upon the tribe of Levi. Within the tribe of Levi, however, only Aaron and his sons could hold the office of priest. From the firstborn of Aaron's sons (after Aaron) was selected the high priest, (or president of the priests, also called bishop). In the Levitical Priesthood, then, Aaron and his sons after him had greater offices in the Levitical Priesthood than did other Levites. (BD p 599-600)

A distinction between the Aaronic and Levitical Priesthood is evident as seen in the scripture that speaks of them as "the priests (of Aaron) and the Levites. (I Kgs 8:4) Among their duties the priests could offer sacrifices for the people, burn incense on the altar, and teach the law; whereas the more menial tasks such as housekeeping of the tabernacle, keeping oil in the lamps, transporting the Ark of the Covenant, taking down and setting up the tabernacle when moving and other tasks assisting the priests were performed by the

Levites.(BD p 600)

Making a point of contrast between the lineal requirement of the lesser priesthood [i.e. the right of this priesthood to be conferred was based on lineage from Levi and worthiness], and the non-lineal Melchizedek Priesthood which was not limited to those of only one tribe, the Apostle Paul declared the law of Moses was fulfilled. Lineal restrictions of the Aaronic (Levitical) Priesthood were lifted when the law of Moses was fulfilled in the coming of the Savior and thereafter the offices of this priesthood were conferred upon worthy men without limitation to the tribe of Levi. Appearing to be the case in the Church as recorded in the New Testament and in the Book of Mormon, it is presently operative in the Church as it has been restored in the latter days. John the Baptist was a priest in the Aaronic Order, and by this authority he prepared the way for and baptized Jesus. (BD p 600)

"... the lesser priesthood continued, which priesthood holdeth the key of the ministering of angels and the preparatory gospel; which gospel is the gospel of repentance and of baptism, and the remission of sins, and the law of carnal commandments, which the Lord in his wrath, caused to continue with the house of Aaron among the children of Israel until John, whom God raised up being filled with the Holy Ghost from his mother's womb ... ordained by an angel of God ... to overthrow the kingdom of the Jews, and to make straight the way of the Lord before the face of his people, to prepare them for the coming of the Lord, in whose hand is given all power ... the offices of teacher and deacon are necessary appendages belonging to the lesser priesthood which priesthood was confirmed upon Aaron and his sons." (D&C 84:26-27)

"Although the Aaronic Priesthood is conferred in the Church today without restriction to the lineage of Aaron, the keys to this priesthood rightly belong to the firstborn of the seed of Aaron, and in the restoration of all things, the office of Bishop (President of the Priests) will once again be conferred on one of that lineage (Aaron's), as it is designated by revelation to the president of the Church." (BD p 600, D&C 84:14-21, 107:13-17)

Aaron was the firstborn son of Amram, who was the firstborn

son of Kohath, who was the second born son of Levi. [Levi's firstborn son had unspecified problems]. Israel had conferred the temporal priesthood powers upon his son Levi because Reuben, Israel's firstborn son, had forfeited this right through sin. Israel or Jacob received these priesthood powers from his father Isaac. Jacob had received them rather than Esau, because Esau had also forfeited these rights of priesthood through sin. Isaac had received these priesthood powers from his father Abraham, because Isaac was Abraham's first and only son born in the covenant. (Abraham, Isaac and Jacob p 133-136,142-56,190, The Twelve Sons of Israel p 26-28)

With reference to the law of Moses, it was "a whole collection of laws given through Moses to the house of Israel as a replacement of the higher law that they failed to obey. The law of Moses consisted of many ceremonies, rituals and symbols, to remind the people frequently of their duties and responsibilities. It included a law of carnal commandments and performances, added to the laws of the gospel.

"Faith, repentance, baptism in water, and remission of sins were part of the law, as were also the Ten Commandments. Although inferior to the fullness of the gospel, there were many provisions in the law of Moses of high ethical and moral value that were equal to the divine laws of any dispensation. The law of carnal commandments and much of the ceremonial law was fulfilled at the death and resurrection of Jesus Christ. The law functioned under the Aaronic Priesthood and was a preparatory gospel to bring its adherents to Christ." (BD p 722, JST Ex 34:1-2, Rom 3:20, Gal 3:19 Eph 2:14-16, Heb 7:11, 18-19, 9:7-14, Ne 25:24-30, Mosiah 12:27 to 13:32, 3 Ne 9:17. 15:18; D&C 8:23-27)

.."John the Baptist was the embodiment of the law of Moses, designed to prepare the way for the Messiah and make ready a people to receive him. He was the outstanding bearer of the Aaronic Priesthood in all history (son of Zacharias and Elizabeth of priestly descent), and was entrusted with its most noble mission ... He was a child of promise with prophecies of his mission having been given by Isaiah and Malachi [and by Book of Mormon prophets]. He grew up in the desert until the time arrived for his ministry to prepare the way for the Savior. The sign of the dove, as an emblem of the Holy Ghost, was a pre-appointed signal by which John knew he had baptized Jesus. (John 1:29-34, BD p.714) At the baptism of Jesus: "John saw the sign and heard the voice of the Father bearing record that Jesus was the Beloved Son in whom the Father was well pleased."(Matt 3:13-17; BD p 714)

John filled his mission in every particular. "His ministry has operated in three dispensations: he was the last of the prophets under the law of Moses, he was the first of the New Testament prophets, and he brought the Aaronic Priesthood to the dispensation of the fullness of times by conferring the keys of his priesthood upon Joseph Smith and ordaining him May 15, 1829." (BD p 715)

THE RESTORATION OF THE MELCHIZEDEK PRIESTHOOD

Not long after the appearance of John the Baptist and the restoration of the Aaronic Priesthood in the spring of 1829, another very significant event took place, "in the wilderness between Harmony, Susquehanna County, Pennsylvania and Coleville, Broome County, New York." (D&C 128:20)

There, the "Apostles Peter, James and John appeared to and conferred upon Joseph Smith and Oliver Cowdery the higher powers of the priesthood and they became apostles and special witnesses of Christ. With this ordination there was restored to the earth the same authority to act in God's name that had been enjoyed in the primitive Church." (Truth Restored p 22)

These three had conferred upon Joseph Smith "the keys of the kingdom, and the dispensation of the fullness of times." (D&C 128:20) "... Unto whom I have committed the keys of my kingdom, and the dispensation of the gospel for the last times; and for the fullness of times, in the which I will gather together in one all things, both which are in heaven and which are on earth,..." (D&C 12-13)

Though the higher or greater priesthood is named after the great high priest Melchizedek, the Bible gives few particulars concerning the functions of that priesthood, except that Christ was a high priest of that order. Within the Melchizedek Priesthood are the offices of elder, seventy, high priest, patriarch, apostle and president. Whenever the kingdom of God is upon the earth in its fullness, this priesthood must be present and functional. (BD p.739). The patriarchs and prophets in every dispensation had this authority. (D&C 84:6-17, TPJS p 180- 1)

"The president of the Church of Jesus Christ of Latter-day Saints is the President of the higher or Melchizedek Priesthood, and by virtue of this position, he possesses and exercises , as necessary, all the keys that pertain to the kingdom of God on earth. This office or calling is held by only one man at a time, and he is the only one on the earth at that time in whom all the powers and keys of the Melchizedek Priesthood are functional." (BD p 731)

Prior to the confirmation of the higher powers of the Melchizedek Priesthood upon Joseph Smith and Oliver Cowdery in 1829, some seventeen revelatory sections had been received which were later accepted as scripture by the body of the latter day Church. Of these, one, [number 2] related to Moroni's first message that Elijah was to come to plant in the hearts of the children the promises made to their fathers and to turn children's hearts to their fathers; another [number 7] declared John the Revelator tarried in the flesh and had not died; and a third, [number 13] sets forth the words pronounced by John the Baptist on Joseph Smith and Oliver Cowdery when he conferred the Priesthood of Aaron and the keys to that Priesthood upon them. The remaining fourteen were revelatory sections addressed to early church leaders individually or collectively, such as Martin Harris, Joseph Smith Sr., Oliver Cowdery, Hyrum Smith, Joseph Knight Sr., David Whitmer, John Whitmer, Peter Whitmer, all of whom would become witnesses to the Book of Mormon plates.

By April 1830 the Lord had begun to reveal how He wanted His Church to be organized and governed. With the powers of and keys to the Aaronic and Melchizedek Priesthood returned to earth and vested in worthy individuals, buttressed by Another Testament of Jesus Christ, the Book of Mormon and the seventeen revelatory sections received by that date, His Church was organized and named.

This was accomplished April 6, 1830. While in the process, the Lord reaffirmed the doctrines of creation, the fall, the atonement and baptism. Set forth for the first time in this dispensation were the duties of priesthood holders, namely elders, priests, teachers and deacons. The mode of baptism was revealed, the blessing of children and duties of members were discussed, sacramental prayers and regulations governing Church membership were given, all in Section 20. (D&C 20:1-84)

Within the next six years some ninety-six additional revelatory sections were received from the Almighty pertaining to the newly restored Church, its purposes, duties and doctrines. Of these Sections 84, 107 and 110 are especially important as they relate to the priesthood or power to act for God. We learn that a New Jerusalem and Temple are to be built in Missouri, and the line of priesthood authority from Moses to Adam; we learn that the greater priesthood administers the gospel ordinances, that the lesser priesthood administers the preparatory gospel, that men and women gain eternal life through the oath and covenant of the priesthood, that the Saints must testify of those things they have received, that every man [and woman] must stand in his own office and labor in his own calling. (D&C 84:1-120)

From Section 107 we see the two priesthoods reaffirmed, the Melchizedek and the Aaronic; those who hold the Melchizedek Priesthood have power to officiate in all offices of the Church, the Bishopric presides over the Aaronic Priesthood, which administers the outward ordinances; the Melchizedek Priesthood holds the keys of all spiritual blessings; the Aaronic Priesthood holds the keys of the ministering of angels, the First Presidency, the Twelve, and Seventy constitute the presiding quorums whose decisions are made in unity and righteousness; the Twelve set the offices of the Church in order; Bishops serve as common judges in Israel; and the First Presidency and Twelve constitute the highest court in the Church and that priesthood presidents govern their respective quorums. (D&C 107:1-100)

From Section 110 we learn that the Lord Jehovah appeared and accepted the newly constructed Kirtland Temple as His house;

that Moses appeared to Joseph Smith and Oliver Cowdery and committed unto them the keys of the gathering of Israel from the four parts of the earth, and the leading of the ten tribes from the land of the North; that Elias appeared and committed the dispensation of the gospel of Abraham, saying that in us and our seed all generations after us should be blessed; and that Elijah, the prophet, came and said that the time had fully come spoken of by Malachi, to turn the hearts of the fathers to the children, and the children to the fathers, lest the whole earth be smitten with a curse. (D&C 110: 1-16)

Three years later in 1839 in Section 121 the Lord would reveal that "the rights of the priesthood are inseparably connected with the powers of heaven, and that the powers of heaven cannot be controlled nor handled only upon the principles of righteousness"; and declared: "No power or influence can or ought to be maintained by virtue of the priesthood, only by persuasion, by long suffering, by gentleness, and meekness, and by love unfeigned; By kindness, and pure knowledge, which shall greatly enlarge the soul without hypocrisy and without guile." (D&C 121:36,41)

Thus the priesthood keys of this dispensation were committed to Joseph Smith. Other leaders were called. The Lord's Church, The Church of Jesus Christ of Latter-day Saints was organized, and functioning as of April 6, 1830.

Within ten years the Aaronic and Melchizedek Priesthoods with their respective keys, including keys to the gathering of Israel held by Moses, keys to the sealing power held by Elijah, and the keys to the dispensation of the gospel of Abraham, which contained a higher law than the law of Moses, keys essential to perfecting the members, were restored by Elias. The stage was now set for the literal and adopted seed of Abraham, who having entered the new and everlasting covenant, to now fulfill a promise of the Lord to Abraham and Sarah, made centuries before, that through them and their seed all generations after them shall be blessed.

CHAPTER VIII

LATTER-DAY SCRIPTURE
THE BOOK OF MORMON, THE DOCTRINE AND COVENANTS, THE PEARL OF GREAT PRICE INCLUDING PORTIONS OF THE JOSEPH SMITH TRANSLATION OF THE BIBLE AND THE BOOK OF ABRAHAM

AN OVERVIEW

Another Testament of Jesus Christ, a subtitle ascribed to the Book of Mormon, may well be its better title because it is more descriptive of its contents. Just as the central message of the Old Testament is a Messiah would appear on earth to save the world's people from their real enemies, death and sin, the central message of the New Testament is that He did come for these same purposes. In like manner, the Book of Mormon is Another Testament of Jesus Christ which bears witness over its one thousand plus year history, before and after His birth, that a Savior would and did come to save all mankind from death and to save those from sin who choose to qualify themselves for eternal life through repentance, and by patterning their lives after the life, teachings and example of Jesus Christ.

Much of the five hundred plus page book is revelatory in nature and is better understood when this is kept in mind. Revelation from God is knowledge of things as they are, as they were and as they are to come (D&C 43:24), and when given through His chosen servants it is very important in answering the questions: Where did we come from, why are we here, and where will we go after this life is over?

Books based on scanty evidence may help us understand the past, but unless they are tied to sources of information that experienced that past, they may prove to be of limited value. On the other hand, if information about the past comes from God, who actually experienced it directly, then what He says, when we understand it, becomes knowledge of things as they were.

Taken together, the Old and New Testaments with restorations made to them by a prophet of God, the Book of Mormon, the Doctrine and Covenants, and the Book of Abraham, set forth in the Pearl of Great Price, become powerful witnesses that all human beings who ever lived, or whoever will live on earth are the spirit children of God the Eternal Father. These scriptures also give us greater light and knowledge respecting our first earthly parents, Adam and Eve, and what they knew and understood from the very beginning. Being spirit children of God makes all humans brothers and sisters, not being on earth by accident, but by design of a loving Father who wants His children to grow, develop, become more like Him and return to His presence.

These books of scripture, the Old and New Testaments, the Book of Mormon, the Doctrine and Covenants, and the Pearl of Great Price which includes the Book of Abraham and portions of the Joseph Smith Translation of the Bible, are also called the standard works of the Church of Jesus Christ of Latter-day Saints. As a further test of the divine link between these books, in 1985 the Church of Jesus Christ of Latter-day Saints, after extensive study, provided annotated scriptures that show their doctrinal compatibility. If their sources were different the doctrines would not link with this meticulous cross referencing. Revelation from God, as it pertains to the past, present and future of God's children taken individually and collectively, underpins each of these books of scripture, so it is important we understand what the word revelation means.

Translated from the Greek word apocalypse, revelation means to make known or to uncover. Because these scriptures are very much revelatory books, they make known, uncover and add to answers to the questions: where did we come from, why are we here on earth, and where we will go after death. For nearly two thousand years the world's people have relied mostly on the Old and New Testaments to answer these questions, but due to many translations, omissions and errors therein, God's plans and purposes, His work and glory, and His design for all mankind had been obscured and confused, until the advent of the dispensation of the fullness of times, which began in

1820, the period in which we now live.

With reference to the Old and New Testaments of the Bible, one might ask: do these two books of scripture contain all of God's words for mankind, and are all the words, phrases end ideas accurately translated from the original languages from which they sprang?

While generally speaking, sound guidelines were established that helped preserve the authoritative books of the Old and New Testaments, it is becoming increasingly clear that the process used in qualifying books for the canon of scripture systematically excluded many sacred writings previously accepted as scripture which were revelatory in nature.

"The Old Testament and Jewish Masoretic Texts of the Holy Scriptures, many writers say, contain only one apocalypse: the Book of Daniel. However, apocalyptic sections are found in Ezekiel Chapter 40-48; Isaiah Chapters 24-27, 34, 56-66; and Zechariah Chapters 9-14. [In addition to the Chapters listed here latter-day prophets have identified several more Chapters in Ezekiel and Isaiah as containing revelatory material and in other Old Testament books as well.] The New Testament adds one apocalypse: the Book of Revelation; but Mark Chapter 13, 1 Thessalonians Chapter 4, and I Corinthians Chapter 15, also contain apocalyptic material. These writings were selected from numerous apocalypses popular during the time the canon of scripture was still open. One might justifiably ask why the decision makers included a few of the apocalypses in the canon of scripture and excluded an array of others".(Adam, Enoch and Noah p 266)

To make sure they did not include false writings from apostates or spurious authors, many documents were excluded because authorship could not positively be established. It is safe to say that the farther back in time one researches the more difficult it is to positively and conclusively identify authorship. It is also easier for those who do not believe God reveals the truth of things as they are, as they were and as they are to come to His authorized servants and prophets; to disregard and discard revelatory books, especially if those books were translated into another language by uninspired men.

97

Joseph Smith, the prophet, put it this way: "Many points touching the salvation of men, had been taken from the Bible, or lost, before it was compiled." He also said that the Bible was correct as "it came from the pen of the original writers," but that "ignorant translators, careless transcribers, or designing and corrupt priests have committed many effors." (HC 1:245, 6:57)

With the advent of the Dead Sea Scrolls in the latter part of the twentieth century it has been established that more than nineteen apocalyptic documents plus seven others with apocalyptic sections relating to the Old Testament, form just part of the pool of documents which appear to contain revelation or disclosure by the Lord, or information uncovered by Him for the benefit and blessing of the world's people, but were excluded from the canon of scripture because authorship could not positively be identified. They include the Apocalypses or Revelations of Enoch, Sedrach, Baruch, Adam, Abraham, Elijah and Daniel, and the Testaments of Abraham, Moses, Isaiah, Jubilees and the Twelve Patriarchs. (Adam, Enoch and Noah p 267) Fourteen other source documents mentioned in the Old Testament have been lost, another dozen documents covering the New Testament times are extant, but were excluded from the canon, along with a second dozen documents of New Testament times no longer extant, which were left out of the scriptures called the Bible.

The Book of Mormon also makes reference to other Old Testament times books which the people brought with them to the Americas along with the brass plates of Laban from Jerusalem. The writings of the prophets Zenoch, Zenos, and Neum along with an extensive prophecy by Joseph, son of Israel, and of Jacob-Israel himself, not found in the Bible, were among the Book of Mormon records. (I Ne 19: 10, Alma 33:3-17, 11 Ne 3:4-22, Alma 46:24-26)

THE BOOK OF MORMON

With so many revelatory books left out of the canon of scripture called the Bible because authorship was unknown or were left out by design of the decision makers, the Book of Mormon, as Another Testament of Jesus Christ and as a revelatory book, takes on

98

added significance. So do the Doctrine and Covenants and the Pearl of Great Price, which include portions of the Joseph Smith Translation of the Bible and the Book of Abraham, because they reveal the truth of many things as they are, as they were and as they are to come; revelations which have come through the gift and power of God.

The history of the process by which the books of the Bible were collected and recognized as a sacred authority is almost hidden in obscurity. There are several legends extant and there may have been some truth in them, but certainly are not complete or totally accurate." (BD p. 630) As a non-Catholic Bible the King James Version contains sixty-six books total, thirty-nine in the Old Testament and twenty-seven New Testament books. In recent years the actual authorship of some of the books of the Bible had been called into question. The discovery of the Dead Sea Scrolls at mid twentieth century [some are believed to have been written as early as the second century B.C.] gives evidence that the Old Testament text was corrupted at least by that time." (BD p 623) This lends credence to Joseph Smith's assessment that the Bible is the word of God as far as it is translated correctly. (Article of Faith 8)

By contrast, the Book of Mormon manuscripts were engraved on metal plates which were tightly controlled as they were passed from prophet to prophet beginning with Lehi in 600 B.C. and ending with Moroni in about 421 A.D. Those responsible for adding to the record or abridging it were authorized prophets and representatives of God. The prophet-historian Mormon is responsible for the major abridgement of these records which he entrusted to his son Moroni, also a prophet, who had seen and conversed with the resurrected Lord. The metal plates lay buried where Moroni had placed them for about 1,400 years, until God gave the signal for them to be brought forth in these latter days. The Lord chose Moroni as His messenger to the newly called prophet Joseph Smith, [who had already spoken with Him face to face] and commissioned the new prophet to translate the sacred record of Lehi's posterity and their dealings with the Lord, from reformed Egyptian to English. Aided by the use of an Urim and Thummim, the new prophet completed the translation and returned custody of the plates to Moroni.

The Book of Mormon is one of the few records in history that addresses future generations, foreshadowing events to come in the day the sacred record would be revealed to the earth. Very few persons living during its one thousand plus year history had access to all these records, and there is no indication additional copies of these plates were ever made. The plates Joseph Smith had access to were an abridgement of a much larger cache of records accumulated over more than a thousand years. Only one person, Moroni, as far as it is known, had access to the complete abridged record, and he had access at a time when he was the sole known survivor of those in America who believed in the divinity of Jesus Christ as God's Only Begotten Son. The Book of Mormon, then, was written to and for readers of the latter and last days, the period in which we now live.

Ezra Taft Benson, President of the Church of Jesus Christ of Latter-day Saints, for the November, 1985 through May, 1994 period, and who was sustained by Church members as Prophet, Seer, and Revelator, and the only person on earth authorized to exercise all priesthood keys during that period, called the Book of Mormon one of the most significant gifts God has given to the world in modern times; a gift greater in value than the advances of modern medicine, of flight or of space travel. He reminded hearers the Lord has born witness by His own mouth (1) that it is true, (D&C 17:6), (2) that it contains the truth and His own words (D&C 19:26), (3) that is was translated by power from on high (D&C 20:8), (4) that it contains the fullness of the Gospel of Jesus Christ (D&C 20:9, 42:12), (5) that it was given by inspiration and confirmed by the ministering of angels (D&C 20:10), (6) that it gives evidence that the holy scriptures are true (D&C 20:11), and (7) that those who receive it in faith shall have eternal life. (D&C 20:14)

Its importance is signaled, said President Benson, by the timetable of its coming forth. Only the First Vision and the restorations of the Aaronic and Melchizedek Priesthoods preceded the Book of Mormon's complete publication. President Benson reiterated Joseph Smith's declaration the Book of Mormon is the keystone of our religion, and added it is the keystone to the witness of Christ, to Church doctrine, and to individual testimony. (Conf Report Oct 1986, p 3-7 Ensign Nov 1986)

The Book of Mormon has much to say about the choice Adam and Eve, our first parents made, the Fall, the plan of salvation or redemption, Christ's atonement, and the gathering, perfection and redemption of Israel, and other topics which are quoted freely in the pages ahead.

THE COMING FORTH OF MANY LATTER-DAY SCRIPTURES WERE NEAR SIMULTANEOUS EVENTS

The coming forth of the Book of Mormon, the translation of many of the books of the Bible, by Joseph Smith, most of the revelations in the Doctrine and Covenants, and the translation of the Book of Abraham record were near simultaneous events wrought by the power of God, all coming forth during the 1829 through 1836 period. Together they give us great insight into pre-earth life and post-mortal life and the purpose of mortal life, lost for nearly two thousand years. The Dead Sea Scrolls were discovered in 1947, and it took scholars many years to translate and publish them. By contrast, Joseph Smith translated the Book of Mormon in just a few short weeks. Joseph Smith explained that he translated by the power of God. The Book of Mormon has stood the test of doctrinal query for more than 150 years without one credible discredit. Can the truth be anything but Joseph Smith's explanation?

All we know about pre-earth life and post-mortal life was revealed to us by God through His servants and prophets like Joseph Smith and his predecessors. Their knowledge of things as they are, as they were and as they are to come, as revealed to them by Deity, and as written in the records they left behind, tell us what truths we must know, and this knowledge forms the basis for things we must do, to obtain immortality, eternal life and to be exalted in the presence of God the Eternal Father and His Son, Jesus Christ.

Joseph Smith had become thoroughly familiar with the contents of the Book of Mormon and what its prophets had to say about the creation, our first parents Adam and Eve, their knowledge of the plan of salvation and Christ's atonement. The Lord and His angels also taught him other important things and declared them for the establishment and regulation of the kingdom of God on earth. During this period the Lord commissioned Joseph to review and add to the King James Version of the Bible as necessary. Later the first portions of the restored Genesis text, named the writings of Moses and the 24th Chapter of Matthew were included in a separate book called the Pearl of Great Price. These were actual excerpts from the Joseph Smith Translation of the Bible. The Book of Abraham was also included in the Pearl of Great Price published at a later date. While carrying out his commission regarding the King James Version of the Bible, Joseph Smith, no doubt, was influenced by what he already knew from his translation of the Book of Mormon. This influence under the direct guidance of the Lord made it possible for him to add whole segments to the original King James Version of Genesis, such as those relating to the prophet Enoch, which are enormously helpful and an invaluable aid to biblical interpretation and understanding. (BD p 717)

CHAPTER IX

LATTER-DAY SCRIPTURE
(continued)
THE DOCTRINE AND COVENANTS

As the restoration unfolded: first, with the appearance of God the Father and His Son, Jesus Christ, to Joseph Smith in answer to Joseph's question concerning which church to join; second, the visitation of the angel Moroni which led to the translation of Another Testament of Jesus Christ, the Book of Mormon; third, the restoration of the Aaronic and Melchizedek Priesthoods through John the Baptist and Peter, James and John; fourth, the Lord's command to Joseph Smith, as His prophet, to restore many concepts lost from the Old and New Testaments; He the Lord God and His angels, simultaneously taught the new prophet Joseph many other important things and declared them for the establishment and regulation of the kingdom of God on earth, in the last days. This collection of divine regulations and inspired declarations was eventually published under the title: "A Book of Commandments for the Government of the Church of Christ," in 1833 in Independence, Missouri. An enlarged compilation was published two years later in 1835 in Kirtland, Ohio, with the title, "Doctrine and Covenants of the Church of Jesus Christ of Latter-day Saints" as the Lord continued to communicate with His servants Joseph Smith and his associates. Additional revelations on other matters of record were added, as received and as accepted by competent assemblies or conferences of the Church.

Included for the first time in the current edition are sections 137 and 138 setting forth the fundamentals of salvation for the dead, and an official declaration announcing that all worthy male members of the Church may be ordained to the priesthood without regard for race or color. (Doctrine and Covenants Explanatory Introduction)

These revelations, inspired declarations and divine regulations cover a wide range of topics, some are addressed to individuals, others to groups, some to the Church as a whole, and still others to the world's people at large, some relating to temporal and others to spiritual affairs. While most of them are published in chronological order of their receipt, not all of them are. Chronologically Section Two was the first of eighteen sections received before the organization of the church April 6, 1830. (2,3,10,4,5,6,7,8, 9,11,12,13,14,15,16,17,18,19)

Section Two is an extract from the words of the Angel Moroni to Joseph Smith the Prophet, in the house of the Prophet's father on the evening of September 21, 1823, and represents God's first reference to priesthood power in this dispensation.

"Behold, I will reveal unto you the Priesthood, by the hand of Elijah the prophet, before the coming of the great and dreadful day of the Lord. And he shall plant in the hearts of the children the promises made to the fathers, and the hearts of the children shall turn to their fathers. If it were not so , the whole earth would be utterly wasted at his coming." (D&C 2:1-3)

Leading off with reference to the sealing power, the Angel Moroni foreshadowed the restoration of that power which was accomplished thirteen years later when Elijah the prophet returned at the completion of the Kirtland Temple in April, 1836, and conferred the keys to this power upon Joseph Smith and Oliver Cowdery. (See D&C Section 110) Elijah held the sealing power of the Melchizedek Priesthood and was the last prophet to do so before the time of Christ. (BD p. 664)

Still in existence today is a Jewish tradition at Passover which leaves the door open and an empty chair for Elijah whom they expect to return. The Latter-day Saints testify to the world that Elijah has already returned and has restored to earth the keys of the sealing power which he held.

Sections Three and Ten were given in the summer of 1828 and relate to the first one hundred sixteen pages called the Book of Lehi, representing the first portion of the Book of Mormon to be translated, with Martin Harris serving part of the time as scribe. These pages were lost when Joseph allowed custody of them to be passed to Martin, temporarily. The original manuscript was not recovered, nor were these portions of the plates re-translated, because wicked men planned to trap the young prophet by altering his translation and discrediting him. However, the Lord was not pleased with His prophet's negligence in allowing custody of this sacred translation to pass to another even for a short period of time. So Joseph Smith was denied the power to translate the rest of the Book of Mormon record for a season, allowing him time to contemplate the consequences of his actions, repent and recognize that he should not have feared man more than God. Joseph was then informed God is merciful to those who repent, commanded to do so, and if he did repent, assured he was still chosen and called to the work.

In these sections God reminds all readers that He does not forget His promises; for He had promised through His prophets, the knowledge and testimonies of some of Lehi's sons who were of the house of Israel and who had left Jerusalem about 600 B.C. [and their subsequent posterity] who were righteous, would be restored and brought to the attention of other members of Lehi's posterity who had dwindled in unbelief, because of the iniquity and failing away of their fathers. The Book of Mormon record afterwards referred to those in its history who were righteous and kept the commandments of God, as the Nephites, and those who were unrighteous and who ignored God's commandments, and who fell away, as the Lamanites. God's purpose in preserving these plates was to fulfill His promise that the posterity of the Lamanites might come to a knowledge of their fathers, that they might know of God's promises, that they might believe the gospel, rely on the merits of Christ, be glorified through faith in His name, and be saved through their repentance.(D&C 3:1-20)

In Section Ten the Lord discusses at length the plans of wicked men influenced by Satan to discredit and destroy Joseph Smith's credibility and his testimony. They planned to alter the translation of these one hundred sixteen pages, but God, knowing of their plans, explained the Book of Mormon record could accomplish its purpose without these one hundred sixteen pages. He restored to Joseph the power to translate and reminded him the plates of Nephi contained a more detailed account of the period covered by the lost Book of Lehi record, and instructed him to set aside the plates covering the one hundred sixteen pages and translate other portions of the Book of Mormon record instead.

"And now, because the account which is engraven upon the plates of Nephi is more particular concerning the things which in my wisdom, I would bring to the knowledge of the people in this account. Therefore, you shall translate the engravings which are on the plates of Nephi, down even till you come to the reign of King Benjamin, or until you come to that which you have translated, which you have retained .... and behold, all the remainder of this work does contain all those parts of my gospel which my holy prophets, yea ,also my disciples, desired in their prayers should come forth unto this people. And I said unto them, that it should be granted unto them according to their faith in their prayers; Yea, and this was their faith- that my gospel, which I gave unto them that they might preach in their days, might come unto their brethren, the Lamanites and also all that had become Lamanites because of their dissensions. Now, this is not all - their faith in their prayers was that this gospel should be made known also, if it were possible that other nations should possess the land; And thus they did leave a blessing upon this land in their prayers, that whosoever should believe in this gospel in this land might have eternal life. Yea, that it might be free unto all of whatsoever nation, kindred, tongue or people they may be." (D&C 10:40-51)

Again and again over the centuries the Lord invited disciples and groups of disciples to pray; to knock and it shall be open to you, seek and ye shall find, ask and it shall be given you; and the Lord promised to hear the prayers of the righteous and answer them. The above verses clearly indicate God does not forget His promises. This is especially true for the persistent prayers of the prophets who knew the covenant "cycle" which contained the hope of a righteous return to Christ and ultimately to the Father. These were the prayers the Lord honored. So happy and so grateful for the gospel were the Nephite prophets and righteous disciples of Israel in America through Joseph, son of Israel's descendants who were led there, that they prayed the posterity of their brethren and sisters who had fallen away and who were called Lamanites, might at some future day have their words of testimony, and not only their Lamanite relations of the latter days, but they prayed the posterity of those from other nations who would possess the land of America might also have their words of testimony. These Nephite prophets and righteous disciples had left their blessing upon the land of America that it might be free for all who come of whatsoever nation, kindred, tongue and people they may be. In answering, the Lord granted their desires according to their faith in their prayers, and brought forth their records as contained in the Book of Mormon, and wicked men of the latter-days were not going to frustrate His promises.

Concluding this revelation the Lord declared: "Behold, I am Jesus Christ, the Son of God. I came unto mine own, and mine own received me not. I am the light which shineth in darkness, and the darkness comprehendeth it not. I am he who said- Other sheep have I which are not of this fold-unto my disciples and many there were that understood me not. And I will show unto this people that I had other sheep and that they were a branch of Jacob; And I will bring to light their marvelous works, which they did in my name; Yea, and I will also bring to light my gospel which was ministered unto them, and behold they shall not deny that which you have received, but shall build it up, and shall bring to light the true points of my doctrine, yea, and the only doctrine which is in me.

"And this I do that I may establish my gospel, that there may not be so much contention; yea, Satan doth stir up the hearts of the people to contention concerning the points of my doctrine; and in these things they do err ... Behold, this is my doctrine- whosoever repenteth and cometh unto me, the same is my church .... And now, behold, whosoever is of my church, and endureth of my church to the end, him will I establish upon my rock, and the gates of hell shall not prevail against them. And now remember the words of him who is the life and light of the world, your Redeemer, your Lord and your God. Amen". (D&C 10:52-70)

Towards the end of His ministry Jesus referred to himself in metaphor as the good shepherd, that He knew His sheep and they were known of Him, that He would lay down His life for the sheep and: "other sheep I have, which are not of this fold: them also I must bring, and they shall hear my voice; and there shall be one fold and one shepherd." (John 10: 16)

Speaking to the Nephites in America after his resurrection the Savior, Jesus Christ said unto them: "Ye are my disciples; and ye are a light unto this people, who are a remnant of the house of Joseph. And behold, this is the land of your inheritance: and the Father hath given it unto you. ... And verily I say unto you, that ye are they of whom I said: Other sheep I have which are not of this fold; them also I must bring, and they shall hear my voice; and there shall be one fold and one shepherd. And they understood me not, for they supposed it had been the gentiles; for they understood not that the Gentiles should be converted through their preaching.,

"And they understood me not that I said they shall hear my voice; and they understood me not that the Gentiles should not at any time hear my voice that I should not manifest myself unto them save it were by the Holy Ghost. But, behold, ye have both heard my voice and seen me; and ye are my sheep, and ye are numbered among those whom the Father hath given me." (3 Ne 15:12-24)

The remaining fifteen of the eighteen pre-church organization sections of the Doctrine and Covenants were received shortly before, during, or shortly after the translation of the Book of Mormon resumed and was completed. Ten of these sections (4,5,8,9,11,12,14,15,16,17) were addressed to early associates of Joseph Smith, some of whom inquired of their duty through the prophet. Seven of these men later became witnesses to the Book of Mormon as reported in its introductory pages.

Believing in the sacred experiences of his son Joseph Jr. beginning with the visitation of God the Father and His Son, Jesus Christ, believing in the Angel Moroni's visit with his son and instruction relating to the Book of Mormon translation, knowing of the progress being made in the translation of that sacred book, and providing whatever assistance, succor and support he could; Joseph Smith Sr. desired to know what role the Lord would have him play in the work of the restoration. Inquiring of the Lord in behalf of his father Joseph Sr., Joseph Jr. received an answer in February, 1829.

To Joseph Smith Sr. the Lord said in part: "...behold, a marvelous work is about to come forth among the children of men,

Therefore, 0 ye that embark in the service of God, see that ye serve him with all your might, mind, and strength.... if ye have desires to serve God, ye are called to the work. For behold, the field is white already to harvest; and lo, he that thrusteth in his sickle with his might, the same layeth up in store that he perisheth not, but bringeth salvation to his soul; and faith, hope, charity, and love, with an eye single to the glory of God, qualify him for the work. Remember faith, virtue, knowledge, temperance, patience, brotherly kindness, godliness, charity, humility, diligence. Ask and ye shall receive, knock and it shall be opened unto you." (D&C 4:1-7) Shortly after this revelation was given, now called section four, Joseph Smith Sr. became one of the Eight Witnesses to the Book of Mormon.

A month later, Martin Harris requested that a similar inquiry be made of the Lord through Joseph Smith Jr. for him. Made clear in the Lord's response was that Martin was to serve in a support role to Joseph Smith, the prophet, and that this generation would receive the Lord's word through Joseph. In addition to Joseph's testimony was the testimony of three other witnesses to the Book of Mormon, whom God would call and have ordained, in fulfillment of Book of Mormon prophecy. Among these three witnesses Martin Harris could be one, if he humbled himself in mighty prayer and faith, and repented. (D&C 5:1-35) As indicated in Section Five, Martin learned what he was to do to become one of the three witnesses; he repented and humbled himself and did become one of the three witnesses to the Book of Mormon soon thereafter.

Beginning his labors as scribe for Joseph Smith in the translation of the Book of Mormon April 7, 1829, Oliver Cowdery had already received a divine manifestation of the truth of the prophet's testimony representing the plates on which were engraved the Book of Mormon record. The Lord had spoken to him through the prophet as recorded in Section Six, as previously mentioned, and further counseled Oliver to hold out faithful to the end, and if he did he would be saved in the kingdom of God "which is the greatest of all gifts of God; for there is no gift greater than the gift of salvation." (D&C 6:13) Oliver was to look unto Christ and do good continually, to doubt not, or fear not and keep God's commandments, and if he did, he would inherit the kingdom of heaven. (D&C 6:14-37)

As previously mentioned, not long after the appearance of John the Baptist and the restoration of the Aaronic Priesthood in May of 1829, an even more significant event took place "in the wilderness between Harmony, Susquehanna County, Pennsylvania and Coleville, Broome County, New York." (D&C 128:20) In June, 1829 the "Apostles Peter, James and John appeared to and conferred upon Joseph Smith and Oliver Cowdery the higher powers of the priesthood and they became apostles and special witnesses of Christ.

With this ordination there was restored to earth the same authority to act in God's name that had been enjoyed in the primitive Church." (Truth Restored p 22) These three had conferred upon Joseph Smith "the keys of the kingdom, and the dispensation of the fullness of times," (D&C 128:20)

"unto whom I have committed the keys of my kingdom, and the dispensation of the gospel for the last times; and for the fullness of times, in the which I will gather together in one all things, both which are in heaven and which are on earth..." (D&C 27:12-13)

Simultaneously with these events, the Lord was preparing the remainder of the eight witnesses to the Book of Mormon including John and Peter Whitmer, Jun. each of whom had sought to know what role the Lord would have them play in the restoration. Joseph Smith inquired of the Lord in their behalf, and the Lord responded in June, 1829 saying to each of them in identical revelations, in part: "...I speak unto you with sharpness and with power, for mine arm is over all the earth. And I will tell you that which no man knoweth save me and thee alone-- For many times you have desired of me to know that which would be of the most worth unto you. Behold, blessed are you for this thing, and for speaking my words which I have given you according to my commandments. And now, behold, I say unto you, that the thing which will be of the most worth unto you will be to declare repentance unto this people, that you may bring souls unto me, that you may rest with them in the kingdom of my Father, Amen." (D&C 15 &16:1-6)

Nearing completion of the Book of Mormon translation, sometime in June 1829, Joseph and his scribe Oliver translated the third reference to three special witnesses who were to be designated for this sacred book. (Ether 5:2-4, 2 Nephi 11:3, and 27:12) Oliver Cowdery, David Whitmer, and Martin Harris were moved with an inspired desire to be these three witnesses. The Prophet inquired of the Lord through the Urim and Thummim and received what is known as Section Seventeen, which reads in part:..."you shall have a view of the plates, and also of the breastplate, the sword of Laban, the Urim and Thummim, which were given to the brother of Jared upon the mount, when he talked with the Lord face to face, and the miraculous directors which were given to Lehi while in the wilderness, on the borders of the Red Sea... And after that you ... have seen them with your eyes, you shall testify of them by the power of God ... And ye shall testify that you have seen them, even as my servant Joseph Smith Jun. has seen them; ... And I, Jesus Christ, your Lord and your God, have spoken it unto you, that I might bring about my righteous purposes unto the children of men..." (D&C 17:1-8 See the Testimony of Three Witnesses in front of the Book of Mormon.)

John the Baptist in his resurrected state explained that he was acting under the direction of Peter, James and John, who would later confer a higher priesthood power upon them. Anticipating this event the Prophet, Oliver Cowdery and David Whitmer sought further knowledge on the matter and the Lord gave it to them through Section Eighteen which reads in part speaking directly to Oliver and David:

"I speak unto you, even as unto Paul mine apostle, for you are called even with that same calling with which he was called. Remember the worth of souls is great in the sight of God; For behold, the Lord your Redeemer suffered death in the flesh; wherefore he suffered the pain of all men, that all men might repent and come unto him. And he hath risen again from the dead, that he might bring all men unto him, on conditions of repentance. and how great is his joy in the soul that repenteth!

"Wherefore, you are called to cry repentance unto this people. And if it so be that you should labor all your days in crying repentance unto this people, and bring save it be one soul unto me, how great shall be your joy with him in the kingdom of my Father! And now, if your joy will be great with one soul that you have

111

brought unto me into the kingdom of my Father, how great will be your joy if you would bring many souls unto me."(D&C 18:9-16)

To gain salvation, however, those who have been brought into the kingdom as new members must take upon them the name of Christ. More specifically, now having His gospel, rock and salvation before them, the new fellow citizens with the Saints are encouraged to ask the Father for their needs in the name of Christ, and the Holy Ghost will manifest all things that are expedient for them to know, and informed that without faith, hope and charity they can do nothing.

They were and are to contend with no church except the church of the devil, to speak the truth with soberness, assuring that those who repent and are baptized in Christ's name and endure to the end shall be saved, and that there is no other name given whereby men can be saved, that they shall be called by that name [Christ] at the last day, else they cannot have place in the kingdom of the Eternal Father. (D&C 18:17-25)

With the Book of Mormon translation essentially complete and awaiting its publication, the Lord was now preparing Joseph Smith, Oliver Cowdery, and David Whitmer to organize a church based on a foundation of apostles and prophets with Himself, Jesus Christ, as the chief cornerstone. These three men were informed that,

"there are others who are called to declare my gospel, both to the Gentile and unto Jew, Yea, even twelve; and the Twelve shall be my disciples and they shall take upon them my name; and the Twelve are they who shall desire to take upon them my name with all purpose of heart... they are called to go into all the world to preach my gospel unto every creature ... ordained of me to baptize in my name, according to that which is written ... And now I speak unto you the Twelve, behold my grace is sufficient for you, you must walk uprightly before me and sin not ... you are ordained of me to ordain priests and teachers to declare my gospel, according to the power of the Holy Ghost which is in you, according to the callings and gifts of God unto men; And 1, Jesus Christ, your Lord and your God have spoken it. These words are not of men, nor of man, but of me, where fore ye shall testify they are of me and not of man." (D&C 18:26-36)

In the next three verses Oliver Cowdery and David Whitmer

were commissioned to search out the Twelve whom they shall know by their desires and works. (v37-39)

The major message of the Twelve to the world's people is that each person should repent and be baptized in the name of Jesus Christ, not just men, but women and children who have arrived at the years of accountability. [eight years or older] (D&C 18:40-46, 68:25)

A marvelous work and a wonder unto the convincing of many of their sins, that they may come unto repentance and unto the kingdom of the Father, would soon be wrought by the hands of these apostles and others. Section Eighteen ends with the declaration: "Behold, I am Jesus Christ, your Lord and your God, and your Redeemer, by the power of my Spirit I have spoken it, Amen". (D&C 18:47)

About nine months later in March, 1830, the last pre-church organization revelation was given through Joseph Smith to Martin Harris. In it Christ reminds them that He retains all power, even to destroying Satan and his works at the end of the world, and the last great day of judgment, when He will judge every man according to his works and the deeds he has done. (D&C 19:13) He declared to them: Every man and woman must repent or suffer, and that eternal punishment is God's punishment. However, the effect of God's punishment on an individual is ameliorated through repentance:

"For behold, I, God, have suffered these things for all, that they might not suffer if they should repent. But if they would not repent they must suffer even as I; Which suffering caused myself, even God, the greatest of all, to tremble, because of pain, and to bleed at every pore and to suffer both body and spirit ... Wherefore, I command you to repent, lest I humble you with my mighty power; and that you confess your sins, lest you suffer these punishments of which I have spoken ... And I command you that you might preach naught but repentance ... For they cannot bear meat now, but milk they must receive; wherefore ... Learn of me, and listen to my words; walk in the meekness of my Spirit, and you shall have peace in me. I am Jesus Christ; I came by the will of the Father, and I do his will." (D&C 19:4-24)

Instructing Martin Harris not to covet his own property the

Lord commanded him to impart of it for the printing of the Book of Mormon, "which contains the truth and the word of God-Which is my word to the Gentile, that soon it may go to the Jew [house of Israel] of whom the Lamanites are a remnant, that they may believe the gospel, and look not for a Messiah to come who has already come." (D&C 19:25-28)

Martin Harris was also to declare the glad tidings contained in the Book of Mormon and publish it on the mountains, every high place and among every people he was permitted to see. He was to do it humbly, trusting in God, and declare repentance, and faith on the Savior, and remission of sins by baptism, and by fire, yea, even the Holy Ghost. Martin was to pay the debt contracted with the printer for the Book of Mormon, and go out into the world speaking freely to all, to preach, exhort and declare the truth with a sound of rejoicing, crying: "Hosanna, Hosanna, blessed be the name of the Lord God!" (D&C 19:25-37) Section nineteen ends with an appeal for Martin Harris to be humble and meek and come unto Christ. (D&C 19: 38-41)

Thus the third of the three witnesses to the Book of Mormon was prepared for his role as a Book of Mormon witness who would later join Oliver Cowdery and David Whitmer in searching out the Twelve especial witnesses in the years ahead.

Further references to these eighteen and the remaining one hundred and twenty sections of the Doctrine and Covenants are interwoven by subject matter in other standard works: the Book of Mormon, the Old and New Testaments and the Pearl of Great Price which contains portions of the Joseph Smith Translation of the King James Version of the Bible and the Book of Abraham. Selected concepts and doctrines revealed in Latter-day scripture and related observations are discussed in the pages ahead, after a brief overview of the Joseph Smith Translation of the Bible and the Book of Abraham.

THE JOSEPH SMITH TRANSLATION OF THE BIBLE

Genesis as a book of the Bible did not come as imaginations

from Moses'mind. Instead, material in Genesis was revealed to him by the God of heaven and earth. Characters in Genesis were long since dead when Moses began to write. The manuscripts he left behind are no longer extant. Subsequent manuscripts based on the original have gone through many translations by uninspired men over the centuries. Passages difficult to understand and even more difficult to translate into another language may well have been confused, obscured, mistranslated or omitted altogether.

As Another Testament of Jesus Christ, the Book of Mormon was just off the presses when the Lord commanded Joseph Smith, His newly appointed prophet, to restore to Moses'record in Genesis of the King James Version important information lost from the original record; information lost through many translations, confused, obscured, mistranslated or omitted altogether by uninspired men. Restorations to Moses'record in Genesis were made by Joseph Smith the first year of the Church's organization from June 1830 through February 183 1. Restorations to many other books of the Bible were made by Joseph within the next few years.

To reiterate, while carrying out his commission regarding the King James Version of the Bible, Joseph Smith, no doubt, was influenced by what he already knew from his translation of the Book of Mormon. This influence under the direct guidance of the Lord made it possible for him to add whole segments to the original King James Version of Genesis, such as those relating to the prophet Enoch, which are enormously helpful and an invaluable aid to biblical interpretation and understanding. (BD p 717)

These restorations in the Bible text, plus the Book of Mormon, plus the revelations in the Book of Abraham brought about five years later, and those in the Doctrine and Covenants, also coming forth during the 1829 through 1836 period, contain a number of concepts important to our understanding of pre-earth life, including the council in heaven, the agency of man, the plans offered, the acceptance of Jehovah's plan and the rejection of Satan's plan, Satan's rebellion and his being cast out, the creation or organization of planet earth, our first parents Adam and Eve, their knowledge of the plan of salvation, and Christ's anticipated atonement, and many other

115

concepts important to our understanding of where we came from, why we are here and where we are going after this life is over.

THE BOOK OF ABRAHAM

Through providential circumstances a manuscript buried with a mummy found in the Middle East containing some of the prophet Abraham's writings was brought to America and fell into the hands of Joseph Smith the prophet in 1835. In that record we see that as God's prophet, seer and revelator, with the help of a Urim and Thummim, Abraham shared a number of concepts important to our understanding of pre-earth or pre-mortal life which help answer the question, when did we come from.

He learned, for example, that each person born to earthly parents existed as a spirit child of God the Eternal Father in pre-earth or pre-mortal life. Though our physical bodies begin at conception, our spiritual selves already existed and came to earth from the presence of God. Our spiritual selves brought with us intelligence and the power to make choices. This power to make choices for ourselves is called the agency of man. Our spirit selves took up residence in a newly formed physical body. The spirit and body constitute the soul of man. (D&C 88:15, Abr. Chapter 3)

Abraham also learned that some spirits were and are greater than others, and that the firstborn spiritual son of God the Eternal Father was and is the greatest of them all, and that He was chosen for the role He would play on earth when bom in the flesh. Abraham and others also were chosen for the roles they were to play on earth before they were born in the flesh, such as Jeremiah. Thus, this concept of being chosen before the time is called foreordination.

Abraham learned that God's purpose in sending His spirit children to earth to take physical bodies included proving each soul "herewith to see if they will do all things whatsoever the Lord their God shall command them"; that earth life is a second estate for man, those coming to earth having made the right choices in pre-mortal life; and that those who keep their second estate, i.e. make the right choices in this life, shall have glory added upon their heads forever

116

and ever. (Abr 3:25-28)

Acting as God's revelator, Abraham also learned of the creation, or organization of planet earth, a past event, and wrote it down for future generations. Comparing his record of the creation and that of Moses, we gain additional truths.

The focus of Abraham's account of the creation is on the plans that were made for the creation or organization of planet earth, while the Genesis account emphasizes the implementation of those plans. A much clearer picture as to why Abraham left Ur is obtained from his own record than from the Moses' record. Abraham sought the blessings of the patriarchal order or priesthood. He understood the origins and government of Egypt. All of the gospel blessings were promised Abraham and his seed, and through his seed to all mankind. He understood much about the sun, the moon, and the stars. He learned and wrote about pre-earth life, foreordination, the choosing of a Redeemer and the second estate of man as previously mentioned; and that through his priesthood power and that of his righteous posterity all the families of the earth were and are to be blessed; and through that priesthood power all of his righteous posterity literal and adopted may be protected from their real enemies of death and sin as discussed in Chapter IV. These and other truths from the Book of Abraham are interwoven by subject matter in the Chapters ahead.

CHAPTER X

SELECTED CONCEPTS AND DOCTRINES SET FORTH IN LATTER-DAY SCRIPTURE AND RELATED OBSERVATIONS

ORIGINS OF PLANET EARTH AND THE DEVELOPMENT OF ITS LIFE FORMS

Some theorize that planet earth was once part of a huge mass of white hot elements and inorganic compounds which exploded, sending material in all directions from an unidentified and un-referenced place in the cosmos. Eventually, the surface of that spherical globe we call earth cooled, a crust formed and life began, spontaneously or accidently; first, as strands of DNA and other organic chemicals that developed into single celled organisms with varying life cycles. These cells began reproducing, and that over many millennia progressed to multiple celled, multiple purposed organisms with specialized functions which took on infinite varieties and forms, one of which is modern man. Conspicuously absent from such theories is the role a higher form of intelligence, or God, may have played in the process.

On the other hand, the Old Testament book of scripture called Genesis makes clear the process of creation or organization of planet earth and its flora and fauna, including man were in hands of God who spelled out the order of creation beginning with light, heat and sources of water, all essential for living organisms. Separating the light from the darkness by way of a spinning sphere at an appropriate distance from a sun around which the earth circled, temperature is controlled within certain tolerances essential for earth's life forms including man.

Leading off with "In the beginning God created the heaven and earth. And the earth was without form, and void, and darkness was upon the face of the deep," (Gen 1:1-2) Genesis makes no mention as to where God got the materials for planet earth or whether they always existed. While silent on the origins of the materials from which planet earth was organized, it does make clear it was the Spirit of God which

119

moved upon the water, and through a series of commands and subsequent actions carried out, the heaven and earth and all of its life forms came into being during six creative or organizing periods. (Gen 1:1-33)

One might justifiably ask: whom was God commanding? Were they the inorganic compounds. and elements of the earth, which were without form and void, or were they of a much higher intelligence capable of carrying out complex commands which required great understanding of chemicals, chemical reactions and the interrelated life cycles of billions of organisms ?

That God was not acting alone as a single entity is made clear in Chapter I verse 26: "And God said, Let us make man in our image, after our likeness, and let them have dominion over the fish of the sea, and over the fowl of the air, and over the cattle, and over all the earth, and over every creeping thing that creepeth upon the earth." Later King David testified: "The earth is the Lord's, and the fullness thereof, the world, and they that dwell therein. For he founded it upon the seas, and established it upon the floods." (PS 24:1-2) Making man in the image of God and giving him dominion over earth's flora and fauna implies man's intelligence is superior to all other life forms, and when controlled under guidelines set forth by God, capable of subduing the earth, as commanded.

Several Old Testament scriptures imply there was a spiritual creation which preceded the natural or physical creation. For example, from Genesis 2:5. "And every plant before it was in the earth, and every herb of the field before it grew; for the Lord God had not caused it to rain upon the earth, and there was not a man to till the ground."

From Psalms 82:6 ..."you are children of the most high."; from Ecclesiastes 12:7 "... and the spirit shall return unto God who gave it;" from Hosea 1:10 "...Ye are the sons of the living God"; from Acts 17:29 "...we are the offspring of God..."; and Hebrews 12:9 "... shall we not much rather be in subjection unto the Father of spirits and live?"

However, when latter-day scripture is read in concert with the Old and New Testaments, especially the Joseph Smith Translation of

Genesis it becomes evident there was not one, but two creations, the first spiritual and the second natural or physical. From the JST Genesis text in the Pearl of Great Price:" And every plant of the field before it was in the earth, and every herb of the field before it grew. For I, the Lord God created all things, of which I have spoken, spiritually, before they were naturally upon the face of the earth. For, I, the Lord God, had not caused it to rain upon the face of the earth. And I, the Lord God, had created all the children of men; and not yet a man to till the ground; for in heaven created I them; and there was not yet flesh upon the earth, neither in the water, neither in the air. ...all things were before created; but spiritually were they created and made according to my word." (Moses 3:5, Pearl of Great Price)

More than one intelligence participated in creating and organizing the earth and making it ready for the billions upon billions of living organisms with interrelated life cycles that would soon live on planet earth. Jehovah, or Yahweh, as the pre-mortal Christ is the living God of planet earth which He created under the direction of His Father Elohim. Life on earth represents a second stage of existence for human beings, who in the premortal world existed as spirit children of God. Those who come to earth and take physical bodies qualified to do so by the choices they made and the lives they lived while they were in the pre-mortal world. Some spirits are greater than others and Jehovah is the greatest of them all. Each is a spirit son or daughter of God the Eternal Father, Elohim, and each had to come to earth and receive a physical body to fill the full measure of his or her creation. (Moses, Aaron and Joshua, Prologue)

GOD'S WORK AND GLORY

Sometime after his experience with the burning bush, where he was called to deliver Israel and before his departure for Egypt, Moses had an astonishing face to face encounter with God. The Almighty revealed the creation of planet earth and rehearsed the early history of its first inhabitants with Moses, beginning with Adam. Revelations included (1) the condition under which a man may see God and still live in the flesh; (2) information that Moses was made in the

121

similitude of God's only Begotten Son, the Savior, yet to be born in the flesh; (3) descriptions of the power of Satan, who is allowed to tempt and persuade man; (4) making it clear that planet earth is but one of the numberless worlds God has created; (5) an account of the creation which was clearly of planet earth only; (6) setting forth the work and glory of God; and (7) a command for Moses to write it all down. (Moses 1:1-42, Pearl of Great Price)

As revealed to Moses, God's work and glory is to bring to pass the immortality and eternal life of man. He, God, created the heaven and earth, all forms of life including man, and gave him dominion over all else. To bring to pass the immortality and eternal life of man presupposes God the Eternal Father has a plan to bring it about for all mankind who choose to embrace it. It is called the Plan of Salvation. (Moses 1:39-42, Pearl of Great Price)

THE AGENCY OF MAN

Freedom to choose to accept the plan or reject it, and each of its provisions along the way was had from the beginning, a principle God will not preempt. A latter-day prophet, David O. McKay, declared that next to the bestowal of life itself, the right to direct that life is God's greatest gift to man. (Conf Report Apr 1950, p. 32)

Adam and Eve were free to choose, even if the choices had important consequences. The command to be fruitful, multiply and replenish the earth and subdue it, was introduced before the command to refrain from eating the forbidden fruit. Of special significance is the phrase, **nevertheless thou mayest choose for thyself**, restored to the Genesis text.(Moses 3:17)

Adam and Eve were free choose as long as they knew of the consequences. They could refrain from eating the fruit and live forever in the Garden, without children, or they could eat the fruit which would bring about the necessary changes in their bodies so they could have children and fulfill the command to be fruitful, multiply and replenish the earth, but in partaking of the fruit they would bring death to themselves and all their posterity. But bringing death to themselves would also bring life to billions of others even if for a limited duration.

Choosing between these two choices was not easy. The first choice was to do something, that is, to be fruitful, multiply replenish and subdue the earth. The second choice was not to do something, that is, do not partake of the forbidden fruit. Both choices had consequences. They could not do both simultaneously. Through guile or trickery, Satan persuaded Eve to believe she could have knowledge of good and evil without tasting death. Some say Satan lied to Eve when he said she would not die if she touched and ate the fruit, but told her the truth when he said, as a result, she would be as God, knowing good and evil. Others characterize Satan's statement as a half truth intended to deceive. She did not die immediately. She did gain knowledge, but when cast out of the garden she and Adam experienced spiritual death, being unable to dwell in the presence of God without reconciliation with Him. They also subjected the earth and all of its creatures to physical death.

With reference to consequences, another latter-day prophet, Ezra Taft Benson, reminds us , "We are free to choose, but we are not free to alter the consequences of those choices."

Concluding the fruit of the tree was good for food and desired to make her wise, Eve partook of it, and gave unto her husband, Adam, and he did eat. After partaking of the fruit herself, had Eve not given Adam of the same fruit, she would have died, and he would have lived forever in the Garden. No children would have been conceived in this situation. Adam recognized this and chose to eat of the fruit also, to fulfill the other command to bring forth children, even if doing so brought death upon himself. Put another way, if he wanted to remain in the Garden, he was not to eat of the fruit. If he wanted to have children, he would have to eat of the fruit, have children and die physically and spiritually. He chose the latter.

Again, this is a pattern. There were two voices or influences seeking to get the attention of Adam and Eve. The same is true for us.. There are at least two, if not multiple choices trying to influnce us. The grea t value of the scriptures is that they show us the way. They help us make choices to listen to the voices that will put us on the straight and narrow path that leads to salvation, perfection and eternal life. But the choice is ours pertaining to which voice we will listen to.

THE FALL

Partaking of the forbidden fruit was contrary to the command of God, and therefore a transgression of His law. It brought about the death of Adam and Eve and all their posterity. But without this transgression the spirit children of Heavenly Father would not have had the experience of earth life. Eating the fruit which brought about the changes in their bodies as a result, is called the Fall. (Gospel Principles p 32)

"Latter-day Scripture helps us understand that their fall was a necessary step in the plan of life and a great blessing to all of us. Because of the Fall, we are blessed with physical bodies, the right to choose between good and evil, and the opportunity to gain eternal life. None of these privileges would have been ours had Adam and Eve remained in the Garden." (Gospel Principles p 32-3)

As Eve put it, "were it not for our transgression we never would have had seed (children) and never should have known good and evil, and the joy of our redemption, and the eternal life which God giveth unto all the obedient." (Moses 5:11, PGP) The Book of Mormon Lehi, clarified: "And now behold, if Adam had not transgressed he would not have fallen (been cut off from the presence of God), but he would have remained in the Garden of Eden. And all things which were created must have remained in the same state in which they were after they were created; ... And they would have had no children, wherefore they would have remained in a state of innocence, having no joy, for they knew no misery, doing no good, for they knew no sin. But behold, all things have been done in the wisdom of him who knoweth all things. Adam fell that man might be; and men are that they might have joy." (2 Ne 2:22-25)

Note the additions made to the King James Version of the Bible by Joseph Smith, at the command of God, and the words of Book of Mormon prophet Lehi indicate, while in the Garden, Adam and Eve lived in the pleasant state of bliss, but that no progression was possible without the Fall, and that Adam and Eve's posterity benefitted from their disobedience and transgression of a law of God. But one might argue, is it right or just for all mankind to benefit from Adam

124

and Eve's transgression; that is, to be blessed with physical bodies, the right to choose between good and evil, and with the opportunity to gain eternal life because of their fall? Justice demands that it would only be right or acceptable for others to benefit from Adam and Eve's transgression if they, or someone else paid the price for that transgression, and made things right with the greatest lawgiver of them all, God the Eternal Father.

Another view is that God allowed Adam and Eve to offer their innocence as a sacrifice so all of His spirit children would experience mortality, their second estate, following a pattern set by Heavenly Father from the beginning whereby selected individuals, including His Only Begotten Son, sacrifice themselves for the greater good of all. Each sacrifice was voluntary, and the consequences of the sacrifice were known in advance. For Adam and Eve their choices brought death unto themselves, but also brought temporary life to their posterity and all reproductions of creation, the right of their posterity to choose between good and evil with an opportunity for eternal life for each soul. For God's Only Begotten Son, His sacrifice in the Garden of Gethsemane and on the cross, which was voluntary, brought immortality for all mankind and the possibility of eternal life with the Father for those who choose to qualify.

With reference to their innocence before the Fall, when compared to mature married, men and women of today, Adam and Eve may be likened to pre-puberty children, at least in terms of the feelings and emotions connected with sexual attraction, and the hormones and the chemical reactions necessary to produce children. They also had no basis for comparing good and evil. They were free to eat of the fruit of all the trees of the Garden, except the tree of the knowledge of good and evil, of which they were commanded not to eat, or even to touch, because to do so would bring upon themselves death. Nevertheless they were free to choose for themselves whether to eat it or not, constrained only by the command of God.

As the first man and woman on earth, they had had no experience with death. No one they knew had ever died, and they had no understanding of the chemical, hormonal, emotional, mental and physical changes in their bodies and minds, eating the fruit of the tree of knowledge of good and evil might bring. Also commanded to bring forth children before the Fall took place, being in a state of innocence they likely did not know how to produce children, nor had the chemical, hormonal, emotional, and mental reactions and sexual attractions become operative in them before the fruit was eaten.

"Before the Fall, Adam and Eve had physical bodies, but no blood. There was on sin, no death, and no children among any of the earthly creations. With the eating of the 'forbidden fruit', Adam and Eve became mortal, sin entered, blood formed in their bodies, and death became a part of life. Adam became the"first flesh" upon the earth. (Moses 3:7 PGP), meaning that he and Eve were the first to become mortal. After Adam fell, the whole creation fell and became mortal. Adam's fall brought physical and spiritual death into the world upon all mankind." (BD p 670) From the Book of Mormon prophet Samuel we learn: "... for all mankind, by the fall of Adam being cut off from the presence of the Lord, are considered as dead, both as to things temporal and to things spiritual." (Helaman 14:16-17) Through the Fall, Eve literally became the 'mother of all living", when her action of eating the fruit of the tree of knowledge of good and evil caused the life cycle of all living things to commence.(Gen 3:20)

All creation had been prepared to produce offspring, but this power lay dormant until Eve's action in partaking of the fruit, and that action brought temporary physical life through each organisms reproductive processes, followed by physical death when each's life cycle is over. Through the atonement of Jesus Christ physical death for all humans becomes temporary as each awaits resurrection, and through the atonement of Jesus Christ all may be redeemed from the spiritual fall or spiritual death who choose to qualify.

"Because Adam and Eve had eaten of the fruit of the tree of knowledge of good and evil, the Lord sent them out of the Garden of Eden into the world as we now know it. Their physical condition changed as a result of their eating the forbidden fruit. As God had promised, they became mortal. They were able to have children. They and their children would experience sickness, pain, and physical death. Because of their transgression, Adam and Eve suffered spiritual death. This meant they and their children could not walk and talk face to face with God. (except for a few prophets at His invitation, when they were filled with the glory of God). Because Satan had introduced evil into the world, Adam and Eve and their children were separated from God both physically and spiritually." (Gospel Principles p 33)

If by the Fall all mankind were cut off from the presence of the Lord both as to things temporal and to things spiritual, what good is it, one might ask, if men and women are blessed with physical bodies, the right to choose between good and evil, and the opportunity to gain eternal life, if physical bodies die and people are cut off from the presence of the Lord, and they are, thereby, considered both physically and spiritually dead? How then will the work and glory of God, which is to bring to pass the immortality and eternal life of men and women be accomplished, if the result of Adam and Eve's Fall brought mankind physical bodies that die separating them physically from God, and Satan in the world influences them to sin, and sinning cuts them off spiritually from God, thereby denying them opportunity for eternal life?

Answers to these questions lie in the scriptures restored to the Genesis text, in the Book of Mormon, supplemented by those in the Doctrine and Covenants, by way of Joseph Smith, the prophet.

THE FALL WAS ANTICIPATED ESTABLISHING THE NEED FOR A SAVIOR OR REDEEMER WHO WOULD SET THE PLAN OF SALVATION IN MOTION

"The Fall was no surprise to the Lord. It was a necessary step in the progress of man, and provisions for a Savior had been made even before the Fall had occurred. Jesus Christ came to atone for the fall of Adam and also for man's individual sins. Latter-day revelation supports the biblical account of the Fall, showing that it was a historical event that literally occurred in the history of man. Many points in latter-day revelation are also clarified that are not discernible from the Bible. Among other things it makes clear that the fall is a blessing, and that Adam and Eve should be honored in their station as the first parents of the earth." (BD p 670)

Realization that Adam and Eve should be honored as the first parents of the earth becomes clear through latter-day scripture. After being cast out of the Garden, Adam and Eve began to till the earth and have dominion over the beasts of the field, and to eat bread by the sweat of the brow, as commanded. Eve labored along with Adam. Eve bare unto Adam sons and daughters and they began to multiply and replenish the earth. Their sons and daughters divided two and two, and they began to till the earth, have flocks and herds, and they begat sons and daughters before the birth of Cain and Abel. The gospel was preached from the beginning, sacrifice of the firstlings of flocks was introduced to Adam and Eve in similitude of the sacrifice of the Only Begotten Son of the Father, yet to be born in the flesh. Adam and Eve were counseled to "do all that thou doest in the name of the Son, and thou shalt repent and call upon the name of the Son forevermore." And "the Holy Ghost fell upon Adam, which beareth record of the Father and the Son." Adam was informed that as he had fallen, there was a way for him and all of mankind, if they would repent, to be redeemed, by entering a covenant with God and keep its provisions. (Moses 5:1-9, PGP)

Adam and Eve rejoiced as they realized they could have joy in this life, and again in the flesh see God. Eve was glad saying: "were it not for our transgression we never should have had seed, never known good and evil, the joys of redemption and eternal life with God given to all the obedient. " Adam and Eve blessed the name of God and made all this known unto their sons and daughters. But Satan competed for their souls, and many followed him, and from that time forth many men and women became carnal, sensual and devilish. But the Lord God called upon men and women everywhere through the Holy Ghost that they should repent. (Moses 5:10-14, PGP)

Again, this is a pattern. As parents, Adam and Eve had to sacrifice in order to have a family. Eve, as all women that have followed, had to literally put her life in jeopardy to have children. Hence, in perspective, the Fall could be viewed as a transgression of mortals, while in another perspective, it could be viewed as a marvelous sacrifice that perpetuated the cycle of life.

Enoch, seventh generation from Adam, explained that Adam and Eve knew the Redeemer to come in the Meridian of Time would be known as Jesus Christ, in the flesh, and taught that by "transgression cometh the fall which fall bringeth death, and inasmuch as ye were born into the world by water and blood, and the spirit, which I have made, and so became of dust a living soul, even so must ye be born again into the kingdom of heaven, of water, and of the spirit, and be cleansed by blood, even the blood of mine Only Begotten; that ye might be sanctified from all sin, and enjoy the words of eternal life in this world, and eternal life in the world to come, even immortal glory: For by the water ye keep the commandment; by the spirit ye are justified, and by the blood ye are sanctified; Therefore it is given to abide in you; the record of heaven; the Comforter; the peaceable things of immortal glory; the truth of all things; that which quickeneth all things, which make alive all things: that which knoweth all things, and hath all power according to wisdom, mercy, truth, justice and judgment. And now behold, I say unto you: This is the plan of salvation, unto all men, through the blood of mine Only Begotten, who shall come in the Meridian of time". (Moses 6: 59-62, PGP)

Thus birth and baptism require the same three elements: water, blood and spirit, with the implication that baptism of the recipient becomes a birth into the family of God, more specifically of Jesus Christ, who thereby becomes our Father by adoption, and our personal Savior who can lead us, as we obey, back into the presence of our Eternal Heavenly Father. We the children of the covenant are characterized by Book of Mormon prophet Abinadi as the Son of God's seed in these words: ..."when his (the Savior 's)soul has been made an offering for sin he shall see his seed....Behold I say unto you, that whosoever has heard the words of the prophets (and) ... hearkened unto their words, and believed that the Lord would redeem his people, and have looked forward to that day for a remission of their sins, I say unto you that these are his seed, or they are the heirs of the kingdom of God. For these are they whose sins he has borne; these are they for whom he has died, to redeem them from their transgressions." (Mosiah 15:10-13)

So Adam and Eve knew of the plan of salvation from the beginning, entered into a covenant with God, were baptized in water by immersion and with fire and with the Holy Ghost, and they taught their sons and daughters, using their agency to also follow God's plan for them too.

Revelation to His servants the prophets since the days of Adam makes clear that mankind needed to be reconciled to God and the provisions of His justice be satisfied, or their temporary estrangement and physical and spiritual separation from God would become permanent. A persons physical body would die never to rise again, and his/her spirit being separated from God would succumb to the influences of Satan forever.

Anticipating these conditions, God the Eternal Father prepared a way for Adam and Eve and all their posterity to be reconciled to Him. That reconciliation would come through His first son born in the spirit, even Jehovah, the name by which He was known in the premortal world before being born in the flesh as Jesus Christ. Information restored to the Genesis text by the Lord through Joseph Smith reveals that the premortal Christ was also referred to frequently by the Father as Mine Only Begotten Son, or the Only Begotten, and that He, the Only Begotten, yet to be born in the flesh played a key role there, proposing that those coming to earth to gain physical bodies be free to choose the courses of their lives on earth.

THE SELECTION OF A REDEEMER

Should Adam and Eve choose to eat the forbidden fruit, and the Eternal Father anticipated they would, someone would need to be sent to make amends for their transgression of the Father's law, which forbade eating of the tree of knowledge of good and evil lest they die. The Son of the Morning or Satan, wanted to be that someone, and declared: "Here am I, send me, and I will be thy son and I will redeem all mankind, that one soul shall not be lost, and surely I will do it; wherefore give me thine honor. But, behold, my Beloved Son, which was my Beloved and Chosen from the beginning, said unto me -- Father, thy will be done, and the glory be thine forever." (Moses 4:1-2, PGP)

The difference between the plans offered was, in the main, Satan's plan called for people to be compelled in all things. They would be like robots, simply responding to the commands of their masters, never able to rise above their servile state. The other plan called for agency and ability to choose the course of action in their lives, using intelligence and knowledge gained from life's experiences and the commands of God to guide their choices between good and evil. If they made the right choices between good and evil, and repented of wrong choices as life progressed, they could become as God and return to His presence.

Satan's plan was rejected. He became angry, rebelled against God the Father, and sought to destroy the agency of man which God had given. The Father caused that Satan be cast down. Satan became the devil, the father of lies, and he sought to deceive and blind men, and lead them captive at his will, even as many as would not hearken to the voice of God. (Moses 2:3-4, PGP)

Based on what is seen in today's world, Satan's plan appeals to many willing to trade agency or freedom of choice for a few moments pleasure or temporary security. Just as Esau traded his birthright blessings for a mess of porridge, so are many today willing to trade their agency, or right to choose, which is a God given birthright, for the momentary pleasures of addictive drugs from which they may never escape, or for political systems promising anything and everything if the people will give up rights of self-determination. Once given up agency may be impossible to regain.

AN ATONEMENT OR PRICE HAD TO BE PAID TO RECONCILE MANKIND TO THE FATHER

Using their agency, Adam and Eve did choose to eat the fruit of the tree of knowledge of good and evil, and their choice resulted in two barriers they could not overcome by themselves; barriers for themselves and all their posterity: death and sin. Mankind, thereby became estranged from God, and would always remain estranged without the intervention of a higher power who would bring about an atonement, pay the price and reconcile man to God the Father. Death, brought about by Adam's transgression, on himself and all his posterity, had to be overcome for each soul. The individual sins of each soul resulting from the choices they made between good and evil, would also have to be overcome.

The purposes then of an atonement are, to overcome the consequences of Adam's transgression which brought about death to himself and his posterity, and to overcome the consequences of his individual sins and the sins of each of his posterity resulting from the choices each of them made in life, should each of them repent. In this manner each individual becomes accountable for their choices, and literally thereafter for their eternal destiny.

"Jesus Christ, as the Only Begotten Son of God and the only sinless person to live on this earth, was the only one capable of making an atonement for mankind. By his selection and foreordination in the Grand Council before the world was formed, his divine Sonship, his sinless life, the shedding of his blood in the Garden of Gethsemane, his death on the cross and subsequent resurrection from the grave, he made a perfect atonement for all mankind. All are covered unconditionally, as pertaining to the fall of Adam. Hence, all shall rise from the dead with mortal bodies, because of Jesus' atonement. 'For as in Adam all die, even so in Christ shall all be made alive.' and all little children are innocent at birth."(I Cor 15:22, BD p 617)

"The atonement is conditional, however, so far as each person's individual sins are concerned, and touches everyone to the degree that he has faith in Jesus Christ, repents of his sins, and obeys the gospel. The services of the Day of Atonement foreshadowed the atoning work of Christ.(Lev 4:23, 26-32; Heb 9) The scriptures point out that no law, ordinance, or sacrifice would be satisfactory if it were not for the atonement of Jesus Christ. (He 10:1-9, 2 Ne 9:5-24; Messiah 13:27-32)."

"Sin is lawlessness (1 Jn 3:4); it is a refusal on man's part to submit to the law of God (Rom 8:7). By transgression man loses control over his own will and becomes the slave of sin, (Rom 7:14) and so incurs the penalty of spiritual death, which is alienation from God. (Rom 6:23) The atonement of Jesus Christ redeems all mankind from the fall of Adam and causes all to be answerable for their own manner of life. This means of atonement is provided by the Father (John 3:16-17) and is offered in the life and person of his son, Jesus

132

Christ. (2 Cor 5:19." (BD p 617)

Through the atonement of Jesus Christ all will be resurrected, so no individual or group of persons may be held accountable for Adam's transgression which brought about the Fall. However, each individual is accountable for his own manner of life, hence Joseph Smith declared: "We believe that men will be punished for their own sins and not for Adam's transgression." (Second Article of Faith.)

The interrelationship of men 's agency and the role of Jesus Christ as Savior of mankind, and his atonement for the transgression of others is discussed by several prophets God raised up in the Americas. These prophets had access to the uncorrupted text of Genesis, as part of the records their forebears brought with them when the prophet Lehi, (contemporary with Jeremiah) and his family were commanded to leave Jerusalem about ten years before the city was overrun by the Babylonians, and the people of Judah were carried away captive. They also had access to revelation from God, as God so chose to reveal it to them. The Book of Mormon records some important concepts which enlighten our understanding of God's plan for all. Some of them are:

SINCE OPPOSITION IS NECESSARY TO LEARNING GOOD FROM EVIL, SATAN IS ALLOWED TO PROVIDE THAT OPPOSITION

The prophet Lehi taught: ...."to bring about his eternal purposes in the end of man, after he had created our first parents, and .... all things which are created, it must needs be that there was an opposition; even the forbidden fruit in opposition to the tree of life; the one being sweet and the other bitter. Wherefore, the Lord God gave unto man that he should act for himself. Wherefore, man could not act for himself save it should be that he was enticed by the one or the other." (2 Ne 2:15-16)

Given opposition was necessary, the Lord God allowed Satan to tempt and persuade man in opposition to the Plan of Salvation ..." an angel of God, according to that which is written, had fallen from heaven; wherefore he became a devil, having sought that which was evil before God. And because he had fallen from heaven, and had become miserable forever, he sought also the misery of all mankind. Wherefore, he said unto Eve, yea, even that old serpent, who is the devil, who is the father of all lies, wherefore he said; Partake of the forbidden fruit, and ye shall not die, but ye shall be as God, knowing good and evil." (2 Ne 2:17-18)

While Satan is allowed to tempt and persuade man in opposition to the plan of salvation his power is limited. The Book of Revelations teaches that Satan has limits. He is not all powerful like God. He has power over us only to the extent we allow it. Our choices of righteousness prevent Satan from influencing us. Our choices of disobedience subject us to the influence of Satan. Obedience can save us. Disobedience will damn us.

After Adam and Eve had partaken of the forbidden fruit they were driven out of the Garden of Eden, to till the earth."And they brought forth children, yea, even the family of all the earth. And the days of the children of men were prolonged, according to the will of God, that they might repent while in the flesh; wherefore their state became a state of probation ... For he (God) gave commandment that all men must repent; for he showed unto all men that they were lost, because of the transgression of their parents... And the Messiah cometh in the fullness of time, that he may redeem the children of men from the fall. And because that they are redeemed from the fall they have become free forever, knowing good and evil; to act for themselves and not be acted upon..." (2 Ne 2:17-26)

NATURAL MAN MAY BE REDEEMED THROUGH THE ATONEMENT OF CHRIST

Foreshadowing the importance and magnificence of Christ's atonement as a blessing to all mankind, Lehi's son Jacob, also a prophet, declared: " For as death passed upon all men, to fulfill the merciful plan of the great Creator, there must needs be a power of resurrection, and the resurrection must needs come unto man by reason of the fall; and the fall came by reason of transgression; and because man became fallen they were cut off from the presence of the Lord.

Wherefore it must needs be an infinite atonement .... wherefore, the first judgment (death) which came upon man must needs have remained to an endless duration. And if so, this flesh must have laid down to rot and to crumble to its mother earth, to rise no more....For behold, if the flesh should rise no more, our spirits must become subject to that angel who fell from the presence of the Eternal God, and become a devil to rise no more, and our spirits must have become like unto him, and we become devils, angels to a devil, to be shut out of the presence of our God, and to remain with the father of lies, in misery, like unto himself; yea, to that being who beguiled our first parents... O how great the goodness of our God, who prepareth a way for our escape from the grasp of this awful monster, yea, that monster, death and hell, which I call death of the body, and also the death of the spirit.

"And because of the way of deliverance of our God, the Holy One of Israel, this death of which I have spoken, which is the temporal, shall deliver up its dead; which death is the grave. And this death of which I have spoken, which is the spiritual death, shall deliver up its dead; which spiritual death is hell; wherefore, death and hell must deliver up their dead, and hell must deliver up it's captive spirits, and the grave must deliver up its captive bodies, and the bodies and the spirits of men will be restored one to another; and it is by the power of the resurrection of the Holy One of Israel.

" O how great the plan of our God! For on the other hand, the paradise of God must deliver up the spirits of the righteous, and the grave deliver up the bodies of the righteous; and the spirit and the body is restored to itself again, and all men become incorruptible and immortal, and they are living souls, having a perfect knowledge like unto us in the flesh, save it be that our knowledge shall be perfect."(2 Ne 9:11-13)

Foreshadowing the earthly appearance of the great Redeemer and Savior of mankind, the prophet Jacob continues: " And he cometh into the world that he may save all men if they will hearken unto his voice; for behold, he suffereth the pains of all men yea, the pains of every creature, both men, women, and children, who belong to the family of Adam. And he suffereth this that the resurrection might pass upon all men, that all might stand before him at the great and judgment day.

"And he commandeth all men that they must repent, and be baptized in his name, having perfect faith in the Holy One of Israel, or they cannot be saved in the kingdom of God ... For the atonement satisfieth the demands of his justice upon all those who have not the law given unto them, that they are delivered from that awful monster death and hell, and the devil ... and they are restored to that God who gave them breath which is the Holy One of Israel." (2 Ne 9:21-26)

King Benjamin, another prophet centuries later, about 124 B.C., also foreshadowing the coming of the Messiah taught: "For behold the time cometh and is not far distant, that with power the Lord Omnipotent ...shall come down from heaven among the children of men, and shall dwell in a tabernacle of clay, and shall go forth among men working mighty miracles ... he shall suffer temptation, and pain of body, hunger, thirst and fatigue, even more than man can suffer, except it be unto death; for behold, blood cometh from every pore, so great shall be his anguish for the wickedness and abominations of his people. And he shall be called Jesus Christ, the Son of God ... And he shall rise the third day from the dead ... and also his blood atoneth for the sins of those who have fallen by the transgression of Adam, who have died not knowing the will of God concerning them, or who have ignorantly sinned. But wo, wo, unto him who knoweth that he rebelleth against God! For salvation cometh to none such except it be through repentance and faith on the Lord Jesus Christ. And the Lord hath sent his holy prophets among all the children of men, to declare these things to every kindred, nation and tongue, that thereby whosoever should believe that Christ should come, the same might receive remission of their sins, and rejoice with exceedingly great joy, even as though he had already come among them.

"... And many signs and wonders and types and shadows showed he (Jehovah/ Christ) concerning his coming; and also holy prophets spake unto them concerning his coming; and yet they (the children of Israel) hardened their hearts, and understood not the law of Moses availeth them nothing except it were through the atonement of his blood ... little children are blessed; for behold, as in Adam, or by nature they fall, even so the blood of Christ -atoneth for [them] ... there shall be no other name given nor any other way, nor means whereby salvation can come unto the children of men, only in and through the name of Christ. The Lord Omnipotent ... and the infant perisheth not that dieth in infancy, but men drink damnation to their souls except they humble themselves and become as little children, and believe that salvation was, and is, and is to come, in and through the blood of Christ, the Lord Omnipotent.

"For the natural man is an enemy to God, and has been from the fall of Adam, and will be forever and ever, unless he yields to the enticings of the Holy Spirit, and putteth off the natural man and becometh a saint through the atonement of the Christ the Lord, and becometh as a child, submissive, meek, humble, patient, full of love, willing to submit to all things which the Lord seeth fit to inflict upon him, even as a child doth submit to his father." (Mosiah 3:5-19)

Note the doctrinal point that none who die shall be found blameless before God except little children who are automatically accepted into the kingdom of heaven. For the rest of us, we must become as little children. How do we do that? We must be born again and submit ourselves to the teachings of Christ, and as a little child learns and does, we follow the example of our leader, Jesus Christ.

About fifty years later, (90-77 B.C.) Aaron, grandson of King Benjamin, expounded

"the scriptures from the creation of Adam, laying the fall of man before him, and their carnal state and also the plan of redemption, which was prepared from the foundation of the world, through Christ, for all whosoever would believe on his name. And since man had fallen he could not merit anything of himself; but the sufferings and death of Christ atone for their sins, through faith and repentance and so forth; and that he breaketh the bands of death, that the grave shall have no victory, and that the sting of death should be swallowed up in the hope of glory." (Alma 22:13-14)

MORTALITY IS A PROBATIONARY TIME TO PREPARE, TO REPENT, TO LEARN THE POWER OF FAITH AND TO SERVE GOD

Ten or more years later, Alma, a great prophet in his day, explained to his son, Corianton, that mortality is a probationary time to enable men to repent and serve God, that the Fall brought temporal and spiritual death upon all mankind, that redemption comes through repentance, that God himself atoned for the sins of the world, that mercy is for those who repent, that all others are subject to God's justice, that mercy comes because of the atonement, and that only the truly penitent are saved. Alma explained that after Adam and Eve had partaken of the tree of knowledge of good and evil, and brought death upon themselves, had they put forth their hands and eaten the fruit of the tree of life, they would not have had the opportunity to repent of their wrong choices and would not have had the opportunity to serve God, but would have lived forever in their sins.

Without space for repentance and service to God, the great plan of salvation would have been frustrated. Therefore, once the forbidden fruit was eaten, cherubim and a flaming sword were placed at the east end of the Garden of Eden to protect the fruit of the tree of life from being eaten prematurely, and to allow mankind time for repentance, a probationary time, and to allow opportunity for men to choose to serve God and to actually serve Him.

God's plan calls for mankind to choose whom they will serve and to demonstrate their sincerity with action and subsequent choices. When in the presence of God the choice to serve Him required very little on our part. Making choices in mortality, however, is a different matter. In mortality, we live in a non-spiritual environment, so we need to declare our initial choice and ongoing choices for God and against the adversary.

Continuing Alma's writings:

"... Our first parents were cut off temporally and spiritually

138

from the presence of the Lord; and thus we see they became subjects to follow after their own will. Now, behold, it was not expedient that man should be reclaimed from this temporal death for that would destroy the great plan of happiness. Therefore, as the soul could never die, and the fall had brought upon all mankind a spiritual death as well as a temporal, that is, they were cut off from the presence of the Lord, it was expedient that mankind should be reclaimed from spiritual death. Therefore, as they [the posterity of Adam and Eve] had become carnal, sensual and devilish, by nature, this probationary state became a state for them to prepare; it became a preparatory state ... were it not for the plan of redemption ... as soon as they were dead their souls were miserable, being cut off from the presence of the Lord.

"And now, there was no means to reclaim men from this fallen state, which man had brought upon himself because of his own disobedience. Therefore, according to justice, the plan of redemption could not be brought, only on conditions of repentance of men in this probationary state, yea, this preparatory state, for except it were for these conditions mercy could not take effect, except it should destroy the work of justice. Now the work of justice could not be destroyed; if so, God would cease to be God. And thus we see that all mankind were fallen. And they were in the grasp of justice; yea, the justice of God which consigned them forever to be cut off from his presence.

"And now, the plan of mercy could not be brought about except an atonement be made; therefore God himself atoneth for the sins of the world, to bring about the plan of mercy, to appease the demands of justice, that God might be a perfect, just God, and a merciful God also ... there is a law given, and a punishment affixed, and a repentance granted, which repentance, mercy claimeth, otherwise justice claimeth the creature and executeth the law; and the law inflicteth the punishment; if not so, the works of justice would be destroyed and God would cease to be God. But God ceaseth not to be God, and mercy claimeth the penitent, and mercy cometh because of

139

the atonement; and the atonement bringeth to pass the resurrection of the dead [temporally and spiritually] bringeth back men into the presence of God; and thus they are restored into his presence to be judged according to their works, according to the law and justice. For behold, justice executeth all his demands, and also mercy claimeth all which is her own, and thus none but the truly penitent can be saved ... And thus God bringeth about his great and eternal purposes, which were prepared from the foundation of the world." (Alma 42:2-26)

SUMMARY

In this chapter we have discussed (1) the origins of planet earth and the development of its life forms; (2) God's work and glory; (3)the agency of man; (4) the Fall; (5) the need for a Savior or Redeemer who would set God's plan of salvation in motion; (6) the selection of a Redeemer; (7) the atonement or price paid to reconcile mankind to the Father and its payment by Jesus Christ as Redeemer; (8) the introduction of opposition which was considered necessary as part of the Fall for mankind to learn good from evil; (9) God's decision to allow Satan to provide that opposition; (10) the redemption of natural man from sin and death through the atonement of Jesus Christ was made possible; and (11) we have characterized mortality as a probationary time for mankind to prepare, to repent, to learn the power of faith and to serve God, thereby making operational the atonement of Jesus Christ in the lives of all.

From previous chapters in this book we have learned that the Lord's plan of salvation and His work and glory, which is to bring to pass the immortality and eternal life of men and women, were known from the beginning, but were lost over the centuries and had to be restored through a latter-day prophet. Book of Mormon prophets had access to the uncorrupted and more complete text of Genesis through the brass plates they brought with them from Jerusalem to America. Their writings were recorded under the inspiration of God. Joseph

Smith translated the Book of Mormon through the gift and power of God. Thus the Lord's plans and purposes are much more clearly seen from Book of Mormon and latter-day scripture and how He plans to carry them out.

The more we understand about the Creation, the Fall and the Atonement, the more we understand the great love God has for His children and the wise plan He has put into place for them. Some mistakenly confuse the consequences that are ordained for our sins as the sign of a vengeful God. The patterns of restoration are evidence that God loves all of His children, in all ages. As man follows the path of faith in the Lord Jesus Christ, repentance, baptism and obedience, the wisdom of God is shed forth as a light to show the way. It has been this way since Adam, and continues today.

Vast amounts of material from prophets of previous dispensations and others, pertaining to God's work and glory, was summarized in these ten chapters. The efforts of Adam, Enoch, Noah, Abraham, Moses and other prophets including the Savior Himself, all have pointed to this the final dispensation of the fulness of times and to Joseph Smith, God's chosen prophet, seer, revelator and dispensation leader during which He, the Lord, is pruning His vineyard for the last time. Through Joseph Smith the Lord has restored His Gospel to the earth and has invited the gathering of scattered Israel and all true believers in Messiah/Christ that they be perfected and redeemed.

Attention is again called to the many patterns Heavenly Father uses in His dealings with mankind including the seven outlined in the introduction of this book. Over-arching all of His patterns is this: that He deals with His children through prophets and the making of covenants. Note in the restoration of His Gospel the seven patterns listed in the introduction still apply: the cyclical pattern of obedience and disobedience; the teaching pattern; the discovery pattern; the pattern of calling prophets; the pattern of limited acceptance; the pattern of two choices or voices; and the pattern of revelation from

God to man through His servants the prophets, evident in all dispensations.

By April, 1830 the heavens were again open. God had answered Joseph Smith's prayer, and sent the Angel Moroni to him. Moroni showed Joseph Smith where the Book of Mormon plates were buried. The Lord gave Joseph Smith the gift and power to act for Him in translating the Book of Mormon into English; sent John the Baptist and Peter, James and John to restore the temporal and spiritual priesthoods through Joseph Smith and others, and reestablished the related ordinances. However, Christ's church was not yet fully organized and all the doctrines were not yet in place that would assure the gathering, perfection and redemption of Israel and all true believers in Messiah/Christ. Revealing all the doctrines essential for gathering, perfecting and redeeming Israel and true believers and tying them to the words of His previous prophets was yet to be accomplished. The first order of business, therefore, was to officially organize His Church under the laws of the land, thereby providing the vehicle through which His plans and purposes could be accomplished.

Heavy emphasis was initially placed on the gathering of elect officials through a process more frequently referred to as missionary work, followed by the work of perfecting the lives of those entering the covenant, called perfecting the Saints, and thirdly, increasing emphasis pertaining to the redemption of the dead. Note also that God's first reference to priesthood power in this dispensation was to the sealing power held by Elijah. Sealing ordinances are performed in temples. Generally, revelations on temple construction and temple ordinances followed the revelations on early missionary work and revelations on perfecting the lives of those entering the covenant. Ultimately, however, the crowning ordinances of the temple will increasingly take center stage as the Savior's return approaches, and will remain center stage throughout the Millennium.

Elijah's words from Kings and Chronicles reminds us that the

142

sealing power transcends earthly powers and reaches beyond the veil. As Malachi tells us, the second coming of the Lord will be both great and dreadful. It will be <u>great</u> for the true believers because they will have aligned themselves with the priesthood and sealing powers, following the fathers as Abraham did, thereby allowing their children to turn their hearts to their fathers, and bind all generations into one family under Jesus Christ. It will be a <u>dreadful</u> day, for the non-believers, because they will not have their covenant ties or the promises.

The Lord God has revealed so much to His servants the prophets, particularly Joseph Smith, in these latter days. We now transition to relatively less paraphrase and more direct quotation from the Lord as revealed in the Doctrine and Covenants. We shall let His words speak directly to the reader except for occasional comments which hopefully tie certain threads together. Emphasis is on the gathering, perfection and redemption of Israel and all true believers in Messiah/Christ through the establishment of a Zion Society in these latter days with an eventual headquarters city in the old Jerusalem for the kingdom of Judah, led by the lineage of Judah, the kingdom which fell and was scattered by the Babylonians, and another city called the New Jerusalem in America for the kingdom of Israel which fell and was scattered by the Assyrians, led by the lineage of Ephraim, which incorporates the other tribes of Jacob/Israel, son of Isaac and grandson of Abraham.

We return now to the organization of the Lord Jesus Christ's Church founded on apostles and prophets with Himself being the chief cornerstone, beginning April 6, 1830; along with selected events and revealed doctrines over the next six years, which laid the foundation necessary to gather all Israel, to perfect the lives of those entering the covenant, place them in position to be redeemed, and which assured His Church would be fitly framed through the establishment of a Zion Society built upon eternal principles capable of exalting its members in the kingdom of God. And consistent with the patterns the Lord uses to teach His children, we will be able to recognize that Church because the teachings, ordinances and organization will be in harmony with past teachings and patterns of the past.

CHAPTER XI

MORE ON DOCTRINE AND RELATED COVENANTS FOR THE GATHERING AND PERFECTION OF ISRAEL
From April 6, 1830 through March 1831

As was the case in preceding dispensations, man departed from God's teachings. They lost the authority to act for Him and the heavens were closed. The teachings of God were slowly replaced with the doctrines of man, mingled with the doctrines of God, but denied the power thereof. Hence, for the true church to be on earth another restoration was needed. One might suppose that if the Lord should give commandments in this dispensation, he would also prepare a way for them to be fulfilled. In essence that is what He did.

At the command of God, The Church of Jesus Christ of Latter-day Saints was organized April 6, 1830. The Lord had taken a number of steps previous to the Church's organization laying the ground work and identifying the leaders necessary to get the organization up and operating. It soon became clear that the Church and its members are the vehicles through which the work and glory of God would be accomplished.

The promises God has made to His children must all be fulfilled. The restoration of the Church, along with the priesthood authority, ordinances and sealing power were required so this could happen. Again, without the sealing power, earthly ordinances would not have effect beyond the grave.

Interestingly, Joseph Smith was persecuted for saying he had seen God. This is the pattern the Bible clearly shows. God selects whom He will speak to, and they are usually not the popular leaders or the heads of the established sects. God's chosen were not always popular, after they stepped forward and declared His word. But they, like Joseph did not deny it either.

The work and glory of God may also be portrayed as the

gathering, perfection and redemption of Israel. It is the members of the Church or the Zion Society who help gather, help perfect and help redeem Israel, the true believers in Messiah/Christ.

For purposes of this presentation, latter-day revelation from the Doctrine and Covenants reported in this chapter and other subsequent chapters will emphasize the gathering, perfection and redemption of Israel, the true believers in Messiah/Christ; under the canopy of an evolving Zion Society, which ultimately will be the New World Order at the Second Coming of the Savior.

In a way, this is like building a house while living in it. Some materials are brought on site but are not immediately used until such time as other parts of the house are completed. Thus, to help clarify what the Lord is doing or saying, when He references future events and when He positions doctrinal concepts essential for those plans; some sections of the Doctrine and Covenants and other scriptures which describe a Zion Society, past and future, and which describe work for the dead are reported in separate chapters. The final chapter deals with the Second Coming, the Millennial Reign of Messiah /Christ and the Final Judgment.

One would expect God to provide new guidance, since He declared that doctrine which existed in the early eighteen hundreds was corrupted and had a form of godliness, but denied the power thereof. Hence, the revelations which were incorporated into the Doctrine and Covenants in the 1830's and 1840's, outline the will of the Lord for this dispensation.

Revelation Received in Sections 20 Through 45
April 6, 1830 Through March 7, 1831

[Section 20]

During April, 1830, the month the Church was organized in this dispensation, a revelation was received on Church organization and government. In fact, Joseph Smith declared the revelation, now known as Section Twenty, was received "by the spirit of prophecy and revelation, which... pointed out to us the precise day upon which ... we should proceed to organize his Church once more upon the earth." The date was April 6, 1830. (HC 1:64-70)

By this date Joseph Smith and Oliver Cowdery had been called and ordained apostles of the Lord Jesus Christ, having been identified as the first and second Elders of the Church, respectively. (D&C 20:2-3)

Joseph's ordination was alluded to as early as March, 1829, before the Book of Mormon translation was complete and the book published. An 1829 revelation in that month declared this generation would receive the Lord's word through Joseph Smith who was soon to be ordained and would "go forth and declare my words unto the children of men." (D&C 5:6)

By June 1829 the Melchizedek Priesthood had been restored by the laying on of the hands through Peter, James and John, acting in behalf of the Lord. These three also had power to bestow the holy apostleship upon others.

Section Twenty describes the Book of Mormon as a

"record of a fallen people, and contains the fulness of the gospel of Jesus Christ to the Gentiles and unto the Jews also; which was given by inspiration... proving to the world that the holy scriptures are true, and that God does inspire men and call them to his holy work in this age and generation, as well as in generations of old." (v 9-11)

Reaffirmed are the doctrines of the creator and the creation, the fall, the atonement, and of the need for baptism and enduring to the end in faith. (v 17-29) Laws governing repentance, justification, and sanctification were also declared.

With reference to baptism, the Lord said:

"All those who humble themselves before God, and desire to be baptized, and come forth with broken hearts and contrite spirits, and witness before the Church that they have truly repented of all

147

their sins, and are willing to take upon them the name of Jesus Christ, having a determination to serve him to the end, and truly manifest, by their works, that they have received of the Spirit of Christ unto a remission of their sins, shall be received by baptism into his Church." (v 37)

Some of the duties of deacons, teachers, priests, and elders were also enumerated, as well as the duties of members after they are received by baptism.

The leadership of the Church is vested in the priesthood and its offices. The priesthood conducts what is known as sacrament meeting in local units. (v 68) The members of the Church shall manifest ...

"by a godly walk and conversation that they are worthy of it", [the sacrament], have faith and do works agreeable to the holy scriptures... walking in holiness before the Lord." (v 69) Parents having children are to bring them unto the elders before the Church, who are to "lay their hands upon them in the name of Jesus Christ, and bless them in his name." (v 70) Only those who have arrived at the age of accountability before God are capable of repentance and can be received officially into the Church. (v 71) That age was later defined as eight years. (D&C 68:25,27) The Lord also later declared that Satan cannot tempt little children until they begin to become accountable before the Lord, (D&C 29:47) and that those children "who die before they arrive at the years of accountability are saved in the celestial kingdom of heaven." (D&C 137:10)

Thus the Lord established the ordinance of the blessing of children, defined what is expected of new members' state of mind before entering the waters of baptism, defined who may be baptized and what is expected of them after baptism, as they take part in the sacrament service. Following these instructions the Lord described how baptism is to be administered and prescribed the precise words which are to be used in performing this ordinance,

"in the following manner unto all those who repent. The

person who is called of God and has authority from Jesus Christ to baptize, shall go down into the water with the person who has presented himself or herself for baptism, and shall say, calling him or her by name: Having been commissioned of Jesus Christ, I baptize you in the name of the Father, and of the Son and of the Holy Ghost, Amen. Then shall he immerse him or her in the water, and come forth again out of the water." (v 72-74)

Made clear is that the Church should meet together often to partake of the bread and of the wine in remembrance of the Lord Jesus. An elder or priest shall administer the sacrament, which serves as a reminder of the covenants members made at baptism.

Four months following this revelation on the sacrament, the Lord declared: "it mattereth not what ye shall eat or what ye shall drink when ye partake of the sacrament, if it so be that ye do it with an eye single to my glory -remembering unto the Father my body which was laid down for you and my blood which was shed for the remission of your sins." (D&C 27:2)

He advised the Church members not to purchase strong drink of their enemies. Wine is to be used, only if it is made new by Church leaders themselves. Church leaders afterwards decided to simply use water as the emblem of His blood. The priest or elder administering the sacrament is to kneel and utter orally the prayers set forth for the bread and the water verbatim, as prescribed in verses 76 through 79 of Section Twenty. The Section closes with some regulations governing Church membership. (D&C 20:1-84)

[Sections 21, 22 and 23]

Three other revelations were received during the first month of the Church's restoration. Section Twenty-one was received on the day of organization April 6, 1830, at the home of Peter Whitmer Sr.

"Six men who had previously been baptized, participated... They also voted to accept and sustain Joseph Smith, Jun., and Oliver Cowdery as the presiding officers of the Church. With the laying on of hands, Joseph then ordained Oliver an elder in the Church; and

Oliver similarly ordained Joseph. After administration of the sacrament Joseph and Oliver laid hands upon the participants individually, for the bestowal of the Holy Ghost, and for the confirmation of each as a member of the Church." (D&C 21 heading)

In Section Twenty-one the Lord declared a record should be kept among the Church members. Joseph Smith is to be called a seer, translator, prophet, apostle of Jesus Christ and an elder in the Church; with the charge to lay the foundation of the Church under the inspiration of the Holy Ghost and "to build it up unto the most holy faith." (v 1-3)

Joseph Smith was to guide the course of Zion and the members were to believe his words as he spoke under the inspiration of the Holy Ghost. "Him have I inspired to move the cause of Zion in mighty power for good, and his diligence I know, and his prayers I have heard," said the Lord. (v 7, HC 1:74-79, D&C 21:1-12)

A third revelation given through Joseph Smith in April 1830, Section Twenty-two, declared baptism is a new and everlasting covenant, a covenant from the beginning, but all baptisms must be authoritative, that is, performed by one having authority, or they mean nothing. (HC 1:79-80, D&C 22:1-4)

A fourth revelation was received in April, 1830, Section Twenty-three, through Joseph Smith to Oliver Cowdery, Hyrum Smith, Samuel H. Smith, Joseph Smith, Sr., and Joseph Knight, Sr. All were early disciples. They were called to preach, exhort, and strengthen the Church. (D&C 23:1-7)

[Sections 24, 25 and 26]

By July 1830 intense persecution in upper New York state made it necessary for Church leaders to seek safety in partial seclusion, hence Joseph Smith and Oliver Cowdery returned to Harmony, Pennsylvania where a revelation was received in July 1830. Section Twenty-four was received to strengthen, encourage and instruct them. Joseph Smith was called to translate, preach, and expound the scriptures and Oliver Cowdery was to preach the gospel.

Set forth were laws relating to miracles, cursings, casting the dust off one's feet and going without purse or script. They were called to "prune my vineyard with a mighty pruning for the last time...", said the Lord. (v 19, D&C 24:1-19)

A second revelation also received in July 1830, Section Twenty-five. It was addressed to Emma, Joseph Smith's wife. In it, Emma is identified as an "elect lady." She was called to aid and comfort her husband, to write, expound the scriptures and to select hymns for the members to sing. Emma was to receive the Holy Ghost from her husband by the laying on of hands. Her time was to be given to writing, and learning much, and she was counseled to "lay aside the things of this world and seek things of a better." (v 10)

Emma also was "to make a selection of sacred hymns, as it shall be given thee, which is pleasing unto me, [the Lord] to be had in my Church. For my soul delighteth in the song of the heart; yea, the song of the righteous is a prayer unto me, and it shall be answered with a blessing upon their heads." (v 11-12)

Section Twenty-five closes with an admonition for Emma to lift up her heart and rejoice and to cleave unto the covenants she had made; and for her to continue in meekness, to beware of pride, to delight in her husband, and the glory which shall come upon him, and to keep God's commandments continually, so that a crown of righteousness, Emma might also receive. (v 13-15, D&C 25:1-16)

A third revelation was received in July 1830, Section Twenty-six. This one was to Joseph Smith, Oliver Cowdery, and John Whitmer. It instructed them to devote their time to studying the scriptures, to preaching and earning their daily bread, performing their labors on the land, until the next conference, at which time it would be made known unto them "what you shall do, and all things shall be done by common consent in the church, by much prayer and faith, for all things you shall receive by faith."... (D&C 26: 1-2)

[Section 27]

An August, 1830 revelation, Section Twenty-seven, referred

151

to the emblems of the sacrament previously reported. The remaining portion of Section Twenty-seven was written in September. It deals with a prophesied future great and grand meeting where Christ and His prophets from previous dispensations are to partake of the sacrament together.

Addressing Joseph Smith the Lord said:

"... I will drink of the fruit of the vine with you on the earth, and with Moroni, whom I sent unto you to reveal the Book of Mormon, containing the fulness of my everlasting gospel to whom I have committed the keys of the record of the stick of Ephraim And also with Elias, to whom I have committed the keys of bringing to pass the restoration of all things spoken by the mouth of all the holy prophets since the world began, concerning the last days; And also John the son of Zacharias ... which John I have sent unto you my servants Joseph Smith Jun., and Oliver Cowdery, to ordain unto you the first priesthood [Aaronic] which you have received, that you might be called and ordained even as Aaron; [see Hebrews 5:4] And also Elijah, unto whom I have committed the keys of the power of turning the hearts of the fathers to the children, and the hearts of the children to the fathers that the whole earth may not be smitten with a curse; And also with Joseph and Jacob [Israel] and Isaac and Abraham, your fathers, by whom the promises remain; And also with Michael, or Adam, the father of all, the ancient of days; And also with Peter, James and John, whom I sent unto you, by whom I have ordained you and confirmed upon you to be apostles, and especial witnesses of my name, and bear the keys of your ministry and of the same things which I revealed unto them; Unto whom I have committed the keys of my kingdom, and a dispensation of the gospel for the last times; and for the fulness of times, in the which I will gather together in one all things both which are in heaven and which are on earth; And also with all those whom the Father hath given me out of the world." (D&C 27:5-14; see also Ezekiel 37)

The Lord closed this revelation with an admonition to: "Take

152

upon you my whole armor... having your loins girt about with truth, having on the breastplate of righteousness, and your feet shod with the preparation of the gospel of peace, which I have sent mine angels to commit unto you; Taking the shield of faith whereby ye shall be able to quench all the fiery darts of the wicked; And take the helmet of salvation and the sword of my Spirit, which I will pour out upon you, and my word which I reveal unto you ... be faithful until I come, and ye shall be caught up, that where I am ye shall be also.." (D&C 27:15-18)

[Section 28]

Continuing His communication in September, 1830, the Lord revealed Oliver Cowdery's relationship to Joseph Smith was to be similar to Aaron's relationship to Moses. Oliver was to declare the content of the revelations and commandments received, teaching them under the influence of the Comforter, or Holy Ghost, but the commandments and revelations from God were to be received through Joseph Smith, "for he receiveth them even as Moses." Oliver was to take his cues from Joseph and not vice versa, for God had given him [Joseph] "the keys of mysteries, and of revelation." For now, Oliver was given further instructions with reference to his missionary labors. While reaffirming Joseph Smith receives revelation for the Church, the Lord made clear Hiram Page, an early disciple, was deceived by Satan, who had given him false revelations. (D&C 28:1-6)

[Section 29]

Introducing Section Twenty-nine in September 1830, the Lord reminded Joseph Smith and the six elders present that He had atoned for their sins, that their sins had been forgiven, that they were to remember to sin no more lest perils come upon them. They were to

"lift up your [their] hearts and be glad for I am in your midst;" (v 5) and it was the good will of the Father to give them the kingdom,

"Whatever ye shall ask in faith, being united in prayer according to my command ye shall receive. And ye are called to bring to pass the gathering of mine elect; for mine elect shall hear my voice and harden not their hearts." (v 6-7)

Reminding them that He, the Savior, would soon come, He declared the proud and those who do wickedly will be burned at His coming, and that which was spoken by

"mine apostles must be fulfilled; for as they spoke so shall it come to pass; For I will reveal myself from heaven with power and great glory, with all the hosts thereof, and dwell in righteousness with men on earth a thousand years, and the wicked shall not stand." (v 9-11) Thus Christ's coming ushers in the Millennium and at his coming the unrepentant wicked will be destroyed.

At the day of Christ's second coming, in a pillar of fire, "being clothed with robes of righteousness, with crowns upon their heads, in glory even as I am," shall the apostles who were with Jesus in His ministry at Jerusalem, stand at His right hand, "to judge the whole house of Israel, even as many as have loved me and kept my commandments, and none else," said the Lord. (v 12)

At His coming a trump shall sound long and loud, all the earth shall quake, and those who have loved Jesus Christ and kept His commandments shall come forth; "yea, even the dead which died in me, to receive a crown of righteousness, and to be clothed upon, even as I am, to be with me, that we may be one." (v 13) Thus, those who are to come forth in the first resurrection are identified.

But before that day the sun shall be darkened, the moon shall turn into blood, and the stars shall fall from heaven; there shall be weeping and wailing among the people; a great hailstorm will be sent forth to destroy the crops of the earth, Christ will take vengeance upon the wicked. He will send flies which shall take hold of the wicked, eat their flesh and breed maggots. Their tongues shall not utter against the Lord, their flesh shall fall off their bones, and their eyes from their sockets. Beasts and fowls shall devour them up and the great and abominable church shall be destroyed by fire. (v 14-21)

As the thousand years of Christ's reign during the Millennium

154

comes to a close, those last to be resurrected shall come forth.

"And the end shall come, and the heaven and the earth shall be consumed and pass away, and there shall be a new heaven and a new earth.... But... before the earth shall pass away, Michael, mine arch-angel, shall sound his trump, and then shall all the dead awake, for their graves shall be opened, and they shall come forth yea, even all. And the righteous shall be gathered on my right hand unto eternal life, and the wicked on my left hand will I be ashamed to own before my Father." (v 23-26)

The wicked who repent not, cannot dwell in the presence of Jesus Christ, "for where I am they cannot come, for they have no power." (v 29)

The Savior also declared in this section there is no separation of temporal and spiritual things, that to Him, all things are spiritual. Clarifying what He meant, the Lord referred to the choices Satan made in rebelling against God, and that He, God, chose to allow the devil and his followers to tempt the children of men. If it were not so,

"they could not be agents unto themselves, for if they never should have the bitter they could not know the sweet." (v 39)

Adam and Eve's choices in the Garden caused them to be cast out of God's presence because of transgression, and because of transgression, Adam became "spiritually dead, which is the first death, even that same death which is the last death, which is spiritual, which shall be pronounced upon the wicked when I shall say: Depart ye cursed. But, behold, I say unto you that I, the Lord God, gave unto Adam and unto his seed that they should not die as to the temporal death until I, the Lord God, should send forth angels to declare unto them repentance and redemption through faith on the name of mine Only Begotten Son.

"And thus did I, the Lord God, appoint unto man the days of his probation - that by his natural death he might be raised to immortality, unto eternal life, even as many as would believe. And they that believe not unto eternal damnation; and they cannot be

155

redeemed from their spiritual fall because they repent not;" (v 41-44)

"But ... little children are redeemed from the foundation of the world through mine Only Begotten.[Christ] Wherefore they cannot sin, for power is not given unto Satan to tempt little children until they begin to become accountable before me; ... I say unto you that whoso having knowledge, have I not commanded to repent?"(v 44-49, D&C 29:1-50)

[Sections 30, 31, 32 and 33]

Section Thirty, given in September, 1830 contained instruction related to missionary work for David Whitmer, Peter Whitmer Jr. and John Whitmer. These Book of Mormon witnesses of three and eight respectively in number, were to open their mouths in the Lord's cause and not fear what man can do. (D&C 30:1-11)

Section Thirty-one, also given in September, 1830, was for Thomas B. Marsh, who was called to preach the gospel, assured his family would be taken care of ,and counseled to be patient, to pray and to follow the prompting of the Holy Ghost. (D&C 31:1-12)

In October, 1830 Section Thirty-two was given through the Prophet Joseph Smith to Parley P. Pratt and Ziba Peterson. They were called to preach to the Lamanites, but to pray first for an understanding of the scriptures. (D&C 32:1-5)

Ever ready to instruct those who diligently seek in faith, the Lord did instruct Ezra Thayre and Northrop Sweet in October, 1830 through Section Thirty-three. They were called to declare the Lord's gospel and informed,

"the field is white and already to harvest; and it is the eleventh hour, and the last time that I shall call laborers into my vineyard." (v 3)

The Lord said His vineyard was corrupted, that His church was called forth out of the wilderness, that He will gather His elect from the four quarters of the earth, and that these brethren should open their mouths and they shall be filled:

"open your mouths and ye shall be laden with sheaves for I am

156

with you, Yea open your mouths and they shall be filled, saying: Repent, repent and prepare ye the way of the Lord and make his paths straight for the kingdom of heaven is at hand. Yea, repent and be baptized, every one of you, for a remission of your sins; yea be baptized even by water and then cometh the baptism of fire and of the Holy Ghost. ... this is my gospel." (v 8-12)

The Lord closed Section Thirty-Three by telling them the Book of Mormon and the Holy Scriptures were given "of me for your instruction", and by admonishing them to "be faithful, praying always, having your lamps trimmed and burning and oil with you that you may be ready at the coming of the Bridegroom ... verily ... I come quickly." (v 17-18)

[Section 34]

Parley P. Pratt had introduced his brother Orson to the gospel six weeks prior to receipt of Section Thirty-four, addressed to Orson through Joseph Smith November 4, 1830. Parley and Orson would later be called as apostles of the Lord Jesus Christ. In Section Thirty-four the Lord refers to John the Beloved's words [John 3:16] saying,

"Jesus Christ your Redeemer ... so loved the world that he gave his own life that as many as would believe might become the sons of God." (v 2-3; Luke 8:21; John 1:12)

Orson was to cry repentance, preparing the way for the Lord's second coming.

"For ... the time is soon at hand that I shall come in a cloud with power and great glory ... and all nations shall tremble." (v 6-8)

After rehearsing again events to precede His coming the Lord counselled Orson to,

"Lift up your voice and spare not for the Lord God hath spoken; therefore prophecy, and it shall be given by the power of the Holy Ghost." (v 10)

Joseph Smith Translation of Bible Continues
[Section 35]

157

At the command of God, beginning in June 1830, Joseph Smith had been making corrections to the King James Version of the Bible and also adding inspired segments. By December, 1830, this had become a regular daily task. Oliver Cowdery and John Whitmer had served as scribes, writing down what Joseph dictated. By December these scribes were called to other duties. Sidney Rigdon had taken the scribe's duties. Section Thirty-five was given to Joseph Smith and Sidney Rigdon. (HC 1:128-131)

In this revelation the Lord describes how men may become the sons of God. Sidney Rigdon's assignment to baptize and confirm the Holy Ghost, was given and clarified, since Sidney had been a leader in another church at the time of his conversion. The Lord declared,

"the time speedily cometh that great things are to be shown unto the children of men; But without faith shall not anything be shown, except desolations upon Babylon..." (v 10-11) He also said he would call upon the weak things of the world, those who are unlearned and despised, to thrash the nations by the power of His spirit,

"And the poor and the meek shall have the gospel preached unto them, and they shall be looking forth for the time of my coming, for it is nigh at hand ... and I have sent forth the fulness of my gospel by the hand of my servant Joseph; and in weakness have I blessed him; And I have given unto him the keys of the mystery of those things which have been sealed, even things which were from the foundation of the world, and the things which shall come from this time until the time of my coming ... thou [Sidney] shalt write for him; and the scriptures shall be given ... to the salvation of mine own elect; For they shall hear my voice and shall see me and shall not be asleep, and shall abide the day of my coming; for they shall be purified, even as I am pure." (v 15-21)

Closing Section Thirty-five the Lord admonished these five men and the Church to,

"Keep all the commandments, and covenants by which ye are bound; and I will cause the heavens to shake for your good, and Satan shall tremble and Zion shall rejoice upon the hills and flourish; and Israel shall be saved in mine own due time; and by the keys which I have given you shall they be led, and no more be confounded at all. Lift up your hearts and be glad, your redemption draweth nigh. Fear not, little flock, the kingdom is yours, until I come. Behold, I come quickly, Even so, Amen." D&C 35:1-27)

[Sections 36 and 37]

In that same month, December, 1830, the Lord spoke through Joseph Smith, in Section Thirty-six, to another soon to be Church leader, Edward Partridge. Edward would have the Holy Ghost conferred upon him and be blessed by Sidney Rigdon, another rising star in the early Latter-day Saint Church. As many as receive the Gospel who accept the calling,

"were to be ordained and sent forth to preach the everlasting gospel among the nations - Crying repentance ... I am Jesus Christ, the Son of God, wherefore, gird up your loins, and I will suddenly come to my temple, even so, Amen." (D&C 36:1-8)

The first reference the Lord made to coming to His temple in this dispensation was thus given in Section Thirty-six, and the first commandment concerning a gathering of His covenant people in this dispensation was received, also in December 1830, Section Thirty-seven. They were to gather to the State of Ohio. Oliver Cowdery, who had been sent to preach the gospel to the Lamanites or Indians, farther west, was to meet the Saints as they gathered to the Kirtland, Ohio area. (D&C 37:1-4)

[Sections 38, 39 and 40]

Three more revelations were given through Joseph Smith at Fayette, New York, before the little flock removed themselves to Kirtland, Ohio, where they arrived the first week in February, 1831.

At the last conference of the Church at Fayette, New York before moving to Ohio, Section Thirty-eight was received through the

159

Prophet January 2, 1831.

In it, Christ reminds them that at His command the world was made and all things in it, that he had taken the City of Enoch or Zion to His own bosom,

"Even as many as have believed in my name ... but the residue of the wicked I have kept in chains of darkness until the judgment, the great day, which shall come at the end of the earth." (v 1-5) He told the Saints He was in their midst, though they could not see Him.

"But the day soon cometh that ye shall see me, and know that I am; for the veil of darkness shall soon be rent, and he that is not purified shall not abide the day. Wherefore gird up your loins and be prepared. Behold the kingdom is yours ...

"Verily, I say unto you, ye are clean, but not all and there is none else with whom I am well pleased, For all flesh is corrupted before me; and the power of darkness prevails upon the earth, among the children of men, ... the angels are waiting the great command to reap down the earth to gather the tares that they may be burned ..." (v 6-12)

"for your salvation I give unto you a commandment, for I have heard your prayers, and the poor have complained before me, and the rich I have made, and all flesh is mine, and I am no respecter of persons. And I have made the earth rich ..." (v 13-17)

The Lord told them He has reserved a land of promise for them in time and in eternity, "if you seek it with all your hearts." (v 19)

This land is to have no king but the Messiah, and no laws but His laws. Every man is to esteem his brother as himself and practice virtue, and holiness before the Lord. (v 20-24)

The Lord reminded the Saints to care for the poor and the needy and for them to be one, "and if you are not one ye are not mine.(v 27) He observed that "war in far countries was in the hearts of men, even in your own land." (v 29) The Saints were to treasure up wisdom and prepare themselves, "That ye might escape the power of the enemy, and be gathered unto me a righteous people without spot and blameless." (v 31)

These were the reasons for the Saints removal to Ohio; there to receive more of God's law and "be endowed with power from on high"; (v 32) [Thereby, the Lord alluded to the keys they would receive about six years later, keys to the gathering of Israel held by Moses, keys to the sealing power held by Elijah, and the blessings of the dispensation of Abraham, through whom all the families of the earth would be blessed. D&C 110:11-16]

"for Israel shall be saved..."(v 33)

The poor and the needy were not to be left behind in New York. Instead, certain men were appointed,

"to look to the poor and the needy and administer to their relief that they shall not suffer; and send them forth to the place which I have commanded them." [to Ohio] (v 35) This revelation was closed with the observation that eventually,

"all things shall be gathered into the bosom of the church; and ye shall be the richest of all people, for ye shall have the riches of eternity." (v 39)

Every able bodied priesthood holder was to labor towards the move to Ohio, and at the same time to let their neighbors be warned in mildness and meekness." (v 41)

In Section Thirty-nine, a revelation given January 5, 1831 to James Covill through Joseph Smith, the Lord said, among other things, His servants were to preach the Gospel to all nations prior to His second coming.

"Go forth baptizing with water, preparing the way before my face for the time of my coming." (v 20, D&C 39:1-24)

Section Forty, also given in January 1831, reveals that fear of persecution and cares of the world cause a rejection of the Gospel among many. (D&C 40:1-3)

[Sections 41 and 42]

As the Saints gathered to Kirtland and their numbers increased rapidly, they "were striving to do the will of God so far as they knew it," but strange notions and false spirits crept in among them, so the Lord gave unto the Church what is now Section Forty-one (HC 1:146-7)

In this revelation given February 4, 1831 in Kirtland, Ohio, the Lord emphasized the Elders are to govern the Church by revelation, and that true disciples will receive and keep the Lord's law. In addressing them Jesus said in part,

..."ye whom I delight to bless with the greatest of all blessings ... assemble yourselves together to agree upon my word and by the prayer of your faith ye shall receive my law, that ye may know how to govern my church and have all things right before me ... He that receiveth my law and doeth it the same is my disciple." (v 1-5) But those who receive His law and doeth it not are not His disciples. Edward Partridge, said the Lord,"is like unto Nathaniel of old, in whom there is no guile." Edward was ordained a bishop in the Church at the Lord's command. (D&C 41:11-12)

Five days later February 9, 1831, another revelation was received at Kirtland. Twelve elders were present as Section Forty-two was given in fulfillment of the Lord's promise in Section Forty-one. They would receive His law by their prayers of faith. Joseph Smith said this revelation embraced the law of the Church.

In Section Forty-two the elders were called to preach the gospel, to baptize converts and to build up the Church. They were to be properly called and ordained to preach and teach the principles of the gospel found in the scriptures, doing their work by the power of the spirit.

"And ye shall go forth by the power of my spirit, preaching the gospel, two by two, in my name, lifting up your voices as with the sound of a trump, declaring my word like unto the angels of God. And ye shall go forth baptizing with water, saying, Repent ye, repent ye, for the kingdom of heaven is at hand." (v 6-7)

Thus the outlines of missionary work by the elders of the

Church were set forth in this dispensation.

"...from this place ye shall go forth ... and inasmuch as ye shall find them that will receive you ye shall build up my church in every region - until the time shall come when it shall be revealed unto you from on high, when the city of the New Jerusalem shall be prepared, that ye may be gathered in one, that ye may be my people and I will be your God." (v 8-9) "ye shall teach them [the scriptures] unto all men; for they shall be taught unto all nations, kindreds and tongues and people."(v 58)

Proclaiming the Gospel to every nation, kindred, tongue and people will continue with increased power, knowledge and effort until the Savior comes to the New Jerusalem. Those going forth to do missionary work must be ordained,

"by someone who has authority, and it is known to the Church that he has authority and has been regularly ordained by the heads of the Church." (v 11)

"...the elders, priests and teachers of this church shall teach the principles of my gospel, which are in the Bible and the Book of Mormon, in the which is the fulness of my gospel... observe the covenants and church articles and do them, and these shall be their teachings, as they shall be directed by the Spirit. And the Spirit shall be given unto you by the prayer of faith; and if ye receive not the Spirit ye shall not teach." (v 13-14)

The scriptures are to be the law by which the church is governed. (v 59)

Speaking to church members as a whole, the Lord reiterated provisions of the Ten Commandments; that they were not to kill, steal, lie, lust, commit adultery or speak evil against others.(v 18-27) He spelled out in greater detail at the end of this revelation, laws governing fornication, adultery, killing, stealing and the confession of sins. (v 74-93)

With reference to fidelity the Lord declared:

"Thou shalt love thy wife with all thy heart, and shall cleave

163

unto her and none else." (v 22)

Speaking about the relationship of the material rich in the church to the material poor of His people, the Lord said:

"For I will consecrate of the riches of those who embrace my gospel among the Gentiles unto the poor of my people who are of the house of Israel. And again, thou shalt not be proud in thy heart; let all thy garments be plain; and their beauty the beauty of the work of thine own hands. And let all things be done in cleanliness before me. Thou shalt not be idle; for he that is idle shall not eat the bread nor wear the garment of the laborer."(v 39-42)

Addressing the care of the sick, the Lord said;

"And whoso among you are sick, and have not faith to be healed, but believe, shall be nourished with all tenderness, with herbs, and mild food, ... And the elders of the church, two or more, Shall be called, and shall pray for and lay their hands upon them in my name; and if they die they shall die unto me, and if they live they shall live unto me. Thou shalt live together in love, inasmuch that thou shalt weep for the loss of them that die, and more especially for those that have not hope of a glorious resurrection. And it shall come to pass that those that die in me shall not taste of death, for it shall be sweet unto them ... And again, it shall come pass that he that hath faith in me to be healed, and is not appointed unto death, shall be healed. He who hath faith to see shall see. He who hath faith to hear shall hear. The lame who hath faith to leap shall leap." (v 43-51)

References to the site of the New Jerusalem, and the mysteries of the kingdom and the law of consecration were also made. (D&C 42:1-93)

[Sections 43 and 44]

Also given during the month of February, 1831 was Section Forty-three. In it, the Lord made clear   revelations and commandments for the Church as a whole come only through the one He appoints. i.e. Joseph Smith, for now.

When the Saints are assembled together,

"ye shall instruct and edify each other, that ye may know how to act and direct my church, how to act upon the points of my law and my commandments and be sanctified by which you have received... and ye shall bind yourselves [agree] to act in all holiness before me - That inasmuch as ye do this glory shall be added to the kingdom which ye have received." (v 8-11)

Speaking to the Elders of the Church whom he had appointed to teach the Gospel, He said,

"ye are not sent forth to be taught, but to teach the children of men the things which I have put into your hands by the power of my Spirit; And ye are to be taught from on high. Sanctify yourselves and ye shall be endowed with power, that ye may give even as I have spoken." (v 15-16) These Elders were sent forth to cry repentance and to prepare people for the great day of the Lord.

Again, the Lord foretold the future and spelled out what His authorized servants, the missionaries, are to do and what they are to declare. He reminded them of the day that cometh,

"that the Lord shall utter his voice out of heaven; the heavens shall shake and the earth shall tremble, and the trump of God shall sound both long and loud, and shall say to the sleeping nations; Ye Saints arise and live; ye sinners stay and sleep until I shall call again." (v 18)

Once again through Joseph Smith, the Lord said unto the Elders of the Church:

"Lift up your voices and spare not. Call upon the nations to repent both old and young, both bond and free, saying, prepare yourselves for the great day of the Lord. For I ... do lift up my voice and call upon you to repent, and ye hate me, what will ye say when the day cometh when the thunderings [and lightnings] all utter their voices from the ends of the earth, saying: Repent and prepare for the great day of the Lord? ... and Repent ye, for the great day of the Lord is come? ... Hearken, O ye nations of the earth, and hear the words of that God who made you. How oft have I called upon you by the voice of my servants, and by the ministering of angels, and mine own voice, and by the voice of thunderings ... lightnings ... tempests ... earthquakes ... great hailstorms ... and pestilence of every kind, and by the voice of the great sound of the trump, and by the voice of judgement, and by the voice of mercy all the day long, and the riches of eternal life, and would have saved you with an everlasting salvation but ye would not! Behold the day has come, when the cup of the wrath of mine indignation is full. Behold verily I say unto you, that these are the words of the Lord your God." (v 2--27)

Addressing the Elders and members of the Church at the close of this revelation, the Lord declared,

"labor ye, labor ye, in my vineyard for the last time - for the time call upon the inhabitants of the earth. For in mine own due time will I come upon the earth in judgment, and my people shall be redeemed and shall reign with me on the earth, For the great Millennium of which I have spoken by the mouth of my servants, shall come." (v 20-30)

During this thousand years, "Satan shall be bound, and when he is loosed again [after the thousand years are over] he shall reign for a little season and then cometh the end of the earth, (Matt 24:14) And he that liveth in righteousness shall be changed in the twinkling of an eye, and the earth shall pass away so as by fire ... Hearken to these words, Behold, I am Jesus Christ, the Savior of the world. Treasure these things up in your hearts and let the solemnities of eternity rest upon your minds. Be sober. Keep all my commandments. Even so, Amen." (D&C 43:1-35)

Also revealed to Joseph Smith in February, 1831 was Section Forty-four in which the Lord commands that the Elders of the Church "should be called together from the east ...west ... north... and south," in conference. He promised to pore out, "my Spirit upon them", that are faithful at this conference. The Elders were to go through the regions round about, "and preach repentance unto the people. And many shall be converted." (v 3-4) They were to organize the new members "according to the laws of man". (v 4)

Ohio was just a few years into statehood. This organization would bring to the Church the protection of the laws of Ohio and the laws of the United States. At the close of Section Forty-four, the Lord reminded the Elders once again, "to visit the poor and needy and administer to their relief," while getting better organized to do more in taking care of needy Church members. (D&C 44:1-6)

[Section 45]

Many false reports and foolish stories were published and circulated in the New York, Pennsylvania, and Ohio areas about the new church, their movement to Kirtland, and their efforts to share the Gospels with others. To the joy of the Saints Section Forty-five was given March 7, 1831 at Kirtland. In it the Lord gives the Saints an important overview of future events to occur in the latter days just prior to the Lord's Second Coming.

Reminding the Saints who they are and who He is, the Lord God declared:

"Hearken O ye people of my church to whom the kingdom has been given; hearken ye and give ear to him who laid the foundation of the earth, who made the heavens and all the hosts thereof, and by whom all things were made which live and move, and have a being. And again I say, hearken unto my voice lest death shall overtake you; in an hour when ye think not the summer shall be past, and the harvest ended and your souls are not saved. Listen to him [Christ] who is the advocate with the Father, who is pleading your cause before him saying ... spare these my brethren that believe on my name, that they may come unto me and have everlasting life.

"I came unto mine own and mine own received me not, but unto as many as received me gave I power to do many miracles and to become the sons of God; and even unto them that believed on my name gave I power to obtain eternal life. And even so I have sent mine everlasting covenant into the world to be a light to the world, and to be a standard for my people, and for the Gentiles to seek it, and

167

to be a messenger before my face to prepare the way before me, wherefore, come ye unto it ... hearken ye together and let me show unto you even my wisdom of him ye say is the God of Enoch and his brethren, who were separated from the earth, and were received unto myself - a city reserved until the day which was sought for by all the holy prophets, and they found it not because of wickedness and abomination and confessed they were strangers and pilgrims on the earth; But obtained a promise that they should find it and see it in their flesh. Wherefore ... I will ... prophecy as unto men in days of old." (v 1-15)

The Savior promised the Latter-day Saints He would show the signs of His coming to them as He did to His disciples when he stood before them in the flesh. [Matt 24:3] This time, said the Lord:

"I shall come in my glory in the clouds of heaven, to fulfill the promises that I have made unto your fathers... I will show unto you how the day of redemption shall come, and also the restoration of the scattered Israel." (v 16-18) Jesus then rehearsed prophecies relating to the destruction of the Jerusalem Temple and the scattering of His people among all nations and their fulfillment.

Acknowledging that his disciples knew the end of the world would come and the heavens and the earth would pass away, He declared that would not happen until "all shall be fulfilled." A remnant of the house of Israel was to be scattered among all nations, and then gathered again when,

"the times of the Gentiles be fulfilled. And in that day, shall be heard of wars and rumors of war, and the whole earth shall be in commotion, and men's hearts shall fail them, and they shall say that Christ delayeth his coming until the end of the earth. And the love of men shall wax cold, and iniquity shall abound. And when the times of the Gentiles is come in, a light shall break forth among them that sit in darkness, and it shall be the fulness of my gospel. But they receive it not; for they perceive not the light, and they turn their hearts from me because of the precepts of men. And in that generation shall the times of the Gentiles be fulfilled ... There shall be men [who] shall see an overflowing scourge; for desolating sickness shall cover the land. But my disciples shall stand in holy places, and shall not be moved; but among the wicked men shall lift up their voices and curse God and die ... There shall be earthquakes in divers places and many desolations ... Men will take up the sword ... and kill one another ... Be not troubled for, when all these things shall come to pass, ye may know that the promises which have been made unto you shall be fulfilled ... Even so it shall be in that day when they shall see these things, then shall they know the hour is nigh... And they shall behold blood and fire and vapors of smoke. And before the day of the Lord shall come, the sun shall be darkened and the moon turned into blood, and the stars shall fall from heaven. And the remnant [house of Israel] shall be gathered unto this place." (v 19-43)

As the restoration unfolded in the 1830's the Master reaffirmed it was He who "created the heavens and the earth, a light which cannot be hid in darkness; wherefore I must bring forth the fulness of my gospel from the Gentiles unto the house of Israel." (D&C 14:9-10)

After righteousness and truth sweep the earth as a flood and the fulness of the Gospel has been taught unto the house of Israel, those accepting and receiving it, both literal and adopted members shall be gathered prior to His coming.

"And then they shall look for me [said the Lord] and behold, I will come, and they shall see me in the clouds of heaven, clothed with power and great glory; with all the holy angels; and he that watches for me not shall be cut off. But before the arm of the Lord shall fall ... the Saints shall come forth from the four quarters of the earth. And then shall the Lord set his foot upon the mount [of Olives] and it shall cleave in twain, and the earth shall tremble, and reel to and fro, and the heavens also shall shake. And the Lord shall utter his voice and all the ends of the earth shall hear it; and the nations of the earth shall mourn, and they that have laughed shall see their folly.

"And calamity shall cover the mocker, and the scorner shall be consumed And they that have watched for iniquity shall be hewn down and cast into the fire. .. And at that day, when I shall come in my glory, shall the parable be fulfilled which I spake concerning the ten virgins. For they that are wise and have received the truth, and have taken the Holy Ghost for their guide, and have not been deceived - verily I say unto you, they shall not be hewn down and cast into the fire, but shall abide the day. And the earth shall be given unto them for an inheritance; and they shall multiply and wax strong; and their children shall grow up without sin unto salvation. For the Lord shall be in their midst, and his glory shall be upon them, and he shall be their king and lawgiver," during the Millennium. (D&C 45:45-59)

From these scriptures the Lord helps us understand what will be required for each of us to be numbered among the wise virgins-- we must take the Holy Ghost to be our companion and guide, and build a reserve of spiritual oil through our day to day choices. By contrast, the foolish virgins will not be able to borrow oil because it must be accumulated by obedience. Having oil and not having oil will be the consequences of the choices we make.

Thus we see the earth is the laboratory in which mankind is tried and tested and found worthy to dwell on earth in its permanent upgraded state. In its loveliness it will be like it was before the Fall, without curse, a place where its creator may dwell and its inhabitants enter covenants with God and keep them, doing good works and repenting from evil works; where the humble, the contrite, the meek, the tithe payer, the almsgiver, those who remember the Sabbath, keep it holy and fast with thanksgiving; where those who love the Lord God with all their might, mind and strength dwell, and show it by being in the service of their fellow beings, and are motivated by a sincere desire to help every person made in the express image of God to be found worthy of all that the Father has.

The Lord interrupted this discourse saying more would be

given after Joseph Smith finished the New Testament translation and instructed him to proceed with it. Subsequently returning to the subject of war in foreign lands, the Lord said in 1831:

"behold I say unto you, they are nigh, even at the doors and not many years hence ye shall hear of wars in your own lands." (v 63)

Within fifteen years after this revelation was given, wars in their own land began and included a war between the United States and Mexico in the 1840's and a war between the states of the United States or Civil War in the 1860's.

Just twenty-one months after Section Forty-five was revealed containing these references to wars in their own lands, the Lord was even more specific when He foretold on December 25, 1832, that

"wars that will shortly come to pass, beginning at the rebellion in South Carolina, which will terminate in the death and misery of many souls. For behold the Southern States shall be divided against the Northern States. And it shall come to pass after many days slaves shall rise up against their masters who shall be marshaled and disciplined for war." (D&C 87:1-4)

However, for the immediate future the Lord turned His attention to the conversion of souls. The Elders of the Church were to proselyte further west calling on the inhabitants thereof to repent, and those entering the covenant to "build up churches unto me". (v 64) It was clear Kirtland was to be a temporary gathering place.

"With one heart and one mind, gather up your riches that ye may purchase an inheritance which shall hereafter be appointed unto you. And it shall be called the New Jerusalem, a land of peace, a city of refuge, a place of safety, for the Saints of the Most High God; And the glory of the Lord shall be there - and it shall be called Zion ... And there shall be gathered unto it out of every nation under heaven, and it shall be the only place that shall not be at war one with another ... And it shall come to pass that the righteous shall be gathered out from among all nations, and shall come to Zion, singing songs of everlasting joy." (v 65-71)

171

Because Zion is both a spiritual condition and a geographical location it is easy to confuse the two. Zion, as a spiritual condition, where the pure in heart dwell, could be in a thousand places simultaneously. However, when one is speaking of a particular place called Zion, Zion used in that context, is restricted to one geographical location. When the New Jerusalem or the Old Jerusalem are referred to as Zion, a place where the pure in heart dwell, one should not assume these are the only places where the pure in heart may dwell and still qualify as a place of Zion. More will be reported on Zion as a Society in the New World Order in Chapter XVIII.

While the major thrust of the Church's activities during its first year of existence relates to missionary work, the Lord began referencing Enoch and his city of Zion in the Doctrine and Covenants, which coincides with Joseph Smith's translation of Old Testament Genesis, which led to the addition of whole chapters relating to Enoch not extant in the King James Version, but which are now part of the writings of Moses in the Pearl of Great Price. In Section 45 of the Doctrine and Covenants given less than a year after the Church's organization, the Lord began referring to the New Jerusalem as a place of peace, safety and refuge for the Saints of the Most High God; a place to which they were to gather with one heart and one mind with their riches to purchase an inheritance there. He said His glory would be there, that it shall be called Zion, that righteous people out of every nation under heaven would gather there, and shall come to Zion singing songs of everlasting joy. As of March 7, 1831 when this revelation was given, the location of the New Jerusalem or Zion was not known to the Saints, but soon would be.

When Isaiah saw the future concerning Judah and Jerusalem in the last days, He apparently saw a spiritual condition and geographical location where a Temple would be built. Isaiah said; "And it shall come to pass in the last days, that the mountain of the Lord's house shall be established in the top of the mountains, and shall be exalted above the hills; and all nations shall flow unto it. And many people shall go and say, Come ye, and let us go up to the mountain of the Lord, to the house of the God of Jacob [Israel], and he will teach us of his ways, and we shall walk in his paths: for out of Zion shall go forth the law, and the word of the Lord from Jerusalem and he shall judge among the nations, and shall rebuke many people; and they shall beat their swords into plow shares, and their spears into pruning hooks: nation shall not lift up the sword against nation, neither shall they learn war any more. O house of Jacob [Israel], come ye, and let us walk in the light of the Lord." (Is, 2:2-5)

One thought is that Isaiah saw the Valley of the Great Salt Lake, Utah where a Temple would be built and nations would flow unto that city where the current presiding high priest, prophet, seer, and revelator, his counselors and the Lord's Quorum of Twelve Apostles would be headquartered; they being the foundation of the Church, with Jesus Christ being its chief cornerstone.

Another thought would be that Isaiah saw the mountain of the Lord as the temple, where men and women could flow unto it, be endowed with knowledge and with power from on high and into enter additional covenants that would allow them to be sanctified from the world.

Referring to a New Jerusalem as a place of peace, a city of refuge, a place of safety for the Saints of the Most High God, the Lord added information about this city to that which He gave the previous month when He said,

"a city of the New Jerusalem shall be prepared, that ye may be gathered in one, that ye may be my people and I shall be your God." (D&C 42:9)

The Prophet Micah, who lived after Isaiah, used almost identical words in describing the place where the law would go forth from Zion, where a temple would be built, Israel gathered to it, the commencing of the Millennial era and the reign of the Lord in Zion. (Micah 4:1-13)

Speaking to the remnant of the house of Israel in America not

173

long after the resurrection of the Lord, referencing the prophet Isaiah's words concerning the establishment of Zion in the last days, the Lord said

"that when they shall be fulfilled then is the fulfilling of the covenant which the Father hath made unto his people, O house of Israel. And then shall the remnants [of the house of Israel] which shall be scattered abroad upon the face of the earth, be gathered in from the east and from the west, and from the south and from the north, and they shall be brought to the knowledge of the Lord their God, who hath redeemed them." (3 Ne 20:11-13)

Implied here is that they did not then have a knowledge of the Lord their God who hath redeemed them and needed to be brought to it, indicating a restoration was needed along with massive missionary work.

The Lord said to these people in America that at that time, Israel would be gathered when the Book of Mormon comes forth, after the Gentiles were established in America as a free people, and that if they believed and obeyed they would be saved. (3 Ne 21:1-22)

The Gentiles "shall assist my people, the remnant of Jacob, and also as many of the house of Israel as shall come, that they may build a city which shall be called the New Jerusalem.

"And then they shall assist my people that they may be gathered in, who are scattered upon all the face of the land in unto the New Jerusalem. And then shall the power of heaven come down among them; and I will be in their midst. And then shall the work of the Father commence at that day even when this gospel shall be preached among the remnant of this people, Verily, I say unto you, at that day shall the work of the Father commence among all the dispersed of my people, yea even the tribes which have been lost, which the Father lead away out of Jerusalem. Yea, the work shall commence among all the dispersed of my people with the Father to prepare the way whereby they may call on the Father in my name.

Yea, and then shall the work commence with the Father among all nations in preparing the way whereby his people may be gathered home to the land of their inheritance." (3 Ne 21:23-29)

From Jesus' words in the Bible we are taught that His Father's house is a house of order, and that there are many mansions or potential rewards there. It follows that the gathering would also reflect an organized effort. It would also follow the scriptural pattern-- the children of the covenant, the house of Israel, are to be gathered according to the birthright blessings leading off with Ephraim and Manasseh followed by the other tribes and the general populace of the world as a whole. For an orderly gathering the conditions would need to be right, with the fulness of the gospel, priesthood power and the ordinances of salvation and exaltation fully restored and operational.

Ether, a prophet in America many hundreds of years before Christ's first coming, spoke of the land of America as being a choice land above all other lands where the Lord would have all men serve Him who dwell there, Moroni, commenting on this choice land said,

"it was a place of the New Jerusalem ... that... should be built upon this land unto the remnant of the seed of Joseph ... and they shall build up a holy city unto the Lord like unto the Jerusalem of old ... until the end come when the earth shall pass away."(Ether 13:1-8)

About eight months after Section Forty-five was given, Section 133 was given in which the Lord declared those among the Gentiles were to flee to Zion (D&C 133:12), and in Section Eighty-four given in September, 1832, the Lord referred to "the gathering of his Saints to stand upon Mount Zion which shall be the New Jerusalem. (D&C 84:2). About a year later in August, 1833 the Lord referred to Zion as the city of our God. (D&C 97:19)

Thus we see that the Lord's covenant people are to be gathered spiritually and temporally to Zion, places of peace, safety, and refuge where there is no war, places worthy as a dwelling place for their leader Jesus Christ. Summarizing all this Joseph Smith declared:

"We believe in the literal gathering of Israel and the restoration of the Ten Tribes; that Zion (the New Jerusalem) will be built upon the American continent; that Christ will reign personally upon the earth, and that the earth will be renewed to receive its paradisiacal glory." (Tenth Article of Faith, HC 4:535-541)

Section Forty-five closes with a reiteration that every nation under heaven is to be gathered unto it, [that is, gathered spiritually first to Zion's designated stakes and second, gathered geographically to designated lands promised as an inheritance to the posterity of Abraham both literal and adopted, through Israel's sons, and it shall be the only people that shall not be at war one with another.(D&C 45:68-75)

In this chapter we see the foundation being laid for future major and massive missionary efforts. Outlines of the spiritual condition and geographical location of a Zion Society under whose canopy Israel is to be gathered, and its covenant members, the true believers in Messiah/Christ, perfected, redeemed and returned to the presence of God, are indicated.

Need for more revelation concerning the Church of Jesus Christ, newly restored in this dispensation, was great. The Lord responded with that revelation over the next nine months; most of which can be categorized as relating to gathering, perfecting, and redeeming Israel, the true believers in Christ, and returning them to the presence of God.

CHAPTER XII

MORE ON DOCTRINE AND COVENANTS
FOR THE GATHERING AND PERFECTION OF ISRAEL
March 8, 1831 through October 25, 1831
[Sections 46 through 66]

[Section 46]

Just one day after receiving Section Forty-five, Section Forty-six came through revelation to Joseph Smith March 8, 1831. It related to governing and conducting Church services and meetings. (HC 1: 163-165)

"it always has been given to the elders of the church from the beginning and ever shall be, to conduct all meetings as they are directed and guided by the Holy Spirit." (v 12) Generally everyone is welcome to attend, especially those seeking the kingdom who are not yet members.

"But ye are commanded in all things to ask of God, who giveth liberally; and that which the Spirit testifies unto you even so I would that ye should do in all holiness of heart, walking uprightly before me ... doing all things with prayer and thanksgiving."(v 7)

To guard against doctrines of devils and commandments of men they were advised:

"to seek ye earnestly the best gifts, always remembering for what they are given ... they are given for the benefit of those who love me and keep all my commandments, and him that seeketh so to do, that all may be benefitted." ... (v 8-9)

As revealed by the Lord through the Apostle Paul, (I Cor 12:8-11) implied by the prophet Moroni, (Mor 10:8-17) and the prophet Joseph Smith

"no man can say that Jesus is the Lord, but by the Holy Ghost." (I Cor 12:3)

Thus a testimony of Jesus is received by revelation following the scriptural pattern. Though we are to seek the best gifts, the Lord has made it clear most of us will not have them all. We can collectively benefit from all these gifts as we assemble ourselves with the faithful, but it is not intended for each of us to have all of them independently.

The Lord said through the Joseph Smith,

"all have not every gift given to them; for there are many gifts, and to every man is given a gift by the Spirit of God. To some is given one, and to some is given another, that all may be profited thereby. To some it is given by the Holy Ghost to know that Jesus Christ is the Son of God, and that he was crucified for the sins of the world. To others it is given to believe on their words, that they also might have eternal life if they continue faithful." (v 11-14)

Other gifts include differences of administration, diversities of operations, the word of wisdom, the word of knowledge, faith to be healed, faith to heal, working of miracles, to prophesy, the discerning of spirits, to speak with tongues, to interpret tongues,

"and all these gifts come from God, for the benefit of the children of God." (v 25-26)

The power to discern whether gifts among the Saints are from God, from man, or from the devil, is vested in Bishops and other leaders appointed to watch over the Church. To the head of the Church is given all these gifts,

"in order that every member may be profited thereby." (v 29)

Whatever is done under the influence of these gifts through the Holy Ghost,

"must be done in the name of Christ, And ye must give thanks unto God in the Spirit for whatsoever blessing ye are blessed with ... and ... practice virtue and holiness before me continually." (v 31-32, D&C 46:1-33)

[Sections 47, 48 and 49]

On the same day March 8, 1831 Section Forty-seven was also given. In it John Whitmer was called to "write and keep a regular history," and "to keep the church record and history continually, for Oliver Cowdery I have appointed to another office." (v 1-3)

John was also to assist "Joseph Smith in transcribing all things which shall be given you," and to do so under the influence of the Comforter or Holy Ghost." (D&C 47:1-4)

Section Forty-eight was also given in March 1831. It sets forth procedures for acquiring lands in Ohio for the settlement for the Saints, as per the Lord's command that they should assemble there. They were to save all the money they could to purchase all the lands they could in righteousness, so that in time they could build a city,

..."and then shall ye begin to be gathered with your families, every man according to his family, and as is appointed to him by the presidency and the bishop of the church." (D&C 48:1-6)

As was now his procedure when confronted with perplexing problems, information or practices different from what he already knew as a result of his role as prophet, seer, and revelator and head of the Church, Joseph Smith inquired of the Lord and received an answer.

Such was the case with revelation in Section Forty-nine, received in March 1831 at Kirtland. Some new members converted from other churches brought with them some beliefs from those churches. Those converted from the "United Society of Believers in Christ's Second Coming," for example, brought with them the belief that Christ had already come a second time in the form of a woman, Ann Lee; that baptism by water was not considered essential, that the eating of pork was forbidden, [many ate no meat at all] and they believed that a celibate life was considered higher or superior to a life in marriage. (HC 1:167-169)

Joseph Smith, Sidney Rigdon, Parley P. Pratt and Leman Copley sought clarification from the Lord on these matters and received answers contained in Section Forty-nine.

In this revelation the Lord reviewed His mission, having been sent by the Father into the world, for the redemption of the world, that through Him only can redemption come, that it is He, Jesus Christ, who will come a second time,

"but the hour and day no man knoweth, neither the angels in heaven, nor shall they know until he comes." (v 7)

To gain salvation people must repent, believe the gospel, enter the covenant through baptism and receive the Holy Ghost. The inquirers were to go to the "Shakers", as they were called, like Peter, His Apostle of old, to declare these things. With reference to celibacy the Lord said,

"marriage is ordained of God unto man ... and they twain [husband and wife], shall be one flesh, and all this that the earth might answer the end of its creation; And that it might be filled with the measure of man, according to his creation before the world was made." (v 16-17)

Given God's work and glory is to bring to pass the immortality and eternal life of man, how could He accomplish His work and glory if His billions upon billions of spirit children were not physically born into the world, because celibacy was taught and practiced as a superior form of human experience? About a year later the Lord explained that temporal things are patterned after spiritual things. (D&C 77:2) Learning to live as husband and wife teaches us very important lessons as we learn to become one in this most intimate relationship.

Abstinence from meat is not ordained of God, said the Lord:

"For behold, the beasts of the field and the fowls of the air, and that which cometh of the earth, is ordained for the use of man for food and for raiment, that he might have in abundance." (v 18-19)

However, "wo be unto the man that sheddeth blood or wasteth flesh and hath no need." (v 21)

Two years later the Lord would specify foods good for man, and things not good for man to take internally. He declared: "flesh, also of beasts and of fowls in the air, I, the Lord, have ordained for the use of man with thanksgiving; Nevertheless, they are to be used sparingly."

At this same time, the Lord suggested that alcohol, hot drinks, meaning coffee and tea, and tobacco taken internally are not good for man. It was not until recently that the wisdom of man has caught up with the prior warnings of God. One must ask how many broken lives and homes could have been saved if more had chosen to obey God's word of wisdom. How much abuse could have been prevented and how many lives saved? And how many more could be saved if mankind will yet listen to the Lord and obey this word of wisdom? (D&C 89:1-21)

The Lord made clear the Son of Man cometh not in the form of a woman, neither of a man traveling on the earth. (v 22) The Saints were commanded "be not deceived, but continue in steadfastness."

He referred them again to signs which are to precede His coming which they were and are to watch for,

"looking forth for the heavens to be shaken, and the earth to tremble and to reel to and fro as a drunken man, and for the valleys to be exalted, and for the mountains to be made low, and for the rough places to be made smooth - and all this when the angel shall sound his trumpet." (v 22-24)

Other important events are to come to pass before Christ's coming;

"But before the great day of the Lord shall come Jacob [His covenant people, Israel] shall flourish in the wilderness, and the Lamanites shall blossom as the rose. Zion shall flourish upon the hills and rejoice upon the mountains, and shall be assembled together unto the place which I have appointed." (v 24-25)

Closing this revelation in Section 49, the Lord counseled the Saints to be obedient, to repent, and He will respond to their questions and open the way for them. As with Moses and the children of Israel, the Lord said He," would go before them and would follow behind them, would be in their midst, and they would not be confounded." (D&C 49:1-28)

[Section 50]

The Restoration of Christ's Church on earth was yet in its first year when the Lord reaffirmed the spiritual gifts which were manifest among His covenant people Israel. Satan responded with his counterfeit gifts. A number of members claimed to be receiving visions and revelations prompting Joseph Smith to make inquiry of the Lord in the matter. A revelation, Section Fifty, was received in response in May 1831 at Kirtland, Ohio.

In it, the Lord said Satan had sought to deceive and overthrow the Saints by way of

"false spirits, which have gone forth in the earth, deceiving the world ... verily I say unto you there are hypocrites among you, who have deceived some, which has given the adversary power ... the hypocrites shall be detected and shall be cut off, either in life or in death, even as I will." (v 1-8)

The adversary is a tenacious opponent. He will not give up easily. He knows the plan of salvation and will do all he can to prevent us from progressing on a path of obedience back to God. We can expect his counterfeit gifts to mirror as opposition the true gifts of God.

chastity - fornication/adultery

agency - bondage: drugs, alcohol, tobacco

virtue - pornography, prostitution, etc

Elders should preach the gospel by the true Spirit, and they as well as the hearers need to be enlightened by the Spirit. It is important speaker and the receiver are edified and rejoice together. (v 22)

"That which is of God is light, and he that receiveth light and continueth in God, receiveth more light, and that light groweth

182

brighter and brighter until the perfect day." (v 24)

He that is ordained of God is appointed to be the greatest and servant of all. The faithful are the possessors of all things and the prayers of the purified are answered. At the Section's close the Savior told them He was in their midst, and reaffirmed He was the good shepherd and the stone of Israel, and

"the day cometh that you shall hear my voice and see me, and know that I am." (D&C 50:1-46)

[Sections 51 and 52]

Saints from the eastern states were now arriving in Ohio and the influx of members gathering there made it necessary to settle them as soon as possible. The Lord had already declared this responsibility was to be led by the new bishop, Edward Partridge. Bishop Partridge sought further instruction in these matters and so Joseph Smith inquired of the Lord. The result was Section Fifty-one. In it the Lord reaffirmed Bishop Partridge's role and added specificity to it. He was to oversee stewardships and properties which were to be organized according to the laws of the land. A bishop's storehouse was to be established, every man was to deal honestly with others and was to be alike and receive alike among the people that they "may be one". The Section closes with a note that Ohio was to be a temporary gathering place. The New Jerusalem, already alluded to by the Lord was to be further west. (D&C 51:1-20)

About six months after the first of the Saints had moved to Ohio from New York a conference was held in Kirtland, Ohio, during the third through sixth of June 1831. Received there the day after on the seventh, was a revelation, Section Fifty-two, in which the Lord announced the next conference was

"to be held in Missouri upon the land which I will consecrate unto my people, which are a remnant of Jacob, and those who are heirs according to the covenant." (v 1-2)

In anticipation of the journey there, He also informed them who was to make it, calling the brethren in pairs or companionships.

Joseph Smith and Sidney Rigdon were to take their journey as soon as preparations could be made to leave their homes. Lyman Wight and John Covill were to take their journey speedily. John Murdock and Hyrum Smith were to travel together, but to go to Missouri by way of Detroit.

All were to preach the gospel enroute,

"saying none other things than that which the prophets and apostles have written, and that which is taught them by the Comforter through the prayer of faith. Let them go two by two, and let them preach by the way ... baptizing by water, and the laying of hands at the water's side." (v 3-10)

They were cautioned to beware of Satan and instructed to be contrite in their missionary labors.

"He that speaketh, whose spirit is contrite, whose language is meek and edifieth, the same is of God if he obey mine ordinances ... he that trembleth under my power shall be made strong, and shall bring forth fruits of praise and wisdom according to the revelations and truths which I have given you ... Behold, this commandment is given unto all the elders whom I have chosen." (v 16-21)

Other pairs were called: Thomas B. Marsh and Ezra Thayre, and Isaac Morley and Ezra Booth. Edward Partridge and Martin Harris were to journey with Joseph Smith and Sidney Rigdon. Still other pairs were called to make the journey to Missouri "preaching by the way" unto the same land, including David Whitmer and Harvey Whitlock, Parley P. Pratt and Orson Pratt, Solomon Hancock and Simeon Carter, Edson Fuller and Jacob Scott, Levi W. Hancock and Zebedee Coltrin, Reynolds Cahoon and Samuel H. Smith, Wheeler Baldwin and William Carter, Newell Knight and Seleh J. Griffin.

The latter pair were ordained just prior to their departure. One pair was not to follow another or to follow up on the previous pair's effort even though they were to end up at the same place in Missouri.

On the other hand, Joseph Wakefield and Solomon Humphrey were sent to labor as missionaries "into the eastern lands", with similar messages. Some other brethren were to be advanced in priesthood offices, while still others were to be disciplined. Those not called to the Missouri conference preaching the Gospel by the way, were to watch over the newly formed Church units in Kirtland and environs, to preach in the regions round about, work for their sustenance, and to take care of the poor and the needy, the sick and the afflicted among them.

Official credentials for Joseph Smith, Sidney Ridgon, Edward Partridge and Oliver Cowdery from the Church were to be taken with them. Oliver Cowdery was already in Missouri.

Closing the revelation the Lord reaffirmed His instruction for all those called to assemble in Missouri;

"which is the land of your inheritance, which is now the land of your enemies. But behold, I, the Lord, will hasten the city in its time, and will crown the faithful with joy and rejoicing." (D&C 52: 1-44)

[Sections 53, 54 and 56]

A new member, Algernon Sydney Gilbert, requested of the Prophet Joseph Smith, an inquiry be made of the Lord concerning the role he were to play. Section Fifty-three was given in response, also in June 1831. (HC 1:179-180) In it the Lord revealed Brother Gilbert was to be ordained an elder and called,

"to preach faith and repentance and remission of sins according to my word, and the reception of the Holy Spirit by the laying on of hands." (v 3) In addition, Elder Gilbert was called to serve as

"an agent unto this church in the place which shall be appointed by the bishop ... you shall take your journey [to Missouri] with my servants Joseph Smith Jun. and Sidney Rigdon." (v 4-5) The Lord also told Brother Gilbert he would receive other ordinances "in a time to come," (v 6) and closed by declaring, "that he only is saved who endureth to the end," (D&C 53:1-7) reminding us that our salvation does not depend on a one time decision.

185

If we are to gain the reward, we must demonstrate through our day to day choices that we have placed our agency willingly on the alter of sacrifice. Ten years later in Section 132 the Lord also reminded us we are the children of Abraham, that we are to be tried even as Abraham, and that we should go do the works of Abraham, if we are to receive the exaltation he has received. To gain the same reward as Abraham we will have to do as he has done; that is, endure adversity, demonstrate our willingness to serve the Lord in all conditions, and sacrifice all that we have willingly, if necessary, and endure to the end.

The brethren arriving in Ohio had entered the covenant very recently. Living the provisions of the covenant and following the Lord's prophet meant sacrifice and consecration of time, talent and resources to the Lord's cause far beyond anything they had previously experienced. Property, in the European culture from which their forebears came, especially England, and to those moving west from the eastern seaboard, was very important.

Land opened up for personal acquisition in Ohio and regions west. Those with any money or financial leverage seized the opportunity, including new or prospective members of the Church. New members, who had already acquired property, were called upon to give up land and consecrate it to the Lord for His purposes, including the settlement of the poor and the needy who had answered the prophet's call to leave New York state and move to Ohio.

Some who initially agreed to give their property for that purpose did so, but others backed out. Members in the Branch at Thompson, Ohio were divided on the issue. Leman Copley broke his covenant to consecrate his large farm as a place of inheritance for the mostly poor and needy Saints arriving from Colesville, New York. Newell Knight, President of the Thompson Branch, and others sought counsel from the Prophet on what to do next.

Joseph Smith inquired of the Lord and received two revelations, Sections Fifty-four and Fifty-six, both at Kirtland, Ohio in June 1831. (HC 1:180-181)

In these revelations the Lord changed the assignments of some companionships because of the controversy over property at Thompson. Ezra Thayre wasn't ready to go to Missouri when his companion Thomas B. Marsh was, because he was a party to the Thompson property controversy. The Lord released Ezra Thayre and replaced him with Selah J. Griffin as Elder Marsh's companion. This necessitated releasing Selah J. Griffin as companion to Newel Knight. The Lord told Newel Knight "to stand fast in the office wherein I have appointed you". (v 2) He was to stay behind, resolve the property difficulties and then lead the arriving Colesville, New York Saints on to Missouri.

In the process, the Lord condemned those who had broken the covenant of consecration, called them to repentance, and declared the promises related thereto were void.(v 3-4) He also praised those who kept the covenant of consecration and blessed them. He instructed those who were to settle at Thompson, but were prevented from doing so, because Leman Copley would not give up his large farm for that purpose, that they should travel on to Missouri under the leadership of Thompson Branch President Newell Knight. After arriving in Missouri these Saints were to "seek ye a living like unto men until I have prepared a place for you." (v 9)

Closing the revelation the Lord counseled the Saints to "be patient in tribulation until I come, and behold I come quickly, and my reward is with me, and they who have sought me early shall find rest in their souls." (D&C 54:1-10)

The Lord wanted the Saints to live the law of consecration where all they had was what they needed, where they were of one heart and one mind, and there were no poor among them. But some of the richer members were unwilling to consecrate their properties for these purposes, so after arriving in Missouri with Newell Knight as their leader these poor and needy were to find work outside the covenant of members until the law of consecration could be better established.

In Section 56, to gain salvation, the Lord said, the saints must take up their cross and follow Him. He also said:

"Wo unto you rich men, that will not give your substance to the poor, for your riches will canker your souls; and this shall be your lamentation in the day of visitation, and of judgment, and of indignation: The harvest is past, the summer is ended, and my soul is not saved!

"Wo unto you poor men, whose hearts are not broken, whose spirits are not contrite, and whose bellies are not satisfied, and whose hands are not stayed from laying hold upon other men's goods, whose eyes are full of greediness, and who will not labor with their own hands!

"But blessed are the poor who are pure in heart, whose hearts are broken, and whose spirits are contrite, for they shall see the kingdom of God coming in power and great glory unto their deliverance; for the fatness of the earth shall be theirs. For behold, the Lord shall come and his recompense shall be with him, and he shall reward every man, and the poor shall rejoice; And their generations shall inherit the earth from generation to generation, forever and ever..." (D&C 56:1-20)

Some have wondered if the Lord intends us to wait until we are commanded to live the law of consecration. Would this sacrifice of obedience be more meaningful if it were given as a free will offering, as contrasted to a response to a command of God? If we are blessed with abundance should we be seeking ways to help the poor and less fortunate, instead of building ever bigger barns and houses in which to secure our possessions?

The Savior's counsel to the rich man who wanted to know "what lack I yet" is instructive, as we shall see.

A certain rich man wanted the Savior to tell him what he should do to gain eternal life. The Gospels of Matthew, Mark and Luke each report the man's accomplishments, and what he lacked.

In Matthew we read that Jesus answered that the man should keep the commandments, to which he countered, which? Jesus responded do not commit murder, adultery, don't steal, or bear false witness. He should honor his father and mother and love his neighbor as himself.

The rich man said he was keeping all these commandments and asked, "what lack I yet?" Jesus said to him, "**If thou wilt be perfect,** go and sell that thou hast, and give to the poor, and thou shalt have treasure in heaven; and come and follow me." (Matt 19:21).

The rich man, though he had kept many of the commandments, wasn't ready to keep the command to consecrate all his riches to the Lord and so he went away sorrowing. It was in this context that Jesus said

"That a rich man shall hardly enter the kingdom of heaven. And again I say unto you, It is easier for a camel to go through the eye of a needle, than for a rich man to enter the kingdom of God." (Matt 19:17-25)

Mark reports that the rich man said he had kept all the enumerated commandments from his youth. Jesus countered that to inherit eternal life the rich man lacked one thing:

"sell whatsoever thou hast, and give to the poor, and thou shalt have treasures in heaven ... And he [the rich man] was sad ...and went away grieved, for he had great possessions." (Mark 10:21-22)

In explaining his answer Jesus declared:

"Children, how hard is it for them that trust in riches to enter into the kingdom of God. It is easier for a camel to go through the eye of a needle, than for a rich man to enter into the kingdom of God, and they were astonished ... saying among themselves, Who then can be saved? And Jesus looked upon them and saith, With men that trust in riches, it is impossible, but not impossible with men who trust in God and leave all for my sake, for with such all these things are possible."(Mark 10:24-27, JST Mark 27))

To Peter, Jesus said that to those who give their all for the Gospel's sake and for Jesus' sake shall receive an hundred fold in houses, lands and family in this time and eternal life in the world to come. (v 30) Luke reported much the same and added,

"those who give their all for the kingdom of God's sake will receive manifold more in the present time and in the world to come life everlasting." (Luke 18:30)

[Section 55]

William W. Phelps [W.W.] was a printer just arriving in Kirtland, Ohio in June 1831. Joseph Smith inquired of the Lord concerning him. Section Fifty-five was the result. In it W.W. Phelps was challenged to be baptized:

"if ye do it with an eye single to my glory, you shall have a remission of your sins and a reception of the Holy Ghost by the laying on of hands." (v 1)

Joseph Smith subsequently ordained him an elder and called him "to preach repentance and remission of sins by way of baptism in the name of Jesus Christ, the son of the living God." (v 2)

Phelps would later receive the power to confer the Holy Ghost on others. He was also ordained to assist Oliver Cowdery in selecting, writing and printing books "for the schools of this church, that little children also may receive instruction before me," said the Lord.

Brother Phelps was to accompany Joseph Smith and Sidney Rigdon to Missouri, after which he would serve as Oliver Cowdery's companion and co-worker. Phelps would later write many now famous Latter-day Saint hymns. (D&C 56:1-20; HC 1:186-188)

[Section 57 and 58]

Shortly after these dozens of Elders arrived in Jackson County, Missouri, a land on the borders of the Lamanites, or American Indians, the Prophet Joseph Smith sought help from the Lord repeating back to Him language the Lord had used in previous revelations, inquiring:

"When will the wilderness blossom as the rose? When will

Zion be built up in her glory, and where will thy Temple stand, unto which all nations shall come in the last days?" In His answer the Lord said through Section Fifty-seven received July 20, 1831:

"Hearken O ye elders of my church, saith the Lord your God, who have assembled yourselves together, according to my commandments, in this land, which is the land which I have appointed and consecrated for the gathering of the Saints, Wherefore this is the land of promise, and the place for the city of Zion ... Behold, the place which is now called Independence, [Missouri] is the center place; and the spot for the temple is lying westward, upon a lot which is not far from the courthouse." (v 1-3)

As Church agents, Edward Partridge and Sidney Gilbert were to purchase lands and establish businesses for the Saints as soon as they arrived from Ohio. Every tract of land lying westward from the temple site to the line dividing the Indians and the white settlers was to be purchased as an everlasting inheritance for the Saints. Brother Gilbert was to receive moneys from members for these purchases and Bishop Partridge was to

"divide unto the Saints their inheritance even as I have commanded." (v 7)

Brother Gilbert was also to establish a store,

"that he may sell goods without fraud, that he may obtain money to buy lands for the good of the Saints, and that he may obtain whatsoever the disciples may need to plant them in their inheritance." (v 8)

A license was to be obtained by Brother Gilbert, thus providing an income to help care for the Saints arriving from the east, who were to be "planted" in their inheritance. Further instruction was also given to W. W. Phelps who was designated as the Church printer assisted by Oliver Cowdery. Oliver was to edit Church publications and select materials "as it shall be proved by the spirit through him." (v 13)

"And now concerning the gathering, Let the Bishop

[Partridge] and the agent [Brother Gilbert] make preparations for their families which have been commanded to come to this land, as soon as possible, and plant them in their inheritances."(D&C 57:1-15; HC 1:189-190)

About a dozen days later, on the first Sabbath after arrival of the Prophet and his party in Jackson County, Missouri, a religious service was held and two members were received by baptism. The Colesville, New York Saints who came by way of Thompson, Ohio arrived during that week under the leadership of Branch President Newell Knight, along with others. Eager to learn the will of the Lord concerning them, Joseph Smith did receive a revelation in their new place of gathering August 1, 1831; Section Fifty-eight.

In this revelation the Lord foreshadowed the fledgling flock of Saints would go through many trials and have much tribulation in the near future, and assured them of great blessings if they endure it well....

"blessed is he that keepeth my commandments whether in life or in death; and he that is faithful in tribulation, the reward of the same is greatest in the kingdom of heaven." (v 2)

For now the Saints could not see "the glory which shall follow after much tribulation. For after much tribulation come the blessings". (v 3)

The Saints were to remember they would be crowned with much glory in the future, but for the immediate future they were to ready themselves for the tribulation to come, that their hearts may be prepared to bear testimony of the things to come, and also that they

"might be honored in laying the foundation of the Church and in bearing record of the land upon which the Zion of God shall stand."(v 7)

The poor are to eat a feast of fat things so that,

"the earth may know that the mouths of the prophets shall not fail; a supper of the house of the Lord, well prepared, [is also to come] unto which all nations shall be invited. First, the rich and the learned, the wise and the noble; And after that cometh the day of my power; then shall the poor, the lame, and the blind, and the deaf, come in unto the marriage of the lamb and partake of the supper of the Lord, prepared for the great day to come." (v 8-11)

Apparently the Lord was referencing His parable of the marriage of the King's son contained in Matthew Chapter Twenty-two - The servants of the king bid invited guests to come to the wedding and its feast, but "they made light of it and went their ways." (Matt 22:5) Others treated the kings servants spitefully and slew them. When the king heard of it he sent his armies, destroyed the murderers and burned up the city; and said unto his servants,

"The wedding is ready, but they which were bidden were not ready. So those servants went out into the highways and gathered together all as many as they found both bad and good; and the wedding was furnished with guests." (Matt 22:5-14)

Bishop Partridge, an imperfect man named to a great responsibility, was called to repentance and reminded his role as bishop included being "a judge in Israel like it was in ancient days."

Just as, during the days when Israel free from Egyptian bondage was about to enter their land of promise, and appointed servants of God were "to divide the lands of the heritage of God unto his children." (D&C 58:14-17), Bishop Partridge was

"to judge his people by the testimony of the just, and by the assistance of his [two] counselors, according to the laws of the kingdom which are given by the prophets of God." (v 18)

The Saints were counseled to be

"subject to the powers that be," [i.e. the laws of the land] until he reigns whose right it is to reign, and subdues all enemies under his feet." (v 22) Later Joseph Smith would declare in part "We believe ... in honoring, obeying and sustaining the law ." (A of F 12)

On this and other occasions the Lord used the events of the times to teach the Prophet and his associates principles essential to effective government of His covenant people, principles which will qualify them for eternal life.

He consistently invited and continues to invite members to counsel with Him directly. Prayers were and are to be addressed to the Father in the name of Jesus Christ, regardless of the number of members in the covenant. There was and is to be no intermediator to whom they should pray.

Likewise, in giving further counsel to Bishop Edward Partridge, after calling him to repentance, the Lord advised him and others through Section Fifty-eight to bring their families to the land [of Missouri] as "they shall counsel between themselves and me."(v 25)

The Lord used this situation to teach members in the new Church to follow a very important principle in governing their lives, as they learned more about the higher law.

Heretofore he had declared the two great commandments were to love God with all their might, mind and strength and to love their fellow men as themselves. To those who embraced His new and everlasting covenant He should not have to prescribe in detail how they should demonstrate their love for Him and their fellow men to qualify for eternal life.

"For behold, it is not meet that I should command in all things, for he that is compelled in all things, the same is a slothful and not a wise servant, wherefore he receiveth no reward. Verily I say, men should be anxiously engaged in a good cause, and do many things of their own free will, and bring to pass much righteousness; For the power is in them, wherein they are agents unto themselves. And inasmuch as men do good they shall in nowise lose their reward. But he that doeth not anything until he is commanded, and receiveth a commandment with doubtful heart and keepeth it with slothfulness, the same is damned." (v 26-29)

In other words no man or woman can expect to gain eternal life if s/he keeps the commandments slothfully, are not anxiously engaged in good causes, and feel they are compelled to keep God's

194

commands. We should do what is right for the right reasons, doing good because we want to and not because we feel compelled to out of fear of God's punishment if we don't.

While some of the party newly arrived in Jackson County, Missouri were now "planted" there and advised to bring their families, the rest were to return to Kirtland, Ohio, again they were "to preach by the way, and to bear testimony of the truth in all places, and call upon the rich, the high, and the low, and the poor to repent. And let them build up churches ..." (v 47-48)

Martin Harris was called upon to lay his moneys before the church to help purchase lands in Independence, "for the place of the storehouse, and also for the house of printing." (v 37) A Church agent was to be appointed in Ohio to receive moneys to purchase lands in Zion [Missouri]. Section Fifty-eight is closed with a reminder that " "the gospel must be preached to every creature with signs following them that believe." (D&C 58:1-65)

[Section 59]

Section Fifty-nine containing revelation through the Prophet Joseph Smith in Zion, Jackson County, Missouri was received just six days later, August 7, 1831. In it the land of Zion is described, its consecration for the Lord's purposes is given, and the site of the future temple there was dedicated. (HC 1:196-201) Some of the ten commandments were reiterated, and the Saints were commanded "to thank the Lord thy God in all things" and "offer a sacrifice unto the Lord thy God in righteousness, even that of a broken heart and contrite spirit." (v 7-8)

Appropriate behavior on the Sabbath day is set forth in verses ten through fifteen followed by a description of some of the great blessings which come to those who keep the day in righteousness. (v 16-20)

Closing this section the Lord declared:

"And in nothing doth man offend God, or against none is his wrath kindled, save those who confess not his hand in all things, and obey not his commandments ... he who doeth the works of righteousness shall receive his reward, even peace in this world, and eternal life in the world to come." (D&C 59:1-24)

Every man or woman is expected to express thanks and appreciation to God for all their blessings, and that expression of gratitude is usually a part of every public and private prayer uttered by the faithful.

[Sections 60, 61 and 62]

Section Sixty was received the day after Fifty-nine, by Joseph Smith, August 8, 1831 in Jackson County, Missouri. The Lord said some of the party recently arrived from Ohio were to return to Ohio, but others were to be "planted" in Missouri. Those Elders appointed to return to Ohio desired to know how they should proceed and which route to take, and whether they should go by land or by river-boat. (HC 1:201-202)

In His answer, the Lord said He was pleased with some of those who made the trip west, but not with others, who would

"not open their mouths, but they hide the talent which I have given them because of the fear of man... For I, the Lord rule in the heavens above, and among the armies of the earth; and in the day when I shall make up my jewels, all men shall know what it is that bespeaketh the power of God." (v 2-4)

Isaiah, Zechariah and Malachi had previously referred to the jewels or diadem which were to be part the Lord's crown, with perhaps Zechariah's words conveying the clearest message. Speaking of the Lord's servants in the last days Zechariah declared

"And the Lord their God shall save them in that day as the flock of his people; for they shall be as the stones of a crown, lifted up as an ensign upon the land." (Zech 9:16)

Two and a half years later while in the midst of prophesied trial and tribulation, the Lord referred again to it, indicating His Saints were afflicted, persecuted and cast out of the land of their inheritance as a consequence of their transgressions:

"Yet I will own them, and they shall be mine in that day when I shall come to make up my jewels. Therefore, they must needs be chastened and tried, even as Abraham, who was commanded to offer up his only [covenant] son."(D&C 101: 2-4)

As for the journey, they were to make a craft or purchase one and go down stream to St. Louis. From there Joseph Smith, Sidney Rigdon and Oliver Cowdery were to travel up stream to Cincinnati. The rest were to spread out two by two preaching among the congregations of the wicked. The trip would be partially financed from moneys collected by the Bishop. They, who could later reimburse those funds after they got home to Ohio, were to do so, if they were able. The Elders were to make the journey with purpose and not idle away their time or bury the talents God had given them, on the way back to Ohio. If they wished, the Elders could

"wash their feet in secret as a testimony against those who rejected their messages of salvation.." (D&C 60:1-17)

By August 12, 1831 Joseph Smith and ten Elders were on their way to Ohio traveling in canoes down the Missouri River and had reached McIlwaine's Bend the third day. W. W. Phelps, who was in the group saw the destroyer riding in power upon the face of the waters. This revelation, Section Sixty-one was received on the banks of the Missouri River. In it the Lord told the Elders they should not all be together traveling swiftly upon the waters while inhabitants on either side of the river were perishing in unbelief. With reference to the waters, the Lord said they were many dangers on the waters.

"I, the Lord, in the beginning blessed the waters, [Gen 1:20] but in the last days by the mouth of my servant John, I cursed the waters [Rev 8:10] (v 14-15) In like manner,

"I, the Lord, in the beginning cursed the land [Moses 4:23] even so in the last days have I blessed it, (D&C 57:1-5) in its time for the use of my Saints, that they may partake the fatness thereof." (v 17)

The Lord by His decree said,

"the destroyer rideth upon the face of the waters" and the day

197

will come when no flesh shall be safe upon the waters, and in days to come none will be able to go up to the land of Zion upon the waters but he that is upright in heart." (v 15,16, 19).

Isaiah reminds us the Lord is quite capable of building highways for those being gathered, as He did for Moses and the children of Israel. It is also not difficult to see those highways might be above the water, such as air highways or land bridges appearing out of the depths of the sea etc.

For now, it did not matter whether this party were to return to Ohio by land or water keeping in mind water travel can be dangerous. However, Joseph Smith, Sidney Rigdon and Oliver Cowdery were hereafter to travel by canal if they were to travel by water. These three were not to preach among the congregations of the wicked until they arrived at Cincinnati. Others were to declare their messages as instructed along the way.

Closing the revelation the Lord counseled them to

"be watchful and be sober, looking forth for the coming of the Son of Man, for he cometh in an hour when ye think not. Pray always that you enter not into temptation, that you may abide the day of his coming, whether in life or in death." (D&C 61:1-39; HC 1:202-205))

While the Prophet and his party were en route to Kirtland they met several Elders who were on their way to the land of Zion. They met at or near Chariton, Missouri August 13, 1831. Happy to see one another and after joyful greetings a revelation known as Section Sixty-two was received.

As advocate before the Father for us earth dwellers, Jesus Christ knows the weaknesses of men and how to succor those tempted. Elders preaching while on the trip to and from Independence had borne their testimonies and the Lord informed them those testimonies were recorded in heaven for angels to see. Those Elders whom Joseph and his brethren had met enroute were to continue on to Zion, to assemble there and rejoice together and offer sacrament unto the Most High, before returning to Kirtland.

They could come back as a group or two by two as they chose, but they were to declare the Gospel's glad tidings en route. Instead of traveling by boat they were free to ride horses or mules or ride in chariots [wagons]. The Lord assured them the kingdom was theirs, and that He was always with the faithful. The revelation closed. (D&C 62:1-9; HC 1:205-206)

[Section Sixty-three]

By August 27, 1831 Joseph and his brethren had returned to Kirtland, Ohio. There they were met with many questions asked by the Kirtland Saints. Seeking how to answer them, Joseph inquired of the Lord and received Section Sixty-three. Prefacing his record of this revelation the Prophet wrote,

"In these infant days of the Church, there was a great anxiety to obtain the word of the Lord upon every subject that in any way concerned our salvation; and as the land of Zion was now the most important temporal object in view, I inquired of the Lord for further information upon the gathering of the Saints, and the purchase of the land and other matters." (D&C 63 Heading) In Section Sixty-three the Lord said a day of wrath is to come upon the wicked.

"And he that seeketh signs shall see signs, but not unto salvation ... But, behold, faith cometh not by signs, but signs follow those that believe. Ye, signs come by faith, and not by the will of men, nor as they please, but by the will of God. Yea, signs come by faith, unto mighty works ... he that endureth in faith and doeth my will, the same shall overcome, and shall receive an inheritance upon the earth when the day of transfiguration shall come; When the earth shall be transfigured according to the pattern which was shown unto mine apostles upon the mount of which account the fulness ye have not yet received... But unto him that keepeth my commandments, I will give the mysteries of my kingdom, and the same shall be in him a well of living water, springing up unto everlasting life." (v 7-20)

Though headquartered in Kirtland, Ohio at present, the Saints were to begin to assemble in Independence, Missouri, gathering not in haste, but they were to purchase land there, that they may have claim upon the world. However, the Lord warned that others would seek land by force, and if they did they were under the influence of Satan, because the Saints were forbidden to shed blood.

Foreshadowing the future, the Lord informed the Saints that Satan stirs up the hearts of others to anger against them, and may well seek their newly acquired lands by force and the shedding of blood. The Saints were not to reciprocate in the shedding of blood, and if they did, they would be scourged from city to city, and few shall stand to receive an inheritance. The Lord said He was angry with the wicked and was withholding His Spirit from the inhabitants of the earth. Instead of the righteous slaying the wicked, He decreed that wars between the wicked would result in the wicked slaying the wicked as the day of His coming draws nearer.

..."fear shall come upon every man; And the Saints also shall hardly escape; nevertheless, I, the Lord, am with them, and will come down in heaven from the presence of my Father, and consume the wicked with unquenchable fire. And behold, this is not yet, but by and by." (v 24-35)

For now, the Saints were to assemble upon the land of Zion, taking righteousness in their hands and faithfulness in their loins, lifting up a warning voice to the inhabitants of the earth, delivering by word and by flight that desolation shall come upon the wicked. Some were to sell their Ohio and other properties and use the money acquired to settle their fellow Saints in Missouri.

Joseph Smith was to discern by the Spirit those who were to depart next spring and those disciples who were to tarry. Agents for both places were appointed and those sending treasures or moving to the land of Zion in Missouri were promised an inheritance in this world and in the world to come. Recognizing some may die in the process of moving to and settling in the land of Zion the Lord said,

"He that is faithful, and endureth shall overcome the world ... Yea, and blessed are the dead that die in the Lord, from henceforth, when the Lord shall come, and old things pass away, and all things become new, they shall rise from the dead, and shall not die after, and shall receive an inheritance before the Lord in the holy city." (v 35-49)

In other words, those who build up Zion with their treasures, but die before obtaining their own inheritance there, are promised an inheritance in the holy city of Zion, the New Jerusalem, after his/her resurrection.

Those living when the Lord comes a second time and have kept the faith are blessed, but will still die at the age of man.

"Wherefore, children shall grow up until they become old; old men shall die, but they shall not sleep in the dust, but they shall be changed in the twinkling of an eye wherefore, for this cause preached the apostles unto the world the resurrection of the dead. These things are the things that ye must look for ... they are now nigh at hand... [but] until that hour there will be foolish virgins among the wise; and at that hour cometh an entire separation of the righteous from the wicked; and in that day will I send my angels to pluck out the wicked and cast them into unquenchable fire." (v 53-54)

To summarize, those who are faithful are assured of blessings at the second coming, in the resurrection and during the Millennium.

Just prior to the Lord's coming is a day of warning, and a day in which the Lord is not to be mocked.

... "I am overall, and in all, and through all, and search all things, and the day cometh that all things shall be subject unto me. Behold, I am Alpha and Omega, even Jesus Christ. Wherefore, let all men beware how they take my name in their lips ... many there be who are under condemnation, who use the name of the Lord, and use it in vain, having not authority ... Remember that that which cometh from above is sacred, and must be spoken with care, and by constraint of the Spirit ... and ye receive the Spirit through prayer, wherefore, without this there remaineth condemnation." (v 57-66, D&C 63:1-66)

[Section 64]

In late August, 1831 Joseph Smith and Sidney Rigdon were counseled to seek a home for the Prophet through prayer. By September 11th that home apparently had been found in Hiram, Ohio, nearby Kirtland. The Prophet was preparing to move there and resume his work on the translation of the Bible which he had suspended while he traveled with a party of Elders to Missouri and returned. Those newly called to move to Zion in Missouri were preparing to leave in October. While busily engaged in these activities the revelation in Section Sixty-four was received.

Forgiving and Judging

The newness of the Church, the expansion of the Saints' knowledge, the persecution they encountered, and the challenges endemic to a move for some and for others to tarry in the Kirtland area, were no doubt exciting, stressful and frustrating. Tempers flaired, disagreements over doctrines and over the sacrifices different ones were called to bear, differences in approach and questions concerning Joseph's leadership and instruction resulted in hurt feelings, anger and a desire for revenge or retribution surfaced among some of the Saints.

Leading off this section the Lord told the Elders of the Church that even though they had sinned,

"for this once, for mine own glory, and for the salvation of souls, I have forgiven you your sins." (v 3) Included in the sinners was Joseph Smith, the Lord said, but He also declared,

"I, the Lord, forgive sins unto those who confess their sins before me and ask forgiveness, who have not sinned unto death. My disciples in the days of old, sought occasion against one another and forgave not one another in their hearts; and for this evil they were afflicted and sorely chastened.

"Wherefore, I say unto you, that ye ought to forgive one another; for he that forgiveth not his brother his trespasses standeth condemned before the Lord: for there remaineth in him the greater sin. I, the Lord, will forgive whom I will forgive, but of you it is required to forgive all men." ((v 1-10)

The unrepentant are to be tried in Church courts, but each Saint individually is to forgive the trespasses of others.

"let God be judge between me and thee and reward thee according to thy deeds." (v 11) It seems the Lord is saying we are to do the forgiving and He will do the judging. (v 12-22)

The Tithed Shall Not Be Burned At His Coming

From a time perspective the Lord calls the period now until the coming of the Son of Man **today.**

"Verily it is a day of sacrifice and a day for the tithing of my people; for he that is tithed shall not be burned at his coming. For after today cometh the burning-... for... tomorrow all the proud and they who do wickedly shall be as stubble; and I will burn them up, for I am the Lord of Hosts; and I will not spare any that remaineth in Babylon. Wherefore if ye believe me, ye will labor while it is called today." (v 23-25)

Tomorrow, apparently, will be when the Savior comes, establishes His government and allows the wicked to be burned.

But tithing was restored in this last dispensation called today, and the money collected was and is to be used to finance Church operations, programs and services and for the construction of Church buildings and facilities. Early Church leaders were not to take on debt to finance the Church, but were to pay the costs with tithes and consecrated offerings. Responsible officers were called agents on the Lord's errand,

"... and whatever ye do according to the will of the Lord is the Lord's business. And he hath set you to provide for his Saints in these last days, that they may obtain an inheritance in the land of Zion." (v 29-30)

Two years later in Section Ninety-seven the Lord said,

"let it [His house] be built quickly, and by the tithing of my people. Behold, this is the tithing and sacrifice which I, the Lord, require at their hands, that there may be a house built unto me for the salvation of Zion." (D&C 97:11-12) A more complete revelation on tithing was received in 1838 and will be later discussed.

Fresh from their trip to the land of where Zion's headquarters was to be built, the Saints were now receiving instruction concerning the acquisition of property with tithes and consecrated offerings, when Section Sixty-four was given. With reference to other matters the Lord added:

"Wherefore, be not weary in well doing, for ye are laying the foundation of a great work. And out of small things preceedeth that which is great. Behold, the Lord requireth the heart, and a willing mind; and the willing and obedient shall eat the good of the land of Zion these last days ... Behold, I, the Lord, have made my church in the last days like unto a judge sitting on a hill, or in a high place, to judge the nations. For it shall come to pass, that the inhabitants of Zion shall judge all things pertaining to Zion ... For, behold, I say unto you that Zion shall flourish, and the glory of the Lord shall be upon her, and she shall be an ensign unto the people, and there shall come unto her out of every nation under heaven. And the day shall come when the nations of the earth shall tremble because of her..." (v 33-43, D&C 64:1-43)

[Section 65]

From Section Sixty-five given through Joseph Smith at Hiram, Ohio in October 1831, we learn that after the keys of the kingdom of God were committed to men on earth,

"shall the gospel roll forth unto the ends of the earth as the stone which is cut out of the mountain without hands shall roll forth until it has filled the whole earth." (v 2)

The earth is being prepared for the Lord, for the Supper of the Lamb and made ready for the Bridegroom. The earth's inhabitants, having been warned, having lamps and oil, as wise virgins who have taken the Holy Ghost as their guide, are being readied to meet Him.

As the gospel covers the earth as with a flood, the Millennial kingdom of heaven, led by Christ, the Son of Man,

"shall come down in heaven clothed in the brightness of his glory, to meet the kingdom of God which is set up on the earth," under the leadership of the Lord's apostles and prophets and the presiding high priest at that time. (D&C 65:1-6; HC 1:218)

[Section 66]

On the first day of an important conference in Orange, Ohio October 25, 1831 Joseph Smith made inquiry of the Lord at William E. Mclellin's request and received Section Sixty-six containing in part these revelations:

"blessed are you for receiving mine everlasting covenant, even the fulness of my gospel sent forth unto the children of men, that they might have life and be partakers of the glories which are to be revealed in the last days, as it was written by the prophets and apostles of old." (v 2) Brother Mclellin and other Elders were, to

"proclaim my gospel from land to land, and from city to city ... Go unto the eastern lands, bear testimony in every place unto every people ... Let my servant Samuel H. Smith go with you ... Lay your hands upon the sick, and they shall recover ...Be patient in affliction ... Seek not to be cumbered, Forsake all unrighteousness. Commit not adultery - a temptation with which you have been troubled. Keep these sayings ... magnify thine office... continue in these things even until the end and you shall have a crown of eternal life at the right hand of the Father, who is full of grace and truth." (D&C 66:1-13; HC 1:219-221)

Publication of revelations to date

As October, 1831 came to a close some sixty-five revelations had been received and written down since the heavens first opened in this dispensation, but they were not yet in book form. A special conference of the Elders of the Church was convened at Hiram, Ohio November, 1831. The agenda for that conference was the compilation and publication of these revelations in book form. Those assembled, concurred and the matter was referred to those who were to oversee the effort. The Lord chose to use this occasion to introduce the compilation with the words contained in Section One, now constituting the Lord's Preface to the Doctrines and Covenants.(HC 1: 221-224) Chapter XIII begins with Section One.

CHAPTER XIII

THE LORD'S PREFACE, PUBLICATION OF THE FIRST SET OF REVELATIONS AND THE RECEIPT OF MORE PERTAINING TO SALVATION AND EXALTATION OF THE LIVING AND THE DEAD
(November 1, 1831 through December 26, 1835)

[Section 1]
Nineteen months after the Church was organized and eleven years after the magnificent vision of the Father and the Son to Joseph Smith in the now sacred grove of trees in upper New York state; the Lord chose to introduce what is now an open ended book of scripture covering the revelations He had given to date. While all quotations are direct, some have been underlined and given a number for emphasis.

"Section One constitutes the Lord's preface to the doctrines, covenants and commandments given in this dispensation.(D&C 1 Heading)

People entering the covenant are to hearken unto His voice and listen together, for

"the voice of the Lord is unto all men, and there is none to escape; and there is no eye that shall not see, neither ear that shall not hear, neither heart that shall not be penetrated ... the voice of warning shall be unto all people, by the mouths of my disciples, whom I have chosen in these last days ... Behold this is mine authority, and the authority of my servants, and my preface unto the book of my commandments, which I have given them to publish unto you, O inhabitants of the earth ... And verily I say unto you that [1] they who go forth, bearing these tidings unto the inhabitants of the earth, [2] to them is power given to seal both on earth and in heaven... Unto the day when the Lord shall come to recompense unto every man according to his work, and measure to every man according to his measure which he has measured to his fellow man.

"Wherefore, the voice of the Lord is unto the ends of the earth; that all that will hear may hear: Prepare ye, prepare ye, for that which is to come, for the Lord is nigh... and the day cometh that they who will not hear the voice of the Lord, neither the voice of his servants, neither give heed to the words of the prophets and apostles, shall be cut off from among the people... Wherefore I the Lord, knowing the calamity which should come upon the inhabitants of the earth, called upon my servant Joseph Smith, Jun., and spake unto him from heaven and gave him commandments ... and to ... others that they should proclaim these things unto the world; and all this that it might be fulfilled, which was written by the prophets." (v 1-18) The Lord said that these commandments are proclaimed to the world so that:

[3]"every man might speak in the name of God, the Lord, even the Savior of the world; [4] That faith might increase in the earth; [5] That mine everlasting covenant might be established; [6] That the fulness of my gospel might be proclaimed by the weak and simple unto the ends of the world, and before kings and rulers. Behold I am God and have spoken it." (v 19-24)

We see that God's plan is for each person to receive revelation for him or herself, and each should develop a personal relationship with the Savior, and seek to become more like Him. As we become like Him we, along with other faithful, will return to the presence of God and receive our eternal inheritance.

Speaking of the Prophet Joseph Smith and other Church leaders, the Lord said He had given these commandments to them in their weakness, that as they were humble they might be made strong and be blessed from on high, and that after receiving the record of the Nephites, contained in the Book of Mormon, Joseph might have the prerogative to translate it by the power of God. The Lord also said that these commandments were given to early Church leaders that they:

[7]"might have power to lay the foundation of this church, and to bring it forth out of obscurity, and out of darkness, the only true and living church upon the face of the whole earth, with which I, the Lord, am well pleased, speaking unto the church collectively and not individually.

[8]"... Search these commandments, for they are true and faithful, and the prophecies and promises which are in them shall be fulfilled." (D&C 1:1-39; HC 1:221-224)

[Section 67]

During the special conference convened to consider and act upon the revelations to date, to which was added the Lord's preface, many of the brethren bore testimony that these revelations were verily true. But there were a few who were embarrassed by the language used in some of the revelations, claiming there were imperfections in them, implying they could have done better.

Section 67 was received in response. In it, the Lord challenged the wisest of the critics to duplicate the least of these revelations. If they could not, they were under condemnation for not bearing record that those received through Joseph Smith were true. The Lord also gave a promise to those ordained to this ministry, declaring if each were to:

[9] "strip yourselves from jealousies and fears and humble yourselves before me ... [10] the veil shall be rent and you shall see me and know that I am-- not with the carnal, neither the natural mind, but with the spiritual. For no man has seen God at any time in the flesh, except quickened by the Spirit of God. Neither can any natural man abide the presence of God, neither after the carnal mind. Ye are not able to abide the presence of God now, neither the ministering of angels; [11] wherefore continue in patience until ye are perfected." (D&C 67:1-14)

THE THREE FOLD MISSION OF A ZION SOCIETY AND REVELATIONS PERTAINING THERETO

Undergirding all latter-day revelation is the purpose of the Church, which is to establish a Zion Society on earth, through implementation of that society's three fold mission: to preach the gospel to every, nation, kindred, tongue and people, to perfect the Saints [those entering the covenant], and to redeem the dead. Missionary work, perfecting the Saints and redeeming the dead, are all to be accomplished in an organized way, the Lord's way.

To assist the reader in better understanding the revelations of God in the Doctrine and Covenants, pertaining primarily to missionary work, i.e. the gathering and redemption of Israel, the true believers in Messiah/Christ, and the doctrine necessary for the perfecting of the Saints and the redemption of the dead; various Doctrine and Covenant sections are reported in different chapters of this book. Missionary work and perfecting the Saints are reported in chapters XIII and XIV. Those revelations pertaining primarily to the redemption of the dead are also reported in chapter XX. Those revelations primarily pertaining to the laying the foundation of the Church, the establishment of a Zion Society, the Second Coming of Messiah/Christ, the Millennium and the Final Judgment are referenced to and reported in upcoming chapters XV, XVI, XVII, XVIII, XIX, and XXI.

[Section 68]

Also received in November, 1831 was revelation through Joseph Smith at Hiram, Ohio, at the request of Orson Hyde, Luke S. Johnson, Lyman E. Johnson and William E. McLellin. All four of these brethren would later be called to serve in the quorum of twelve apostles in 1835 when it was first organized in this dispensation.

In it the Lord declared that those acting in the office and calling to which they have been appointed by the President of the Church, such as missionaries, should;

[12] "speak as they are moved upon by the Holy Ghost. [13] And whatsoever they shall speak when moved upon by the Holy Ghost shall be scripture, shall be the will of the Lord, shall be the

mind of the Lord, shall be the word of the Lord, shall be the voice of the Lord, and the power of God unto salvation.

[14] "ye shall bear record of me, even Jesus Christ, that I am the Son of the living God, that I was, that I am, and that I am to come... [15] Go ye into all the world, preach the gospel to every creature,[16] acting in the authority which I have given you, [17] baptizing in the name of the Father, and of the Son, and of the Holy Ghost." (v 3-12)

Within the next four years a Quorum of Twelve Apostles would be established, the Lord having chosen them. Under this charge they and those appointed by the President of the Church were to bear record of Him, to preach the gospel to every creature, and to act under the authority given, baptizing in the name of the Father, Son and Holy Ghost.

The Lord foretold the calling of other bishops as the Church grew and continues to grow as the need arises, indicating they are to be

"appointed by the First Presidency of the Melchizedek Priesthood, except they be literal descendants of Aaron. No man has a legal right to this office, to hold the keys of this Priesthood, except he be a literal descendant and the firstborn of Aaron.

[18] "But as a high priest of the Melchizedek Priesthood has authority to officiate in all the lesser offices he may officiate in the office of bishop when no literal descendant of Aaron can be found, provided he is called and set apart and ordained unto this power, under the hands of the First Presidency of the Melchizedek Priesthood." (v 13-20)

Other issues addressed by this revelation include the trial of bishops and other high priests accused of crime, and [19] the responsibility parents have in Zion for teaching their children the doctrines of repentance, faith in Christ, and of baptism and the gift of the Holy Ghost by the time their children are eight years old. Failure to teach them thusly results in the sin being on the heads of the parents.

The Lord noted [20] the inhabitants of Zion are to observe the Sabbath day to keep it holy and [21] to remember to labor in all faithfulness; that some children in Zion were growing up in wickedness; that there were idlers among them,

"that they seek not earnestly for the riches of eternity, for their eyes are full of greediness. These things ought not to be, and must be done away from among them..." (D&C 68:1-35; HC 1:227-229)

[Section 69]

November, 1831 was a very eventful month. Some sixty-five revelations received to date intended for publication had been passed upon at a special conference, November 1st. Section 133 was first added as an appendix on November 3, 1831 and given a number ten years later in 1843. Sections 67, 68, 69 and 70 were also received in November 1831.

A printing shop had been set up the previous summer at Independence, Missouri. W. W. Phelps, a printer by trade, had been called to labor there assisting Oliver Cowdery in the printing of books and articles for the Church. By action of the conference, Oliver Cowdery was appointed to convey the manuscript of the compiled revelations to Independence for printing, taking with him moneys that had been contributed for the build up of the Church there. In this revelation a traveling companion for Oliver, John Whitmer, a Book of Mormon witness, is identified as that person.

John had previously been appointed as a writer and historian for the church, and was to continue in those duties. He was to take with them an account of the stewardships of the Lord's servants to the future and more permanent headquarters of the Church in Missouri which,

"shall be a seat and a place to receive and do all these things. Nevertheless, let my servant John travel many times from place to place, and from church to church, that he may the more easily obtain knowledge--

[22] "Preaching and expounding, writing, copying, and obtaining all things which shall be for the good of the church, and for the rising generations that shall grow up on the land of Zion, to possess it from generation to generation, forever and ever..." (D&C 69:1-8; HC1:234-235)

[Section 70]

According to Joseph Smith's history, written by the Prophet, four special conferences were held the first twelve days of November 1831. In the last of these conferences the Book of Commandments or Doctrine and Covenants was considered. The prophet referred to this book as being:

[23] "the foundation of the Church in the last days, and a benefit to the world, showing the keys of the mysteries of the kingdom of our Savior are again entrusted to man." (HC 1:235-237)

In this revelation speaking to the inhabitants of Zion and the members of the Church, the Lord appointed Joseph Smith, Martin Harris, Oliver Cowdery, John Whitmer, Sidney Rigdon and William W. Phelps as stewards to publish the compilation of revelations received to date. The Lord also declared

[24] "an account of this stewardship will I require of them in the day of judgment...this is their business in the church of God, to manage them, and the concerns thereof, yea, the benefits thereof." (v 1-6)

The money collected to publish these commandments and other money received from the sale thereof, was to be used by these stewards to pay the expenses of publication and to pay for their own expenses.[25]Any excess of funds was to be given to the Lord's storehouse,

[26] "the benefits shall be consecrated to the inhabitants of Zion and unto their generations, inasmuch as they become heirs according to the laws of the kingdom."(v 7-8)

[27] Thus outlines of the law of consecration, essential to the

213

exaltation of every man and woman entering the covenant were introduced including [28] "a sufficient for the need" principle, with any excess to be given to the Lord's storehouse for the benefit of current and future generations of the inhabitants of Zion, according to the laws of the kingdom. No one in Zion is exempt from this law of stewardship and accountability, which is very much a part of the law of consecration, meaning the "sufficient for the need" principle applies to all, including those who are appointed to administer spiritual things, as well as those appointed to administer temporal things in Zion.The Lord further made clear all members in Zion are to be equal in temporal things, otherwise the abundance of the manifestations of the spirit shall be withheld.

"Behold, this is what the Lord requires of every man in his stewardship, even as I, the Lord, have appointed or shall hereafter appoint unto every man. And behold, none are exempt from this law who belong to the church of the living God. Yea, neither the bishop, neither the agent, who keepeth the Lord's storehouse, neither who is appointed in a stewardship over temporal things.

"He who is appointed to administer spiritual things, the same is worthy of his hire, even as those who are appointed to a stewardship to administer temporal things; Yea, even more abundantly, which abundance is multiplied unto them through the manifestations of the Spirit. Nevertheless, in your temporal things you shall be equal, and this not grudgingly, otherwise the abundance of the manifestations of the Spirit shall be withheld.

"Now, this commandment I give unto my servants for their benefit while they remain, for a manifestation of my blessings upon their heads, and for a reward of their diligence and for their security; For food and for raiment, for an inheritance; for houses and for lands, in whatsoever circumstances I, the Lord, shall place them, whithersoever I, the Lord, shall send them. For they have been faithful over many things, and have done well inasmuch as they have not sinned. Behold, I, the Lord, am merciful and will bless them, and they shall enter into the joy of these things." (D&C 70:1-18) For more on the law of consecration, see Chapter XIX, A Zion Society Is To Be The New World Order.

[Section 71]

Unfriendly feelings had developed against the Church as a result of newspaper articles related to Ezra Booth's apostasy. This necessitated a change in the work schedules of Joseph Smith and Sidney Rigdon. The Prophet was continuing his translation of the Bible and Sidney was serving as scribe when Section 71 was received December 1, 1831 at Hiram, Ohio. ((HC 1:238-239)

The instruction given in this revelation caused them to temporarily lay aside their translating work. Addressing them the Lord declared:

"you should [28] open your mouths in proclaiming my gospel, the things of the kingdom, expounding the mysteries thereof out of the scriptures, according to that portion of the Spirit and power which shall be given you... Verily I say unto you, proclaim unto the world in the regions round about, and in the church also, for the space of a season, even until it shall be made known unto you... labor in my vineyard. Call upon the inhabitants of the earth, and bear record, and prepare the way for the commandments and revelations which are to come.

"Now. behold, this is wisdom; whoso readeth, let him understand and receive also; For unto him that receiveth it shall be given more abundantly, even power." (v 1-6)

They were to confront their enemies meeting them in public and in private, challenging them to "bring forth their strong reason against the Lord. [29] Verily... there is no weapon that is formed against you [that] shall prosper.And if any man lift up his voice against you he shall be confounded in mine own due time..."(D&C 71:1-11)

[Section 72]

Newell K. Whitney was called as a bishop in Section 72,

received through Joseph Smith December 4, 1831 at Kirtland, Ohio. He and other future bishops were given additional information as to a bishop's duties. (HC 1:239-241)

The thrust of this revelation relates to the keeping of a storehouse, caring for the poor and needy, and accounting for stewardships; hallmarks of a Zion Society and the law of consecration which are reported in Chapter XVIII.

"... it is required of the Lord, at the hand of every steward, to render an account of his stewardship both in time and in eternity. For he who is faithful and wise in time is accounted worthy to inherit the mansions prepared for him of my Father.

"... the elders of the church ... shall render an account of their stewardship unto the bishop, who shall be appointed of me in this part of my vineyard. These things shall be had on record, to be handed over unto the bishop in Zion.

[30] "... the duty of the bishop who has been ordained unto the church in this part of the vineyard, which is verily this--

"To keep the Lord's storehouse; to receive the funds of the church in this part of the vineyard; To take an account of the elders; as before has been commanded; and to administer to their wants, who shall pay for that which they receive, inasmuch as they have wherewith to pay; That this also may be consecrated to the good of the church, to the poor and the needy."(D&C 72:3-12)

[Section 73]

For about five weeks the prophet Joseph Smith, and his companion Sidney Rigdon, had been preaching the Gospel as assigned, and as a result, diminished the unfavorable feelings that had arisen concerning Ezra Booth's departure from the Church.

This revelation, Section 73, given to Joseph Smith and Sidney Rigdon at Hiram, Ohio, January 10, 1832 called for the Elders to continue to preach, but for Joseph Smith and Sidney Rigdon,

"... saith the Lord, it is expedient to translate again; And inasmuch as it is practicable, to preach in the regions round about until conference; and after that it is expedient to continue the work of translation [of the Bible] until it is finished." (D&C 73: 1-6; HC 1:241-242)

[Section 74]

After returning to the work of translation in January 1832 a revelation was received at Hiram, Ohio. Laboring diligently until just before a scheduled conference on January 25th, Joseph Smith received a revelation in explanation of I Corinthians 7:14, which sets forth Paul's counsel to the church of his day. They were not to keep the law of Moses, especially as it related to circumcision, and that little children are sanctified through the atonement of Jesus Christ. (HC 1:242)

"For the unbelieving husband is sanctified by the wife, and unbelieving wife is sanctified by the husband; else were your children unclean, but now they are holy. Now in the days of the apostles, [Peter, James John, etc] the law of circumcision was had among all of the Jews who believed not the gospel of Jesus Christ.

"And it came to pass that there arose a great contention among the people concerning the law of circumcision, for the unbelieving husband was desirous that his children should be circumcised, and become subject to the law of Moses, which law was fulfilled. And it came to pass that the children being brought up in subjection to the law of Moses, gave heed to the traditions of their fathers and believed not the gospel of Jesus Christ, wherein they became unholy.

"Wherefore for this cause the apostle wrote unto the church, giving unto them a commandment, not of the Lord, but of himself, that a believer should not be united to an unbeliever; except the law of Moses should be done away among them. That their children might remain without circumcision, and that the tradition might be done away, which saith that little children are unholy; for it was had among the Jews; [31] <u>But little children are holy, being sanctified through the atonement of Jesus Christ; and this is what the scriptures mean.</u>"(D&C 74:1-7)

217

[Section 75]

At a scheduled conference of the Church at Amherst, Ohio, January 25, 1832, Joseph Smith was sustained and ordained President of the High Priesthood. It was learned at that conference some elders were having difficulty in communicating the restored gospel's message and were uncertain where to go to do it. Seeking assistance the Prophet inquired of the Lord and received the response contained in Section 75, including the calling of many pairs of elders and giving them specific areas to proscylite.

All were assured that elders who lift up their voices

"... as with the sound of a trump, proclaiming the truth according to the revelations and commandments which I have given you... if ye are faithful ye shall be laden with many sheaves, and crowned with honor, and glory, and immortality and eternal life. [William E. McLellin and Luke Johnson were to] proclaim the things which I have commanded them-- Calling on the name of the Lord for the Comforter, which shall teach them all things that are expedient for them...

"... let my servant Orson Hyde and my servant Samuel H. Smith take their journey into the eastern countries... Lyman Johnson and ... Orson Pratt ... take their journey into the eastern countries ...Asa Dodds and ...Calves Wilson ... shall take their journey unto the western countries, ... Major N. Ashley, and my servant Burr Riggs, let them take their journey also unto the south country, ...going from house to house, and from village to village, and from city to city.... leave your blessing upon that house." (v 1-22)

In the context of the law of consecration and an operational united order the Lord answered those elders who had given their names that they might know His will concerning them:

"... it is the duty of the church to assist in supporting the families of those, and also to support the families of those who are called and must needs be sent into the world to proclaim the gospel unto the world." (v 23-24)

Elders called to serve as missionaries were to secure places for their families to be domiciled while they were away, preferably in the care of existing Church members. Everyone was to help out and not be idle. Additional missionaries were sent forth, including Simeon Carter and Emer Harris; Ezra Thayre and Thomas Marsh; Hyrum Smith and Reynolds Cahoon; Daniel Stanton and Seymour Brunson; Sylvester Smith and Gideon Carter; Ruggles Eames and Stephen Burnett and Micah B. Welton and Eden Smith." ((D&C 75:1-36; HC 1:242-245)

[Section 76]

Returning home to Hiram, Ohio the prophet Joseph Smith wrote that this revelation was given February 16, 1832 after he had translated John 5:29.

"Upon my return from [the] Amherst conference I resumed the translation of the Scriptures. From sundry revelations which had been received, it was apparent that many important points touching the salvation of man had been taken from the Bible, or lost before it was compiled. It appeared self-evident from what truths were left, that if God rewarded every one according to the deeds done in the body, the term 'Heaven', as intended for the Saints' eternal home, must include more kingdoms than one. Accordingly, while translating St. John's Gospel, myself and Elder Rigdon saw the following vision."(HC 1:245-252)

In it the Lord said the mysteries of the kingdom will be revealed to all the faithful; that all shall come forth in the resurrection of the just and the unjust; that the inhabitants of many worlds are begotten sons and daughters unto God through the atonement of Jesus Christ; that an angel fell and became the devil; that the sons of perdition suffer eternal damnation; that all others gain some degree of salvation; that some receive the glory and reward of exalted beings in the celestial kingdom; that others receive the reward of a terrestrial or a telestial kingdom. The status of those in the telestial, terrestrial and celestial kingdoms is discussed and the faithful are assured they also may see the vision of the degrees of glory. More Specifically:

"... For while we were doing the translation, which the Lord had appointed unto us, we came to the twenty-ninth verse of the fifth chapter of John, which was given as follows-- Speaking of the resurrection of the dead, concerning those who shall hear the voice of the Son of Man: And shall come forth; they who have done good, in the resurrection of the just; and they who have done evil, in the resurrection of the unjust.

"Now this caused us to marvel, for it was given unto us of the Spirit. And while we meditated upon these things, the Lord touched the eyes of our understandings and they were opened, and the glory of the Lord shone round about.

"And we beheld the glory of the Son on the right hand of the Father, and received of his fulness; And saw holy angels, and them who are sanctified before his throne, worshiping God, and the Lamb, who worship him forever and ever. And now after the many testimonies which have been given of him, this is the testimony last of all, which we give of him: That he lives!

[32] "For we saw him, even on the right hand of God, and we heard the voice bearing record that he is the Only Begotten of the Father-- That by him, and through him and of him, the worlds are and were created, and the inhabitants thereof are begotten sons and daughters unto God." (D&C 76:1-24) For a discussion of the remaining verses 25 through 119 see Chapter XXI, THE SECOND COMING, CHRIST'S MILLENNIAL REIGN, AND THE FINAL JUDGMENT.

[Section 77]

Revelation given to Joseph Smith was received as he continued to translate the Book of Revelation of St. John in March 1832. In it John's revelation is embellished and we learn that beasts have spirits as well as men, that they shall dwell in eternal gladness on an immortal earth, that the earth has a temporal existence of 7,000 years, that various angels minister on earth, the lineage of the 144,000 high priests is through the tribes of Israel, that Christ will come in the beginning of the seventh thousand years, and that two prophets will be slain in Jerusalem.

These things are explained in greater detail in upcoming Chapter XIX on a Zion Society and in Chapter XXI, the ushering in of the Millennium. (D&C 77:1-15; HC 1:2 53-255)

[Section 78]

Revelation was received in March 1832 through Joseph Smith at Hiram, Ohio in which the order was given for the purpose of establishing a storehouse for the poor. The Lord said a wise use of their properties would lead to salvation, that the church should be independent of earthly powers, that Michael [Adam} serves under the direction of the Holy One, Jesus Christ, and that the faithful will be blessed and inherit all things.

The first sixteen verses of this section dealing with the law of consecration, establishing a storehouse for the poor, and the church becoming independent of earthly powers, are reported in Chapter XIX A Zion Society To Be The New World Order.

Section 78 closes with the Lord declaring these early latter-day church members were yet little children who,

"have not as yet understood how great blessings the Father hath in his own hands and prepared for you. And ye cannot bear all things now, nevertheless, be of good cheer, for I will lead you along. The kingdom is yours, and the riches of eternity are yours.

"And he who receiveth all things with thankfulness shall be made glorious; and the things of this earth shall be added unto him, even an hundred fold, yea, more. Wherefore, do the things I have commanded, you, saith your Redeemer, even the Son, Ahman who prepareth all things before he taketh you;

[33] "For ye are the church of the firstborn, and he will take

221

you up in a cloud, and appoint every man his portion. And he that is a faithful and wise steward shall inherit all things." (D&C 78: 1-22; HC 1:255-257))

[Section 79]

Revelation was given through Joseph Smith at Hiram, Ohio in March 1832 calling Jared Carter to preach the gospel. Jared was to serve in the eastern part of the United States in the power of his ordination,

"proclaiming glad tidings of great joy, even the everlasting gospel. And I will send upon him the Comforter, which shall teach him the truth and the way whither he shall go; And inasmuch as he is faithful I will crown him again with sheaves... let your heart be glad, my servant Jared Carter, and fear not, saith your Lord..." (D&C 79: 1-4; HC 1:257)

[Section 80]

Revelation was given through Joseph Smith in March 1832 at Hiram, Ohio, calling Stephen Burnett and Eden Smith to preach in whatever place they chose.

"... go ye and preach my gospel whether to the north, or to the south, to the east or to the west, it mattereth not, for ye cannot go amiss. Therefore, declare the things which ye have heard, and verily believe, and know to be true. Behold, this is the will of him who hath called you, your Redeemer, even Jesus Christ. Amen." (D&C 80: 1-5; HC 1: 257)

[Section 81]

Historical records show that a revelation at Hiram, Ohio in March 1832 contained a call for Frederick G. Williams to be a high priest and a counselor to Joseph Smith in the Presidency. This revelation is regarded as a step in the formal organization of the First Presidency of the Church.

"... you are called, even to be a high priest in my church, and a counselor unto [34] my servant Joseph Smith, Jun.; Unto whom I have given the keys of the kingdom, which belong always unto the

<u>Presidency of the High Priesthood</u>... be faithful, stand in the office which I have appointed you; succor the weak, lift up the hands which hang down, and strengthen the feeble knees. And if thou art faithful unto the end thou shalt have a crown of immortality, and eternal life in the mansions which I have prepared in the house of my Father..." (D&C 81 1:1-7; HC 1:267-269)

[Section 82]

Joseph Smith had been ordained as President of the High Priesthood at a conference of high priests, elders and members January 25, 1832. He was again sustained in this calling at a general church council on April 26, 1832 at which time he also received revelation in Section 82.

In it the Lord said that where much is given, much is required; that darkness reigns in the world; that the Lord is bound when we do what he says; that Zion must increase in beauty and holiness; and that every man should seek the interest of his neighbor; all important characteristics of a Zion Society which are discussed in Chapter XIX ahead. (D&C 82:1-24; HC 1:267-269)

[Section 83]

Revelation was received through Joseph Smith at Independence, Missouri April 30, 1832 declaring women and children have claim upon their husbands and fathers for their support. Widows and orphans have claim upon the Church for their support. For greater detail see Chapter XIX, A Zion Society To Be the New World Order. (D&C 83:1-6; HC 1:269-270)

[Section 84]

Missionary elders had begun to return and report their labors in the eastern states. While they were together is this season of joy, revelation was received through Joseph Smith at Kirtland, Ohio September 22 and 23, 1832, which he designated as a revelation on priesthood.

In it, the Lord declared the city of the New Jerusalem and its temple are to be built in Missouri, gave the line of priesthood from

Adam to Moses, explained that the greater priesthood administers the gospel ordinances, the lesser priesthood administers the preparatory gospel, that men gain eternal life through the oath and covenant of the priesthood, that it is the Spirit of Christ which enlightens men, that the world lies in sin, that the Saints must testify of those things they have received, that they are to preach the gospel and signs will follow, that elders are to go forth without purse or scrip, and the Lord will care for their needs, that plagues and cursings await those who reject the gospel, that every man is to stand in his own office and labor in his own calling, and that the Lord's servants are to proclaim the abomination of desolation of the last days.

The Lord traced the priesthood Moses held back to Abraham, then to Noah, then to Enoch, then to Abel. Moses was ordained by his father-in law Jethro, who was ordained by Caleb, who was ordained by Elihu, who was ordained by Jeremy, who was ordained by Gad, who was ordained by Esaias, who was received it from the hand of God. Esaias lived in the days of Abraham and was blessed of him. Abraham was ordained by Melchizedek, who was ordained through Noah to Abel who received the priesthood by the commandments of God, by the hand of his father Adam.

Drawing a distinction between the Aaronic and Melchizedek Priesthoods, the Lord said a priesthood was continued through Aaron and his seed, throughout all their generations, but that the greater or Melchizedek Priesthood administers the gospel and holds the key of the mysteries of the kingdom even the key of the knowledge of God, that the power of godliness is manifested in the ordinances, and without them and the authority of the priesthood, the power of godliness is not manifest unto men in the flesh. Moses taught these things to the children of Israel in the wilderness, but they weren't ready for it so a lesser priesthood was substituted. (5-25)

This lesser priesthood holds:

"the key of the ministering of angels and the preparatory gospel, Which gospel is the gospel of repentance and of baptism, and the remission of sins, and the law of carnal commandments..." (v 26-27) "the offices of teacher and deacon are necessary appendages belonging to the lesser priesthood, which was confirmed upon Aaron and his sons..." (v 30) But "the offices of elder and bishop are necessary appendages belonging to the high [Melchizedek] priesthood." (v 29)

"Therefore, as I said concerning the sons of Moses--for the sons of Moses and of Aaron shall offer an acceptable offering and sacrifice in the house of the Lord... And the sons of Moses and of Aaron shall be filled with the glory of the Lord, upon Mount Zion in the Lord's house, whose sons are ye; and also many whom I have called and sent forth to build up my church.

(35a) "For whoso is faithful unto the obtaining these two priesthoods of which I have spoken, and the magnifying their calling, are sanctified by the Spirit unto the renewing of their bodies. They become the sons of Moses and of Aaron and the seed of Abraham, and the church and kingdom, and the elect of God. And also all they who receive this priesthood receive me, saith the Lord; For he that receiveth my servants receiveth me; And he that receiveth me receiveth my Father;

"And he that receiveth my Father receiveth my Father's kingdom; therefore, all that my Father hath shall be given unto him."(v 33-38)

"And this is according to the oath and covenant which belongeth to the priesthood.

Therefore, all those who receive the priesthood, receive the oath and covenant of my Father, which he cannot break, neither can it be moved. But whoso breaketh the covenant after he hath received it, and altogether turneth therefrom, shall not have forgiveness of sins in this world nor in the world to come. And wo unto all those who come not unto this priesthood which ye have received, which I now confirm upon you who are present this day, by mine own voice out of the heavens; and even I have given the heavenly hosts and mine angels

225

charge concerning you.

"And I now give unto you a commandment to beware concerning yourselves, to give diligent heed to the words of eternal life. (35b) For you shall live by every word that proceedeth forth from the mouth of God. For the word of the Lord is truth, and whatsoever is truth is light, and whatsoever is light is Spirit, even the Spirit of Jesus Christ. And the Spirit giveth light to every man that cometh into the world, and the Spirit enlighteneth every man through the world that hearkeneth to the voice of the Spirit. And every one that hearkeneth to the voice of the Spirit cometh unto God, even the Father." (v 39-47)

Interrelationships of the priesthood, missionary work and the principles of a Zion Society as contained in the remainder of Section 84, including the new song of the redemption of Zion, are reported Chapter XIX ahead. (D&C 84:1-120; HC1:286-295)

[Section 85]

An extract from of a letter of the prophet to W. W. Phelps who was living in Independence, Missouri dated November 27, 1832, is treated as a revelation, answering questions about those saints who had moved to Zion in Missouri, but who had not received their inheritances according to the established order of the Church. Its contents are reported in Chapter XIX concerning a Zion Society. (D&C 85: 1-11, HC 1:298-299)

[Section 86]

While reviewing and editing the manuscript for his translation of the Bible, Joseph Smith received a revelation, Section 86, December 6, 1832 at Kirtland, Ohio. In it the Lord gives meaning to the parable of the wheat and the tares and indicates that priesthood blessings are for those who are lawful heirs according to the flesh. Its contents are reported in Chapter XVI the Gathering, Perfection and Redemption of Israel Begins. (D&C 86 :1-11; HC 1:300)

[Section 87]

During the Christmas season of 1832 the leading brethren of

the Church were discussing the importation of African slaves on the American continent as well as slavery through out the world. On Christmas day December 25, 1832 a revelation and prophecy was received by Joseph Smith. In it we see that the Lord not only foretold the outbreak of the United States Civil War or the War between the States, but foreshadowed the inhabitants of all the earth would "feel the wrath, and indignation and chastening hand of an Almighty God, until the consumption decreed hath made a full end of all nations." (v 6)

In other words the outbreak of Civil War over slavery in the United States marked the beginning of warfare which will end only when all nations will end, and the Savior returns as the earth's God and King.

"Verily, thus saith the Lord concerning the wars that will shortly come to pass, beginning at the rebellion of South Carolina, which will eventually terminate in the death and misery of many souls; And the time will come that war will be poured out upon all nations, beginning at this place.

"For behold, the Southern States shall be divided against the Northern States, and the Southern States will call on other nations, even the nation of Great Britain, as it is called, and they shall also call upon other nations, in order to defend themselves against other nations, and then war shall be poured out upon all nations. And it shall come to pass, after many days, slaves shall rise up against their masters, who shall be marshalled and disciplined for war. And it shall come to pass also that the remnants who are left of the land will marshal themselves, and shall become exceedingly angry, and shall vex the Gentiles with a sore vexation.

"And thus, with the sword and by blood shed the inhabitants of the earth shall mourn; and with famine and with plague, and earthquake, and the thunder of heaven, and the fierce and vivid lightning also, shall the inhabitants of the earth be made to feel the wrath and indignation and chastening hand of an Almighty God, until the consumption decreed hath made an end of all nations;

"That the cry of the saints, and the blood of the saints shall cease to come up unto the ears of the Lord of the Sabaoth, from the earth, to be avenged of their enemies. Wherefore, stand in holy places and be not moved until the day of the Lord come; for behold, it cometh quickly, saith the Lord, Amen." (D&C 87:1-8; HC 3:101-302)

[Section 88]

From the historical records it appears that portions of revelation in Section 88 were received December 27 and 28, 1832 and January 3, 1833. Given through Joseph Smith at Kirtland, Ohio, the Prophet designates it as the "olive leaf ... plucked from the Tree of Paradise, the Lord's message of peace unto us." (HC1:302-303)

In it, the Lord declares that faithful Saints will receive that Comforter which is the promise of eternal life; that all things are controlled and governed by the light of Christ; that the resurrection comes through the redemption; that obedience to celestial, terrestrial, or telestial law prepares men for their respective kingdoms and glories; that those who will to abide in sin, remain filthy still; that all kingdoms are governed by law; that God hath given a law unto all things; that man shall comprehend even God. The Lord relates the parable of the man sending his servants into the field and visiting them in turn; that they who draw near unto the Lord shall see his face.

The Saints were to sanctify themselves and teach one another the doctrine of the kingdom and were counseled that every man that has been warned should warn his neighbor; that signs, upheavals of the elements and angels prepare the way for the coming of the Lord; that angelic trumps shall call forth the dead in their order; that angelic trumps proclaim the restoration of the gospel, the fall of Babylon, and the battle of the great God. The Saints are counseled to seek learning, establish a house of God or temple and clothe themselves with a bond of charity; and the order of the school of the prophets was set forth, including the ordinance of washing of feet. (D&C 88:1-141)

Adding more specificity to doctrine designed to prepare the

saints to help gather, help perfect, and help redeem the true believers in Messiah/Christ, and help them understand the differences in kingdoms, and what one needs to do to inherit the celestial kingdom, the Lord declared that "all kingdoms have a law given; and there are many kingdoms; for there is no space in the which there is no kingdom; and there is no kingdom in which there is no space, either a greater or a lesser kingdom.

"And unto every kingdom is given a law; and unto every law there are certain bounds also and conditions. All beings who abide not in those conditions are not justified. For intelligence cleaveth unto intelligence; wisdom receiveth wisdom; truth embraceth truth; virtue loveth virtue; light cleaveth unto light; mercy hath compassion on mercy and claimeth her own; justice continueth its course and claimeth its own; judgment goeth before the face of him who sitteth upon the throne and governeth and executeth all things." (v 36-40)

Several metaphors were used to help describe kingdoms and laws governing them, but the Lord then returns to what individuals must do to inherit the celestial glory saying:

"...call upon me while I am near---Draw near unto me and I will draw near unto you; seek me diligently and ye shall find me; ask and ye shall receive; knock and it shall be opened unto you. Whatsoever ye ask the Father in my name it shall be given unto you, that is expedient [beneficial] for you... if your eye be single to my glory, your whole bodies shall be filled with light, and there shall be no darkness in you; and that body which is filled with light comprehendeth all things. Therefore sanctify yourselves that your minds become single to God, and the days will come that you shall see him; for he will unveil his face unto you, and it shall be in his own time, and in his own way, and according to his own will. (v 62-68)

These revelations are also discussed in greater detail in Chapter XIX A ZION SOCIETY, and in Chapter XXI THE SECOND COMING.

[Section 89]

Some of the early brethren meeting as the school of the prophets, used an upstairs bedroom for a classroom. The crowded room soon became thick with tobacco smoke and spit. Joseph Smith inquired of the Lord and received Section 89 at Kirtland, Ohio on February 27, 1833 as a result.

The use of wine, strong drinks, tobacco and hot drinks was not approved said the Lord. Herbs, fruits and grain were appointed for the use of man and of animals, and obedience to gospel law, including this new word of wisdom, brings temporal and spiritual blessings. The word of wisdom would later become a distinctive characteristic of the Zion Society under development. More on the word of wisdom, its promises and blessings in the Chapter XIX, A ZION SOCIETY TO BE THE NEW WORLD ORDER. (D&C 89:1-21; HC 1:327-329)

[Section 90]

Revelation fleshing out and establishing more completely the First Presidency as the Church's leading ecclesiastical and administrative body was received through Joseph Smith at Kirtland, Ohio March 8, 1833.

In this revelation the Lord made clear the keys of the kingdom of God on earth were committed to Joseph Smith and through him to the Church; that Sidney Rigdon and Frederick G. Williams were to serve as counselors in the First Presidency; that the Gospel is to be preached to the nations of Israel, to the Gentiles, and to the Jews, every man hearing in his own tongue; that Joseph Smith and his counselors were to set in order the Church and various individuals were also counseled to walk uprightly and serve in his kingdom. Specific plans were outlined for those bound for Zion in Missouri which included elements of the law of consecration, which will be discussed in Chapter XIX, A ZION SOCIETY TO BE THE NEW WORLD ORDER. (D&C 90:1-37; HC 1:329-331)

[Section 91]

While engaged in the translation of the Old Testament, Joseph Smith received a revelation March 9, 1833 at Kirtland, Ohio, pertaining to ancient writings called the Apocrypha. Joseph asked whether the Apocrypha should be translated. In this revelation the Lord said:

"There are many things contained therein that are true, and it is mostly translated correctly. There are many things contained therein that are not true, which are interpolations by the hands of men. Verily, I say unto you, that it is not needful that the Apocrypha be translated. Therefore, whoso readeth it, let him understand, for the Spirit manifesteth truth;

"And whoso is enlightened by the Spirit shall obtain benefit therefrom. And whoso receiveth not by the Spirit, cannot be benefitted..." (D&C 91:1-6; HC 1:331-332)

[Section 92]

Revelation given to Joseph Smith directed to Frederick G. Williams, counselor in the First Presidency, was received March 15, 1833 at Kirtland Ohio. Brother Williams was to be received into the United Order and counseled that if he is faithful in keeping all former commandments he shall be blessed forever. A description of the United Order or the law of consecration is contained in Chapter XIX, A ZION SOCIETY TO BE THE NEW WORLD ORDER.. (D&C 92: 1-2; HC 1:333)

[Section 93]

Revelation given through Joseph Smith May 6, 1833 at Kirtland, Ohio covers doctrines and concepts important to our understanding of the Son of God's command to be perfect, as He or His Father in Heaven is perfect, understanding His work and glory, which includes bringing to pass the eternal life of all who enter the new and everlasting covenant and keep its provisions, and placing them on a path of eternal progression eventually leading to inheritance of all that the Father has.

We are informed that all who are faithful shall see the Lord;

that John bore record that the Son of God went from grace to grace until he received a fulness of the glory of the Father; that faithful men and women who progress from grace to grace, shall also receive of his fulness; that those who are begotten through Christ are the Church of the Firstborn; that Christ received a fulness of all truth, and man by obedience may do likewise; that man was in the beginning with God; that the elements are eternal; that man may receive a fulness of joy in the resurrection; that the glory of God is intelligence; that children under the age of accountability are innocent before God because of the redemption of Christ; that the leading brethren are commanded to teach their children light and truth and otherwise set their families in order, as they undertake their Church responsibilities, thereby setting an example for the members of the Church. More specifically,

"... saith the Lord: [35] every soul who forsaketh his sins and cometh unto me, and calleth on my name, and obeyeth my voice, and keepeth my commandments, shall see my face and know that I am; And that I am the true light that lighteth every man that cometh into the world;

[36]" ... John saw and bore record of the fulness of my glory, and [37] the fulness of John's record is hereafter to be revealed.[38] And he bore record, saying: I saw his glory, that he was in the beginning, before the world was; Therefore, in the beginning the Word was, for he was the Word, even the messenger of salvation-- The light and the Redeemer of the world; the spirit of truth, who came into the world because the world was made by him, and in him was the life of men and the light of men.

[39]"The worlds were made by him; through him and of him. And I, John [40] bear record that I beheld his glory, as the glory of the Only Begotten of the Father, full of grace and truth, even the truth which came in the flesh, and dwelt among us. And I, John, [41] saw that he received not of the fulness at the first, but received grace for grace; And he received not of the fulness at first, but continued from grace to grace, until he received a fulness; And thus he was called the

Son of God, because he received not of the fulness at the first.

[42]" ... And I, John, bear record that he received a fulness of the glory of the Father; And he received all power, both in heaven and on earth, and the glory of the Father was with him ... [43] And it shall come to pass, that if you are faithful, you shall receive a fulness of the record of John.

[44]"I give unto you these sayings that you may understand and know how to worship, and know what you worship, that you may come unto the Father in my name, and in due time receive of his fulness. [45]" For if you keep the commandments you shall receive of his fulness, and be glorified in me as I am in the Father, therefore, I say unto you, you shall receive grace for grace.

"And now, verily I say unto you,[46] I was in the beginning with the Father, and am the Firstborn.[47] And all those who are begotten through me [born again] are partakers of the glory of the same, and are the church of the Firstborn. Ye were also in the beginning with the Father; that which is Spirit even the Spirit of truth; [48] And truth is knowledge of things as they are, as they were, and as they are to come; And whatsoever is more or less than this is the spirit of that wicked one who was a liar from the beginning.

[49] "The Spirit of truth is of God. I am the Spirit of truth, and John bore record of me, saying: He received a fulness of truth, yea, even all truth; And no man receiveth a fulness unless he keepeth his commandments. [50] He that keepeth his commandments receiveth truth and light,until he is glorified in truth and knoweth all things.

"Man was also in the beginning with God. Intelligence, or the light of truth, was not created or made, neither indeed can be.[51] All truth is independent in that sphere in which God has placed it, to act for itself, as all intelligence also; otherwise there is no existence. Behold, here is the agency of man, and here is the condemnation of man; because that which was from the beginning is plainly manifest unto them, and they receive not the light.

"And every man whose spirit receive not the light is under

condemnation. [52]" For man is spirit. The elements are eternal, and spirit and element inseparably connected receive a fulness of joy; And when separated man cannot receive a fulness of joy. The elements are the tabernacle of God; yea, man is the tabernacle of God, even temples; and whatsoever temple is defiled, God shall destroy that temple.

[53] "The glory of God is intelligence, or in other words, light and truth. Light and truth forsake that evil one. [54] Every spirit of man was innocent in the beginning; And God having redeemed man from the fall, men became again, in their infant state, innocent before God. And that wicked one cometh and taketh away light and truth, through disobedience, from the children of men, and because of the tradition of their fathers. [55] But I have commanded you to bring up your children in light and truth."

The revelation closes with an admonition for Joseph Smith and Frederick G. Williams to

"hasten to translate my scriptures, and to obtain a knowledge of history, and of countries, and of kingdoms, of laws of God and men, and all this for the salvation of Zion. Amen." (D&C 93:1-53; HC 1:343-346)

[Section 94]

By the spring of 1833 the Missouri Saints were suffering intense persecution which eventually forced them to leave Missouri. The need was upon them to establish a city and stake of Zion, and build a House of the Lord or temple as its center piece. A revelation was received May 6, 1833 by Joseph Smith appointing Hyrum Smith, Reynolds Cahoon, and Jared Carter as members of a Church building committee. Temples, tabernacles, meeting houses, places of residence and businesses are hallmarks of a Zion Society inhabited by Saints consecrating their all for the good of the whole. The specifics of this revelation pertaining to the erection of a house for the work of the presidency, a printing house and the first latter-day temple are reported in Chapter XIV.(D&C 94:1-17; HC 1:346-347))

[Section 95]

About six months after beginning to give divine direction to build houses of worship and instruction contained in Section 88: 119-136, followed up by Section 94, the Lord gave, through Joseph Smith, on June 1, 1833 more direction on building construction, especially the House of the Lord or Temple. In this revelation the Saints are chastened for failure to build the House of the Lord. He desires to use his house to endow his people with power from on high, as a place of worship and a school for the apostles. Specifics are reported in Chapter XIV pertaining to building the first latter-day temple. (D&C 95:1-17; HC 1: 350-352)

[Section 96]

Three days later on June 4, 1833 a conference of high priests was convened to consider the disposal of certain lands possessed by the Church including a property known as the French farm. Agreement was not reached so all agreed to inquire of the Lord through Joseph Smith. The Lord responded with revelation in Section 96. In it the Lord emphasized the Kirtland Stake of Zion was to be made strong; that the bishop was to divide inheritances for the Saints and that John Johnson was to be a member of the United Order. Specifics are reported in Chapter XIX A ZION SOCIETY TO BE THE NEW WORLD ORDER. (D&C 96:1-9; HC 1:352-353)

[Section 97]

By August 1833 persecution of the small body of Saints in the Missouri Zion became so great they were forced to sign an agreement to leave Jackson County. Inquiry was made of the Lord as to what they should do. Revelation was received through Joseph Smith in Kirtland, Ohio pertaining to the struggling Saints in Missouri. Among other things the Lord declared many of the saints in the Jackson County, Missouri Zion were blessed for their faithfulness including Parley P. Pratt who is commended for his labors in the school in Zion. The Lord also noted that those who observe their covenants are accepted by Him. He reaffirms a house is to be built in Zion in which the pure in heart shall see God, defines Zion as THE PURE IN HEART, and assures them Zion shall escape the Lord's scourge if she is faithful. More in Chapter XIX on A ZION SOCIETY TO BE THE NEW WORLD ORDER. (D&C 97: 1-28; HC 1:400-402)

[Section 98]

Revelation came at Kirtland, Ohio August 6, 1833 as a consequence of the persecution upon the Saints in Missouri. In it the Lord declared that the afflictions on the Saints would ultimately be for their good; that the Saints were to befriend the constitutional law of the land; that honest, wise, and good men should be supported for secular offices; that those who lay down their lives in the Lord's cause shall have eternal life; that the Saints should renounce war and proclaim peace; that the Lord reproved the Kirtland Saints and commanded them to repent; that the Lord will reveal his laws governing the toleration of the persecutions and afflictions of his people; that war is justified only when the Lord commands it; and that the Saints are to forgive their enemies, who, if they repent, shall also escape the Lord's vengeance. More specifically,

"... all things wherewith you have been afflicted shall work together for your good, and to my name's glory saith the Lord... it is my will that my people should observe to do all things whatsoever I command them. And that law of the land which is constitutional, supporting that principal of freedom in maintaining rights and privileges, belongs to all mankind, and is justifiable before me. Therefore, I, the Lord, justify you, and your brethren of my church, in befriending that which is the constitutional law of the land; And as pertaining to law of man, whatsoever is more or less than this cometh of evil.

"I, the Lord your God, make you free, therefore ye are free indeed; and the law also maketh you free. Nevertheless, when the wicked rule the people mourn. Wherefore, honest men and wise men should be sought for diligently, and good men and wise men ye should observe to uphold; otherwise whatsoever is less than these cometh of evil. And I give unto you a commandment, that ye shall forsake all evil and cleave unto all good, that ye shall live by every word which proceedeth forth out of the mouth of God. For he will give unto the faithful line upon line, precept upon precept; and I will try you and prove you herewith.

"And whoso layeth down his life in my cause for my name's sake, shall find it again, even eternal life. Therefore be not afraid of your enemies, for I have decreed in my heart, saith the Lord, that I will prove you in all things, whether you abide in my covenant, even unto death, that you may be found worthy. For if ye will not abide in my covenant ye are not worthy of me." (v 3-15)

As the Lord counseled the Church, through Joseph Smith, to renounce war and proclaim peace, He also seems to be saying that there is a connection between peace and the turning of the hearts of children to their fathers and the hearts of fathers to their children; and that the hearts of the Jews should be turned to the prophets and the hearts of the prophets should be turned unto the Jews;

"lest I come and smite the whole earth with a curse, and all flesh be consumed before me. Let not your hearts be troubled; for in my Father's house are many mansions, and I have prepared a place for you; and where my Father and I am, there ye shall be also." (v 16-18)

After reprimanding the Kirtland Saints for pride, covetousness and other sins, the Lord set forth His laws regulating the mistreatment and tribulations inflicted upon His people. They were counseled that if they bore it patiently and revile not or seek revenge against their enemies that smite or physically abuse them; they, the Saints, would be rewarded, the reward being increased a hundred fold each time their enemies repeated the offense. After the third offense, they were to warn the enemy in Christ's name, not to harm them or their families. If the warning were left unheeded the Lord would intervene and take care of it directly. The Lord said these laws governing offenses were not new, but were given to Nephi, to Joseph, to Jacob, or Israel, to Isaac, to Abraham and to all His ancient prophets and apostles. (v 19-32)

Not only were these laws of forgiveness and non-retaliation to apply to His covenant peoples, but apply to any nation, kindred, tongue or people as they contemplate going into battle, unless the Lord commands them to do so. Therefore, the obligation of any nation is to lift a standard of peace to the possible adversary at least three times, before the Lord will justify them going into battle, and after that the Lord will fight their battles for them in similar fashion as described for individuals. This revelation is closed with a description of penalties for individuals abusing others, and penalties for nations being at war without justification and what steps individuals and nations must take to avoid the vengeance of God including a four-fold restoration for their trespasses. (v 33-48; D&C 98:1-48; HC 1:403-406)

[Section 99]

To John Murdock was given a revelation through Joseph Smith in August 1832, but reported a year later. In it the Lord called Brother Murdock to go into the eastern countries and proclaim the Gospel, and those who receive him, receive the Lord and shall obtain mercy. However, he first needed to "send up kindly to the bishop in Zion, his children."(v 6) "... after a few years, if thou desirest of me thou mayest go up also unto the goodly land, to possess thine inheritance; Otherwise thou shalt continue proclaiming my gospel until thou be taken." (D&C 99:1-8)

Here is an illustration the Lord expects bishops in Zion, especially those with a functioning united order to care for an Elder's children while said elder is away on missionary assignment.

[Section 100]

During the early fall of 1833 Joseph Smith and Sidney Rigdon, missionaries in Perrysburg, New York for a short period, received a revelation October 12th, assuring them their families whom they had not seen for several days were,

"well; they are in mine hands, and I will do with them as

seemeth me good; for in me there is all power... I have much people in this place, in the regions round about; and an effectual door shall be opened ... in this eastern land. Therefore I, the Lord, have suffered you to come unto this place; for thus it is expedient in me for the salvation of souls... I say unto you, lift up your voices ... speak the thoughts that I shall put into your hearts... For it shall be given you in the very hour, yea in the very moment, what ye shall say ... declare whatsoever thing ye declare in my name, in solemnity of heart, in the spirit of meekness... And I give unto you this promise, that inasmuch as ye do this, the Holy Ghost shall be shed forth in bearing record unto all things whatsoever ye shall say.

"... And now I give unto you a word concerning Zion. Zion shall be redeemed, although she is chastened for a little season. ... Therefore, let your hearts be comforted; for all things shall work together for good to them that walk uprightly, and to the sanctification of the church. For I will raise up unto myself a pure people, that will serve me in righteousness; And all that call upon the name of the Lord, and keep his commandments, shall be saved." (D&C 100:1-17; HC 1:416, 419-421)

[Section 101]

Mobs had driven the suffering Saints from their homes in Jackson County, Missouri. Some had tried to establish themselves in Van Buren County, but persecution followed them. The main body of the Saints by now was in Clay County. Many received death threats, lost their clothing, furniture, livestock, other personal property, and/or had their crops destroyed. In this context revelation was received by Joseph Smith December 16, 1833 at Kirtland, Ohio.

In this revelation the Lord said the Saints were chastened and afflicted because of their transgressions; that His indignation shall fall upon the nations, but His people will be gathered and comforted; that Zion and her stakes shall be established. The Lord revealed the nature of life during the Millennium; declared the Saints shall be blessed and rewarded then. The Lord signified the troubles and eventual redemption of Zion citing the parable of the nobleman and the olive trees; encouraged the Saints to continue to gather together; noted that He had established the Constitution of the United States; and instructed the Saints to importune for redress of grievances according to the parable of the woman and the unjust judge. Though the Saints were being chastened and afflicted because of their transgressions the Lord said such chastening and trial was necessary even as it was with Abraham, else they could not be sanctified and made holy. If they endured it well He would own them in the day when He makes up His jewels. More specifically,

"Verily, I say unto you, concerning your brethren who have been afflicted, and persecuted, and cast out from the land of their inheritance-- I the Lord have suffered the affliction to come upon them, wherewith they have been afflicted in consequence of their transgressions; Yet I will own them, and they shall be mine in that day when I shall make up my jewels.

"Therefore, they must be chastened and tried, even as Abraham, who was commanded to offer up his only [covenant] son. For all those who will not endure chastening, but deny me, cannot be sanctified. Behold, I say unto yo, there were jarrings, and contentions, and envyings, and strifes, and lustful and contentious desires among them; therefore, by these things they polluted their inheritances. They were slow to hearken unto the voice of the Lord their God; therefore, the Lord their God is slow to hearken unto their prayers, to answer them in the day of their trouble.

"In the day of their peace they esteemed lightly my counsel; but, in the day of their trouble, of necessity, they feel after me. Verily, I say unto you, notwithstanding their sins, my bowels are filled with compassion towards them, I will not utterly cast them off; and in the day of wrath I will remember mercy. I have sworn, and the decree hath gone forth by a former commandment which I have given unto you, that I would let fall the sword of mine indignation in behalf of my people; and even as I have said, it shall come to pass. Mine indignation is soon to be poured out without measure upon all nations; and this will I do when the cup of their iniquity is full. And in that day all who are found upon the watchtower, or in other words, all mine Israel, shall be saved." (v 1-12)

With reference to the Constitution of the United States and the persecution of His people, the Lord said:

"And again I say unto you, those who have been scattered by their enemies, it is my will that they should continue to importune for redress, and redemption, by the hands of those who are placed as rulers and are in authority over you-- According to the laws and constitution of the people, which I have suffered to be established, and should be maintained for the rights and protection of all flesh, according to just and holy principles; That every man may act in doctrine and principle pertaining to futurity, according to the moral agency which I have given unto him, that every man may be accountable for his own sins in the day of judgment.

"Therefore, it is not right that any man should be in bondage one to another. And for this purpose have I established the Constitution of this land, by the hands of wise men whom I raised up unto this very purpose, and redeemed the land by the shedding of blood." (v 76-80)

Referencing and citing the parable of the woman and unjust judge, the Lord likened the children of Zion to the woman in this parable and counseled them to petition appropriate judges for redress. If that did not bring relief, to petition the governor, and if no relief came, to petition the President of the United States of America. If the President gave them no relief, the Lord would eventually

"vex the nation; and in His hot displeasure, and in his fierce anger, in his time, will cut off those wicked, unfaithful, and unjust stewards, and appoint them their portion among hypocrites and unbelievers; ..." (v 81-89)

He advised them to,

"Pray ye, therefore, that their ears may be opened unto your cries, that I may be merciful unto them, that these things may not come upon them. What I have said unto you must needs be, that all men may be left without excuse; That wise men and rulers may hear and know that which they have never considered; That I may proceed to bring to pass my act, my strange act, and perform my work, my strange work, that men may discern between the righteous and the wicked, saith your God."

Even though the Saints were being persecuted and driven out, they were not to sell the Lord's storehouse to these enemies; for such would be an affront to Him. (v 92-98)

[Section 102]

A high council was appointed at Kirtland, Ohio February 17, 1834, to settle important difficulties that arose in the Church. The original minutes prepared by Oliver Cowdery and Orson Hyde were corrected by the Prophet Joseph Smith. They were later amended in 1835 when verses were added pertaining to the Council of Twelve Apostles, when the then most recent edition of the Doctrine and Covenants was being prepared for publication. In it procedures were set forth for hearing cases, including a provision for handling appeals. The president of the high council renders the decision after consultation with the council. (D&C 102:1-34; HC 2:28-31)

[Section 103]

Parley P. Pratt and Lyman Wight while on assignment in Missouri traveled to Kirtland, Ohio to consult with the prophet concerning relief and restoration of the Saints to their lands in Jackson, County, Missouri. This revelation received February 24, 1834 was received in response. In it the Lord sets forth why He permitted the Saints in Jackson County to be persecuted and told the Saints they would prevail if they keep the commandments; that the redemption of Zion shall come by power; that the Lord will go before His people; that the Saints are to gather in Zion; that those who lay down their lives shall find them again; that various brethren were being called to organize Zion's Camp and to go to Zion; and the Saints will be victorious if they are faithful. More specifically the Lord said,

"I will give unto you a revelation and commandment, that you may know how to act in the discharge of your duties concerning the salvation and redemption of your brethren, who have been scattered on the land of Zion; Being driven and smitten by the hands of mine enemies, on whom I will pour out my wrath without measure in mine own due time. For I have suffered them thus far, that they might fill up the measure of their iniquities, that their cup might be full; And that those who cal themselves after my name might be chastened for a little season with a sore and grievous chastisement, because they did not hearken altogether unto the precepts and commandments which I gave unto them." (v 1-4)

Having made His point the Lord said henceforth if the afflicted Saints would listen and obey Him the tide would be turned from this very hour, and that His Saints

"would never cease to prevail until the kingdom do the world are subdued under my feet, and the earth is given unto the saints, to possess it forever and ever." (5-7)

More on this in Chapter XIX pertaining to ZION AS THE NEW WORLD ORDER. (D&C 103:1-40; HC 2:36-39)

[Section 104]

At a council meeting of the First Presidency and other high priests the pressing temporal needs of the people were considered. The United Order at Kirtland was to be temporarily dissolved and reorganized and the properties as stewardships were to be divided among the members of the order. The United Order and the order of the Church for the benefit of the poor are to operate separately, as spelled out by the Lord in this revelation given to Joseph Smith April 23, 1834.

In this revelation the Lord also declared that those Saints who transgress against the United Order shall be cursed; that He provides for His Saints in His own way and that Gospel law governs the care of the poor. Stewardships and blessings of various brethren are designated; the sacred treasury of the Lord is set up for the printing of the scriptures, and the general treasury of the United Order is to operate on the basis of common consent. Those in the United Order are to pay all their debts and the Lord will deliver them from financial bondage. For more specificity see Chapter XIX, A ZION SOCIETY, TO BE THE NEW WORLD ORDER. (D&C 104:1-86; HC 2:54-60)

[Section 105]

By mid-summer 1834 mob violence against the Saints in Missouri had increased to the point organized bodies from several counties had announced their intent to destroy the people. Bringing clothing and provisions from Kirtland, Ohio, Zions Camp had reached Fishing River, Missouri June 22, 1834. While thus encamped Joseph Smith received revelation in Section 105.

In it the Lord informed the Saints that Zion shall be built up by conformity to celestial law; that the redemption of Zion will be deferred for a little season; that the Lord will fight the battles of Zion; that the Saints are to be wise and not boast of mighty works as they gather; that lands in Jackson and adjoining counties should be purchased; that the elders are to receive an endowment in the House of the Lord in Kirtland; that the Saints who are called and chosen shall be sanctified; and that the Saints are to lift up an ensign of peace to the world. For more specificity see Chapter XIX, A ZION SOCIETY, TO BE THE NEW WORLD ORDER. (D&C 105:1-41; HC 2:108-111)

[Section 106]

Directed to Warren A. Cowdery, an older brother to Oliver Cowdery, was a revelation given through Joseph Smith at Kirtland, Ohio November 25, 1834. In this revelation the Lord called Warren A. Cowdery as a local presiding officer and reminded him of the Second Coming:

"the coming of the Lord draweth nigh, and it overtaketh the

world as a thief in the night. Therefore, gird up your loins, that you may be the children of light, and that day shall not overtake you as a thief.

"...if he [Warren] continue to be a faithful witness and a light unto the church I have prepared a crown for him in the mansions of my Father." (D&C 106:1-6; HC 2:170-171)

[Section 107]

Meeting in council, the Twelve just prior to their departure for missions to districts assigned, confessed their individual weaknesses and shortcomings, expressed repentance and humbled themselves seeking further guidance from the Lord. In response, revelation was received March 28, 1835.

Various parts of what is now Section 107 were received earlier, some as early as November 1831. They were aggregated together with that received on March 28, 1835. In these revelations the Lord declared there are two priesthoods, the Melchizedek and the Aaronic; that those who hold the Melchizedek Priesthood have power to officiate in all offices of the Church; that the bishopric presides over the Aaronic Priesthood, which administers in outward ordinances; that the Melchizedek Priesthood holds all the keys of all spiritual blessings; that the Aaronic Priesthood holds the keys of the ministering of angels; and that the First Presidency, the Twelve and the Seventy constitute the presiding quorums, whose decisions are to be made in unity and righteousness.

The Lord set forth the patriarchal order from Adam to Noah and reported that the ancient Saints assembled at Adam-ondi-Ahman three years before Adam's death and that He, the Lord, appeared to them; that the Twelve are to set the officers of the Church in order; that bishops serve as common judges in Israel; that the First Presidency and the Twelve constitute the highest court of the Church; and that priesthood presidents govern their respective quorums.

More specifically, after declaring there are two priesthoods in the Church: the Melchizedek and Aaronic, including the Levitical

Priesthood; He said the higher priesthood was named after Melchizedek because he was such a great high priest. However, before the days of Melchizedek it was called

"the Holy Priesthood, after the Order of the Son of God. But out of respect or reverence to the name of the Supreme Being, to avoid the too frequent repetition of his name, they, the church, in ancient days called that priesthood after Melchizedek, or the Melchizedek Priesthood. All other offices or authorities in the church are appendages to this priesthood. But there are two divisions or grand heads--one is the Melchizedek Priesthood, and the other is the Aaronic or Levitical Priesthood." (v 1-6)

Indicating those who hold the Melchizedek Priesthood have power to officiate in all offices of the Church the Lord said:

"The Melchizedek Priesthood holds the right of presidency, and has power and authority over all the offices in the church in all ages of the world, to administer in spiritual things... The power and authority of the higher or Melchizedek Priesthood is to hold the keys of all the spiritual blessings of the church--To have the privilege of receiving the mysteries of the kingdom of heaven, to have the heavens opened unto them, to commune with the general assembly of the church of the Firstborn, and to enjoy the communion and presence of God the Father, and Jesus the mediator of the new covenant.

By contrast,

"The power and authority of the lesser, or Aaronic Priesthood, is to hold the keys of the ministering of angels, and to administer in outward ordinances, the letter of the gospel, the baptism of repentance for the remission of sins, agreeable to the covenants and commandments."(v 8,18-20)

Signifying the placement of power within the these two priesthoods the Lord has put the Presidency of the High Priesthood at the head of the higher priesthood and the bishopric at the head of the Aaronic Priesthood.

"The second priesthood is called the Priesthood of Aaron,

because it was conferred upon Aaron and his seed, throughout all their generations. Why is it called the lesser priesthood is because it is an appendage to the greater, or the Melchizedek Priesthood, and has power in administering all outward ordinances. The bishopric is the presidency of this priesthood, and holds the keys or authority of the same. But as a high priest of the Melchizedek Priesthood has authority to officiate in all the lesser offices, he may officiate in the office of bishop when no literal descendant of Aaron can be found provided he is called and set apart and ordained unto this power by the hands of the Presidency of the Melchizedek Priesthood." (v 13-18)

Offices growing out of the higher priesthood are elder, seventy, high priest, patriarch, apostle and president. Offices in the Aaronic Priesthood include bishop, priest, teacher and deacon. There are quorums of first presidency, apostles, high priests, seventy, and elders, each with a presidency.

Guiding principles for decision making are that decisions are to be made in all righteousness, in holiness, and lowliness of heart, in meekness and long suffering, and in faith, and virtue, and knowledge, temperance, patience, godliness, brotherly kindness and charity; "Because the promise is if these things abound in them they shall not be unfruitful in the knowledge of the Lord." (v 9-12, 21-31)

Verses 33 through 70 are reported in Chapter XIX concerning ZION AS THE NEW WORLD ORDER. (D&C 107:1-100; HC 2: 209-217)

[Section 134]

At a meeting of Church leaders brought together to consider the contents of the first edition of the Doctrine and Covenants, in Kirtland, Ohio, August 17, 1835, a declaration of belief regarding governments and laws was proposed to a general assembly of the Church and adopted by unanimous vote. To make clear its purpose, a preamble was written:

"That our belief with regard to earthly governments and laws in general may not be misinterpreted nor misunderstood, we have thought proper to present at the close of this volume our opinions concerning the same." (HC 2:247-249)

The declaration includes beliefs:

"that governments were instituted of God for the benefit of man; and that he holds men accountable for their acts in relation to them, both in making laws and administering them for the good of society;

"that no government can exist in peace, except such laws are framed and held inviolate as will secure to each individual the free exercise of conscience, the right and control of property, and the protection of life;

"that all governments necessarily require civil officers and magistrates to enforce the laws of the same; and that such as will administer the law in equity and justice should be sought for and upheld by the voice of the people, if a republic or the will of the sovereign;

"that religion is instituted of God; and that men are amenable to him, and to him only, for the exercise of it, unless their religious opinions prompt them to infringe upon the rights and liberties of others; but we do not believe that human law has a right to interfere in prescribing rules of worship to bind the consciences of men, nor dictate forms of public or private devotion; that the civil magistrate should restrain crime, but never control conscience; should punish guilt, but never suppress the freedom of the soul;

"that all men are bound to sustain and uphold the respective governments in which the reside...

"that every man should be honored in his station, rulers and magistrates as such, being placed for the protection of the innocent and the punishment of the guilty...

"that rulers, states, and governments have a right and are bound to enact laws for the protection of all citizens in the free exercise of their religious belief...

"that the commission of crime should be punished according to the nature of the offense ...

"We do not believe it just to mingle religious influence with civil government, whereby one religious society is fostered and another proscribed in its spiritual privileges, and the individual rights of its members as citizens, denied; that all religious societies have a right to deal with their members for disorderly conduct, according to rules and regulations of such societies; provided that such dealings be for fellowship and good standing; but we do not believe that any religious society has authority to try men on the right of property or life, to take from them this worlds goods, or to put them in jeopardy of either life or limb, or to inflict any physical punishment upon them. They can only excommunicate them from their society, and withdraw from them their membership.

"We believe that men should appeal to the civil law for redress of all wrongs and grievances, where personal abuse is inflicted or the right of property or character infringed where such laws exist as will protect the same; but we believe that all men are justified in defending themselves, their friends and property, and the government, from the unlawful assaults... of all persons in times of exigency, where immediate appeal cannot be made to the laws, and relief afforded.

"We believe it just to preach the gospel to the nations of the earth, and warn the righteous to save themselves from the corruption of the world..." (D&C 134:1-12; HC 2:247-249)

[Section 108]

At the request of Lyman Sherman, previously ordained a high priest and a seventy, Joseph Smith inquired of the Lord concerning Brother Sherman's duty. Revelation on that topic was received December 26, 1835 at Kirtland, Ohio. In it the Lord said:

"Your sins are forgiven you, because you have obeyed my voice ... Therefore, let your soul be at rest, concerning your spiritual standing, and resist no more my voice... Wait patiently until the solemn assembly shall be called of my servants, then you shall be remembered with the first of mine elders and receive right by ordination with the rest of mine elders whom I have chosen.

"... strengthen your brethren in all your conversations, in all your prayers, in all your exhortations, and in all your doings..." (D&C 108:1-8; HC 2:345)

While the members of the Lord's Church were persecuted much and passed through considerable tribulation the first half dozen years since it was organized, even more lay ahead during the next dozen years, including the murder of the Lord's prophet without cause and in cold blood; an exodus of the Lord's covenant people to safety in the west led by another prophet, Brigham Young, a modern day Moses, chosen of the Lord.

But amidst tribulation also came great blessings, including the construction of the first latter-day temples, the appearance of the Lord accepting the Kirtland Temple, the appearance of Moses, and Elias and Elijah returning to earth the keys of the gathering of Israel, the restoration of the Gospel of Abraham or the Abrahamic Covenant which contains higher laws than the law of Moses, and the return of Elijah to restore the sealing power and all the attendant blessings which go with these higher laws and covenants.

Though the construction of the Nauvoo Temple was not quite complete when Israel was forced to vacate the city of Nauvoo, it was complete enough for sacred endowments and other ordinances to be performed during the final three months before departure, giving the departing Saints the strength and faith they needed to endure the hardships endemic to crossing a thousand mile wilderness from Iowa to Salt Lake Valley which then was part of Mexico.

Chapter XIV includes a brief history of the Lord's people from January 1, 1836 through July 24, 1847. The revelations received during that period plus one other received in 1918, which, in essence, completed the restoration of the Lord's Gospel in all of its fulness, set the stage for its messages to be spread throughout the earth.

CHAPTER XIV

FIRST LATTER-DAY TEMPLES BUILT,
MORE DOCTRINE FOR PERFECTION OF SAINTS,
EARLY SAINTS TESTED WITH TRIAL AND TRIBULATION
PROPHET MARTYRED,
EXODUS TO SAFETY IN THE WEST LED BY ANOTHER
PROPHET CHOSEN OF THE LORD
(January 1836 through July 24, 1847)

It was the intent of the Church leadership to build a church headquarters, printing house and temple in Independence, Jackson County, Missouri after the Lord revealed it's location there in 1831. However, by 1833 the members of the Church in Missouri were forced to leave Jackson County and flee to Clay, Davies and Caldwell Counties due to persecution, intolerance and bigotry. But their stay in these counties was also short lived. By 1838 they had to flee Missouri altogether.

As part of a revelation given through Joseph Smith at Kirtland, Ohio received December 27, 1832, the Lord had commanded:

"Organize yourselves; prepare every needful thing; and establish a house, even a house of prayer, a house of fasting, a house of faith, a house of learning, a house of glory, a house of order, a house of God." (D&C 88:119)

Planning of these facilities for Kirtland, Ohio was begun in 1833 instead of Independence, Missouri, since conditions in Missouri were such that these facilities could not be built there. So, a Church Building Committee consisting of Hyrum Smith, Reynolds Cahoon and Jared Carter was created at the Lord's request. It is Section 94, a revelation given at Kirtland May 6, 1833.
[Section 94]
In this revelation they were instructed to

"commence a work of laying out and preparing a beginning and foundation of the city of the stake of Zion, here in the land of Kirtland, beginning at my house... let the first lot on the south be consecrated unto me for the building of a house for the presidency, for the work of the presidency, in obtaining revelations; and for the work of the ministry of the presidency, in all things pertaining to the church and kingdom.

"... And it shall be dedicated unto the Lord from the foundation thereof, according to the order of the priesthood, according to the pattern which shall be given unto you hereafter. And it shall be wholly dedicated unto the Lord for the work of the presidency. And ye shall not suffer any unclean thing to come in unto it; and my glory shall be there, and my presence shall be there. But if there shall come into it any unclean thing, my glory shall not be there; and my presence shall not come into it.

"And again, verily I say unto you, the second lot on the south shall be dedicated unto me for the building of a house unto me, for the work of the printing of the translation of my scriptures, and all things whatsoever I shall command you." (v 1-10)

A description of these facilities and their dimensions was given in this revelation, along with a description of the inheritance of a lot, each of the three members of the committee was to receive, as compensation for their work. After they had completed laying out the plans for these facilities they were to wait for the Lord's approval before actual construction were to begin. (D&C 94:1-17, HC 1:346-347))

Section 95

Four weeks later another revelation was received, Section 95, also at Kirtland June 1, 1833, which was a continuation of directions to build houses of worship, and of instruction, and especially a Temple or House of the Lord.

In this revelation the Lord chastens His leaders for not moving faster in getting His house or temple built, although a lot had been set aside for that purpose. He was anxious to endow His people with power from on high, and anxious to prepare His apostles to prune His vineyard for the last time, that He may pour out His Spirit upon all flesh. The Lord wanted it to be dedicated as a place of worship and a place for the school of the apostles as soon as possible.

"But behold, verily I say unto you, that there are many who have been ordained among you, whom I have called, but few of them are chosen. They who are not chosen have sinned a very grievous sin, in that they are walking in darkness at noon-day...I gave unto you a commandment that you should build a house, in the which house I design to endow those whom I have chosen with power from on high;... Verily I say unto you, it is my will that you should build a house. If you keep my commandments you shall have power to build it..." (v 1-11)

A description of the Kirtland Temple and its dimensions then followed with space for prayer, fasting and for instruction of the school of His apostles. (D&C 95:1-17)

The Kirtland Temple would not contain all the services or ordinances essential to the salvation of the living and the dead, but it would serve as a place for restoration of keys necessary for the salvation of the living and the dead, and as a place for visitation by heavenly messengers, and by the Lord Himself; enabling the prophet and others to receive important ordinances, counsel and instruction there.

Some of the ordinances of the endowment had already been revealed by January 21, 1836 and the Kirtland Temple was sufficiently completed by that date to allow limited use of the building. The Prophet was not immune from tragedy, for he experienced much of it during his life including the death of his father, his mother, four young children and his brother Alvin whom he dearly loved. His mother and father lived long enough to receive the saving ordinances, but Alvin had died before these ordinances were restored to earth, and his young children died before they had reached the age of accountability.

[Section 137]

While in the Kirtland Temple January 21, 1836, the prophet Joseph Smith, to his surprise, saw in vision, his deceased brother Alvin in the celestial kingdom of heaven.

"The heavens were opened upon us, and I beheld the celestial kingdom of God, and the glory thereof, whether in the body or out I cannot tell. I saw the transcendent beauty of the gate through which the heirs of that kingdom will enter, which was like unto circling flames of fire. Also the blazing throne of God, whereon was seated the Father and the Son. I saw the beautiful streets of that kingdom, which had the appearance of being paved with gold.

"I saw Father Adam and Abraham; and my father and my mother; my brother Alvin, that has long since slept; And marveled how it was that he had obtained an inheritance in that kingdom, seeing that he had departed this life before the Lord had set his hand to gather Israel the second time, and had not been baptized for the remission of sins.

"Thus came the voice of the Lord unto me, saying: All who have died without a knowledge of this gospel, who would have received it if they had been permitted to tarry, shall be heirs of the celestial kingdom of God. Also all that shall die henceforth, without a knowledge of it, who would have received it with all their hearts, shall be heirs of that kingdom.

"For I, the Lord, will judge all men according to their works, according to the desire of their hearts. And I also beheld that all children who die before they arrive at the years of accountability are saved in the celestial kingdom of heaven." (D&C 137: 1-10, HC 2:380-381)

Such knowledge must have been a great comfort to Joseph Smith who had lost a brother before the restoration. Two of his small children had died before they had reached the age of accountability i.e. eight years of age.

254

[Section 109]

At a prayer offered to the God of Israel by Joseph Smith at the dedication of the Kirtland Temple March 27, 1836, a prayer in turn was given him by the Lord, said Joseph. It revealed that the Kirtland Temple was built as a place for the Savior or Son of Man to visit; that it was to be a house of prayer, fasting, faith, learning, glory and order and a house of God. An appeal was made that the unrepentant who oppose the Lord's people be confounded. (v 1-33)

Other appeals in the prayer were that the saints may go forth in power to gather the righteous in Zion; that the saints be delivered from the terrible things to be poured out upon the wicked in the last days; and that nations and peoples and churches be prepared for the gospel. Some of these are discussed in Chapter XIX entitled A ZION SOCIETY, TO BE THE NEW WORLD ORDER.(v 34-60)

The remaining verses of Section 109 appeal for the redemption of the Jews and the Lamanites, with the hope that righteous saints shall be crowned with glory and honor and gain eternal salvation, are reported in the Chapter XVI entitled: THE GATHERING, PERFECTION AND REDEMPTION OF ISRAEL BEGINS. (v 60-80; D&C 109:1-80; HC 2:420-426)

[Section 110]

A week following the prayer of dedication offered for the Kirtland Temple, on Sunday April 3, 1836, services were held in the Temple.

"In the afternoon, I assisted the other Presidents in distributing the Lord's Supper to the Church, receiving it from the Twelve, whose privilege it was to officiate at the sacred desk this day. After having performed this service to my brethren, I retired to the pulpit, the veils being dropped, and bowed myself with Oliver Cowdery, in solemn and silent prayer. After rising from prayer... the following vision was opened to both of us."
(HC 2:435-436)

"The veil was taken from our minds, and the eyes of our

understanding were opened. We saw the Lord standing upon the breastplate of the pulpit, before us; and under his feet was a paved work of pure gold, in color like amber. His eyes were as a flame of fire; the hair of his head was white like the pure snow; his countenance shone above the brightness of the sun; and his voice was as the sound of the rushing of great waters, even the voice of Jehovah, saying:

"I am the first and the last; I am he who liveth, I am he who was slain; I am your advocate with the Father. Behold your sins are forgiven you; you are clean before me; therefore, lift up your heads and rejoice. Let the hearts of your brethren rejoice, and let the hearts of all my people rejoice, who have, with their might, built this house to my name.

"For behold, I have accepted this house, and my name shall be here; and I will manifest myself to my people in mercy in this house. Yea, I will appear unto my servants, and speak unto them with mine own voice, if my people will keep my commandments, and do not pollute this holy house. Yea, the hearts of thousands and tens of thousands shall greatly rejoice in consequence of the blessings which shall be poured out, and the endowment with which my servants have been endowed in this house. And the fame of this house shall spread to foreign lands; and this is the beginning of the blessing which shall be poured out upon the heads of my people, Even so, Amen.

"After this vision closed, the heavens were again opened unto us; and Moses appeared before us, and committed unto us the keys of the gathering of Israel from the four parts of the earth, and the leading of the ten tribes from the land of the north. After this, Elias appeared, and committed the dispensation of the gospel of Abraham, saying that in us and our seed all generations after us should be blessed.

"After this vision had closed, another great and glorious vision burst upon us; for Elijah the prophet, who was taken to heaven without tasting death, stood before us and said: Behold, the time is fully come, which was spoken of by the mouth of Malachi--testifying that he [Elijah] should be sent, before the great and dreadful day of the Lord come-- To turn the hearts of the fathers to the children, and the children to the fathers, lest the whole earth be smitten with a curse–

"Therefore, the keys of this dispensation are committed into you hands; and by this ye may know that the great and dreadful day of the Lord is near, even at the doors.(D&C 110:1-16; HC 2:435-436)

[Section 111]

This revelation given through Joseph Smith at Salem, Massachusetts August 6, 1836, was received at a time when the Church was heavily in debt. Joseph Smith, Sidney Rigdon and Oliver Cowdery had made the trip from Kirtland, preaching the gospel and transacting church business along the way. A promise of money they needed did not materialize, but the Lord chose to assure them He is mindful of the temporal needs of His servants, that He will deal mercifully with Zion and arrange all things for the good of His servants. A more complete discussion of this revelation's contents is in Chapter XIX, A ZION SOCIETY TO BE THE NEW WORLD ORDER. (D&C 111: 1-11; HC 2:465-466)

[Section 112]

Shortly after His resurrection, the Lord Jesus Christ appeared to His remaining apostles and charged them to go forth and preach the gospel to all the world and to every creature. In like manner, in the dispensation of the fulness of time; after the quorum of Twelve Apostles has been organized in 1835; and after Moses had appeared in the Kirtland Temple to bestow the keys of the gathering of Israel from where ever they are on earth; the Twelve apostles and prophets, as the foundation of the Church with Christ as its chief cornerstone; under the leadership of their President Thomas B. Marsh were charged with sending the gospel and raising voices of warning to all nations and people in Section 112, received through Joseph Smith July 23, 1837 at Kirtland, Ohio. This revelation was received on the same day the gospel was first preached in England by Heber C.

257

Kimball and others.

In this revelation the Lord admonishes the Twelve to take up their crosses and follow Jesus and to feed His sheep; and informed them that those who receive the First Presidency receive the Lord; that darkness covers the earth, and only those who believe and are baptized are saved; and that the First Presidency and the Twelve hold the keys of the dispensation of the fulness of times, as well as being the foundation of the Church. (D&C 112;1-34; HC 2:499-501)

[Section 113]

In March 1838, the Prophet Joseph Smith asked and the Lord answered selected questions relating to the writings of Isaiah.

"Who is the stem of Jesse spoken of in the 1st, 2d, 3d, 4th and 5th verses of the 11th chapter of Isaiah? Verily, thus saith the Lord: It is Christ?

"What is the rod spoken of in the first verse of the 11th chapter of Isaiah, that should come of the stem of Jesse? Behold, thus saith the Lord: It is a servant in the hands of Christ, who is partly a descendant of Jesse as well as Ephraim, or of the house of Joseph, on whom there is laid much power.

What is the root of Jesse spoken of in the 10th verse of the 11th chapter? Behold, thus saith the Lord, a descendant of Jesse, as well as of Joseph, unto whom rightly belongs the priesthood, and the keys of the kingdom, for an ensign, and for the gathering of my people in the last days." (v 1-6)

The remaining verses in Section 113 are reported in Chapter XIX, A ZION SOCIETY TO BE THE NEW WORLD ORDER.(D&C 113:1-10; HC 3:9-10)

[Section 114]

Revelation given through Joseph Smith at Far West, Missouri April 17, 1838 indicates church positions held by those who are not faithful, that is, those who do not bear testimony of His name and are not willing to go on missions to do the same, shall be given to others. (D&C 114 1-2; HC 3:23)

[Section 115]

Addressed to the presiding officers of the Church, revelation in Section 115, given through Joseph Smith April 26, 1838, the Lord named His Church, The Church of Jesus Christ of Latter-day Saints; that Zion and her stakes are places of defense and refuge for His covenant people, that they were to build a house of the Lord in Far West, and that Joseph Smith holds the keys of the kingdom of God on earth. Verses 1-6 are discussed in greater detail in Chapter XIX, A ZION SOCIETY TO BE THE NEW WORLD ORDER. [where should the remaining verses 7-19 be placed?]

[Section 116]

At a place called Spring Hill, Davies County, Missouri May 19, 1838, revelation was received through Joseph Smith indicating Spring Hill is the place where Adam shall come to visit his people just prior to the Millennium. For more on this verse Chapter XXI, THE SECOND COMING, CHRIST'S MILLENNIAL REIGN AND THE FINAL JUDGMENT. (D&C 116:1, HC 3:35)

[Section 117]

Revelation was received concerning the immediate duties of William Marks, Newell K. Whitney and Oliver Granger July 8, 1838 by Joseph Smith at Far West, Missouri. The Lord said His servants should not covet temporal things, for what is property to the Lord? And that they should forsake littleness of soul.

The Lord reaffirmed that He had created the fowls of heaven, the fish of the sea, and the beasts of the mountains, and that He holds the destinies of the armies of earth's nations in His hands; abd therefore is quite capable of causing solitary places to bud and blossom and bring forth in abundance. He chastised them for coveting temporal things, for neglecting weightier matters and for being reluctant to leave Kirtland, the property there and come to Zion in Missouri. (D&C 117:1-16; HC 3:45-46)

[Section 118]

The early latter-day church faced many crises as they were

attempting do what the Lord required, including a financial depression in the Kirtland, Ohio area, intense persecution there and in Missouri. By the summer of 1838, pressures on some leading brethren proved too much for them, and they became disaffected and/or fell away, including some members of the Quorum of Twelve. Joseph inquired of the Lord's will concerning the Twelve, and received an answer, July 8, 1838 at Far West, Missouri. The Lord's answer:

"...let the Twelve be organized; and let men be appointed to supply the place of those who are fallen. Let my servant Thomas [B Marsh] remain for a season in the land of Zion, to publish my word. Let the residue continue to preach from that hour, and if they will do this in all lowliness of heart, in meekness and humility, and long-suffering, I, the Lord, give unto them a promise that I will provide for their families; and an effectual door shall be opened for them, henceforth.

"And next spring let them depart to go over the great waters, and there promulgate my gospel, the fulness thereof, and bear record of my name. Let them take leave of my saints in the city of Far West, on the twenty-sixth day of April next, on the building spot of my house, saith the Lord.

"Let my servant John Taylor, and also my servant John E. Page, and also my servant Wilford Woodruff, and also my servant Willard Richards, be appointed to fill the places of those who have fallen, and be officially notified of their appointment." (D&C 118:1-6, HC 3:46-47)

[Section 119]

In answer to Joseph Smith's supplication "O Lord, show unto thy servants how much thou requirest of the properties of thy people for a tithing"; revelation was received July 8, 1838, at Far West, Missouri. The Lord answered the Saints were to pay their surplus property and then give, as tithing, one-tenth of their interest annually. For more discussion of tithing see Chapter XIX, A ZION SOCIETY

TO BE THE NEW WORLD ORDER. (D&C 119:1-7; HC 3:44, see also 64:23, 85:, and 97:11)

[Section 120]

The Lord made known the disposition of the properties tithed as named in the previous revelation, Section 119, through Section 129 given July 8, 1838 at Far West, Missouri. See Chapter XIX, A ZION SOCIETY TO BE THE NEW WORLD ORDER. (D&C 120:1)

[Section 121]

As the number of Saints in Missouri increased, persecution reached new heights when then Governor, Lilburn B. Boggs, issued an order October 27, 1838 which called for the Saints to leave the State of Missouri or be exterminated. The prophet and several other members were arrested and incarcerated without just cause.

Jailed with several companions in Liberty, Missouri for many months, in a room with a ceiling not high enough for the prophet to fully stand, and being there for crimes he and they had not committed, having failed in their appeals directed to executive officers and the judiciary; Joseph Smith petitioned the Lord in mighty prayer.

He pleaded in behalf of the suffering and persecuted Saints, the Lord's covenant people, in various parts of Missouri, Illinois and other places, and in his own behalf while languishing in jail.

Note here was the Lord's Prophet and several leading brethren of the Church in jail, not just overnight, but for months. Joseph had been party to many previous heavenly visitations including the visitation of the Father and the Son, many visits by the Angel Moroni, of John the Baptist, of Peter, James and John, of Moses, Elias and Elijah, and again by the Lord Jesus Christ himself, more recently in 1836 at the Kirtland, Ohio Temple.

After much pleading with the Lord for the suffering and persecuted Saints the Lord responded March 20, 1839. He cursed those who raised false cries of transgression against His people. These false accusers were not to have the right of priesthood but were damned instead. Suffering Saints who endure their trials valiantly are

261

promised glorious revelations. Why many are called, but few chosen is made clear. Personal righteousness as a guiding principle is essential to any man's use of the priesthood, or power to act for God.

"... Remember thy suffering saints, O our God; and thy servants will rejoice in thy name forever.

"My son, peace be unto thy soul; thine adversity and thine afflictions shall be but a small moment; And then, if thou endure it well, God shall exalt thee on high; thou shalt triumph over all thy foes. Thy friends stand by thee, and they shall hail thee again with warm hearts and friendly hands. Thou art not yet as Job; thy friends do not contend against thee, neither charge thee with transgression, as they did Job. And they who do charge thee with transgression, their hope shall be blasted, and their prospects shall melt away as the hoar frost melteth before the burning rays of the rising sun; ...

"Cursed are all those that shall lift up the heel against mine anointed, saith the Lord, and cry they have sinned when they have not sinned before me, saith the Lord, but have done that which was meet in mine eyes, and which I have commanded them. But those who cry transgression do it because they are the servants of sin, and are the childr0en of disobedience themselves. And those who swear falsely against my servants, that they might bring them into bondage and death-- Wo unto them; because they have offended my little ones they shall be severed from the ordinances of mine house...

"They shall not have right to the priesthood, nor their posterity after them from generation to generation. It had been better for them that a millstone had been hanged about their necks; and they drowned in the depths of the sea. Wo unto all those that discomfort my people, and drive, and murder, and testify against them, saith the Lord of Hosts; a generation of vipers shall not escape the damnation of hell. Behold, mine eyes see and know all their works, and I have in reserve a swift judgment in the season thereof, for them all. For there is a time appointed for every man, according as his works shall be." (v 6-25)

Switching to the positive and marvelous hope and promise of the future for those who endure their afflictions well, Joseph under the influence of the Lord continues:

"God shall give unto you knowledge by his Holy Spirit, yea, by the unspeakable gift of the Holy Ghost, that has not been revealed since the world was until now; Which our forefathers have awaited with anxious expectation to be revealed in the last times, which their minds were pointed to by the angels, as held in reserve for the fulness of their glory; A time to come in the which nothing shall be withheld, whether there be one God or many gods, they shall be made manifest.

"All thrones and dominions, principalities and powers, shall be revealed and set forth upon all who have endured valiantly for the gospel of Jesus Christ. And also, if there be bounds set to the heavens or to the seas, or to the dry land, or to the sun, moon, or stars--- All the times of their revolutions, all the appointed days, months, and years, and all their glories, laws, and set times, shall be revealed in the days of the fulness of times--According to that which was ordained in the midst of the Council of the Eternal God of all other gods before the world was, that should be reserved unto the finishing and the end thereof, when every man shall enter his eternal presence and into his immortal rest." (v 26-32)

No doubt feeling the euphoria of these uplifting moments while the Lord was guiding his words Joseph becomes even more eloquent.

"How long can rolling waters remain impure? What power shall stay the heavens? As well might man stretch forth his puny arm to stop the Missouri river in its decreed course, or to turn it up stream, as to hinder the Almighty from pouring down knowledge from heaven upon the heads of the Latter-day Saints. Behold, there are many called, but few are chosen? And why are they not chosen? Because their hearts are set so much upon the things of this world, and aspire to the honors of men, that they do not learn this one lesson-- That the rights of the priesthood are inseparably connected with the powers of heaven, and that the powers of heaven cannot be controlled nor handled only upon the principles of righteousness.

"That they may be conferred upon us, it is true; but when we undertake to cover our sins, or to gratify our pride, our vain ambitions, or to exercise control or dominion, or compulsion upon the souls of the children of men, in any degree of unrighteousness, behold, the heavens withdraw themselves; the Spirit of the Lord is grieved; and when it is withdrawn, Amen to the priesthood or authority of that man. Behold, ere he is aware, he is left to kick against the pricks, to persecute the saints and to fight against God.

"We have learned by sad experience that it is the nature and disposition of almost all men, as soon as the get a little authority, as they suppose, they will immediately begin the exercise unrighteous dominion. Hence many are called, but few are chosen. No power or influence can or ought to be maintained by virtue of the priesthood, only by persuasion, by long-suffering, by gentleness and meekness, and by love unfeigned; By kindness, and pure knowledge, which shall greatly enlarge the soul without hypocrisy, and without guile-- Reproving betimes with sharpness, when moved upon by the Holy Ghost; and then showing forth afterwards an increase of love toward him whom thou hast reproved, lest he esteem thee to be his enemy; That he may know that thy faithfulness is stronger than the cords of death.

"Let thy bowels also be full of charity towards all men, and to the household of faith, and let virtue garnish thy thoughts unceasingly; then shall thy confidence wax strong in the presence of God; and the doctrine of the priesthood shall distil upon thy soul as the dews from heaven. The Holy Ghost shall be thy constant companion, and thy scepter an unchanging scepter of righteousness and truth; and thy dominion shall be an everlasting dominion, and without compulsory means it shall flow unto thee forever and ever."(v 33-46; D&C 121:1-46;HC 3:289-300)

[Section 122]

While still in jail in Liberty, Missouri the word of the Lord came to Joseph Smith in March 1839. In it the Lord declared the ends of the earth shall inquire after the name of Joseph Smith, that his tribulations, trials and hardships shall give him experience and be for his benefit; and that the Son of Man had endured them all.

"...If thou art called to pass through tribulation; if thou art in perils among false brethren; if thou art in perils among robbers; if thou art in perils by land or by sea; If thou art accused with all manner of false accusations; if thine enemies fall upon thee; if they tear thee from the society of thy father and mother and brethren and sisters; and if with a drawn sword thine enemies tear thee from the bosom of thy wife, and of thine offspring, and thine elder son, although but six years of age, shall cling to thy garments, and shall say, My father, my father, why canst thou stay with us? O my father, what are the men going to do with you? and if then he shall be thrust from thee by the sword, and thou be dragged to prison, and thine enemies prowl around thee like wolves for the blood of the lamb;

"And if thou shouldst be cast into the pit, or into the hands of murderers, and the sentence of death passed upon thee; if thou be cast into the deep; if the billowing surge conspire against thee; if fierce winds become thine enemy; if the heavens gather blackness; and all the elements combine to hedge up the way; and above all, if the very jaws of hell shall gape open the mouth wide after thee, know thou, my son, that all these things shall give thee experience, and shall be for thy good. The Son of Man hath descended below them all. Art thou greater than he?

"Therefore, hold on thy way, and the priesthood shall remain with thee; for their bounds are set, they cannot pass. Thy days are known, and thy years shall not be numbered less; therefore, fear not what man can do, for God shall be with you forever and ever." (D&C 122:1-9;HC 3:300-301)

[Section 123]

While a prisoner in the jail at Liberty, Missouri, in March,

1839, Joseph Smith received a revelation concerning the Saint's duty in relation to their persecutors. They should collect and publish an account of their sufferings, and persecutions; that the same spirit that established the false creeds also leads to persecution of the Saints; and that notwithstanding persecutions and derision, many among all sects will yet receive the truth. More specifically,

"... not only publish to all the world, but present them to heads of the government... It is an imperative duty that we owe to God, to angels, with whom we shall be brought to stand, and also to ourselves, to our wives and children, who have been made to bow down with grief, sorrow, and care, under the most damning hand of murder, tyranny and oppression; supported and urged on and upheld by the influence of that spirit which hath so strongly riveted the creeds of the fathers, who have inherited lies, upon the hearts of the children, and filled the world with confusion... and is now the mainspring of all corruption, and the whole earth groans under the weight of iniquity...it is an imperative duty ... not only to our own wives and children, but to the widows and fatherless, whose husbands and fathers have been murdered under its iron hand ... also it is an imperative duty ... to all the rising generation, and to all the pure in heart--

"For there are many yet on the earth among all sects, parties, and denominations, who are blinded by the subtle craftiness of men, whereby they lie in wait to deceive, and WHO ARE ONLY KEPT FROM THE TRUTH BECAUSE THEY KNOW NOT WHERE TO FIND IT.[caps added]

"... Therefore, dearly beloved brethren, let us cheerfully do all things that lie in our power; and then may we stand still, with the utmost assurance, to see the salvation of God, and for his arm to be revealed."(D&C 123:1-17; HC 3:302-303)

[Section 124]

Because of illegal procedures, an exterminating order issued against them by the Governor, and other means of persecution the

Saints were compelled to leave the State of Missouri in late 1838 and 1839. By January 19, 1841 when Section 124 was received, the former village of Commerce, Illinois located on a bend in the Mississippi River had been built up and given the name Nauvoo, by the Saints and here the headquarters of the Church was now established.

In this revelation Joseph Smith is commanded to make a solemn proclamation of the gospel to the president of the United States, the governors, and the rulers of all nations; living and dead leaders were blessed for their integrity and virtues; the Saints were commanded to build both a house for the entertainment of strangers and a temple in Nauvoo; Baptisms for the dead heretofore performed in the open were hereafter to be performed in temples; performance of holy ordinances in temples has always been the reason the Lord's people build temples; because of the oppression of their enemies the Saints were excused from building a temple in Jackson County, Missouri; The Lord also gave directions for building the Nauvoo house and called Hyrum Smith to be a patriarch, and to receive keys and stand in the place of Oliver Cowdery, who was under Church discipline. Some general and local officers and their quorums were named and their duties given. More specifically,

"Verily, I say unto you, I now give unto you the officers belonging to my Priesthood, that ye may hold the keys thereof, even the Priesthood which is after the order of Melchizedek, which is after the order of mine Only Begotten son. First, I give unto you Hyrum Smith to be a patriarch unto you to hold the sealing blessings of the church, even the Holy Spirit of promise, whereby ye are sealed up unto the delay of redemption, that ye may not fall notwithstanding the hour of redemption that may come upon you.

"I give unto you my servant Joseph to be a presiding elder over all my church, to be a translator, a revelator, a seer, and a prophet. I give unto him for counselers my servant Sidney Rigdon and my servant William Law, that these may constitute a quorum and

267

First Presidency, to receive the oracles for the whole church.

"I give unto you my servant Brigham Young to be a president over the traveling counsel; Which twelve hold the keys to open up the authority of my kingdom upon the four corners of the earth, and after that, to send my word to every creature. They are Heber C. Kimball, Parley P. Pratt, Orson Pratt, Orson Hyde, William Smith, John Taylor, John E. Page, Wilford Woodruff, Willard Richards, George A. Smith. David Patten I have taken unto myself; behold his priesthood no man taketh from him; but verily I say unto you, another may be appointed unto the same calling." (v 123-130)

After setting forth the First Presidency and the twelve traveling council [Council of Twelve Apostles], the Lord set forth in this revelation the members of the standing high council for the corner-stone [stake] of Zion;

the presidency for the quorum of high priests; the presidency for the quorum of elders as standing ministers; the seven presidents of the quorum of seventies. who were to

"bear record of my name in all the world, wherever the traveling high council [Council of Twelve] mine apostles, shall send them to prepare a way before my face." (131-140)

A bishopric comprised of Vinson Knight, Samuel H, Smith and Shadrack Roundy was also called, as well as presidencies of the lesser offices of the priesthood:

"The above offices I have given unto you [said the Lord], and the leys thereof, for helps and for governments, for the work of the ministry and the perfecting of my saints. And a commandment I give unto you, that you should fill all these offices and approve of those names which I have mentioned, or else disapprove of them at my general conference; And that ye should prepare rooms for all these offices in my house when you build it unto my name, saith the Lord your God..." (v 141-145; D&C 124:1-145; HC 3:175)

[Section 125]

Revelation given through Joseph Smith at Nauvoo, Illinois in

March 1841 concerning the settlement of the Saints in the territory of Iowa. See Chapter XVI, THE GATHERING ... BEGINS. (D&C 125:1-4; HC 4:311-312)

[Section 126]

Addressing Brigham Young, now President of the Quorum of Twelve Apostles, through the Prophet Joseph Smith in Brigham's home at Nauvoo, Illinois July 9, 1841, the Lord commends Brigham for his labors and he is relieved of any future travel abroad.

"...it is no more required at this time at your hand to leave your family as in times past, for your offering is acceptable to me. I have seen your labor and toil in journeying for my name. I therefore command you to send my word abroad, and take especial care of your family from this time, henceforth and forever, Amen."(D&C 126:1-3;HC 4:382)

The President of the Quorum of Twelve currently continues in a similar leading role related to missionary work sending God's word throughout the earth.

The Wentworth Letter

Mr. John Wentworth, Editor and Proprietor of the Chicago Democrat newspaper requested information from Joseph Smith and the Church, to furnish his friend who was writing a history of New Hampshire. The Prophet Joseph Smith responded with a sketch of the rise, progress, persecution and faith of the Latter-day Saints to date which was March 1, 1842. Now considered to be one of the choicest documents in Church history, this letter is the earliest published document of the Prophet's own consecutive narrative of events. Published in the Times and Seasons March 15, 1842, was Joseph's own extractions from his journals. It is "a remarkable full history of the leading events in the Church, and an epitome of her doctrines from the beginning [the birth of the Prophet in 1805] up to the date of publication in March 1842, a period of thirty-six years. "The epitome of the doctrines of the Church, since called the Articles of Faith "... has been carried to all the nations of the earth and tribes of men where the gospel has been preached. "These Articles of Faith were ... "struck off by one inspired mind at a single effort to make a declaration of that which is most assuredly believed by the Church, for one making earnest inquiry about the truth. The combined correctness, perspicuity, simplicity and comprehensiveness of this statement of our religion may be relied upon as strong evidence of a divine inspiration resting upon the Prophet Joseph Smith." (HC IV: 535)

In this letter Joseph Smith rehearses his birth and early life experiences; his decision to ask God what church was right, the appearance of the Father and the Son, their answer "to go not after them", [the other churches] because at some future date the fulness of the gospel would be made known to him. Joseph rehearsed the appearance of the Angel Moroni, the coming forth of the Book of Mormon, and a brief description of its appearance and contents.

Of the Book of Mormon the Prophet wrote:

"This book also tells us that our Savior made his appearance upon this Continent after his resurrection; that he planted the Gospel here in all of its fulness and richness and power, and blessing; that they had Apostles, Prophets, Pastors, Teachers, and Evangelists; the same order of the same priesthood, the same ordinances, gifts, powers and blessings, as were enjoyed in the eastern continent, that the people were cut off in consequence of their transgressions, that the last of their prophets who existed among them were commanded to write an abridgement of their prophecies, history, etc, and to hide it up in the earth, and that it should come forth and be united with the Bible for the accomplishment of the purposes of God in these last days..."

After describing the Church's organization, its rapid growth, and the persecution that followed, he concluded his letter with a preamble to thirteen Articles of Faith by declaring:

"... the Standard of Truth has been erected; no unhallowed hand can stop the work from progressing; persecutions may rage, mobs may combine, armies may assemble, calumny may defame, but the truth of God will go forth boldly, nobly, and independent, till it has penetrated every continent, visited every clime, swept every country, and sounded in every ear, till the purposes of God shall be accomplished, and the Great Jehovah shall say the work is done - We beleive in God the Eternal Father, and in His Son Jesus Christ and in the Holy Ghost..." (HC IV 535-540)

[Section 127]

Directions pertaining to baptisms for the dead were contained in a letter dated September 1, 1842 at Nauvoo, Illinois. In it Joseph Smith considered it an honor to be persecuted for the Lord's sake. Also in this revelation the Lord specified the need for records to be kept relative to baptisms for the dead. More specific instructions are reported in Chapter XX pertaining the PERFECTION AND REDEMPTION OF THE LIVING AND THE DEAD.(D&C 127:1-12; HC 5:142-144)

[Section 128]

Further directions on baptisms for the dead are set forth dated September 6, 1842 at Joseph Smith's hand in Nauvoo, Illinois. In these revelations the Lord states that local and general recorders are to certify to the fact of baptisms for the dead; that their records are binding and recorded on earth and in heaven; that the baptismal font is a similitude of the grave; and that Elijah restored power relative to baptism for the dead. The Lord reaffirms that all the keys, power, and authorities of past dispensations have been restored, and glad and glorious tidings are acclaimed for the redemption of living and the dead who enter the covenant and keep its provisions. More specifically [to be completed] (D&C 128:1-25; HC 5:148-153)

This section is discussed in greater detail in Chapter XX.

[Section 129]

As the Second Coming approaches and communication from the heavens becomes more frequent, it is important to be able to distinguish true ministering angels and spirits sent from God, from those sent by Satan. On February 9, 1843 the Lord made clear through Joseph Smith at Nauvoo, Illnois there are three grand keys by which they may be distinguished, and revealed that there are both resurrected and spirit bodies in heaven.   More specifcally,

"There are two kinds of beings in heaven, namely: Angels, who are resurrected personages, having bodies of flesh and bones-- For instance, Jesus said: 'Handle me and se, for a spirit hath not flesh and bones as ye see me have.' Secondly: the spirits of just men made perfect, they who are not resurrected, but inherit the same glory.

"When a messenger comes saying he has a message from God, offer him your hand and request him to shake hands with you. If he be an angel he will do so, and you will feel his hand.

"If he be a spirit of a just man made perfect he will come in his glory; for that is the only way he can appear-- Ask him to shake hands with you, but he will not move, because it is contrary to the order of heaven for a just man to deceive, but he will still deliver his message.

"If he be the devil as an angel of light, when you ask him to shake hands, he will offer you his hand, and you will not feel anything; you may therefore detect him. These are three grand keys whereby you may know whether any administration is from God." (D&C 129: 1-9; HC 5:267)

[Section 130]
Instructions given by Joseph Smith at Ramus, Illinois April 2, 1843. See Chapter XX, THE PERFECTION AND REDEMPTION OF THE LIVING AND THE DEAD ARE INTEGRAL PARTS OF A ZION SOCIETY

[Section 131]
Instructions given by Joseph Smith at Ramus, Illinois May 16 and 17, 1843 included
that celestial marriage in temples is essential to exaltation in the highest heaven. It also describes how men are sealed up unto eternal life. For more, see Chapter XX, THE PERFECTION AND

REDEMPTION OF THE LIVING AND THE DEAD ARE INTEGRAL PARTS OF A ZION SOCIETY.

In addition the Prophet said:

"There is no such thing as immaterial matter. All Spirit is matter, but it is more fine and pure, and can only be discerned by purer eyes; We cannot see it; but when our bodies are purified, we shall see that it is all matter." (D&C 131:1-8;HC 5:392-393)

[Section 132]

From historical records it is clear that the doctrines and principles involved in this revelation had been known by the prophet since 1831, but had not been officially recorded. They relate to the new and everlasting covenant the Lord had referenced a number of times and places since the Church's organization in 1830. When recorded July 12, 1843 this revelation included the eternal nature of the marriage covenant.

In this revelation the Lord makes clear that exaltation is gained through the new and everlasting covenant and sets forth the terms and conditions of that covenant; that celestial marriage and a continuation of the family unit enable men to become gods; and that the strait and narrow way leads to eternal lives. The Lord gave the law relative to blasphemy against the Holy Ghost and revealed promises of eternal increase and exaltation made to prophets and Saints in all ages. The Lord declared that Joseph Smith was given the power to bind and seal on earth and in heaven and reported Joseph Smith had sealed upon him his exaltation. Emma Smith is counseled to be faithful and true, and the law of plurallity of wives are set forth. For more specificity see Chapter XX PERFECTION AND REDEMPTION OF THE LIVING AND THE DEAD ARE INTEGRAL PARTS OF A ZION SOCIETY.

[Section 133]
Discussed in Chapter XXI
[Section 134]
Discussed in Chapter XIII

[Section 135]

Much has been written about the martyrdom of Joseph Smith, and his brother Hyrum Smith, June 27, 1844, the events that led up to it and the consequences of those actions for the covenant people of Israel, the true believers in Messiah/Christ; and for the world at large. Therefore, this book contains only a summation by an eyewitness written by John Taylor, member of the Quorum of Twelve, known as Section 135 which is included here.

"To seal the testimony of this book and the Book of Mormon, we announce the martyrdom of Joseph Smith, the Prophet, and Hyrum Smith the Patriarch. They were shot in Carthage jail, on the 27th of June, 1844, about five o'clock p.m., by an armed mob-- painted black-- of men 150 to 200 persons. Hyrum was shot first and fell calmly, exclaiming: I am a dead man! Joseph leaped from the window, and was shot dead in the attempt, exclaiming: O Lord my God! They were both shot after they were dead, in a brutal manner, and both received four balls.

"John Taylor and Willard Richards, two of the Twelve, were the only persons in the room at the time; the former was wounded in a savage manner with four balls, but has since recovered; the latter, through the providence of God, escaped, without even a hole in his robe.

"Joseph Smith, the Prophet and Seer of the Lord, has done more, save Jesus Only, for the salvation of men in this world, than any other man that ever lived in it. In the short space of twenty years, he has brought forth the Book of Mormon, which he translated by the gift and power of God, and has been the means of publishing it on two continents; has sent the fulness of the everlasting gospel, which it contained, to the four quarters of the earth; had brought forth the revelations and commandments which compose this book of Doctrine and Covenants, and many other wise documents and instructions for the benefit of the children of men; gathered many thousands of the Latter-day Saints, founded a great city, and left a fame and name that cannot be slain. He lived great, and he died great in the eyes of God and his people; and like most of the Lord's anointed in ancient times, has sealed his mission and his works with his own blood; and so has his brother Hyrum. In life they were not divided, and in death they were not separated!

"When Joseph went to Carthage to deliver himself up to the pretended requirements of the law, two or three days previous to his assassination, he said: 'I am going like a lamb to the slaughter; but I am calm as a summer's morning; I have a conscience void of offense towards God, and towards all men. I SHALL DIE INNOCENT, AND IT SHALL YET BE SAID OF ME--HE WAS MURDERED IN COLD BLOOD.' The same morning, after Hyrum had made ready to go--shall it be said to the slaughter? yes, for so it was--he read the following paragraph, near the close of the twelfth chapter of Ether, in the Book of Mormon and turned down the leaf upon it:

"'And it came to pass that I prayed unto the Lord that he would give unto the Gentiles grace, that they might have charity. And it came to pass that the Lord said unto me: If they have not charity it mattereth not unto thee, thou has been faithful; wherefore thy garments shall be made clean. And because thou hast seen thy weakness, thou shalt be made strong, even unto the sitting down in the place which I have prepared in the mansions of my Father. And now I ... bid farewell unto the Gentiles; yea, and also unto my brethren whom I love, until we shall meet before the judgment-seat of Christ, where all men shall know that my garments are not spotted with your blood.' The testators are now dead, and their testament is in force.

"Hyrum Smith was forty-four years old in February 1844, and Joseph Smith was thirty-eight in December, 1843; and hence forward their names will be classed among the martyrs of religion; and the reader in every nation will be reminded that the Book of Mormon, and this book of Doctrine and Covenants of the church cost the best blood of the nineteenth century to bring them forth for the salvation of a ruined world; and that if the fire can scathe a green tree for the glory of God, how easy it will burn up the dry trees to purify the vineyard of corruption. They lived for glory; they died for glory; and glory is their eternal reward. From age to age shall their names go down to posterity as gems for the sanctified..." (D&C 135:1-7; HC 6:629-631)

THE RUPP ARTICLE

Just twenty-two days before his death, on June 5, 1844, Joseph Smith acknowledged receipt of a book entitled, **An Original History of the Religious Denominations at Present Existing in the United States,** which had been sent him earlier that spring. The book, edited by I. Daniel Rupp of Lancaster, Pennsylvania, contained an article written by the Prophet called **The History of the Latter-day Saints.** (HC IV, p.428)

The Charles Desilver Company of Philadelphia appears to have printed the article again in 1859, along with others contained in a volume, **The Religious Denominations in the United States.** This volume introduced its contents with these words: "The Religious Denominations in the United States, Their Past History, Present Condition, and Doctrines Accurately Set Forth in Fifty Carefully Prepared Articles Written by Eminent Clerical and Lay Authors Connected with the Respective Persuasions." (Rupp Article Title Page)

The preface of Rupp's volume continues, "Each sect having been afforded an opportunity of presenting its own history, all danger of misrepresentation is thereby completely avoided, and the public may rely upon having a 'History of Religious Denominations' which is free from the objections usually urged against books of this character. (Ibid., Preface)

Joseph Smith was pleased with the article as evidenced by his letter to Rupp dated June 5, 1844: "... The design, the propriety, the wisdom of letting every sect tell its own story, and the elegant manner in which the work appears have filled my breast with encomiums [high praise] upon it; wishing you God Speed.

"... I shall be pleased to furnish further information, at a proper time, and render you such service as the work, and vast extension of our church may demand, for the benefit of truth, virtue and holiness. Your work will be suitably noticed in our paper for your benefit." (Smith, op. sit., p. 428)

The Rupp volume notes that "Smith never redeemed his promises. He, and his brother Hyrum Smith were killed in jail, at Carthage, Illinois, June 28, 1844." (Rupp, op. sit. p. 348)

The History of the Latter-day Saints contained in the Rupp volume resembles the celebrated Wentworth Letter, which "is one of the choicest documents in our church literature." (Smith, op. sit., Vol IV. p . 435)

The Rupp Article contains important information not included in the Wentworth letter. For example, the Rupp Article includes a paragraph on the construction of the Nauvoo Temple, "... being built by the direct revelation of Jesus Christ for the salvation of the living and the dead. It also contains an introductory paragraph which declares, "The Church of Jesus Christ of Latter-day Saints was founded upon direct revelation, as the true Church of God has ever been, according to the scriptures [Amos 3: 7 and Acts 1:2], and through the will and blessings of God, I have been an instrument in His hands, thus far, to move forward the cause of Zion." (Ibid., p. 344) Missionary work was cited indicating that missionaries had also been sent to Egypt and the Islands of the Pacific, and "are now preparing to open the door in the extensive dominions of Russia." (Rupp, op.sit., p.347) However, the killing of Joseph Smith and his brother Hyrum changed all that.

[Section 136]

Pressured out of Illinois two and a half years after Joseph Smith was martyred, the Saints, under the leadership of the Quorum of Twelve Apostles, with Brigham Young as President, the main body of Saints, en route to the Salt Lake Valley, had made their way to a place near Council Bluffs, Iowa. There the Camp of Israel, as the departing body of Saints was called, set up Winter Quarters on the west bank of the Missouri River.

There the Lord spoke through his new prophet Brigham Young, giving His word and will concerning how the Camp of Israel was to be organized for their westward journey; instructed the traveling Saints to live numerous gospel standards; encouraged them to sing, dance, pray and learn wisdom on the way; and addressing the martyrdom of Joseph Smith, informed them prophets are slain that they might be honored and the wicked condemned. See Chapter XIX, A ZION SOCIETY, TO THE THE NEW WORLD ORDER.

[Section 138]

Seventy years after the Saint's arrival in the Salt Lake Valley, following their forced departure from Nauvoo, Illinois and leaving the Lord's Temple there, the Lord provided great additional insight concerning the perfection and redemption of the living and the dead given through the Prophet Joseph F. Smith in a vision October 3, 1918. During this seventy year period four temples had been built and placed into operation: the Saint George, Manti, Logan and Salt Lake Temples, all in Utah.

President Smith declared that he had received several divine communications during the previous months, among them, what is now Section 138. While pondering the writings of Peter and our Lord's visit to the spirit world, he saw the righteous dead assembled in paradise, and Christ's ministry among them; he saw how preaching the gospel was organized among the spirits; he saw Adam, Eve and many of the holy prophets in the spirit world who considered their spirit state before their resurrection as a bondage, and noted that the righteous dead of this day continue their labors in the world of spirits; all of which will be discussed in greater detail in Chapter XX, THE PERFECTION AND REDEMPTION OF THE LIVING AND THE DEAD, ARE INTEGRAL PARTS OF A ZION SOCIETY.

CHAPTER XV

THE GATHERING OF ISRAEL SPIRITUALLY AND GEOGRAPHICALLY IS FORESHADOWED, THE PERFECTION AND REDEMPTION OF ITS MEMBERS IS PROCLAIMED

Before we focus our attention on the gathering, let us briefly mention the scattering which helps us understand the many references to, and the need for the gathering of Israel. As previously mentioned, Israel is the name used to denote Jacob, son of Isaac, grandson of Abraham, through whom the covenant originally made with Adam, Enoch and Noah was continued. As explained by Paul, (Rom. 10:1; 11:17; Gal. 6:16; Eph. 2:12) in a broader sense, Israel means the true believers in Messiah/Christ, regardless of lineage or geographical location.

While all mortals can claim God as the common father of their spirits, the promises made to Israel only apply to those who accept Messiah/Christ through covenant and follow His teachings. Belief in Messiah/Christ therefore, becomes the mechanism for gathering the children of the covenant. Those gathered to the covenant who have kept its provisions will be found heirs and joint heirs with Messiah/Christ to all that the Father has.

Through the allegory of the Olive Tree, Book of Mormon prophet Zenos teaches us the principle of the scattering and gathering of Israel. We are taught that they were and are not random events, but were carefully planned and handled by the master of the vineyard with the outcome in mind. The "Scattering of Israel" means the scattering of Israel's descendants throughout the world and the title of a book with that name which discusses the subject extensively. As a reminder, to set the stage for the topic of the gathering, perfection and redemption of Israel, some of the reasons for the scattering should be set forth.

Some were scattered (1) because of their righteousness to protect them from those who had fallen away and who sought their lives (2) to preserve and add to scriptures previously recorded by righteous prophets.

(3) The main body of Israelites comprised of descendants of all twelve tribes of Israel, who had been placed under covenant by the Lord through His prophets Moses and Joshua, however, were scattered throughout the earth, because they had broken their covenant with God through collective and individual sin, disobedience and idol worship.

To fulfill His promises to their faithful forebears, Abraham and Sarah, Isaac and Rebekah, and Jacob/Israel and his wives, the Lord has turned the scattering of Israel to useful purposes, regardless of the initial reasons for their being scattered. Through the scattering, the covenant blood has been mingled with the blood of most, if not all, nations, tongues and peoples.

Whether by blood or by adoption, all may now lay claim to the blood of Abraham, and to the promise that through Abraham's and Israel's posterity all the families of the earth would be blessed. All of Abraham's and Israel's literal and adopted posterity entering the covenant become candidates for salvation and exaltation in God's kingdom through the atoning sacrifice of Messiah /Christ, by faith in the Lord Jesus Christ, repentance, baptism by immersion for the remission of sins, and by receiving the gift of the Holy Ghost from one having authority.

Foreshadowing the scattering, the Lord promised Abraham, then Isaac and then Jacob before each had any, that their posterity would become as numerous as the dust of the earth and would spread abroad. The same promise was given to the sons of Israel, such as Joseph. To Jacob/Israel, before he met Rachel or Leah or had children, the Lord said:

"thy seed shall be as the dust of the earth, and thou shalt spread abroad to the west ... east ... north ... and to the south; and in thee and in thy seed shall all the families of the earth be blessed." (Gen.28:14)

To Joseph, the Lord said through Israel,

"Joseph is a fruitful bough, even a fruitful bough by a well; whose branches run over the wall." (Gen. 49:22)

To Ephraim, son of Joseph, the Lord said, through Israel,

"he and his seed shall become a multitude of nations", and to his brother Manasseh, the Lord declared, "he also shall become a people, and he also shall be great." (Gen. 49:19)

Other references to the scattering are found in Leviticus, Deuteronomy, 1st and 2nd Kings, Jeremiah, Ezekiel, Hosea, Amos, Matthew, Luke, John, Romans, 1st and 2nd Nephi, Jacob, Omni, Helaman, 3rd Nephi, Ether, and the Doctrine and Covenants. For a more extensive treatment of the Scattering of Israel the reader is referred to the above references and to the author's book by that title soon to be published.

Just as the scattering was foreshadowed by the Lord's prophets so was the gathering, perfection and redemption of Israel. The prophet Moses foreshadowed the scattering and gathering before the children of Israel entered the promised land in these words :

[From Deuteronomy]

"Take heed unto yourselves, lest ye forget the covenant of the Lord your God, which he hath made with you... When thou shalt beget children, and children's children, and ye have remained long in the land, and corrupt yourselves and make a graven image... and shall do evil in the sight of the Lord thy God... I call heaven and earth to witness against you this day, that ye shall soon utterly perish from off the land whereunto ye go over Jordan to possess it ... And the Lord shall scatter you among the nations, and ye shall be left few in number among the heathen whither the Lord shall lead you. And there ye shall serve gods, the work of men's hands, wood and stone, which neither see, nor hear, nor eat, nor smell.

"But if from thence thou shalt seek the Lord thy God, thou shalt find him, if thou seek him with all thy heart and with all thy soul. When thou art in tribulation, and all these things are come upon thee, even in the latter days, if thou turn to the Lord thy God, and be obedient unto his voice; (For the Lord thy God is a merciful God) he will not forsake thee, neither destroy thee, nor forget the covenant of thy fathers which he sware unto them." (Deut. 4:23-31)

Again from the prophet Moses to the children of Israel before they entered the promised land, and reiterated by the prophets Jeremiah and Ezekiel to those remaining in Jerusalem who were about to be taken captive by the Babylonians:

"And it shall come to pass when all these things are come upon thee ... And [thou] shalt return unto the Lord thy God and shalt obey his voice according to all that I command thee this day, thou and thy children, with all thine heart, and with all thy soul; That then the Lord thy God will turn thy captivity, and have compassion upon thee, and will return and gather thee from all the nations, whither the Lord thy God hath scattered thee."(Deut.30:14)

[From Psalms]

In Psalms we read that Israel will rise up and thank the Lord when they are gathered and redeemed.

"O give thanks unto the Lord, for he is good: for his mercy endureth forever. Let the redeemed of the Lord say so, whom he hath redeemed from the hand of the enemy: And gathered them out of the lands, from the east .. west .. north, and ... south."(Ps. 107:1-3)

[From Isaiah, reiterated by Nephi]

"And he will lift up an ensign to the nations from far and will hiss [whistle] unto them from the end of the earth: and behold, they shall come with speed swiftly." (Isa. 5:26; 2Ne 15:26)

[From Isaiah and Nephi]

"And the Lord have removed men far away, and there be a great forsaking in the midst of the land. But yet in it shall be a tenth [remnant] and it shall return ..." (Isa. 6:13; 2Ne:13)

[From Isaiah and Nephi]

"And it shall come to pass in that day, that the remnant of Israel, and such as are escaped of the house of Jacob, shall no more again stay upon him that smote him; but shall stay upon the Lord, the Holy One of Israel in truth. The remnant shall return, even the remnant of Jacob unto the mighty God. For though thy people Israel be as the sand of the sea; yet a remnant of them shall return: the consumption decreed shall overflow with righteousness.(Isa.10:20-22; 2Ne20:20-22)

[From the prophet Isaiah]

After describing aspects of the Millennium Isaiah said:

"And it shall come to pass in that day, that the Lord shall set his hand again a second time to recover the remnant of his people, which shall be left from Assyria, and from Egypt, and from Pathros, and from Cush, and from Elam, and from Shinar, and from Hamath, and from the isles of the sea. And he shall set up an ensign for the nations, and shall assemble the outcasts of Israel, and gather together the dispersed of Judah from the four corners of the earth."(Isa. 11:11-12)

"He [the Lord] shall cause them that come of Jacob to take root: Israel shall blossom and bud and fill the earth with fruit," said Isaiah, "... And it shall come to pass in that day, ... ye shall be gathered one by one, O ye children of Israel ... and shall worship the Lord in the holy mount at Jerusalem." (Isa. 27:6,12)

In the day of restoration:

"The wilderness and the solitary place shall be glad for them; and the desert shall rejoice, and blossom as the rose... No lion shall be there, nor any ravenous beast shall go up thereon, it shall not be found there; but the redeemed shall walk there; And the ransomed of the Lord shall return, and come to Zion with songs of everlasting joy upon their heads: they shall obtain joy and gladness, and sorrow and sighing shall flee away." (Isa. 35: 1,9,10)

"But now thus saith the Lord that created thee O Jacob, and he that formed thee, O Israel, Fear not: for I have redeemed thee, I have called thee by thy name; thou art mine... For I am the Lord thy God, the Holy One of Israel, thy Saviour... Fear not for I am with thee: I will bring thy seed from the east, and gather thee from the west; I will say to the north, give up; and to the south, Keep not back; bring my sons from far, and my daughters from the ends of the earth." (Isa. 43:1,3,5,6)

"Listen, O isles of the sea; and hearken, ye people from far; The Lord hath ... said unto me, Thou art my servant, O Israel, in whom I will be glorified... And now, saith the Lord that formed me from the womb to be his servant, to bring Jacob again to him... It is a light thing that thou shouldst be my servant to raise up the tribes of Jacob, and to restore the preserved of Israel: I will also give thee for a light to the Gentiles, That thou mayest be my salvation unto the end of the earth.... Thus saith the Lord, In an acceptable time have I heard thee, and in a day of salvation have I helped thee: and I will preserve thee, and give thee for a covenant of the people, to establish the earth, to cause to inherit the desolate heritages;

[Note that this and other scriptures refer to Messiah/Christ as the "light of the world". With reference to the Gathering, it implies He will do the Gathering with the help of those in the covenant, and that the ultimate rewards of redemption will be given to those who embrace the Savior by covenant; even those heretofore prisoners who shall go free, and them that are in darkness who now have the light of Messiah/Christ.]

"That thou mayest say to the prisoners, Go forth, to them that are in darkness, Shew yourselves. They shall feed in the ways, and their pastures shall be in all high places. They shall not hunger nor thirst; neither shall the heat nor sun smite them: for he that hath mercy on them shall lead them, even by the springs of water shall he guide them. And I will make all my mountains a way, and my highways shall be exalted. Behold these shall come from far: and lo, these from the north and from the west; and these from the land of Sinim. Sing O heavens; and be joyous O earth; and break forth into singing, O mountains: for the Lord hath comforted his people, and will have mercy upon his afflicted....Lift up thine eyes round about, and behold: all these gather themselves together and come to thee.

[It seems the Lord's reference to "mountains" in metaphor, relates to temples, where the children of God receive covenants.]

"Thus saith the Lord God, Behold, I will lift up mine hand to the Gentiles, and set up a standard to the people: And they shall bring thy sons in their arms and thy daughters shall be carried upon their shoulders. And kings shall be thy nursing fathers and their queens thy nursing mothers... and thou shalt know that I am the Lord: for they shall not be ashamed that wait for me... and all flesh shall know that I the Lord am thy Saviour and thy Redeemer, the mighty One of Jacob." (Isa.49:1-26)

"Therefore the redeemed of the Lord shall return, and come with singing unto Zion; and everlasting joy shall be upon their head: they shall obtain gladness and joy; and sorrow and mourning shall flee away." (Isa. 51:11, re-iterated by the Book of Mormon prophet Nephi 2Ne 8:11)

[Metaphorically the Lord refers to Himself as the "husband" who has a duty to take care of His "wife", to protect her and provide for her, and to Israel, the children of the covenant, as His "wife".]

To Israel the Lord said:

"For thy Maker is thine husband; the Lord of hosts is his name; and thy Redeemer thy Holy One of Israel; the God of the whole earth shall he be called. For the Lord hath called thee as a woman forsaken and grieved in spirit ... For a small moment have I forsaken thee; but with great mercies will I gather thee. In a little wrath hid I my face from thee for a moment; but with everlasting kindness will I have mercy on thee, saith the Lord thy Redeemer." (Isa. 54:5-8)

"The Lord God which gathereth the outcasts of Israel saith, Yet will I gather others to him, beside those that are gathered unto him." (Isa. 56:8; Ps 147:20)

[From the prophet Jeremiah]

"Turn, O backsliding children, saith the Lord, for I am married unto you; and I will take you one of a city, and two of a family, and

I will bring you to Zion. And I will give you pastors according to mine heart, which shall feed you with knowledge and understanding ... At that time they shall call Jerusalem the throne of the Lord; and all the nations shall be gathered unto it, to the name of the Lord, to Jerusalem... In those days the house of Judah shall walk with the house of Israel and they shall come together out of the land of the north to the land that I have given for an inheritance unto their fathers." (Jer. 3:14,15,17,18)

[Those gathered will be on the basis of their covenant relationship to Him and not on the basis of their geographical proximity to Him or His covenant people. Animosity between Judah's posterity and the posterity of the other tribes of Israel will cease and they will work together under the leadership of Messiah/Christ as King of Kings and Lord of Lords.]

"Thus saith the Lord against all my evil neighbors, that touch the inheritance which I have caused my people Israel to inherit; Behold, I will pluck out the house of Judah from among them. And it shall come to pass, after that I have plucked them out I will return, and have compassion on them, and will bring them again, every man to his heritage and every man to his land. (Jer. 12:14-15)

"Therefore, behold, the days come, saith the Lord, that it shall no more be said, The Lord liveth, that brought up the children of Israel out of the land of Egypt; But, The Lord liveth, that brought up the children of Israel from the land of the north, and from all the lands whither he had driven them; and I will bring them again into their land that I gave unto their fathers. Behold, I will send forth many fishers, saith the Lord, and they shall fish them; and after will I send for many hunters, and they shall hunt them from every mountain, and from every hill, and out of the holes of the rocks." (Jer. 16:14-16)

"And I will gather the remnant of my flock out of all countries whither I have driven them, and will bring them again unto their folds; and they shall be fruitful and increase. And I shall set up shepherds over them which shall feed them; and they shall fear no more, nor be dismayed, neither shall they be lacking saith the Lord.

"In his [King Messiah's] days Judah shall be saved, and Israel shall dwell in safety: and this is his name whereby he shall be called, THE LORD IS OUR RIGHTEOUSNESS. Therefore, behold, the days come sayeth the Lord, that they shall no more say, The Lord liveth, which brought up the children of Israel out of the land of Egypt; But the Lord liveth, which brought up and which led the seed of the house of Israel out of the north country, and from all countries whither I have driven them; and they shall dwell in their own land." (Jer. 23:3-8)

[Jeremiah seems to be saying that as great as the gathering of ancient Israel out of Egypt and the Lord's leading them to the promised land of Canaan was; the latter-day gathering of Israel from the lands of the north and from all the world, and bringing them to their lands of inheritance will be much greater; and the Lord will be so recognized for it. In Moses' day the children of covenant, or Israel, no doubt, knew something important was happening to them, but still did not fully accept it as a divine manifestation that over-arched everything in their lives. They repeatedly turned to idol worship rather that submit themselves, by obedience, to the Lord.

As the massive movement of people from the lands of the north and other places, to the lands of their inheritance, commences in these last days, the world's people will witness a great event is taking place. But will they be motivated to change behaviors and become part of it, or will they, in their unrepentant and wicked state remain knowing bystanders, who are gathered and burned as stubble during His coming?]

"And ye shall seek me, and find me, when ye shall search for me with all your heart. And I will be found of you, saith the Lord: and I will turn away your captivity and I will gather you from all the nations and from all the places whither I have driven you, saith the Lord, and I will bring you again unto the place whence I caused you to be taken away captive ... and I will cause them to dwell safely: and they shall be my people, and I will be their God: And I will give them one heart and one way ... and I will make an everlasting covenant with them ... Yea, I will rejoice over them to do them good, and I will plant them in this land assuredly with my whole heart and with my whole soul." (Jer. 28:13-14; 32:37-41)

[Here Jeremiah, without naming it as such, suggests gathered Israel will dwell safely in Zion, where the people shall be recognized as God's people, planted there by him, living in the harmony of one heart and one way, under a {new} and everlasting covenant; and that the Lord would bring all this about with all His heart and soul.]

" For lo, the days come, saith the Lord ... Israel and Judah ... I will cause them to return to the land that I gave to their fathers, and they shall possess it."(Jer.30:3)

"Hear the word of the Lord, O ye nations, and declare it in the isles afar off, and say, He that scattered Israel will gather him, and keep him, as a shepherd doth his flock." (Jer. 31:10)

"In those days, and in that time, saith the Lord, the children of Israel shall come, they and the children of Judah together, going and weeping; they shall go, and seek the Lord their God. They shall ask the way to Zion with their faces northward, saying, Come let us join ourselves to the Lord in a perpetual covenant that shall not be forgotten... And I will bring Israel again to his habitation ...

"In those days, and in that time, saith the Lord, the iniquity of Israel shall be sought for, and there shall be none; and the sins of Judah, and they shall not be found: for I will pardon them whom I reserve."(Jer. 50: 4,5,19,20)

Reconciliation of the kingdoms of Judah and Israel after their estrangement, following the United Kingdom's breakup and their members being scatttered, will take place as part of Israel's gathering in the last days. Another Testament of Jesus Christ, the Book of Mormon, explains the Savior's role as mediator of the covenant helps dissolve the estrangement of Judah and Israel. That dissolution has already begun.

Of note is that the title page of this other testament of Jesus Christ, or the Book of Mormon, suggests that one of its purposes is to "show the remnant of the house of Israel what great things the Lord hath done for their fathers, and that they may know the covenants of the Lord that they are not cast off forever..."

It is conceivable that other groups who were scattered could also come forward with similar records, and that the Lord will follow a comparable pattern established with the people of the Americas. Given father Israel's blessing to Joseph, that his posterity would be "as a fruitful bow whose branches run over the wall," should we be surprised if other records surface confirming how the Lord deals consistently with His children?

[From the prophet Ezekiel]

"Therefore say, thus saith the Lord God; Although I have cast them [Israel] far off among the heathen, and although I have scattered them among the countries, yet will I be to them as a little sanctuary in the countries where they shall come. Therefore say, Thus saith the Lord God; I will even gather you from the people, and assemble you out of the countries where ye have been scattered, and I will give you the land of Israel. And they shall come thither, ... And I will give them one heart, and I will put a new spirit within you ... That they may walk in my statutes, and keep mine ordinances, and do them: and they shall be my people, and I will be their God." (Ez. 11:16-20)

[Ezekiel thus foreshadows the formation of Zion where gathered Israel will dwell with one heart and one spirit, a people who will walk in the statutes and ordinances of God, who will view them as His people, and they accept Him as their God.]

" I will accept you ... when I bring you out from the people, and gather you out of the countries wherein you have been scattered; and I will be sanctified in you before the heathen, and ye shall know that I am the Lord, when I shall bring you into the land of Israel, into the country for which I lifted up mine hand to give it to your fathers." (Ez. 20:41; 36:24)

"Therefore thus saith the Lord; Because ye are all become as dross, behold, therefore, I gather you into the midst of Jerusalem." (Ez. 22:19)

"Thus saith the Lord God; When I shall have gathered the house of Israel from the people among whom they are scattered, and shall be sanctified in them in the sight of the heathen, then shall they dwell in their land that I have given to my servant Jacob. And they shall dwell safely therein, and shall build houses, and plant vineyards, yea, they shall dwell with confidence, when I have executed judgments upon those that despise them round about them; and they shall know that I am the Lord their God." (Ez. 28:25-26)

[Ezekiel foresaw the gathering of Israel to places of permanent dwelling where they would build and plant, and the people would dwell together in confidence. Using sheep and shepherd metaphors, Ezekiel describes the blessed state of gathered Israel where there will be plenty of temporal and spiritual nourishment. This is also consistent with the husband/wife metaphor and the husband's role, which Messiah/Christ assumed for His covenant people, confirming the rewards of entering and obeying the covenant are protection from their long term enemies of death and sin, in a place of safety, food, shelter, and peace, and freedom from the concerns of the world.]

"For thus saith the Lord God; Behold, I, even I, will both search my sheep and seek them out. As a shepherd seeketh out his flock in the day that he is among his sheep that are scattered; so will I seek out my sheep, and will deliver them out of all places where they have been scattered in the cloudy and dark day. And I will bring them out from the people, and gather them from the countries, and will bring them to their own land, and feed them upon the mountains of Israel by the rivers, and in all the inhabited places of the country. I will feed them in a good pasture and upon the high mountains of Israel shall their fold be: there shall they lie in a good fold, and in a fat pasture shall they feed upon the mountains of Israel." (Ez. 34:11-

14)	[Mountains are high places. Living and feeding in the fat pastures thereon imply the people are high and lifted up from the rest. Their physical and spiritual covenants and ordinances are of a higher order, like in sacred temples, where those who receive endowments, or gifts of knowledge, indeed feed in the best of pastures, both spiritually and temporally. Thus the gathering is two fold: both a spiritual and a geographical, to the best the Lord has.

Referring to the resurrection and the reign of the Lord during the Millennium, the Lord said to Ezekiel:]

"Therefore prophecy and say unto them, thus saith the Lord God; Behold, O my people, I will open your graves, and cause you to come up out of your graves, and bring you into the land of Israel....

"Thus saith the Lord God; Behold, I will take the children of Israel from among the heathen, whither they be gone, and will gather them on every side, and bring them into their own land: And I will make them one nation in the land upon the mountains of Israel; and one king shall be king to them all; and they shall be no more two nations, neither shall they be divided into two kingdoms anymore at all:

"Neither shall they defile themselves any more with their idols, nor with their detestable things, nor as with any of their transgressions: but I will save them out of their dwelling places, wherein they have sinned, and will cleanse them: so shall they be my people, and I will be their God.

..."and they all shall have one shepherd: they shall also walk in my judgments, and observe my statutes, and do them. And they shall dwell in the land that I have given unto Jacob my servant, wherein your fathers have dwelt: and they shall dwell therein, even they, and their children, and their children's children for ever: ... Moreover I will make a covenant of peace with them; it shall be an everlasting covenant with them; and I will place them, and multiply them, and will set my sanctuary in the midst of them evermore. My tabernacle also shall be with them: yea, I will be their God, and they shall be my people. And the heathen shall know that I the Lord do sanctify Israel, when my sanctuary shall be in the midst of them for evermore." (Ez. 37:12,21-28)

"...Thus saith the Lord God; Now will I ... have mercy upon the whole house of Israel... After that they have borne their shame, and all their trespasses whereby they have trespassed against me, when they dwelt safely in their land, and none made them afraid. When I have brought them again from the people, and gathered them out of their enemies lands, and am sanctified in them in the sight of many nations; Then shall they know that I am the Lord their God, which caused them to be led into captivity among the heathen: but I have gathered them unto their own land, and have left none of them any more there. Neither will I hide my face any more from them: for I have poured out my spirit upon the house of Israel, saith the Lord God." (Ez. 39:25-29)

[From the prophet Hosea]

"Yet the number of the children of Israel shall be as the sand of the sea, which cannot be measured nor numbered; and it shall come to pass, that in the place where it was said unto them, Ye are not my people, there it shall be said unto them, Ye are the sons of the living God. Then shall the children of Judah and the children of Israel be gathered together, and appoint themselves one head, and they shall come up out of the land:" (Hosea 1:10-11)

[Not only will the children of Israel be innumerable, they are to be gathered together in unlikely places. There they will become known as the sons of the living God. The posterity of Judah and the posterity of the other tribes of Isarel under Ephraim, will be reconciled under one leader and work together]

[From the prophet Amos]

"And I will bring again the captivity of my people of Israel, and they shall build the waste cities, and inhabit them; and they shall plant vineyards, and drink the wine thereof; they shall also make gardens, and eat the fruit of them. And I will plant them upon their land, and they shall no more be pulled up out of their lands which I have given them, saith the Lord thy God." (Amos 9:14-15)

[Land once inhabited by the Lord's people Israel, which they were forced to abandon by enemies, is to be re-inhabited by them, as they are gathered together. The Lord's covenant people Israel will rebuild the waste cities, cultivate the land, eat of its fruits, and put down roots to stay, never again to be forced out, not only in the old Jerusalem, but in the New Jerusalem as well.

This does not mean that while the rebuilding is taking place the covenant people Israel will not have enemies. They will have enemies, with much attendant strife and conflict. The Lord is confirming that He will be their protector, and if they abide in His covenant, wrongs suffered will be redressed. Yes, the Lords promises will all be fulfilled]

[From the prophet Micah]

"I will surely assemble, O Jacob, all of thee; I will surely gather the remnant of Israel; I will put them together as the sheep of Bozrah [the sheepfold], as the flock in the midst of their fold: they shall make great noise by reason of the multitude of men."(Micah 2:12)

[When the great masses of the ten tribes return, such a return will be highly visible. Their movement and the movement of those of these tribes already in the new and everlasting covenant will be accompanied by visible, physical changes in the earth, such as highways coming out of the depths of the sea, events clearly in the future.

However, the movement of large numbers of people, signifying a trek to the New Jerusalem lands of inheritance, by its rightful heirs, will follow an advance party of Israel's millions already in the new and everlasting covenant, whose lineage has heretofore been revealed in patriarchal blessings. They have already been gathered spiritually to Messiah/Christ and are now being gathered temporarily in stakes of Zion throughout the world. They await the Lord' signal to occupy their lands of inheritance.

On the other hand, the geographical gathering of the house of Judah to the Old Jerusalem is well under way and evidence of attendant strife and conflict around that gathering is front page news almost daily. The spiritual gathering of the house of Judah, in large measure, lies ahead, giving rise to the notion that the tribes of Israel headed by Ephraim are being gathered spiritually, first, followed by a geographical gathering to their lands of inheritance; while the gathering of Judah or Jews is in reverse order; first, a geographical gathering followed by a spiritual gathering as spelled out in greater detail in Chapter XVI.

Clarifying who would lead them the Lord said in latter days: "in time ye shall have no king nor ruler, for I will be your king and watch over you." (D&C 38:21)]

"In that day, saith the Lord, will I assemble her that halteth, and I will gather her that was cast far off a strong nation: and the Lord shall reign over them in mount Zion from henceforth, even for ever." (Micah 4:6 Zeph. 3:19)

[Eventually Israel will be gathered as a shepherd gathers his sheep. Leaders of nations will be replaced by the Lord who will reign over His people and all the world forever.]

[From the prophet Zechariah]

"And I will strengthen the house of Judah, and I will save the house of Joseph, and I will bring them again to place them; for I have mercy upon them: and they shall be as though I had not cast them off; for I am the Lord their God, and will hear them.

"And they of Ephraim shall be like a mighty man, and their heart shall rejoice as through wine: yea, Their children shall see it, and be glad; their heart shall rejoice in the Lord. I will hiss [whistle] for them, and gather them; for I have redeemed them; and they shall increase as they have increased. I will sow them among the people: and they shall remember me in far countries..." (Zech. 10:6-9)

[The posterity of father Israel's sons Judah and Joseph, though scattered in far countries will remember the Lord, be strengthened, increased in number, saved and restored to the places originally promised, for the Lord will hear and answer them.]

[From the book of Matthew]

Speaking to the multitude, and to his disciples, Jesus criticized the scribes and Pharisees, condemned them as hypocrites, called them a generation of vipers, and attributed the death of Zacharias, John the Baptist's father, to them. He also forecast their ultimate fate and declared how oft he would have gathered them, in this lament:

"Ye bear testimony against your fathers, when ye, yourselves, are partakers of the same wickedness. Behold your fathers did it through ignorance, but ye do not; wherefore, their sins shall be upon your heads.

"O Jerusalem, Jerusalem, thou that killest the prophets, and stoned them which are sent unto thee, how oft would I have gathered thy children together, even as a hen gathereth her chickens under her wings, and ye would not!

"Behold, your house is left unto you desolate. For I say unto you, Ye shall not see me henceforth, till ye shall say, Blessed is he that cometh in the name of the Lord." (JST Matt.23:34-35, KJV Matt. 23:37, Luke 13:34; D&C 10:65;43:24)

Eventually the posterity of those responsible for the death of the prophets and for the death of the Savior Himself, will be humbled to the point they will recognize who He is. They will recognize His servants who come in His name and enter the covenant again.

[From John the Beloved]

Caiaphas the high priest in Jerusalem, in council with other priests, were trying to decide what to do with Jesus, eventually deciding he must die. In the process, Caiaphas prophesied Jesus would die for their nation, and set the stage for the gathering of Israel in these words:

"Ye know nothing at all, Nor consider it expedient for us, that one man should die for the people, and that the whole nation perish not. And thus spake he not of himself; but being high priest that year, he prophesied that Jesus should die for that nation; And not for that nation only, but that also he should gather together in one the children of God that were scattered abroad." (John 11:52)

[From Apostle Paul's epistle to the Ephesians]

"Blessed be the God and Father of our Lord Jesus Christ, who hath blessed us with all spiritual blessings... Having predestinated [foreordained, from the Greek] us ...Having made known unto us the mystery of his will, according to his good pleasure which he hath purposed in himself:

"That in the dispensation of the fulness of times he might gather together in one all things in Christ, both which are in heaven, and which are on earth; even in him: In whom also we have obtained an inheritance, being [foreordained] according to the purpose of him who worketh all things after the counsel of his own will. In whom also we have obtained an inheritance... In whom ye also trusted, after that ye heard the word of truth, the gospel of your salvation: in whom also after that ye believed, ye were sealed with that holy Spirit of promise." (Eph. 1:3-13)

Paul was saying there is a special promise the Lord's covenant people Israel, the true believers in Messiah/Christ, will receive in the last days, or dispensation of the fulness of times; and that promise was foreordained, or planned for, in the original scheme of things. The covenant people Israel, who live the provisions of the covenant and were sealed by the holy spirit of promise will receive an inheritance including salvation.

[From Nephi quoting the prophet Lehi]

"Yea, even my father [Lehi] spake much concerning the Gentiles, and also concerning the house of Israel, that they should be compared like unto an olive tree, whose branches should be broken off and should be scattered upon all the face of the earth. Wherefore, he said it must needs be that we should be led with one accord into the land of promise, unto the fulfilling of the word of the Lord that we should be scattered upon all the face of the earth.

"And after the house of Israel should be scattered they should be gathered together again; or, in fine, after the Gentiles had received the fulness of the Gospel, the natural branches of the olive-tree, or the remnants of the house of Israel should be grafted in, or come to a knowledge of the true Messiah, their Lord and their Redeemer." (1Ne.10:12-14; 3Ne 16:4, 11-12)

Clarifying to his brothers what Lehi meant relating to the olive-tree, Nephi said:

"the house of Israel was compared unto an olive-tree, by the Spirit of the Lord, which was in our father; [Lehi] and behold are we not broken off from the house of Israel, and are we not a branch of the house of Israel?

"And now, the thing which our father meaneth concerning the grafting in of the natural branches through the fulness of the Gentiles, is, that in the latter days, when our seed shall have dwindled in unbelief, yea, for the space of many years, and many generations after the Messiah shall be manifested in body unto the children of men, then shall the fulness of the gospel of the Messiah come unto the Gentiles unto the remnant of our seed-

"And at that day shall the remnant of our seed know that they are of the house of Israel, and that they are the covenant people of the Lord; and then shall they know and come to a knowledge of their forefathers, and also to the knowledge of the gospel of their Redeemer, which was ministered unto their fathers by him; wherefore, they shall come to the knowledge of their Redeemer and the very points of his doctrine, that they may know how to come unto him and be saved...

"Behold, I say unto you, Yea; they shall be remembered again among the house of Israel; they shall be grafted in, being a natural branch of the true olive-tree...

"Wherefore, our father hath not spoken of our seed alone, but also of all the house of Israel, pointing to the covenant which should be fulfilled in the latter days; which covenant the Lord made to our father Abraham, saying: In thy seed shall all the kindreds of the earth be blessed. [also] I spake unto them concerning the restoration of the Jews in the latter days. And I did rehearse unto them the words of Isaiah, who spake concerning the restoration of the Jews, or of the house of Israel, and after they were restored they should no more be confounded, neither should they be scattered again..."(1Ne. 15:12-20)

[From Nephi quoting the prophet Zenos]

"the God of Abraham, and of Isaac, and of Jacob, yieldeth himself, according to the words of the angel, as a man, into the hands of wicked men, to be lifted up, according to the words of Zenock, and to be crucified, according to the words of Neum, and to be buried in a sepulchre, according to the words of Zenos which he spake concerning the three days of darkness, which should be a sign given of his death unto those who are of the house of Israel.

"For thus spake the prophet: The Lord God surely shall visit all the house of Israel at that day, some with his voice because of their righteousness, unto their great joy and salvation, and others with the thunderings and lightnings of his power, by tempest, by fire, and by smoke, and vapor of darkness, and by the opening of the earth, and by mountains which shall be carried up. And all these things must surely come, saith the prophet Zenos. And the rocks of the earth must rend; and because of the groanings of the earth, many of the kings of the isles of the sea shall be wrought upon by the Spirit of God, to exclaim: the God of nature suffers.

"As for those who are at Jerusalem, [the Jews] saith the prophet, they shall be scourged by all people, because they crucify the God of Israel, and turn aside, rejecting signs and wonders, and the power and glory of the God of Israel. And because they turn their hearts aside, saith the prophet, and have despised the Holy One of Israel, they shall wander in the flesh, and perish, and become a hiss and a byword, and be hated among all nations.

"Nevertheless, when that day cometh, saith the prophet, that they no more turn aside their hearts against the Holy One of Israel, then will he remember the covenants which he made to their fathers. Yea, then will he remember the isles of the sea; yea, and all the people who are of the house of Israel, will I gather in, saith the Lord, according to the words of the prophet Zenos, from the four quarters of the earth. Yea, and all the earth shall see the salvation of the Lord, saith the prophet; every nation, kindred, tongue and people shall be blessed."(1Ne.19:10-17)

[We can recognize that day when all the earth shall see the salvation of the Lord and every nation, kindred, tongue and people shall be blessed by paying careful attention to the 24th Chapter of Matthew, the parable of the ten virgins and the parable of the sheep and the goats. Those prepared and ready for the bridegroom, through the choices they have made throughout their lives and the works have have done, will receive their eternal inheritances.]

[Again from the prophet Nephi]

Isaiah is to be the Lord's servant in advancing the tribes of Jacob/Israel and to help rejuvenate the spared of Israel; [through his recorded words, for thus saith the Lord, "great are the words of Isaiah"]

"And now saith the Lord-- that formed me from the womb that I should be his servant, to bring Jacob again to him--though Israel be not gathered yet shall I be glorious in the eyes of the Lord, and my God shall be my strength. And he said: it is a light thing, that thou shouldst be my servant to raise up the tribes of Jacob, and to restore the preserved of Israel, I will also give thee for a light to the Gentiles, that thou mayest be my salvation unto the ends of the earth." (1Ne:21:5-6; Isa.49:5-6)

Speaking to the remnant of Israel in America who had not yet returned to the Lord, and about others not of the literal descent of Israel, who would yet embrace the gospel and be grafted in or adopted by Israel, in the last days, the Lord said:

"Lift up thine eyes round about and behold; all these gather themselves together, and they shall come to thee. And as I live, saith the Lord, thou shalt surely clothe thee with them all, as with an ornament, and bind them on even as a bride...

"Thus saith the Lord God: Behold, I will lift up mine hand to the Gentiles, and set up my standard to the people; and they shall bring thy sons in their arms, and thy daughters shall be carried on their shoulders. And kings shall be thy nursing fathers, and their queens thy nursing mothers; they shall bow down to thee with their face towards the earth, and lick the dust of thy feet; and thou shalt know that I am the Lord; for they shall not be ashamed that wait for me. For shall the prey be taken from the mighty, or the lawful captives delivered? But thus saith the Lord, even the captives of the mighty shall be taken away, and the prey of the terrible shall be delivered; for I will contend with him that contendeth with thee, and I will save thy children... All flesh shall know that I, the Lord, am thy Saviour and thy Redeemer, the Mighty One of Jacob." (1Ne 21:18,22-26; Isa. 49:18,22-26)

Not only was the main body of the house of Israel to be scattered upon all the face of the earth, and among all nations, so were the descendants of Lehi in America to be scattered in the last days. And just as the main body of scattered Israel is to be gathered so is the remnant of Israel, Lehi's seed in America to be gathered in the last days. From the prophet Nephi, son of Lehi:

[Again from the prophet Nephi, son of Lehi]

"...the time cometh that after all the house of Israel have been scattered and confounded, that the Lord God will raise up a mighty nation among the Gentiles, yea, even upon the face of this land; [America] and by them shall our seed be scattered. And after our seed is scattered the Lord God will proceed to do a marvelous work among the Gentiles, which shall be of great worth unto our seed; wherefore, it is likened unto their being nourished by the Gentiles and being carried in their arms and upon their shoulders.

"And it shall also be of worth unto the Gentiles; and not only

300

unto the Gentiles but unto all the house of Israel, unto the making known of the covenants of the Father of heaven unto Abraham, saying: In thy seed shall all the kindreds of the earth be blessed.

"And I would, my brethren, that ye should know that all the kindreds of the earth cannot be blessed unless he shall make bare his arm in the eyes of the nations. Wherefore, the Lord God will proceed to make bare his arm in the eyes of all the nations, in bringing about his covenants and his gospel unto those who are of the house of Israel. Wherefore, he will bring them again out of captivity, and they shall be gathered together to the lands of their inheritance; and they shall be brought out of obscurity and out of darkness; and they shall know that the Lord is their Saviour and their Redeemer, the Mighty One of Israel.

..."And the time cometh speedily that the righteous must be led up as calves of the stall, and the Holy One of Israel must reign in dominion, and might, and power, and great glory. And he gathereth his children from the four quarters of the earth; and he numbereth his sheep, and they know him; and there shall be one fold and one shepherd; and he shall feed his sheep, and in him they shall find pasture. And because of the righteousness of his people, Satan has no power; wherefore, he cannot be loosed for the space of many years; for he hath no power over the hearts of the people, for they dwell in righteousness, and the Holy One of Israel reigneth." 1Ne 22:7-12, 24-26)

As previously mentioned, the children of Lehi came to America under the guidance of the Lord, in about 600 B.C. They brought with them plates of brass which included the five books of Moses and the Hebrew scriptures up through the writings of the prophet Isaiah, some of the writings of Jeremiah, and other scriptures not found in the Bible, including some of the writings of Joseph, son of Jacob/ Israel.

Lehi, later speaking to his youngest son, whom he had named Joseph, born in the wilderness while enroute to America, told him:

301

"I am a descendant of Joseph who was carried captive into Egypt. And great were the covenants of the Lord which he made unto Joseph. Wherefore Joseph [son of Israel] truly saw our day and he obtained a promise of the Lord, that out of his loins the Lord God would raise up a righteous branch unto the house of Israel; not the Messiah, but a branch which was to be broken off, nevertheless to be remembered in the covenants of the Lord that the Messiah should be made manifest unto them in the latter days, in the spirit of power, unto the bringing of them out of darkness unto light -- yea, out of hidden darkness and out of captivity unto freedom...

"a seer will I raise up out of the fruit of thy loins; and unto him will I give power to bring forth my word unto the seed of thy loins and not only, saith the Lord, but to the convincing them of my word, which shall already gone forth among them.

"Wherefore, the fruit of thy loins shall write; and the fruit of the loins of Judah shall write; and that which shall be written by the fruit of thy loins, and also that which shall be written by the fruit of the loins of Judah, shall grow together unto the confounding of false doctrines and laying down of contentions, and establishing peace among the fruit of thy loins, and bringing them to the knowledge of my covenants saith the Lord.

"... And thus prophesied Joseph saying: Behold a seer will the Lord bless; and they that seek to destroy him shall be confounded; for this promise, which I have obtained of the Lord, of the fruit of my loins, shall be fulfilled. Behold, I am sure of the fulfilling of this promise; And his name shall be called after me; and it shall be after the name of his father. And he shall be like unto me; for the things, which the Lord shall bring forth by his hand, by the power of the Lord shall bring my people unto salvation.

"Yea, thus prophesied Joseph: I am sure of this thing, even as I am sure of the promise of Moses; for the Lord hath said unto me, I will preserve thy seed forever." (2Ne 3:4-16)

The seer spoken of in this revelation is Joseph Smith, Junior, son of Joseph Smith Senior, both descendants of Joseph, son of Israel. Closing out his discussion with Joseph in the America's, Lehi declared:

"And now, behold, my son Joseph, after this manner did my father [Joseph of Israel] of old prophesy...

"And there shall rise up one mighty among them [the descendant of Joseph, son of Israel] who shall do much good, both in word and in deed, being an instrument in the hands of God, with exceeding faith, to work mighty wonders, and do that thing which is great in the sight of God, unto the bringing to pass much restoration unto the house of Israel, and unto the seed of thy brethren. And now blessed art thou Joseph [son of Lehi]. Behold thou art little; wherefore hearken unto the words of thy brother, Nephi, and it shall be done unto thee even according to the words I have spoken. Remember the words of thy dying father, Amen." (2Ne 3:24-5)

Jacob, the prophet-brother of Nephi knew through revelation that the Jews had been taken captive by the Babylonians and foretold the ministry and crucifixion of the Holy One of Israel. At Nephi's behest Jacob related Isaiah's words concerning all the house of Israel, reiterating the Gentiles would carry their sons and daughters upon their shoulders and serve as nursing father's and nursing mothers to the remnant of the house of Israel. Jacob forecast the Holy One of Israel would manifest himself in the flesh, but his own people would scourge him and decree his crucifixion, and because of what his own people did to him. Jacob prophesied the day would come when they, his own people would be smitten and afflicted. Rather than let them perish outright, the prayers of the faithful were answered with their scattering, though they were smitten and hated in the process. But when they come to a knowledge of the Redeemer, the Lord will be merciful unto them and they "shall be gathered again to the lands of their inheritance.

"... And behold, according to the words of the prophet, the Messiah will set himself again, the second time to recover them;

303

wherefore, he will manifest himself unto them in power and great glory, unto the destruction of their enemies, when that day cometh when they shall believe in him; and none will he destroy that believe in him." (2Ne 6:1-11,14 ;21:11; 25:17; 29:1; Jacob 6:2; Isa. 11:11)

[From the prophet Nephi]

"And now my beloved brethren, I have read these things that ye might know concerning the covenants of the Lord that he has covenanted with all the house of Israel--That he has spoken unto the Jews, by the mouth of his holy prophets, even from the beginning down, from generation to generation, until the time comes that they shall be restored to the true church and fold of God; when they shall be gathered home to the lands of their inheritance, and shall be established in all their lands of promise." (2 Ne 9:1-2)

Summarizing the words of these American prophets, we see that through the gathering God remembers His covenant to restore Israel to a knowledge of Messiah; that He considers them to be natural branches of the olive-tree to be grafted in; that He will gather all people who are of the house of Israel spiritually through the faith, repentance, baptism, gift of the Holy Ghost sequence; that through Isaiah's prophetic words, he [Isaiah] is to be the servant of the Lord instrumental in raising up and restoring the tribes of Israel; that a seer of the posterity of Joseph, son of Israel, named after him, Joseph, and his own immediate father, Joseph, Senior, is to be raised up to bring to pass much restoration of Israel in the last days; that Messiah will set His hand a second and last time to recover His covenant people; and that the Lord will speak to Israel through prophets until the time when the house of Israel is restored to the true church and are gathered geographically to their respective lands of inheritance.

Jacob, also a prophet and brother of Nephi, knowing that his father, mother, brothers and sisters were of the house of Israel, through Joseph, Israel's son sold into Egypt; while speaking to his brethren in about 550 B.C., concerning their future posterity, the descendants of the Nephites and the Lamanites, said:

304

"For behold the promises which we have obtained are the promises unto us according to the flesh; wherefore, as it has been shown unto me that many of our children shall perish in the flesh because of unbelief, nevertheless God will be merciful unto many; and our children shall be restored and that they may come to that which will give them the true knowledge of their Redeemer.

"Wherefore, ... it must needs be expedient that Christ ...should come among the Jews... But because of priestcrafts and iniquities, they at Jerusalem will stiffen their necks against him, that he be crucified. Wherefore, because of their iniquities, destructions, famines, pestilences and bloodshed shall come upon them; and they who shall not be destroyed, shall be scattered among all nations.

"But thus saith the Lord God: When the day cometh that they shall believe in me, that I am Christ, then have I covenanted with their fathers that they shall be restored in the flesh, upon the earth, unto the lands of their inheritance. And it shall come to pass that they shall be gathered in from their long dispersion, from the isles of the sea, and from the four parts of the earth; and the nations of the Gentiles shall be great in the eyes of me, saith God, in carrying them forth to the lands of their inheritance." (2Ne 10:1-8; 30:5; Hel. 15:11; 3Ne 5:23)

Because those of the house of Israel at Jerusalem did stiffen their necks against Messiah, did cause his crucifixion and did many other iniquities; destructions, famines, pestilences and bloodshed did come upon them, and those not destroyed were scattered among all nations. But as their posterity believe in Messiah again, they are to be gathered in from their long dispersion and returned to the lands of their inheritance; and the Gentiles will be very helpful to them in this geographical restoration.

Prophesying of the descendants of Judah [Jews] of the house of Israel Nephi declared:

"And after they have been scattered, and the Lord God hath scourged them by other nations for the space of many generations, yea, even down from generation to generation until they shall be persuaded to believe in Christ, the Son of God, and the atonement, which is infinite for all mankind--and when that day shall come that they shall believe in Christ, and worship the Father in his name, with pure hearts and clean hands, and look not forward any more for another Messiah then, at that time, the day will come that it must needs be expedient that they should believe these things. And the Lord will set his hand again a second time to restore his people from their lost and fallen state. Wherefore he will proceed to do a marvelous work and a wonder among the children of men.

"Wherefore, he shall bring forth his words unto them, which words will judge them at the last day, for they shall be given them for the purpose of convincing them of the true Messiah, who was rejected by them; and unto the convincing of them that they need not look forward any more for a Messiah to come... for there is ... one Messiah spoken of by the prophets, and that Messiah is he who should be rejected by the Jews." (2Ne25:16-18)

Nephi prophesied that in the latter days when his words shall hiss forth many will reject the Book of Mormon because they think the Bible contains all of his words, but they are reminded that there are more nations than one, that the Lord created all men and is capable of raising up other prophets and scriptures to spread the word, fulfill their words and gather Israel.

"But behold, there shall be many-- at that day when I shall proceed to do a marvelous work among them, that I may remember my covenants which I have made unto the children of men, that I may set my hand again the second time to recover my people, which are of the house of Israel...and my words shall hiss forth unto the ends of the earth, for a standard unto my people, which are of the house of Israel." (2Ne 29:1-7)

Nephi prophesied that in the latter days converted Gentiles shall be numbered with the covenant people and that many of the Lamanites and Jews shall believe the word and become a delightsome people, and that Israel shall be restored and the wicked destroyed.

"And now, I would prophesy somewhat more concerning the Jews and the Gentiles. For after the book of which I have spoken shall come forth, and be written unto the Gentiles, and sealed up again unto the Lord, there shall be many which shall believe the words which are written; and they shall carry them forth unto the remnant of our seed. And then shall the remnant of our seed know concerning us, how that we came forth out from Jerusalem, and that they are the descendants of the Jews.

"And the gospel of Jesus Christ shall be declared unto them; wherefore they shall be restored unto the knowledge of their fathers, and also to the knowledge of Jesus Christ, which was had among their fathers. And then shall they rejoice for they shall know that it is a blessing unto them from the hand of God;

"... And it shall come to pass that the Jews which are scattered also shall begin to believe in Christ; and they shall begin to gather in upon the face of the land; and as many as shall believe in Christ shall become a delight-some people. And it shall come to pass that the Lord God shall commence his work among all nations, kindreds, tongues and people, to bring about the restoration of his people upon the earth." (2Ne 30:3-8, 3Ne 20:31-33; Mormon 5:14)

Nephi's brother Jacob, quoted Zenos relative to the allegory of the tame and wild olive trees likening them to Israel and the Gentiles, which foreshadowed the prefigured scattering and gathering of Israel; noting that the Gentiles themselves would eventually be grafted into Israel, along with Israel's remnants, and that the grafting process includes pruning the dead wood from all the olive trees in the Lord's vineyard, and eventually the vineyard itself would be burned. Thus the Lord is to recover Israel, the true believers in Messiah/Christ by grafting of the trees of the vineyard [world] and pruning the vineyard, before burning it by fire; referring to that day as a day that the Lord sets his hand again a second time to recover his people, "yea, even the last time, that the servants of the Lord shall go forth in his power to nourish and prepare the vineyard, and after that the end cometh." (Jacob 5:52-74; 6:2)

[From the Prophet Mormon]

Mormon, a prophet who lived in the fourth century A.D. and the person who abridged the records of Lehi's descendants in America, under the inspiration of God, made these observations concerning the gathering.

"Surely he [the Lord] hath blessed the house of Jacob, and hath been merciful unto the seed of Joseph. And inasmuch as the children of Lehi have kept his commandments he hath blessed them and prospered them according to his word. Yea, and surely shall he again bring a remnant of the seed of Joseph to the knowledge of the Lord their God. And as surely as the Lord liveth, will he gather in from the four quarters of the earth all the remnant of the seed of Jacob, who are scattered abroad upon all the face of the earth.

"And as he hath covenanted with all the house of Jacob, even so shall the covenant wherewith he hath covenanted with the house of Jacob be fulfilled in his own due time, unto the restoring all the house of Jacob unto the knowledge of the covenant that he hath covenanted with them. And then shall they know their Redeemer, who is Jesus Christ, the Son of God; and then shall they be gathered in from the four quarters of the earth unto their own lands, from whence they have been dispersed; yea, as the Lord liveth so shall it be, Amen." (3Ne. 5:21-26)

Speaking to the Nephites during His visit
among them in America after His resurrection
the Lord said:

"O ye people of these great cities which have fallen, who are descendants of Jacob, yea, who are of the house of Israel, how oft have I have gathered you as a hen gathereth her chickens under her wings, and have nourished you. And again, how oft would I have gathered you as a hen gathereth her chickens under her wings, yea, O ye people of the house of Israel, who have fallen: yea, O ye people of

the house of Israel, ye that dwell at Jerusalem, as ye that have fallen; yea, how oft would I have gathered her chickens, and ye would not. O ye house of Israel whom I have spared, how oft will I gather you as a hen gathereth her chickens under her wings, if ye will repent and return unto me with full purpose of heart. But if not, O house of Israel, the places of your dwellings shall become desolate until the time of the fulfilling of the covenant to your fathers."
(3Ne. 10:4-7; Matt.23:37)

In the latter days the Gospel will go unto the Gentiles and then to the house of Israel, said the Lord, that they:

"may be brought in, or may be brought to a knowledge of me, their Redeemer. And then will I gather them in from the four quarters of the earth; and then will I fulfill the covenant which the Father hath made unto all the people of the house of Israel." (3Ne. 16:4-5)

Continuing this discourse the Lord said:

"... blessed are the Gentiles, because of their belief in me, in and of the Holy Ghost, which witnesses unto them of me and of the Father. Behold, because of their belief in me, saith the Father, and because of the unbelief of you, O house of Israel, in the latter day shall the truth come unto the Gentiles, that the fulness of these things shall be made known unto them. [additionally]

"... because of the mercies of the Father unto the Gentiles, and also the judgments of the Father upon my people who are of the house of Israel, verily, verily, I say unto you, that after all this, and I have caused my people who are of the house of Israel to be smitten, and to be afflicted, and to be slain, and to be cast out from among them, and to become hated by them, and to become a hiss and a byword among them,-- [after the Gentiles have been given the opportunity if they] "... shall reject the fulness of my gospel, behold, saith the Father, I will bring the fulness of my gospel from among them. And then will I remember my covenant which I have made unto my people, O house of Israel, and I will bring my gospel unto them. And I will show thee, O house of Israel, that the Gentiles shall not have power over you; but

I will remember my covenant unto you, O house of Israel, and ye shall come unto a knowledge of the fulness of my gospel. But if the Gentiles will repent and return unto me, saith the Father, behold they shall be numbered among my people, O house of Israel." (3Ne 16:6-13)

In the mercy, equity and justice of God, the descendants of the northern kingdom of Israel comprising ten of the twelve tribes of Israel, who were scattered and carried away by the Assyrians, would again be introduced to the provisions of the covenant they once entered into with the God, and those accepting the Messiah/Christ would again be numbered as His people and receive all that the Father hath as they comply fully with the covenant's provisions. In like manner would those descendants of the people of the southern kingdom of Judah, comprising two of the tribes of Israel who were scattered and carried away by the Babylonians be again introduced to the provisions of the covenant they once entered into with God, and again be numbered as His people and receive all that the Father hath, as they comply with the covenant's provisions.(See Ezekiel 18:21-32)

The posterity of those descendants of the southern kingdom of Israel's two tribes who returned after seventy years, comprised the main body of Israel's descendants in the Holy Land when the Savior lived upon the earth. Their leaders were the ones primarily responsible for the Savior's crucifixion and death. Their posterity too shall be restored to the covenant as they accept Jesus Christ as Messiah and Savior of mankind. However, the sequence or order in which the Gospel messages are presented to the world is important.

Note that it is the Gentiles who were to be the first to be gathered spiritually by receiving the messages of the restoration, and given the opportunity to embrace it; followed by known descendants of the Joseph, in America and other places; followed by other tribes of the northern kingdom of Israel, followed by the posterity of the southern kingdom of Judah.

The recently resurrected Lord said to the assembled covenant people in America, that the remnant of Jacob in America shall come to a knowledge of the Lord their God, and shall inherit the Americas, and that He Jesus, is the prophet like unto Moses, that the Nephites are the children of the prophets; and that others of the Lord's people shall be gathered to Jerusalem in these words:

"Ye remember that I spake unto you, and said that when the words of Isaiah should be fulfilled ... then is the fulfilling of the covenant which the Father hath made unto his people, O house of Israel. And then shall the remnants, which shall be scattered abroad upon the face of the earth, be gathered in from the east and from the west, and from the south and from the north; and they shall be brought to the knowledge of the Lord their God, who hath redeemed them.

"And the Father hath commanded me that I should give unto you this land, for your inheritance. And I say unto you, that if the Gentiles do not repent after the blessing which they shall receive, after they have scattered my people--

"Then shall ye, who are a remnant of the house of Jacob, go forth among them; and ye shall be in the midst of them who shall be many; and ye shall be among them as a lion among the beasts of the forest, and as a young lion among the flocks of sheep, who, if he goeth through both treadeth down and teareth to pieces and none can deliver. Thy hands shall be lifted up upon thine adversaries, and thine enemies shall be cut off.

"And I will gather my people together as a man gathereth his sheaves into the [thrashing] floor. For I will make my people with whom the Father hath covenanted, yea, I will make thy horn iron, and I will make thy hoofs brass. And thou shalt beat in pieces many people; and I will consecrate their gain unto the Lord, and their substance unto the Lord of the whole earth. And behold, I am he who doeth it.

"And it shall come to pass, saith the Father, that the sword of justice shall hang over them at that day; and except they repent it shall fall upon them, saith the Father, yea, even upon all the nations of the Gentiles.

"And it shall come to pass that I will establish my people, O house of Israel. And behold, this people will I establish in this land, unto the fulfilling of the covenant which I made with your father Jacob; and it shall be a New Jerusalem. And the powers of heaven shall be in the midst of this people; yea, even I will be in the midst of you.

"Behold, I am he of whom Moses spake, saying: A prophet shall the Lord your God raise up unto you of your brethren, like unto me; him shall ye hear in all things whatsoever he shall say unto you. And it shall come to pass that every soul who will not hear that prophet shall be cut off from among the people. Verily I say unto you, yea and all the prophets from Samuel and those that follow after, as many as have spoken have testified of me.

"And behold, ye are the children of the prophets; and ye are of the house of Israel; and ye are of the covenant which the Father made with your fathers, saying unto Abraham: In thy seed shall all the kindreds of the earth be blessed. The Father having raised me up unto you first, and sent me to bless you in turning away everyone of you from his iniquities; and this because ye are the children of the covenant.

" And after that ye were blessed then fulfilleth the Father the covenant which he made with Abraham, saying: In thy seed shall all the kindreds of the earth be blessed--unto the pouring out of the Holy Ghost through me unto the Gentiles, which blessing upon the Gentiles shall make them mighty above all, unto the scattering of my people, O house of Israel. And they shall be a scourge unto the people of this land. Nevertheless, when they shall have received the fulness of my gospel, then if they harden their hearts against me, I will return their iniquities upon their own heads, saith the Father.

"And I will remember the covenant which I have made with my people; and I have covenanted with them that I would gather them together in mine own due time, that I would give unto them the land of their fathers for their inheritance, which is the land of Jerusalem, which is the promised land unto them forever, saith the Father."(3Ne. 20:11-29)

Thus in the restoration the Lord said that He would establish His covenant people in America where the descendants of Lehi, to whom He was speaking, lived, and that a New Jerusalem would be built in America to which some of His covenant people would be gathered geographically in the last days. He also reminded them of His promises concerning the original Jerusalem, still to be fulfilled, in which He said He would give them the land of their fathers [Abraham, Isaac, and Jacob] for an inheritance, which is the land of Jerusalem.

One should keep in mind that, with the march of time, Israel's posterity through his twelve sons have become as the dust of the earth in number, and that the space needed to provide for them if they embrace the covenant again, would overwhelm the current capacity of the Holy Land to house them many times over. By establishing a gathering place for four fifths of the posterity of Israel and those adopted into the same, in the Americas, with its vast geographical and natural resources, space enough to provide a place of inheritance for all the posterity of Israel entering the covenant still exists.

When the Book of Mormon comes forth Israel will begin to be gathered, after the Gentiles have been "set up as a free people by the power of the Father, that these things might come forth from them unto a remnant of your seed, [said the Lord to the Nephites] that the covenant of the Father may be fulfilled which he hath covenanted with his people, O house of Israel...

"For it behooveth the Father that it [the restored gospel] should come forth from the Gentiles, that he may show forth his power unto the Gentiles, if they will not harden their hearts that they may repent and come unto me and be baptized in my name and know of the true points of my doctrine, that they may be numbered among

313

my people, O house of Israel; ...

"And they [the Gentiles] shall assist my people, the remnant of Jacob, and also as many of the house of Israel as shall come, that they may build a city, which shall be called the New Jerusalem. And they shall assist my people that they may be gathered in who are scattered upon all the face of the land, in unto the New Jerusalem.

"And then shall the power of heaven come down among them; and I also will be in their midst. And then shall the work of the Father commence at that day, even when the gospel shall be preached among the remnant of this people. Verily I say unto you, at that day shall the work of the Father commence among all the dispersed of my people, yea, even the tribes which have been lost, which the Father hath led away out of Jerusalem.

"Yea, the work shall commence among all the dispersed of my people, with the Father to prepare the way whereby they may come unto me, that they may call on the Father in my name. Yea, and then shall the work commence, with the Father among all nations in preparing the way whereby his people may be gathered home to the land of their inheritance. And they shall go out from all nations, and they shall not go out in haste nor go by flight, for I will go before them, saith the Father, and I will be your rearward." (3Ne 21:1-6,23-29)

From the 29th Chapter of 3rd Nephi we learn that the coming forth of the Book of Mormon is a sign that the Lord has commenced to gather Israel and fulfill his covenants.

"And now, behold, I say unto you that when the Lord shall see fit, in his wisdom, that these sayings shall come unto the Gentiles according to his word, then ye may know that the covenant which the Father hath made with the children of Israel, concerning their restoration to the land of their inheritance, is already beginning to be fulfilled.

"... and ye need not say that the Lord delays his coming unto the children of Israel... ye need not any longer spurn at the doings of the Lord, for the sword of justice is in his right hand;...Yea, wo unto them that shall deny the revelations of the Lord, and that shall say the Lord no longer worketh by revelation, or by prophecy, or by gifts, or by tongues, or by healing, or by the power of the Holy Ghost...

Yea, and ye need not any longer hiss, nor spurn, nor make game of the Jews, nor any remnant of the house of Israel; for behold, the Lord remembereth his covenant unto them, and he will do unto them according to that which he hath sworn. Therefore ye need not suppose that ye can turn the right hand of the Lord unto the left, that he may not execute judgment unto the fulfilling of the covenant which he hath made unto the house of Israel." (3Ne 29:1-9)

Speaking to the Gentiles of the last days the Lord commands them to repent and come unto Him:

"Hearken, O ye Gentiles, and hear the words of Jesus Christ, the Son of the living God, which he hath commanded me that I should speak concerning you for, behold he commandeth me that I should write saying:

"Turn, all ye Gentiles, from your wicked ways; and repent of your evil doings, of your lyings and deceivings, and of your whoredoms, and of your secret abominations, and your idolatries and of your murders and your priestcrafts and your envyings and your strifes, and from all your wickedness and abominations and come unto me and be baptized in my name, that ye may receive a remission of your sins and be filled with the Holy Ghost, that ye may be numbered with my people who of the house of Israel." (3Ne. 30:1-2)

From the Prophet Mormon

Again the prophet Mormon wrote after abridging the records of the Savior's words to the Nephites:

"Therefore I [Mormon] write unto you, Gentiles, and also unto you, house of Israel, when the work shall commence, that ye shall be about to prepare to return to the land of your inheritance." (Morm.3:17)

"Now these things [the writings of the Book of Mormon] are

315

written unto the remnant of the house of Jacob;... and they are to be hid up unto the Lord that they may come forth in his own due time... and behold they shall come forth according to the commandment of the Lord, when he shall see fit, in his wisdom.

"And behold, they shall go unto the unbelieving of the Jews; and for this intent shall they go--that they may be persuaded that Jesus is the Christ, the Son of the living God; that the Father may bring about, through his most Beloved, his great and eternal purpose, in restoring the Jews, or all the house of Israel, to the land of their inheritance, which the Lord their God hath given them, according to the fulfilling of his covenant. And also that the seed of this people [Lehi's posterity] may more fully believe the gospel, which shall go forth unto them from the Gentiles..." (Morm. 5:12-15)

From the Book of Ether, the Prophet Moroni reports the words of the brother of Jared and of Ether speaking in behalf of the Lord

"Come unto me, O ye Gentiles, and I will show unto you the greater things, the knowledge which is hid up because of unbelief.

"Come unto me, O ye house of Israel, and it shall be made manifest unto you how great things the Father hath laid up for you, from the foundation of the world;..." (Ether 4:14)

"And then, cometh the New Jerusalem; and blessed are they who dwelleth therein, for it is they whose garments are made white through the blood of the Lamb; and they are they who are numbered among the remnant of the seed of Joseph, who were of the house of Israel.

"And then also cometh the Jerusalem of old; and the inhabitants thereof, blessed are they, for they have been washed in the blood of the Lamb; and they are they who were scattered and gathered in from the four quarters of the earth, and from the north countries, and are partakers of the fulfilling of the covenant which God made with Abraham."
(Ether 13:10-11)

It is believed the promised gathering spiritually and geographically for the purpose of perfecting and redeeming Israel, the true believers of Messiah/Christ, began with the restoration of the Gospel in 1820, thereby ushering in the last dispensation before the return of the Savior, the dispensation of the fulness of times, the subject of Chapter XVI.

SUMMARY

From the scriptures we see that the Lord established a covenant people through whom He would work to achieve His purposes; His purposes being to bring to pass the immortality and eternal life of those willing to enter a covenant with Him and keep its provisions. This covenant was established first through Adam. When the people dwindled in unbelief, broke the covenant and fell away, the covenant was reestablished or restored through Enoch. When Enoch's city was taken to a place akin to the Garden of Eden, the people left behind were far from righteousness. Though the gospel was mightily preached through Noah, only eight souls were found worthy enough to survive the Flood.

The earth was repeopled by Noah's descendants through Shem, Japheth and Ham. Ten generations later the descendants of Noah, in the main, had broken the covenant and had fallen away from the Lord. The covenant was restored, this time, through Abraham. In each of these previous dispensations a body of scripture was written at the command of God, as were books of remembrance, and prophets were raised up to teach the people. Covenants were made and the people were blessed for having kept the covenant's provisions. Some of the blessings promised those who kept the provisions of the covenant all their days, related to their future posterity.

In Abraham and Sarah's case, through whom the covenant was restored, because they endured to the end in faithfulness, the Lord made good on a promise concerning their posterity, fulfilled through their grandson Jacob/Israel. The covenant God made with Abraham was continued through Isaac, then Jacob/Israel and Israel's posterity.

317

It included lands of everlasting inheritance.

After the children of Israel moved to Egypt from their promised land in Canaan, to escape the famine, they lived in righteousness for awhile. By Moses' day they had become beholden, not only to the Egyptian task masters, but to their gods of wood and stone that could neither hear, speak nor deliver. The Lord raised up Moses to lead them out of Egypt to their promised land in Canaan. But the children of Israel were not ready to live the higher law, embodied in the Abrahamic Covenant, with God. A lesser law was substituted, a law of carnal commandments led be a lesser a priesthood. This was the operable law until the ministry of Jesus Christ. The Savior reintroduced the higher law operable in the days of Abraham, as stipulated in the Sermon of the Mount, clearly a higher law. The Savior served in a dual capacity during His ministry, as the prophet of the dispensation of the meridian of time, and as the Savior and Redeemer of mankind and the God of planet earth.

But the scriptures clearly indicate the Savior would make not one, but two appearances on earth, and that prior to His second coming Israel's posterity would have the gospel preached to them, and they would enter a new and everlasting covenant with God, which included some of the provisions once operable in the Abrahamic Covenant. The scriptures also indicate that previous prophets such as Moses, knew that the children of Israel would be scattered to the ends of the earth, but their posterity would be gathered again in the Lord's own due time, and that they would embrace the provisions of this new and everlasting covenant, along with some Gentiles, all becoming true believers in Messiah/Christ. Thus the gathering of Israel includes preaching the gospel to all peoples of the earth thereby searching out the true believers in Messiah/Christ, and ultimately leading them to their lands of promise.

From the scriptures of the western hemisphere we learn that there will be two Jerusalem's built worthy for the appearance and return of the Messiah/Christ; one the site of the Old Jerusalem in the mid-east, and the other in America, in Jackson County, Missouri, in the United States of America.

Keys to the gathering of Israel were restored to the earth through Joseph Smith in 1836, as previously reported in Chapter XIV.

Many different metaphors were used in the above scriptures to symbolize the future gathering of Israel, the true believers in Messiah/ Christ. They include fishers and fish, hunters and the hunted, shepherd and the sheep, the tame and wild olive trees, the grafting in of branches, a hen and her chicks under her wing, and the gathering of sheaves. Each of these metaphors underscores the justice of God and that he is no respecter of persons, even though He has a planned sequence in accomplishing it. All of God's children will have a chance to accept or reject the Gospel of Jesus Christ. And each will gain their eternal inheritance as a direct consequence of their choices.

Worthy of note is that on several occasions the Lord has said the first shall be last and the last shall be first. As applied to the gathering of Israel, the Lord introduced the gospel to the children of Israel through Abraham, Isaac and Jacob/Israel. When the people began to fall away He sought to recover Israel from their fallen state before and after the break-up of the united kingdom. A consequence of the covenant people's failure to keep its provisions lead to their scattering by the Assyrians and Babylonians.

Now that it is time to recover Israel, the Lord said they, the known posterity of Israel had received their initial chance, so the restored gospel would be taught first to the Gentiles and then to the house of Israel, and that the house of Israel would receive the gospel from the Gentiles. But after the Gentiles had received an opportunity to hear it and embrace it, the gospel would be taken to the house of Israel in America, whose lineage from Jacob/Israel has been established through scripture. After that, the gospel would be taken to the lost tribes of Israel, as their identity is revealed by the Lord, and He signals the time to commence.

With reference to the order in which the gospel would be

preached to the house of Israel, other than those remnants surviving in America through their father Lehi already mentioned, the Lord placed the lineage of Ephraim, son of Joseph, son of Israel, son of Isaac, son of Abraham in the key position to bring His plans for gathering about. According to Archibald F. Bennett, noted Genealogical Researcher, the prophet of the dispensation of the fulness of times, Joseph Smith, whom God raised up in these last days is a descendant of both Joseph and Judah. Joseph had had the birthright blessing conferred upon him by father Israel, and Judah had had the right of kings conferred upon him also by father Israel.

It has been learned through revelation that those entering the new and everlasting covenant in the initial days of the dispensation of the fulness of times, are of the lineage of Ephraim. They are the descendants of Joseph, son of Israel, that son who had the birthright blessing bestowed upon him by father Israel. Simultaneously Manasseh had the birthright blessing conferred upon him, though the greater blessing went to Ephraim.

Those whose lineage was not known at the time of the restoration were classified as Gentiles and it was among them the gospel was first preached in this dispensation. In reality precious few of them entered the covenant, but those who did enter the covenant in the initial years of the restoration would learn by revelation through patriarchal blessings that they indeed were of the lineage of Ephraim.

As the Lord has revealed, the order of gathering to the gospel is, first to the Gentiles, that is, wherever there are ears to hear, the gospel will be preached in every nation, kindred, tongue and people without reference to whether they are of the house of Israel or not. However, those accepting the covenant and entering it, are, by and large, of one of the twelve tribes of Israel with the preponderance of members thus far being of the lineage of Ephraim and Manesseh. At this writing a few from the lineage of Judah, Benjamin, Levi, and others are now coming into the Church. A preponderance of Church leaders at this date are from these the lineage of Ephraim and Manesseh.

This pattern, however, most likely will change as the gospel is introduced to more and more countries of the earth, where scattered remnants of other tribes now live. When the Lord gives the signal, great numbers of the lost tribes of Israel will make their appearances after which they will be taught and gathered. Finally, those of the house of Judah, whose lineage has been known all along through the centuries, from the records they kept, their traditions and culture retained, will receive the Gospel and recognize the Jesus Christ was and is Messiah.

CHAPTER XVI

THE GATHERING, PERFECTION AND REDEMPTION OF ISRAEL
THE TRUE BELIEVERS IN MESSIAH/ CHRIST, BEGINS

The gathering, perfection and eventual redemption of Israel, the true believers in Messiah/Christ, have spiritual and geographical dimensions. Initially, as the gospel was restored the spiritual and geographical dimensions were inseparable, since the restoration had to start somewhere. That somewhere was with the elect of God who were prepared for their roles in the restoration before coming to earth, and included such choice people as Joseph Smith, Brigham Young, John Taylor, Wilford Woodruff, and Lorenzo Snow the first five presidents of the Church. Other elect persons include Joseph's brother Hyrum, his father and mother, Joseph Senior and Lucy Mack Smith, his wife Emma and the wives of other elect. Key players in the early days of the restoration also include Oliver Cowdery, Sidney Rigdon, Martin Harris, various members of the Whitmer family, and others.

But the literal descendants of Israel have been scattered throughout the earth, so, for them to hear the appeal to come unto Christ, and gather spiritually and geographically, means the gospel has to be preached to every nation, kindred, tongue and people.

Were and are the world's people to be taught in random order, or does the Lord have a plan to teach, gather, perfect and redeem all mankind who voluntarily respond to His voice? And what about those not of Israel's literal descent; when and where are they to be taught, by whom, and where are their gathering places? What are the evidences the spiritual and geographical gathering of Israel has begun? And what doctrines did He reaffirm or proclaim anew in these last days which will lead to perfection, redemption and eternal life for those who enter the covenant and keep its provisions? Answers to these questions are contained in the early instructions to the elect who joined the Church.

Section 10

In the summer of 1828, before the Book of Mormon was published, the Church organized, or the first portions of the Doctrine and Covenants had been published, in a revelation given to Joseph Smith the Lord referenced His "other sheep have I which are not of this fold" proclamation, contained in John 10:16.

In it, the Lord said that these other sheep were a branch of the house of Jacob that He had brought to America. He wanted to

"bring to light their marvelous works, which they did in my name; Yea, and I will also bring to light my gospel, which was ministered unto them, ... and shall bring to light the true points of my doctrine, yea, and the only doctrine that is in me. And this I do that I may establish my gospel... For, behold, I will gather them [the remnant of Israel in America] as a hen gathereth her chickens under her wings, if they will not harden their hearts; Yea, if they will come, they may, and partake of the waters of life freely. Behold, this is my doctrine-- whosoever repenteth and cometh unto me, the same is my church." (D&C 10:59-70; HC 1:20-23)

Section 14

To David Whitmer, a witness to the Book of Mormon plates through the prophet Joseph Smith in June 1829 at Fayette, New York the Lord said:

"Behold, I am Jesus Christ, the Son of the living God, who created the heavens and the earth, a light which cannot be hid in darkness; Wherefore, I must bring forth the fulness of my gospel from the Gentiles, unto the house of Israel."(D&C 14:9-10; HC 1:48-50)

Section 29

To the Prophet Joseph Smith in the presence of six elders, September, 1830 at Fayette, New York the Lord declared:

"Listen to the voice of Jesus Christ, your Redeemer, the Great I Am, whose arm of mercy hath atoned for your sins; Who will gather his people even as a hen gathereth her chickens under her wings, even as many as will hearken to my voice and humble themselves before me, and call upon me in mighty prayer..

"And ye are called to bring to pass the gathering of mine elect, for mine elect hear my voice and harden not their hearts; Wherefore the decree hath gone forth from the Father that they shall be gathered in unto one place upon the face of this land to prepare their hearts and be prepared in all things against the day when tribulation and desolation are sent upon the wicked.

"The hour is nigh and the day soon at hand when the earth is ripe; and all the proud and they that do wickedly shall be as stubble; and I will burn them up, saith the Lord of Hosts, that wickedness shall not be upon the earth.

"For the hour is nigh, and that which was spoken by mine apostles must be fulfilled; for as they spoke so shall it come to pass; For I will reveal myself from heaven with power and great glory, with all the hosts thereof, and dwell in righteousness with men on earth for a thousand years, and the wicked shall not stand.

"And again verily, verily, I say unto you, and it hath gone forth in a firm decree, by the will of the Father, that mine Apostles, the Twelve which were with me in my ministry at Jerusalem, shall stand at my right hand at the day of my coming in a pillar of fire, being clothed with robes of righteousness, with crowns upon their heads, in glory even as I am, to judge the whole house of Israel, even as many as have loved me and kept my commandments, and none else." (D&C 29:1-12; HC 1:111-115)

Section 35

To Joseph Smith and Sidney Rigdon as Joseph translated and Sidney recorded portions of the Bible at the Lord's command in December 1830 at Fayette, New York.

"the scriptures shall be given, even as they are in mine own bosom, to the salvation of mine own elect; For they will hear my voice, and shall see me, and shall not be asleep, and shall abide the day of my coming; for they shall be purified, even as I am pure.

"...And Israel shall be saved in mine own due time; and by the keys which I have given shall they be led, and no more be confounded at all. Lift up your hearts and be glad, your redemption draweth nigh." (D&C 35:20-26; HC 1:128-131)

Section 38

Through the prophet Joseph Smith at a conference of the Church January 2, 1831 at Fayette, New York the Lord said:

"whosoever I will shall go forth among all nations, and it shall be told them what they shall do; for I have a great work laid up in store, for Israel shall be saved, and I will lead them whithersoever I will, and no power shall stay my hand." (D&C 38:33, HC 1:140-143)

Section 39

Through the prophet Joseph Smith to James Covill, long term former Baptist minister, January 5, 1831.

"Thou shalt preach the fulness of my gospel, which I have sent forth in these last days, the covenant which I have sent forth to recover my people, which are of the house of Israel...

"Go forth baptizing with water, preparing the way before my face for the time of my coming; For the time is at hand; the day or hour no man knoweth; but it surely shall come. And he that receiveth these things receiveth me; and they shall be gathered unto me in time and in eternity." (D&C 39:11,20-22; HC 1:143-145)

Section 42

Through the prophet Joseph Smith in the presence of twelve elders February 9, 1831 at Fayette, New York.

"ye shall go forth into the regions westward; and inasmuch as ye shall find them that will receive you ye shall build up my church in every region- Until the time shall come when it shall be revealed unto you from on high, when the city of the New Jerusalem shall be prepared, that ye may be gathered in one, that ye may be my people, and I will be your God." (D&C 42:8-9; HC 1:148-154)

[Section 45]

This section was given through Joseph Smith the Prophet to the Church March 7, 1831 at Kirtland, Ohio at a time when many false and foolish stories were circulated and published to prevent people from investigating the work or embracing the faith. To the joy of the Saints the Lord said:

"... As ye have asked of me concerning the signs of my coming, in the day when I shall come in my glory in the clouds of heaven, to fulfill the promises that I have made unto your fathers... I will show unto you how the day of redemption shall come, and also the restoration of the scattered Israel... Ye say that ye know that the end of the world cometh; ye say also that ye know that the heavens and the earth shall pass away; And in this ye say truly; for so it is; but these things which I have told you shall not pass away until all shall be fulfilled. And this I told you concerning Jerusalem; and when that day shall come, shall a remnant be scattered among all nations;

"But they shall be gathered again; but they shall remain until the times of the Gentiles be fulfilled. And in that day shall be heard of wars and rumors of wars, and the whole earth shall be in commotion, and men's hearts shall fail them, and they shall say that Christ delayeth his coming until the end of the earth. And the love of men shall wax cold, and iniquity shall abound.

"And when the times of the Gentiles is come in, a light shall break forth among them that sit in darkness, and it shall be the fulness of my gospel. But they receive not the light, and they turn their hearts from me because of the precepts of men. And in that generation shall the times of the Gentiles be fulfilled.(D&C 45:17,25; HC 1:158-163)
D&C 45:51 (Zech 13:6)

Section 77

Explanations given to Joseph Smith the Prophet in connection with the translation of the Revelation of St. John received in March 1832. at Hiram, Ohio.

"Q. What are we to understand by the little book which was eaten by John, as mentioned in the 10th chapter of Revelation?

"A. We are to understand that it was a mission, and an ordinance, for him to gather the tribes of Israel; behold, this is Elias, who, as it is written, must come and restore all things.

"Q. What is to be understood by the two witnesses, in the eleventh chapter of Revelation?

"A. They are two prophets that are to be raised up to the Jewish nation in the last days, at the time of the restoration, and to prophecy to the Jews after they are gathered and have built the city of Jerusalem in the land of their fathers." (D&C 77:14-15; HC 1:253-255)

Section 84

In a revelation given at Kirtland, Ohio September 22, 1833 the Lord said His Church was

"established in the last days for the restoration of his people, as he has spoken by the mouth of his prophets, and for the gathering of his saints to stand upon Mount Zion, which shall be the city of Jerusalem." (D&C 84:2; HC 1:286-295)

Section 86

Given through Joseph Smith at Kirtland, Ohio when he was translating the New Testament, the Lord revealed more insight concerning the parable of the tares. During His ministry He explained the parable to His disciples, saying in part, that the good seed was sown by the Son of man; that the field is the world; that the good seed are the children of the kingdom; that the tares are the children of the wicked one; that the enemy that sowed the tares is the devil; that the harvest is the end of the world or the destruction of the wicked; that the reapers are the angels or messengers sent of heaven; that the gathering out of His kingdom all things that offend and burning of the tares is a description of the destruction of the wicked by fire before the Son of Man comes; and that the righteous that remain shall shine forth as the sun in the kingdom of their Father. (Matt 13:24-49,JST Matt 13:29-44)

On December 6, 1832 speaking through Joseph Smith in Section 86, the Lord added:

"... concerning the parable of the wheat and the tares: Behold, verily I say, the field was the world, and the apostles were the sowers of the seed; And after they had fallen asleep the great persecutor of the church, the apostate, the whore, even Babylon, that maketh all nations to drink of her cup, in whose hearts the enemy, even Satan, sitteth to reign- behold, he soweth the tares; wherefore, the tares choke the wheat and drive the church into the wilderness.

"But behold, in the last days, even now while the Lord is beginning to bring forth the word, and the blade is springing up and is yet tender--Behold, verily, I say unto you, the angels are crying unto the Lord day and night, who are ready and waiting to be sent forth the reap down the fields; But the Lord saith unto them, pluck not up the tares while the blade is yet tender (for verily your faith is weak), lest you destroy the wheat also. Therefore, let the wheat and the tares grow together until the harvest is fully ripe; then ye shall first gather out the wheat from among the tares, and after the gathering of the wheat, behold and lo, the tares are bound in bundles, and the field remaineth to be burned.

"Therefore, thus saith the Lord unto you, with whom the priesthood hath continued through the lineage of your fathers- For ye are lawful heirs, according to the flesh, and have been hid from the world with Christ in God--Therefore your life, and the priesthood have remained, and must needs remain through you and your lineage until the restoration of all things spoken by the mouths of all the holy prophets since the world began.

"Therefore, blessed are ye if ye continue in my goodness, a light unto the gentiles, and through this priesthood, a savior unto my people Israel." (D&C 86:1-11; 113:8; HC 1:300)

Note that this clarification indicates that the sowers of the good seed were the Savior and His apostles and that the wheat and the tares are to grow together until the harvest is fully ripe; then the wheat is to be first gathered out from among the tares in the field or world; leaving the tares in the field to be bundled and burned.

Hence, at this writing the Lord's covenant people are hard at work gathering the wheat with a force of some 60,000 full-time missionaries, under the direction of the Prophet of the Church and the Quorum of Twelve Apostles, with the help of all other members of the covenant acting under the counsel that every member is a missionary; each being "a light unto the Gentiles through this priesthood and a savior unto my people Israel."

[Section 90]

Putting in place the ecclesiastical and administrative structure necessary to gather, perfect and redeem Israel the Lord established the office of First Presidency. Through revelation He called two counselors to Joseph Smith: Sidney Rigdon and Frederick G. Williams, the three constituting a Quorum of First Presidency. Instructing Joseph Smith and subsequently his counselors the Lord said, March 8, 1833:

"... And when you have finished the translation of the prophets, you shall henceforth preside over the affairs of the church and the school; And from time to time, as shall be manifested by the Comforter, receive revelations to unfold the mysteries of the kingdom; And set in order the churches, and study and learn, and

329

become acquainted with all good books, and with languages, tongues and people.

"And this shall be your business and mission in all your lives, to preside in council, and set in order all the affairs of this church and kingdom. Be not ashamed neither confounded; but be admonished in all your high-mindedness and pride for it bringeth a snare unto your souls. Set in order your houses; keep slothfulness and uncleanness far from you." (v 13-18)

Getting organized to carry out their duties, they were to take care of some family business: a place for Frederick G. Williams and his family was to be provided, Sidney Rigdon was to continue to reside where he already was living, Joseph's father, aged Joseph Senior, was to live where he currently was living; the bishop was to search for an agent, a man of strong faith, a man of God, and a man with some money; a man who would help discharge every debt; that the storehouse of the Lord may not be brought into disrepute; and a handmaid, a faithful woman, Vienna Jacques, was to receive money to bear the expenses of a move from Ohio to Missouri to receive an inheritance from the hand of the bishop there, since she was a faithful saint.

The Lord closed this revelation by reiterating Joseph's call to preside over Zion, and let him know that He, the Lord would contend with Zion, would plead with her leaders, and chasten her until she overcomes and is clean before Him, "For she shall not be removed out of her place." (D&C 90:19-37, 1-37, HC 1:329-331)

Section 101

To Joseph Smith in Kirtland, Ohio the Prophet on December 16, 1833, the Lord gave explanations at a time when the Saints gathered in Missouri were suffering intense persecution. Though the Lord's indignation shall fall upon the nations, his people shall yet be gathered and comforted.

"I, the Lord, have suffered the affliction to come upon them [His people] wherewith they have been afflicted, in consequence of their transgressions; Yet I will own them, and they shall be mine in that day when I shall make up my jewels. Therefore, they must be tried, even as Abraham, who was commanded to offer up his only

330

[covenant] son. For all those who will not endure chastening, but deny me, cannot be sanctified...

"Mine indignation is soon to be poured out without measure upon all nations; and this will I do when the cup of their iniquity is full. And in that day all who are found upon the watchtower, or in other words, all mine Israel, shall be saved. And they that have been scattered shall be gathered. And all they who have mourned shall be comforted. And all they who have given their lives for my name shall be crowned. Therefore, let your hearts be comforted concerning Zion; for all flesh is in mine hands: be still and know that I am God. Zion shall not be moved out of her place, notwithstanding her children are scattered." (D&C 101:2-5,11-17; HC 1:458-464)

Section 109

A prayer was offered at the dedication of the temple at Kirtland, Ohio, March 27, 1836. This temple was built at great sacrifice by the fledgling group of Church members. The prayer was given the prophet by revelation.

"And now we ask thee, Holy Father, in the name of Jesus Christ... That all the ends of the earth may know that we, thy servants, have heard thy voice, and that thou hast sent us; That from among all these, the sons of Jacob, may gather out the righteous to build a holy city to thy name, as thou has commanded them.

"We ask thee to appoint unto Zion other stakes besides this one which thou hast appointed, that the gathering of thy people may roll on in great power and majesty, that thy work may be cut short in righteousness...

"thou knowest that thou hast a great love for the children of Jacob [Israel], who have been scattered upon the mountains for a long time, in a cloudy and dark day. We therefore ask thee to have mercy upon the children of Jacob, that Jerusalem, from this hour, may begin to be redeemed; And the yoke of bondage may begin to be broken off from the house of David; And the children of Judah may return to the lands which thou didst give to Abraham, their father.

..."And may all the scattered remnants of Israel, who have been driven to the ends of the earth, come to a knowledge of the truth, believe in the Messiah, and be redeemed from oppression, and rejoice before thee." (D&C 109:4,57-67; HC 2:420-426)

Section 110

In a vision manifested to Joseph Smith the prophet and Oliver Cowdery in the temple at Kirtland, Ohio April 3, 1836 Joseph Smith affirmed:

"We saw the Lord standing on the breastwork of the pulpit, before us; and under his feet was a paved work of pure gold, in color like amber. His eyes were as a flame of fire, the hair on his head was white like the pure snow; his countenance shone above the brightness of the sun; and his voice was as the sound of the rushing of great waters, even the voice of Jehovah saying: I am the first and the last; I am he who liveth, I am he who was slain; I am your advocate with the Father.

..."After this vision closed, the heavens were again opened unto us; and Moses appeared before us, and committed unto us the keys of the gathering of Israel from the four parts of the earth, and the leading of the ten tribes from the land of the north..." (D&C 110:2-4,11; HC 2:435-436)

Section 113

In response to questions raised by some who entered the covenant of baptism, given in March 1838.

Q. "What is the rod spoken of in the first verse of the 11th chapter of Isaiah, that should come of the Stem of Jesse?

A. "Behold, thus saith the Lord: it is a servant in the hands of Christ, who is partly a descendant of Jesse as well as of Ephraim, or of the house of Joseph, on whom there is laid much power.

Q. "What is the root of Jesse spoken of in the 10th verse of the 11th chapter?

A. "Behold, thus saith the Lord, it is a descendant of Jesse, as well as of Joseph, unto whom rightly belongs the priesthood, and the keys of the kingdom, for an ensign, and for the gathering of my people in the last days.

Q. "What is meant by the command in Isaiah, 52d chapter, 1st verse, which saith-

Put on thy strength O Zion-- and what people had Isaiah reference to?

A. "He had reference to those whom God should call in the

last days, who should hold the power of priesthood to bring again Zion, and the redemption of Israel; and to put on her strength is to put on the authority of the priesthood which she, Zion, has a right to by lineage; also to return to that power which she had lost.

Q. "What are we to understand by Zion loosing herself from the bands of her neck; 2d verse?

A. "We are to understand that the scattered remnants are exhorted to return to the Lord from whence they have fallen; which if they do, the promise of the Lord is that he will speak to them, or give them revelation... The bands of her neck are the curses of God upon her, or the remnants of Israel in their scattered condition among the Gentiles."(D&C 113:1-10; HC 3:9-10)

Section 125

Concerning the Saints in Iowa Territory, revelation was received through Joseph Smith at Nauvoo, Illinois March 1841. In it the Lord said the Saints were and are to build cities and gather to the stakes of Zion. More specifically:

"Verily, thus saith the Lord, I say unto you, if those who call themselves by my name and are essaying to be my saints, if they will do my will and keep my commandments concerning them, let them gather themselves together unto the places which I shall appoint unto them by my servant Joseph, and build up cities unto my name, that they may be prepared for that which is in store for a time to come.

"Let them build up a city unto my name upon the land opposite the city of Nauvoo, and let the name of Zarahemla [Iowa] be named upon it. And let all those who come from the east, and the west, and the north and the south, that have desires to dwell therein, take up their inheritance in the same, as well as in the city of Nashville, [Iowa], or in the city of Nauvoo, [Illinois] and in all the stakes which I have appointed, saith the Lord."(D&C 125:1-4; HC 4:311-312)

Section 133

In a revelation November 3, 1831 given through the prophet Joseph Smith the Lord directed:

"Send forth the elders of my church unto the nations which are afar off; unto the isles of the sea; send them forth unto foreign lands;

call upon all nations, first upon the Gentiles, and then upon the Jews. And behold and lo, this shall be their cry, and the voice of the Lord unto all people: Go forth unto the land of Zion, that the borders of my people may be enlarged, and that her stakes may be strengthened and that Zion may go forth unto the regions round about.

...'Let them, therefore, who are among the Gentiles flee unto Zion. And let them who be of Judah flee unto Jerusalem, unto the mountains of the Lord's house. Go ye out from among the nations, even Babylon, from the midst of wickedness, which is spiritual Babylon." (D&C 133:8-14; HC 1:229-234)

Summarizing all this the Prophet Joseph Smith declared in 1842 that one of the articles of faith espoused by the Church of Jesus Christ of Latter-day Saints is

"We believe in the literal gathering of Israel and in the restoration of the Ten Tribes; that Zion (the New Jerusalem) will be built upon the American continent; that Christ will reign personally upon the earth; and that the earth will be renewed and receive its paradisiacal glory." (Tenth Article of Faith)

That the spiritual gathering unto Messiah/Christ, through the Lord's authorized agents holding His priesthood had begun in earnest by the early 1840's is evident by an editorial in the Norwalk, Connecticut Gazette, located more than a thousand miles to the east of Nauvoo, Illinois.

"One or two of Joe Smith's disciples are traveling through the vicinity and edifying the curious with the dogmas of their creed, and defending from common reprehension the character of their interesting earthly head. We have not had time to give these gentlemen much of a hearing... If we do so we shall tell all our readers something about them and their new fangled latter dayism. All we can say with certainty now is, that they are not lacking in lungs or volubility."

From a February 9, 1842 editorial the Norwalk Gazette wrote under the heading of:

The Mormons:

"This singular sect, which has so recently sprung up and is so rapidly increasing, is sending its agents abroad without stint, judging

334

from the supply which has fallen to our lot. For several weeks, regular periodical meetings have been held in this and neighboring towns.

"Many are drawn to hear their doctrines, and as might be supposed, a few have embraced them and been baptized. This ordinance is performed after the manner of the Baptists, by dipping. Much zeal and industry is manifested in the propagation of their creed. They boldly challenge investigators, and shrink not from the closest scrutiny.

"Whatever may be thought of their theories, or the delusions they are playing off on the world, we believe it is a fact, that they are increasing in numbers as rapidly as any Christian denomination, if indeed they are not entirely outstripping them. It was stated in a discourse delivered in this place that the Mormons have a foothold on every territory and state in the Union and that their city of Nauvoo contains a population of 10,000 souls and increasing rapidly."

A neighboring paper the Danbury, Connecticut Times wrote January 26, 1842:

"Two Mormon madcaps who had got the hang of the Mormon story made their appearance in Danbury."

A Litchfield, Connecticut paper under a March 20, 1842 date discussed Joseph Smith's translation of the Book of Abraham from manuscripts discovered in Egyptian catacombs; the New York Mechanic reported under date of July 6, 1842 the Mormons had ten churches in New England; and the Journal of Commerce reported November 24, 1841, that of the 17,068,666 people in the 1840 United States Census about 100,000 were members of the Church of Jesus Christ of Latter-day Saints.

As of mid-1998 worldwide Church membership has surpassed 10,000,000, and with a missionary force of 60,000 those numbers will likely increase even more rapidly. Indeed Israel, those who are the true believers of Messiah/Christ, are being gathered spiritually to Him. But what of the geographical gathering to the Old and New Jerusalems?

The Spiritual and Geographical Gathering

The gathering of the Lord's elect few who participated in the early days of the restoration was a simultaneous spiritual gathering to Messiah/Christ and a geographical gathering to designated lands, of perhaps less than five thousand souls, who set the stage for the return of priesthood keys which were restored after the Kirtland Temple was completed; keys to the gathering, perfection and redemption of Israel, the true believers of Messiah/Christ committed to Joseph Smith and Oliver Cowdery by Moses, Elias and Elijah.

In these early days all those who were baptized were, in effect, gathered spiritually to Messiah/Christ by virtue of their entrance into the covenant, and were encouraged to gather geographically to Church headquarters or to settle in communities nearby. Gathering places included the Kirtland, Ohio area, then Jackson County, Missouri and neighboring counties.

With the move to Missouri in 1831, it was the Lord's intent to begin building the New Jerusalem with its related center stake of Zion, and several temples, as the geographical gathering place for the descendants of tribes of the northern kingdom of Israel who had already been gathered spiritually by entrance into the covenant through baptism.

With the dedication of the land of Palestine by Apostle Orson Hyde for the gathering of the descendants of Judah in 1841, it seems the Lord intended to begin their geographical gathering first to Jerusalem and environs, followed by their spiritual gathering to Christ the true Messiah. In like manner, but in reverse order, the descendants of Ephraim and the other tribes were to be gathered first spiritually followed by their geographical gathering to the New Jerusalem in Independence, Jackson County, Missouri, and other places in America.

However, when the Saints already gathered spiritually through entering the covenant, were forced to move, they left the designated geographical gathering places in Jackson and other Missouri Counties and settled in Nauvoo, Hancock County, Illinois and environs. When they were forced out of Nauvoo, they moved west taking with them all who voluntarily joined them. Hence, the geographical gathering of the Lord's covenant people to their places of inheritance in the New Jerusalem has been delayed.

During the administrations of President Brigham Young and several Presidents that followed, many of those who gathered to Messiah/Christ by entering the covenant and who had emigrated to Salt Lake City were sent out to build communities and church units in places where none existed before.

During this period those entering the covenant in foreign lands were encouraged to emigrate to Utah, and to some extent Idaho and Arizona, in the United States of America, to help build up Zion, in temporary gathering places, by becoming members of stakes already organized. However, as the twentieth century arrived, it became clear that Zion, which includes people entering the covenant from every nation, kindred, tongue and people, would be gathered to the Savior more quickly, if stakes of the Church were organized around clusters of members wherever they lived in the world. This enables missionary work to proceed unimpeded until such time as the Lord again signals that the geographical gathering for building the New Jerusalem in Jackson County, Missouri has been restarted, and the rebuilding of the Old Jerusalem is upon us.

With reference to the gathering of Israel, it has also become clear, that generally, those descendants of Israel's ten northern tribes were and are the first to be gathered spiritually to Messiah/Christ, and will be the last to be gathered geographically to their lands of inheritance in the New Jerusalem and environs; and that the descendants of Judah and Benjamin were and are the first to be gathered geographically to the land of their inheritance in Palestine and the last to be gathered spiritually to Messiah/ Christ. Evidences that the spiritual gathering of Israel to Messiah/Christ is well under way have already been indicated.

Words from a hymn entitled, "Come, O Thou Kings of Kings," by Parley P. Pratt, a member of the first Quorum of Twelve Apostles in this dispensation, foreshadow the geographical gathering of the Jews to their home.

Originally this land was given by the Lord to Abraham, then Isaac, then Jacob and their posterity some 3,600 years ago. The Jews, the descendants of Judah, son of Jacob/Israel, though retaining their ethnic identity, were scattered throughout the earth and had not occupied Jerusalem [and environs] as a people for almost 2,000 years. Elder Pratt's hymn pleads for the gathering of the long scattered house of Israel of which the lineage of Judah, or Jews, is a part. The geographical gathering of the Jewish people to the land of Palestine is now taking place. Chapter XVII, LET ISRAEL NOW BE GATHERED HOME, addresses that topic.

CHAPTER XVII

LET ISRAEL NOW BE GATHERED HOME

****

The Geographical Gathering of Judah

Harry Truman, in his third year as President of the United States, knew May 14, 1948 would be a special day. This was the day the Jewish state was to be declared. The name of the new state was not yet known.

From his studies of ancient history and the Bible, Truman saw the parallel of present events with the time of Cyrus. Cyrus, the Persian leader, was then in control of Babylon, more than half a century after the kingdom of Judah fell and many of its people had been taken captive by the Babylonians.

Cyrus allowed the Judean exiles in Babylon to return to their homes some seventy years after their capture. [This fulfilled a prophecy of Jeremiah.]

Truman gave much needed assistance to the newly created state of Israel. Seeing the parallel, Truman said later that he had felt like saying, "I am Cyrus"!

Truman was a supporter of the idea of a Jewish homeland in Palestine. He had aggressively worked for the passage of the United Nations resolution which partitioned Palestine into a Jewish state and an Arab state. This resolution passed November 29, 1947.

Although there was great support throughout the United States for the creation of a Jewish state, President Truman faced opposition on this issue from many advisers. The Pentagon and the State Department were opposed to any further American support for the new state and did not advise official recognition by our country. The military Chief of Staff estimated the new nation would need 100,000 American troops to protect it from expected invasion by Arab armies. The Secretary of Defense, Forrestal, reminded Truman of our critical need for Saudi Arabian oil. Truman told him he would make his

339

decision based on justice, not oil.

The State Department said that all our legations and consulate offices in the middle east and all the members of the State Department who had responsibility for that area were opposed to further support for partition. One of his advisers, however, noted that a separate Jewish state was inevitable, and that it was scheduled to take place in the near future. He quoted lines from Deuteronomy regarding the Jewish claim to Palestine.

"Behold, I have set the land before you. Go in and possess the land which the Lord swear unto your fathers, Abraham, Isaac and Jacob, and gave unto them and their seed forever."

The new Jewish state, the first Jewish state in nearly 2,000 years, was proclaimed on schedule, at midnight, May 14, 1948. David Ben-Gurion read over the radio the new nation's Declaration of Independence.

"The land of Israel was the birthplace of the Jewish people. Here they wrote and gave the Bible to the world." Continuing, he said "The state of Israel will be open to the immigration of the Jews from all the countries of the dispersion." He also said the state's values "will be based on the precepts of liberty, justice and peace taught by the Hebrew prophets."

Eleven minutes after the Jewish state was created, at midnight, the White House Press Secretary, Charlie Ross, announced that the United States was giving defacto recognition to Israel, the first country to do so. The following year Israel's Chief Rabbi visited President Truman and told him, "God put you in your mother's womb so that you could be the instrument to bring about the birth of Israel, after two thousand years."

The new state was named Israel. Its flag is white and light blue with a star of David in the center.

Orson Hyde Dedication

Orson Hyde, in his sixth year as a member of the Quorum of Twelve Apostles of the Church, visited Jerusalem. On Sunday morning October 24, 1841, before daybreak, he walked out of the city as soon as the gates were open, crossed the brook Kedron, and went up upon the Mount of Olives. Here he offered a prayer, dedicating the land of Palestine for the gathering of the Jews.

In this prayer he said in part:

"O, Thou, who didst covenant with Abraham, Thy friend, and who didst renew that covenant with Isaac, and confirm the same with Jacob with an oath, that Thou wouldst not only give them this land for an everlasting inheritance, but that Thou wouldst also remember their seed forever...

"Their children are scattered and dispersed abroad among the nations of the Gentiles like sheep that have no shepherd and are still looking forward for the fulfillment of these promises.

"Grant therefore ... to remove the barrenness and sterility of this land and let springs of living water break forth to water its thirsty soil. Let the vine and the olive produce in their strength and the fig tree bloom and flourish. Let the land become abundantly fruitful when possessed by its rightful heirs ... Let the flocks and herds greatly increase and multiply upon the mountains and the hills ...

"Incline them to gather in upon this land according to thy word. Let them come like clouds and like doves to their windows. Let the large ships of nations bring them from the distant isles...

"Thou, O Lord, did once move upon the heart of Cyrus to show favor unto Jerusalem and her children, Do Thou now also be pleased to inspire the hearts of kings and powers of the earth to look with a friendly eye towards this place ... Let them know it is thy good pleasure to restore the kingdom unto Israel -- raise up Jerusalem as its capital, and constitute her people a distinct nation and government."

He then made an unequivocal statement regarding the powers who would help in the endeavor and those who would not assist in this work.

"Let this nation or people who shall take an active part in behalf of Abraham's children, and in the raising up of Jerusalem, find favor in thy sight. Let not their enemies prevail against them, neither let pestilence of famine overcome them ... while that nation or kingdom that will not serve Thee in this glorious work must perish according to Thy word-- Yea, those nations shall be utterly destroyed." (HC IV. p 456-457)

In his travels Elder Hyde said he had found many Jews who were interested in the subject. He said the idea of the Jews being restored to Palestine "is gaining ground in Europe almost every day." Already there were Jews who had immigrated to Palestine and were living in small groups. He estimated that the population of Jerusalem at that time was twenty thousand. Of these about seven thousand were Jews and the rest were Turks and Armenians.

PALESTINE

Palestine is the territory along the eastern coast of the Mediterranean Sea. From early times this land was occupied by many different tribes. This land is a bridge between Africa, Asia and Europe. For centuries lines of caravans traveled across this land to trade with the far flung areas of the world.

As previously mentioned, Abraham, his family and followers entered Palestine in the second millennium B.C. The scriptures refer to Palestine as Canaan. Abraham was called "the father of the many nations." (Gen. 17:5) and "the friend of God". (2 Chron. 20:7) He was the father of Isaac and the grandfather of Jacob, whose name was changed to Israel. Jacob's twelve sons and their descendants are known as the children of Israel.

Jacob's family, the Israelites, left Canaan, their land of promise, and moved to Egypt at their brother Joseph's invitation. After Joseph died the children of Israel were eventually held there in captivity and servitude. They were liberated and led to freedom by Moses. Joshua led them back to Palestine, the Promised Land, the land that had been promised by the Lord to Abraham and his posterity.

A monarchy was eventually established under David and his son Solomon. Solomon's reign in the tenth century B.C. was a very prosperous time for Israel. The temple was built at Jerusalem. At his death the united kingdom was divided into two parts; the northern part was named, Israel, and the southern part, Judah.

In 722 B.C. the Kingdom of Israel was destroyed by the

Assyrians and the entire population was deported. That was the end of the kingdom.

In 586 B.C. the Kingdom of Judah was conquered by the Babylonians. Judah's inhabitants were carried away into exile in Babylon, except for the poor and infirm who were left behind to care for unharvested crops, and except for Jeremiah the prophet.

The Babylonians destroyed the temple at Jerusalem and carried away its contents. In the scriptures the Jews in exile expressed their feelings: :

> "By the waters of Babyon
> We sat down and wept
> How can we sing the Lord's song
> In a strange land."
> (Psalms 137)

Fifty years later the Persian ruler Cyrus II gained control over Babylon. Twenty years after that he permitted the Judean exiles to return to Palestine and to rebuild the temple.

In the following centuries, hegemony over Palestine was held by the Ptolemias, Seleucids [Syrians] and in 65 B.C. by the Romans. Jesus lived in Palestine at the time of Roman rule.

A rebellion against Rome commenced in 66 A.D. The city of Jerusalem was captured and destroyed in August, 70 A.D. The temple was destroyed. All that was left was one outer wall on the western side. This has been known as the Western Wall and is still standing.

In 135 A.D. another revolt was put down. These two revolts led to the loss of Jewish political authority in Palestine until 1948. One million Jews were killed in these revolts.

With the complete end of the kingdom of Judah, almost all the rest of the Jewish people were dispersed.

From 135 A.D. until 1948 there were several powers who controlled Palestine's real estate. The Romans continued their rule until the division of the Roman empire, and then the Byzantine's were in control until 614. The Persians had a brief rule and the Mohammedans possessed the land for 500 years.

343

The crusaders captured the Holy Land in 1100 and ruled until 1300 A.D. The Mamelukes, a series of Egyptian sultans, gained control for 200 years. In 1517 the Ottoman Turks annexed Palestine. Over the years the Ottoman Empire and its possessions declined until by 1860, Palestine had practically become a barren desert.

THE DISPERSION

After 135 A.D. most of the Jewish people remaining in Palestine turned westward in dispersion. They had been preceded by merchants and traders who had already visited Europe. At the time of Paul there were Jewish communities in Greece, Italy, and Spain. Soon they formed communities in France and in the Rhineland. The leaders of these countries welcomed them during the first three centuries of this dispersion.

But the situation of the Jews changed during the Middle Ages. Restrictive laws began to be enacted against them. They and their children were not permitted to become citizens. They could not own land. Many professions were closed to them. Finally they were forced to live in a certain area of each town, or in what came to be called ghettoes. During the Middle Ages the western European countries began to expel the Jews from their lands; England in 1290, France in 1306, Spain in 1492, Portugal in 1496, and Navarre in 1498. In Germany there was no general expulsion, but there was local banishment and massacres. Following these expulsions the vast majority of the Jews moved eastward and settled in Turkey, Poland, Russia and eastern Europe.

By the nineteenth century the western European countries had invited the Jews to return but the great majority remained in eastern Europe. By 1870 central and western lands had practically all granted equality of rights to their Jewish inhabitants and they were given the right to vote, hold office and all restrictions were removed. The United States had never denied the Jews rights accrued to any of its citizens.

The idea of the actual establishment of a Jewish state began to surface about 1860, nineteen years after Orson Hyde's dedication

344

of Palestine. This happened at a time when a wave of anti-semitism appeared throughout Europe. By the late nineteenth century pogroms or systematic planned massacres of Jewish communities had started in Russia. Those who favored the creation of a Jewish state believed that Jews could never find security by fleeing from one country to another, but needed to have a country of their own.

Several books published between 1860 and 1900 presented this idea. The first was Rome and Jerusalem written in 1862 by Moses Hess. Later an influential essay The Eternal People was published by Peretz Smolenskin. In the 1880's Rabbi Samuel Mohileve inaugurated the first immigration wave to Palestine. He founded a political action organization, named Lovers of Zion. A part of its platform was the purchase of land in Palestine. Its slogan was "On To Palestine". The time was right for the Zionism movement to begin.

THEODOR HERZL

If I forget thee, O Jerusalem

In 1896 a book was published in Vienna, The Jewish State. Its author was Theodor Herzl [1860 to 1904]. Herzl had been raised in a wealthy, Jewish home in Vienna. He had studied law, but later became a well known journalist. He was sent to France to cover the Dreyfus trial. Dreyfus, a Jewish captain in the French army, was falsely accused of spying for the German army. The Dreyfus Affair with its overtones of anti-semitism caused Herzl to write his book. This was the beginning of the movement known as Zionism.

He said the aims of Zionism were "to create for the Jewish people a homeland secured by public law." Zionism was not to be a mere trickle of individual Jews returning to Palestine, but mass movement of farmers, workers, managers, entrepreneurs and scholars. The book created a sensation among the Jewish people. This was to be a voluntary exodus, not to wilderness, but to a recognized Jewish state.

This concept was not a piecemeal program, but a total

concept.

Herzl gained great support, especially from the Jewish people in eastern Europe.

He organized an international Zionist movement, and in 1897 convened the First Zionist Congress in Basel, Switzerland.

Herzl, himself, had a commanding appearance. He was handsome and always dressed in elegantly tailored suits. He was a prophetic figure.

At the first and subsequent meetings of the Zionist Congress Herzl wore full morning dress with a top hat. His appearance and utterances were intended to convey that he headed a dynamic world organization: "We are here to lay the foundation stone of the house which is to shelter the Jewish nation," he stated. He also declared, "If you will it, it is no legend."

In the last speech which he was ever to give to a Zionist Congress he raised his right hand and said in Hebrew quoting Psalm 137, "If I forget thee, O Jerusalem, let my right hand wither." Herzl died in 1904 at the age of forty-four. His work took place during a period of just ten years. He started a movement that became a state.

BEGINNINGS

From the time of Herzl's death to the declaration of Israel's independence was forty-four years. All this time the work of the Zionists continued.

A Zionist Jewish National Fund was set up. The Zionist's decided to buy land for all Jewish settlers. By 1948 the fund had paid millions of dollars to buy 250,000 acres of desert land in Palestine.

Actually Jewish immigration came in five waves. The first wave was 1880 to 1900 comprised mostly of farmers. The second wave 1900 to 1914 included scientific farmers and laborers. The third wave, 1918 to 1924, was made up of young people and entrepreneurs. In the fourth wave, 1924 to 1929, intellectuals, professionals and bureaucrats arrived. After World War II Jews came from every occupation.

During World War II the Holocaust took place, the planned

murder of six million Jews in German death camps. When it became known the world was horrified. When the war ended Jewish survivors needed a home. Many were in Displaced Persons Camps through out Europe. During 1946 and 1947 it was not possible for many people to emigrate to Palestine because of a restrictive policy by the British who held a mandate over Palestine. The British voluntarily gave up their mandate and turned control of Palestine over to the United Nations in 1948.

Shortly after the creation of the state of Israel fifty-two refugee camps in Europe were closed. In just a few years more than 200,000 Holocaust survivors had settled in Israel.

By 1948 the appearance of Palestine had changed, Instead of a barren desert, a modern agricultural and industrial state had appeared. The desert was criss-crossed with fertile farmland, villages, factories and orange groves had sprung up, There were museums, opera houses and theaters. There were also colleges, hospitals, art galleries, newspapers and magazines.

THE RETURN

A few hours after the proclamation of Israel's independence five Arab armies attacked. These were the armies of Egypt, Trans-Jordan, Iraq, Syria and Lebanon. In a few weeks it appeared there would be an Israeli victory. The United Nations arranged a truce. When the truce ended the Arab armies attacked. The Israeli counter attack carried them to enemy territory. Another United Nations truce was arranged. When the truce was broken the Israeli army crossed Egypt's borders. Egypt, and one by one, the other Arab nations sued for peace. The war was won and Israel had gained additional territory. Other wars followed and Israel won those also.

Since independence, Jewish immigrants have arrived from all over the world.

There is a law in Israel called the Law of Return. (Khok ha-Sh'vuk) The law states all Jews have the right to emigrate to Israel and claim immediate citizenship.

ON EAGLES WINGS

Of special interest is the return of the Jews from Yemen and later the return of the Ethiopian Jews.

With the creation of Israel difficulties arose for the Jews who lived in Arab countries. People from Egypt, Iraq and Syria fled in great numbers to Israel.

The Yemenite Jews lived in one of the poorest Arab countries of the world. There were anti-semitic restrictions on them. They could not wear brightly colored clothes, have weapons or use saddles. Arab school children threw stones at them. Yemen itself was very primitive and few inhabitants had ever had the use of electricity.

Israel airlifted the Jews of Yemen and took them to Israel. Many were reminded of the Biblical verse, "Ye have seen ... how I bare you on eagles wings and brought you unto myself." (Ex.19:4)

This became known as "Operation Magic Carpet".

Airlifts were also used to bring the black Jews of Ethiopia to Israel. The Ethiopian Jews were known as Falashas. ("landless people") They called themselves Beta Yisrael (House of Israel"). They had split at a very early time from the rest of the Jewish people.

The Ethiopians Jews were treated in a humane way when Haile Selassie was Emperor, but in the 1970's he was overthrown and a Marxist government came into power. The new government under the Communist dictator, President Mengistu, was strongly anti-Israel. The Ethiopian Jews were in a very dangerous situation.

In the early 1980's, Israel started to bring out by plane as many of the Ethiopian Jews as possible. This was known "Operation Moses." When the Ethiopian government found out how many were leaving they forbade further emigration. Many thousand Ethiopian Jews had been airlifted to Israel, but there were 3500 who remained unable to leave.

The Israeli government contacted former United States President Jimmy Carter and asked him to intercede for these people so they could get emigration permits. Through the Carter Center in Atlanta, Georgia, which he had founded, President Carter had been able to negotiate a number of international problems. He talked with

President Mengistu about this matter. President Mengistu agreed to release the Falashas, if the government of Israel made a direct request to him. This was done and the 3500 Ethiopian Jews were flown to Israel. This was called "Operation Solomon".

Israel has now become the only country where people who were once exiled from their land have returned.

Our hope is not yet lost
The hope of 2,000 years
To be a free people in our own land
The land of Zion and Jerusalem
(Hatikvah)

TODAY

With the barrenness and sterility of the land removed, not only does the land sustain a population in excess of 5,000,000 mostly Jews, agricultural products from Israel, such as citrus, are even being exported to countries in southern Africa.

Evidences of the geographical gathering of Judah to the land of their permanent inheritance abound. These evidences, however, did not gain momentum until after March 27, 1836, when the prophet Joseph Smith appealed to the Lord

"to have mercy upon the children of Jacob, that Jerusalem, from this hour, may begin to be redeemed ... And the children of Judah may begin to return to the lands which thou didst give unto Abraham their father." (D&C 109:62-64).

Seven days following this appeal on April 3, 1836, the Lord sent Moses to restore the keys for the gathering of Israel from the four parts of the earth, and the leading of the ten tribes from the north, which were conferred upon Joseph Smith. On that same day the Lord sent Elias who committed the dispensation of the gospel of Abraham, saying that in us and our seed all the generations after us should be blessed." (D&C 110:11-12)

After Israel was created as a sovereign state, several other prominent leaders, in addition to President's Truman and Carter, helped Israel towards achieving her goals. For example: In the 1980's a large emigration of Jewish people from the Soviet Union took place. This came about because the United States Congress granted Most Favored Nation status to the Soviet Union, on condition that Jewish people be allowed to leave the country. Senator Henry "Scoop" Jackson led this congressional action.

Thus we see that the geographical gathering of the children of Judah to their promised land is well under way. The rebuilding of the Old Jerusalem has not yet begun. An interim geographical gathering of those of other tribes to staging areas is under way, in preparation for receiving their permanent lands in inheritance in the eastern and western hemispheres. At this writing there are nearly 3,000 stakes of Zion throughout the world in which some ten million from various tribes of Israel are temporarily gathered. More than four million of the house of Judah have already gathered to their homeland in Palestine.

The restoration of the ten tribes, as a body of true believers in Messiah/Christ however, the geographical building of the New Jerusalem upon the American continent, and a geographical gathering to the center place of the New Jerusalem are yet to be fulfilled.

The Lord's Zion Society which is to be the new world order, will flower just prior to His Second Coming.

But just what is a Zion Society; what are its characteristics and purposes? Answers and explanations are in Chapters XVIII and XIX..

CHAPTER XVIII

A ZION SOCIETY

WHAT WERE THE PURPOSES AND CHARACTERISTICS OF EARLY ZION SOCIETIES?

The geographical gathering of the Jews to Zion continues as discussed in the previous chapter. Zionism for the Jews relates to their gathering to lands promised by the Lord through Abraham, Isaac and Jacob/Israel. Several presidents of the United States of America have used the powers of the presidency to assist in the creation of and maintenance of the free state of Israel. They have also assisted in relocating Jews to Palestine from Ethiopia and Yemen.

These Presidents: Truman, Nixon and Carter, were and are likely unaware they helped fulfill parts of Orson Hyde's prayer of dedication uttered on the Mount of Olives in October, 1841; and have also helped fulfill some parts of Joseph Smith's prayer of dedication for the Kirtland, Ohio Temple in March, 1836.

But why all the interest in Zion? What were the purposes and characteristics of early Zion Societies and how do those Societies relate to our day?

Answers to questions concerning the purposes and characteristics of a Zion Society in general, and of early Zion Societies in particular, lie in the scriptures, the Old and New Testaments, the Book of Mormon, the Doctrine and Covenants, the Pearl of Great Price and related writings.

Latter-day revelation defines **Zion** as **the pure in heart.** (D&C 97:21)

It is a spiritual condition as well as a geographical location, and therefore those who seek Zion seek both.

For purposes of this presentation, Zion as a spiritual condition as well as a geographical location will be discussed together and no

351

attempt will be made to separate them at the outset. Later the point will be made that the pure in heart need not be in contiguous locations, at least as long as the earth remains divided by oceans. The scriptures and the Prophet Joseph Smith indicate that Zion or the New Jerusalem will be built on the American Continent, but this may refer to the headquarters city for Zion in America and not to the totality of Zion, which may include all the Western Hemisphere.

Similarly, the Old Jerusalem is to be a headquarters city for Zion in the Eastern Hemisphere, and again should not be considered to be the totality of Zion in that part of the world. More on this subject later.

A Zion Society is not new. It existed on earth prior to the Flood in the days of Enoch, a great and powerful prophet in his day. It also appears that characteristics of a Zion Society were present in Salem, now known as Jerusalem, when Melchizedek was king of Salem, and again in the days of Abraham, Isaac and Jacob. Abraham had received the keys to spiritual blessings and priesthood authority from Melchizedek.

Characteristics of a Zion Society are also evident in the records of the people of Lehi, a prophet whom the Lord led to America from Jerusalem about 600 years B.C. Here they developed a mighty civilization and entered into covenants with the Lord. When they lived these covenants, characteristics of a Zion Society surfaced and flourished. Tragically, the posterity of most of those who had set up the Zion Society at that time in America broke their covenants with the Lord and eventually were swept off the earth as a consequence.

But records left behind in the Book of Mormon by the faithful, addressed to us in the dispensation of the fulness of times, in latter-day revelation, contained in the Doctrine and Covenants and in inspired translations of the Bible, provide priceless insights as to what a Zion Society was and is like. These records also make clear that ultimately, a Zion Society is to be the new world order as Israel, the true believers in Messiah/Christ are gathered, perfected and eventually redeemed.

Thus the purposes of a Zion Society were and are to help gather, perfect, and redeem its members from their fallen state, and to return them to the presence of God. The processes of gathering, perfecting and redeeming a Zion Society's members and returning them to the presence of God are achieved by placing the members of the Society under covenant and helping them to keep the covenant's provisions through the choices they make. Those who keep the provisions of the covenant become perfected step by step, principle by principle and are eventually redeemed and returned to God's presence with His approval and blessing.

Those who keep the provisions of the covenant through the choices they make, and perfect themselves with the help of God and their righteous forebears, will be instrumental in setting up a Zion Society, which will be in place when the Savior comes again, this time in all glory and majesty. A Zion Society could be characterized as being the kingdom of God on earth.

To help us flesh out the purposes of a Zion Society and define its characteristics, let us examine that Zion Society which existed before the Flood; after the Flood in Salem under Melchizedek; in Abraham's tents wherever he lived; among Book of Mormon peoples; in the messages of the Savior while He walked the earth, especially in the Sermon on the Mount, and shortly after His resurrection when the Saints had all things in common both in the eastern and western hemisheres; and consider them as prototypes or models of a Zion Society the Messiah/Savior wants us to set up in our day. Let us also examine the life of their leaders and their relationship to the creator of heaven and earth.

In Chapter II, we developed the notion that full accountability to God for choices made pre-supposes individuals are free to choose. Further, that essential to the Lord's plan of salvation and exaltation for all mankind is the principle of agency, the right to choose, or the right of self determination, and that no individual can be held fully accountable for choices made between good and evil unless she/he is able to know good and evil for her/himself, is able to identify which is which, and is free from political, economic and religious perspectives to do so. Persons in poverty are restricted in living spiritual values when they are preoccupied with hunger. Persons are restricted in living fully spiritual laws, if the political state where they reside does not allow them to choose their religion. In like manner, persons are restricted in their ability to develop a Zion Society if the state mandates their religion. In essence, the principle of agency is essential to accountability before God for individual and collective choices made and that agency cannot be fully exercised unless there is freedom from economic, political and religious perspectives to do so. Our review of past Zion Societies will therefore keep these three perspectives in mind.

References to Zion are found in Deuteronomy, Second Samuel, Psalms, Isaiah, Jeremiah, Joel, Micah, and Zechariah in the King James Version of the Old Testament and in Romans, Hebrews and the Book of Revelation in the New Testament. References to Zion are also found in the writings of the first, second, third and fourth books of Nephi, and in Mosiah and Moroni in the Book of Mormon. References to Zion are also found in at least twenty-two sections of the Doctrine and Covenants.

Joseph Smith translated Genesis using the King James Version of the Old Testament as a reference. This translation was undertaken at the command of God commencing in June 1830. It contains significant additions to scripture which relate to Enoch and his city of Zion. These additions are now a part of the Writings of Moses in the Pearl of Great Price. Drawing from these combined sources we learn much more about Enoch and the character of his city of Zion.

We learn that Enoch was twenty-five years old when he was ordained at the hand of Adam; and he was sixty-five when Adam blessed him. Given Adam was the patriarch of the earth at the time of this blessing it is likely Enoch's blessing today would be called a patriarchal blessing. More on patriarchal blessings later.

Enoch saw the Lord, walked with him and was before His face continually for the space of 365 years after having been blessed by Adam, making him 430 years old when he was translated. (D&C 107:48-49) A translated being is one whose body has been changed without tasting death. This state of being permits them to walk the earth among the children of men indefinitely, and also to walk among the beings in the paradise of a terrestrial glory, a place of higher order than the earth is in its current state. More on bodies telestial, terrestrial and celestial later. Translated beings include such persons as Moses, Elijah, and John the Beloved of the Old and New Testaments, and Alma and the three Nephite disciples of Christ in the Book of Mormon. (Index to Book of Mormon, Doctrine and Covenants and Pearl of Great Price p. 373)

Enoch was present when Adam called his righteous posterity together to bless them, three years before his death, along with Enoch's son Methuselah, and Enoch's father Jared, and his forebears Mahalaleel, Cainan, Enos, and Seth. Jared had taught his son Enoch in all the ways of the Lord, and he in turn was taught by his forebears who were "preachers of righteousness who spake and prophesied and called upon all men everywhere to repent; and faith was taught unto the children of men."(Moses 6:23)

After being ordained and blessed by father Adam, Enoch journeyed in the land, and

"the Spirit of God descended out of heaven and abode upon him. And he heard a voice from heaven saying: Enoch my son, prophesy unto this people, and say unto them - Repent, for thus saith the Lord: I am angry with this people, and my fierce anger is kindled against them; for their hearts have waxed hard, and their ears are dull of hearing, and their eyes cannot see afar off... And when Enoch heard these words, he bowed himself to the earth before the Lord, and

355

spake before the Lord saying: Why is it that I have found favor in thy sight, and am but a lad, and all the people hate me; for I am slow of speech; wherefore am I thy servant? And the Lord said unto Enoch: Go forth and do as I have commanded thee, and no man shall pierce thee. Open thy mouth, and it shall be filled; and I will give thee utterance, for all flesh is in my hands..." (Moses 6:21-32)

Open his mouth Enoch did and the Lord gave him utterance. As he conversed with the Lord, Enoch was shown in vision

"the spirits that God had created; and he beheld also things which were not visible to the natural eye; and from thenceforth came the saying abroad in the land: A seer hath the Lord raised up unto his people."

The Lord told Enoch His Spirit was upon him, that He would justify Enoch's words, and give him power to turn rivers of water out of their course and to remove mountains. People were afraid of him and declared,

"a wild man hath come among us... when they heard him, no man laid hands upon him; for fear came on all them that heard him; for he walked with God. And there came a man ... [Mahijah] and said unto him [Enoch] tell us plainly who thou art, and from whence thou comest?" (Moses 6:33-40)

Mahijah gave Enoch the opening he needed so Enoch told them he had come from the land of his fathers. [Jared, Mahalaleel, Cainan, Enos, and Seth]

"And my father [Jared] taught me in all the ways of the Lord". He also rehearsed with his hearers the vision God showed him and told them that God had spoken with him, that God had made the heavens and earth and had brought a host of men and women upon the earth, that by this time death had come upon his fathers including his and their first father Adam, that they had kept a book of remembrance written among them in their own language according to a pattern given by the finger of God. (Moses 6:41-46)

As Enoch spoke God's words the people trembled and could

not stand in his presence.

He told them that

"because that Adam fell, we are and by his fall came death"..., that Satan had come among them, and that they had become carnal, sensual and devilish and were shut out from the presence of God, but through repentance there was a way back to His presence. Enoch rehearsed with them the Plan of Salvation, introduced them to baptism in the name of Jesus Christ and invited them to afterwards receive the Holy Ghost. He explained in greater detail the atonement which would be wrought by God's Only Begotten Son yet to be born in the flesh, even Jesus Christ, and informed them his forebears had submitted to these ordinances including father Adam. (Moses 6:47-68)

Enoch declared the Lord had led him to the top of Mount Simeon. There he beheld the heavens opened and that he was clothed upon with the glory of God. In this condition Enoch said he

"saw the Lord and he stood before my face, and he talked with me, even as a man talketh with another, face to face, and he said unto me, Look and I shall show unto thee the world for the space of many generations." (Moses 7:1-4)

And look Enoch did and the Lord showed him a people that needed to hear his messages.

"...and the Lord said unto me: Go to this people and say unto them - Repent, lest I come out and smite them with a curse, and they die. And he gave unto me a commandment that I should baptize in the name of the Father, and of the Son, which is full of grace and truth, and of the Holy Ghost, which beareth record of the Father and the Son...

"And so great was the faith of Enoch that he led the people of God, and their enemies came to battle against them; and he spake the word of the Lord, and the earth trembled, and the mountains fled, even according to his command; and the rivers of water were turned out of their course; and the roar of lions was heard out of the

357

wilderness; and all nations feared greatly, so powerful was the word of Enoch, and so great was the power of the language which God had given him." (Moses 7:5-13)

Fear drove some of the people to flee to a land recently emerging from the sea,

"and there went forth a curse upon all people that fought against God. And from that time forth there were wars and bloodshed among them; but the Lord came and dwelt with his people, and they dwelt in righteousness. The fear of the Lord was upon all nations, so great was the glory of the Lord, which was upon his people. And the Lord blessed the land, and they were blessed upon the mountains, and upon the high places and did flourish.

"And the Lord called his people Zion, because they were of one heart, and one mind and dwelt in righteousness; and there were no poor among them. And Enoch continued his preaching in righteousness unto the people of God. And it came to pass in his days, that he built a city that was called the City of Holiness, even Zion." Moses 7:14-19)

As Enoch's City comprised of a people of Zion was being built spiritually and geographically, Enoch was shown in vision the future of the people of Zion, by the Lord, and observed that

"Surely Zion shall dwell in safety forever. But the Lord said unto Enoch: Zion have I blessed, but the residue of the people have I cursed." (v 20)

Underscoring the blessings in store for his City of Zion, the Lord,

"showed unto Enoch all the inhabitants of the earth; and he beheld, and lo Zion, in the process of time, was taken up into heaven. And the Lord said unto Enoch, Behold mine abode forever ... And after that Zion was taken up into heaven, Enoch beheld, and lo, all the nations of the earth were before him; And there came generation upon generation; and Enoch was high and lifted up, even in the bosom of the Father, and of the Son of Man; and behold, the power of Satan was upon all the face of the earth." (v 21-24)

Enoch was shown what was going to happen to the City of Zion and its people. They were to be taken to a place of peace and safety where Satan has no power, where the Lord may dwell among them, where there is no long period of separation between spirit and body we call death, but people are changed from mortality to immortality in a twinkling of an eye; a place where the people live a higher law than the laws of men on earth.

After showing him the future of Zion, the Lord turned Enoch's attention to those left behind, including some of Enoch's own posterity. Satan prevailed on earth among the remaining inhabitants,

"And he [Enoch] saw angels descending out of heaven, and he heard a loud voice saying: Wo, wo be unto the inhabitants of the earth. And he beheld Satan; and he saw a great chain in his hand, and it veiled the whole face of the earth with darkness; and he looked up and laughed, and his angels rejoiced." (v 25-26)

Put another way, chains represent power and control and Satan had that power and control which brought darkness upon the land as contrasted to the light of the gospel, which Enoch also saw descending out of heaven bearing testimony of the Father, Son and Holy Ghost.

"And Enoch beheld angels descending out of heaven, bearing testimony of the Father and the Son; and the Holy Ghost fell on many, and they were caught up by the powers of heaven into Zion," [a place of peace and safety]. (v 27)

In other words, after Enoch's city of Zion is taken up to a place of peace and safety, before the Flood, some remaining behind who hear the Gospel, enter the covenant, and live its provisions were to be caught up by the powers of heaven into Zion. [But]

"the God of heaven looked upon the residue of the people [left behind after Zion had fled] and he [and the heavens] wept." (v 28)

At first Enoch wondered how God and the heavens could weep since they were holy, that God was merciful and just, and that the people had had a chance, and those who responded to the Lord and kept their covenant with Him had been or would be taken to heaven with Zion. In answering Enoch the Lord said:

"Behold these thy brethren; they are the workmanship of mine own hands, and I gave them their knowledge in the day that I created them, and in the Garden of Eden, gave I unto them their agency. And unto thy brethren have I said, and also given commandment, that they should love one another, and that they should choose me, their Father, but behold, they are without affection, and they hate their own blood." (v 29-33)

To the unrepentant the Lord said,

"will I send the floods upon them...their sins shall be upon the heads of their fathers. Satan shall be their father ... these which thine eyes are upon shall perish in the floods, and behold, I will shut them [their spirits] up, a prison I prepared for them. And That [Mine Only Begotten] which I have chosen hath pled before my face. Wherefore, he suffereth for their sins; inasmuch as they will repent in the day that my Chosen shall return unto me, and until that day they shall be in torment; Wherefore, for this shall the heavens weep, yea, and all the workmanship of mine hands." (v 34-39)

The Lord seems to be saying that those, who lived the covenant of a Zion Society before the Flood, were taken to heaven to a place of peace, safety and protection, en masse, at the time Enoch and his city departed. Further, that the repentant who entered the covenant and lived its provisions while still on earth after Enoch's departure but before the Flood, would be caught up to Zion. The rest, the unrepentant and therefore unworthy inhabitants of the earth, would be destroyed in the flesh by the Flood, except for eight souls found worthy to repeople the earth through Noah.

However, those whose lives were lost in the Flood were not condemned forever for their sins. They were to remain in the spirit prison in torment until the resurrection of Jesus Christ. Christ would suffer for their sins. Those losing their lives in the Flood, if they repent, accept Jesus Christ and His atonement and live the provisions of the covenant taught them in the world of disembodied spirits; are to be partakers of salvation and will be resurrected sometime during the Millennium.

After being presented the justice and mercy of God in His great plan of salvation, Enoch saw in vision his great grandson Noah and his posterity who would survive the Flood. He also saw the residue of the wicked who were swallowed up by the Flood. Mercy and compassion swelled Enoch's soul and he wept and refused to be comforted. But the Lord counseled him to lift up his heart and be glad and to look some more. And Enoch looked some more and

"saw the coming of the Son of Man even in the flesh; and his soul rejoiced, saying: The Righteous is lifted up, and the Lamb is slain from the foundation of the world, and through faith I am in the bosom of the Father, and behold, Zion is with me...

"And the Lord said: Blessed is he through whose seed Messiah shall come; for he saith - I am Messiah, the King of Zion, the Rock of Heaven... And it came to pass that Enoch cried unto the Lord, saying: When the Son of Man cometh in the flesh, shall the earth rest? I pray thee, show me these things. And the Lord said unto Enoch: Look, and he looked and beheld the Son of Man lifted up on the cross, after the manner of men; And he heard a loud voice; and the heavens were veiled, and all the creations of God mourned; and the earth groaned; and the rocks were rent; and the saints arose, and were crowned at the right hand of the Son of Man, with crowns of glory; And as many of the spirits as were in prison came forth and stood on the right hand of God; and the remainder were reserved in chains of darkness until the judgment of the great day. And again Enoch wept and cried unto the Lord, saying: When shall the earth rest?

"And Enoch beheld the Son of Man ascend up unto the Father; and he called upon the Lord, saying: Wilt thou not come again upon the earth? ... And the Lord said unto Enoch: As I live, even so will I come in the last days ... to fulfill the oath which I have made unto you concerning the children of Noah; And the day shall come that the earth shall rest, but before that day ... great tribulations shall come among the children of men, but my people will I preserve.

"And righteousness will I send down out of heaven; and truth will I send forth out of the earth, to bear testimony of Mine Only Begotten; his resurrection from the dead; yea, and also righteousness and truth will I cause to sweep the earth as with a flood, to gather out mine elect from the four quarters of the earth, unto a place which I shall prepare, an Holy City, that my people may gird up their loins and be looking forth for the time of my coming; for there shall be my tabernacle, and it shall be called Zion, a New Jerusalem.

"And the Lord said unto Enoch: Then shalt thou and all thy city meet them there, and we will receive them into our bosom, and they shall see us and we will fall upon their necks, and they shall fall upon our necks, and we will kiss each other;

"And there shall be mine abode, and it shall be Zion which shall come forth out of all the creations which I have made; and for the space of a thousand years the earth shall rest.

"And it came to pass that Enoch saw the day of the coming of the Son of Man, in the last days, to dwell on earth in righteousness for the space of a thousand years...

"And the Lord showed Enoch all things, even unto the end of the world; and he saw the day of the righteous, the hour of their redemption and received a fulness of joy. And all the days of Zion in the days of Enoch, were three hundred and sixty-five years.

"And Enoch and his people walked with God, and he dwelt in the midst of Zion; and it came to pass that Zion was not, for God received it up into his own bosom; and from thenceforth went forth the saying ZION IS FLED." (Moses 7:48-69)

**The covenant God established with Enoch
is continued through Noah.**

362

Prior to the Flood Methuselah, the son of Enoch, was ordained under the hand of Adam, and Lamech, Methuselah's son, was ordained under the hand of Seth. Methuselah, in turn, ordained Noah his grandson, when Noah was just ten years old. (D&C 107:50-52)

Following the JST Genesis account of Enoch and his city just reviewed, the next reference to Zion, or Enoch or his city is also found in the JST Genesis in the life of Noah after the Flood when he built an altar "and offered burnt offerings on the altar; and gave thanks unto the Lord, and rejoiced in his heart. And the Lord spake unto Noah, and he blessed him...

[And the Lord said unto Noah]

"For a commandment I give, that every man's brother shall preserve the life of man, for in mine own image have I made man. And a commandment I give unto you, Be ye fruitful and multiply, bring forth abundantly on the earth, and multiply therein." (JST Genesis 9:4-14)

At Enoch's pleading the Lord promised there would never again be a universal flood such as the Flood which took the lives of all remaining beings on earth made in the express image of God, except for eight souls.

Remembering that covenant with Enoch the Lord now:

"spake unto Noah and his sons with him saying, And I, behold, I establish my covenant with you which I made with your father Enoch concerning your seed after you ... And I will establish my covenant with you, which I made unto Enoch, concerning the remnants of your posterity, neither shall all flesh be cut off anymore by the waters of a flood, neither shall there anymore be a flood to destroy the earth... I do set my bow in the cloud and it shall be a token of a covenant between me and the earth... And I will remember my covenant which is between me and you and every living creature of all flesh; and the waters shall no more become a flood to destroy the earth.

"And the bow shall be in the cloud; and I will look upon it, that I may remember the everlasting covenant, which I made unto thy father Enoch; that, when men should keep all my commandments, Zion should again come on the earth, the city of Enoch which I have caught up unto myself. And this is mine everlasting covenant, that when thy posterity shall embrace the truth, and look upward, then shall Zion look downward, and all the heavens shall shake with gladness, and the earth shall tremble with joy; And the general assembly of the church of the firstborn, shall come down out of heaven, and possess the earth, and shall have place until the end come. And this is mine everlasting covenant, which I made with thy father Enoch. And the bow shall be in the cloud, and I will establish my covenant unto thee, which I have made between me and thee, for every living creature of all flesh that shall be upon the earth. And God said unto Noah, This is the token of the covenant which I have established between me and thee; for all flesh that shall come upon the earth." (JST Genesis 9:21-25)

The Lord apparently was referencing Noah to the last days when his posterity, after having embraced the truth, entered the covenant, had become part of the Zion Society in the New Jerusalem would look up towards heaven in the last days; and the people of Enoch's City of Zion, who had been taken to paradise before the Flood, without tasting death, would look downward from their current place in paradise. As Enoch's City of Zion and its people return to earth as prophesied, they would see the people of the Zion Society formed on earth in the last days at the New Jerusalem, and as they join together, they will fall on each other's necks and kiss one another, causing the heavens to shake with gladness and the earth to tremble with joy.

Zion, or Enoch's city, also referred to as the general assembly of the church of the firstborn, shall come down and possess the earth alongside those in the Zion Society on earth living on a plane with Enoch's people. Together, they will possess the earth and have place here until the end, or final judgment comes.

The covenant the Lord established
with Enoch and Noah is continued
through Melchizedek and Abraham

Ten generations after Noah, Abraham sought for righteousness, for the blessings of his forefathers and for the right to administer in the same, since his immediate forebears had fallen into idolatry. After much trial and tribulation Abraham was led to the land of Melchizedek who was king of Salem, a man of righteousness, a great high priest and a prince of peace. The covenant the Lord made with Enoch was continued through Noah and thence through Abraham after he was ordained by Melchizedek.

Answering the Lord's call, Abraham and Sarah left the land of their birth traveling to Haran and thence to Canaan, but removed to Egypt to escape a famine. There they were tried and tested before Pharaoh's court. Upon their return to Canaan with great riches in the form of flocks, herds and cattle, Abraham and his nephew Lot part company, due to strife over their cattle. Lot exercised first choice of the land and Abraham took the other.

"And the Lord said unto Abram after that Lot was separated from him, Lift up now thine eyes, and look from the place where thou art northward, and southward, and eastward and westward: And remember the covenant which I make with thee; for it shall be an everlasting covenant; and thou shalt remember the days of Enoch thy father; For all the land which thou seest, to thee will I give it, and to thy seed forever... And I will make thy seed as the dust of the earth: so that if a man can number the dust of the earth, then shall thy seed be numbered." (JST Genesis 14:13:13)

Lot got captured and Abraham rescued him with the help of 318 chosen men. Melchizedek heard of these things and he went out to meet Abraham.

"And Melchizedek, king of Salem brought forth bread and blest it; and he blessed the wine, he being the priest of the Most High

God. And he blessed him, and said, Blessed be Abram of the most high God, possessor of heaven and earth: And blessed be the most high God, which hath delivered thine enemies into thine hand. And he gave him tithes of all." (KJV Genesis 14:17-20)

"And Melchizedek lifted up his voice and blessed Abram. Now Melchizedek was a man of faith, who wrought righteousness; and when a child he feared God, and stopped the mouths of lions, and quenched the violence of fire. And thus, having been approved of God, he was ordained an high priest after the order of the covenant which God made with Enoch, It being after the order of the Son of God; which order came, not by man, nor the will of man: neither by father nor mother; neither by beginnings of days nor end of years; but of God.

"And it was delivered unto men by the calling of his own voice, according to his own will, unto as many as believed on his name. For God having sworn unto Enoch and unto his seed with an oath by himself; that everyone being ordained after this order and calling shall have power, by faith, to break mountains, to divide the seas, to dry up waters, to turn them out of their course; To put at defiance the armies of nations, to divide the earth, to break every band, to stand in the presence of God; to do all things according to his will, according to his command, subdue principalities and powers; and this by the will of the Son of God which was from before the foundation of the world. And men having this faith, coming up unto this order of God, were translated and taken up into heaven.

"And now Melchizedek was a priest of this order; therefore he obtained peace in Salem, and was called the Prince of peace. And his people wrought righteousness, and obtained heaven, and sought for the city of Enoch which God had before taken, separating it from the earth, having reserved it unto the latter days, or the end of the world; And hath said and sworn with an oath, that the heavens and the earth should come together; and the sons of God should be tried so as by fire.

"And this Melchizedek, having thus established righteousness, was called the king of heaven by his people, or, in other words, the king of peace. And he lifted up his voice, and he blessed Abram, being the high priest, and the keeper of the storehouse of God; Him whom God had appointed to receive tithes for the poor. Wherefore, Abram paid unto him tithes of all that he had, of all the riches which he possessed, which God had given him more than which he had need. And it came to pass, that God blessed Abram, and gave unto him riches, and honor, and lands for an everlasting possession; according to the covenant which he had made, and according to the blessing wherewith Melchizedek had blessed him." (JST Genesis 14:25-40)

Note that Melchizedek was the high priest and the keeper of the storehouse whom God appointed to receive tithes for the poor; and that Abraham did pay tithes of all the riches he possessed, which God had given him more than which he had need. Hence we see the "sufficient for the need" principle mentioned in Abraham's day, was very likely the pillar precept operable in Enoch's Zion Society where they were of one heart and one mind and there were no poor among them.

In these last days the Lord has counseled his covenant people to go and do the works of Abraham, which includes living the "sufficient for the need" principle of a Zion Society, and by giving any excess to the Lord's authorized servant/s who use it for approved purposes, including a storehouse with provisions for the poor and needy.

In like manner, those in the covenant who live the "sufficient for the need" principle in these last days will be blessed by the Lord as Abraham was blessed, with eternal riches, honor and lands of inheritance in the geographical Zion, for an everlasting possession.

For a review of the Abrahamic Covenant, please return to Chapter IV of this book and the author's book entitled Abraham, Isaac and Jacob, Servants and Prophets of God.

Elements of the higher law were evident in the lives of the twelve sons of Israel particularly Joseph. His jealous brothers had sought to kill him, but they eventually sold Joseph into Egypt. How Joseph reacted to that adversity is a marvel to behold, and a great example of one who lived the higher law, even in prison.

Not only was he forsaken by his brothers, he was imprisoned for twelve years for spurning the advances of Potiphor's wife. He successfully resisted committing egregious sexual sin, and lived the law of chastity under very difficult circumstances, at a time when he was abandoned by his brethren, and for a moment seemingly abandoned by the Lord.

Amidst it all however, Joseph seemed to know that the promises made by the Lord many years earlier in a dream, when he was only seventeen years old, would come to pass, and that he would somehow be put in a position above his brethren and even his parents, and that he must be ready and worthy of such blessing should it come. Through an unusual series of events familiar to many, he transitioned from ragged prisoner to high government official overnight, and was now in a perfect position to get even with his brothers, when a famine in Canaan drove them to try to buy corn in Egypt. As second in command to Pharaoh, Joseph could have put them to death, or could have meted out any punishment he so desired. Instead, he forgave them, and recognized the hand of the Lord in it, by saying,

"I am Joseph your brother whom you sold into Egypt. Now therefore be not grieved, nor [be] angry with yourselves, that ye sold me thither; for God did send me before you to preserve life. ... And God sent me before you to preserve you a posterity in the earth and to save your lives by a great deliverance. So now it was not you that sent me thither but God, and he hath made me a father to Pharaoh, and lord of all his house, and a ruler throughout the land of Egypt. " (Gen. 45:5-8)

What a great example to each of us, as we try to live the higher law, that regardless of our circumstances the Lord is aware of the events of our lives. In His own way and in His own time, He will bring about His purposes and fulfill His promises to us as He did with Joseph. Our job is to remain faithful and be prepared. The Lord will do the rest.

Had Joseph not brought his father's families to Egypt, but had chosen to get even with his brothers instead, by putting them to death, and/or letting their wives and children die in Canaan for want of bread, the promises the Lord made to father Israel, that his seed would become as the dust of the earth would not have been fulfilled. Joseph was sent ahead by God to preserve the posterity of Israel and saved their lives from a famine of bread, a great deliverance indeed.

Reviewing his life at its end Joseph spoke with his brethren and with his children and children's children, and shared with them his life's experiences which embodies many elements of the higher law which members of a Zion Society are expected to live. He said:

"These my brethren hated me, but the Lord loved me;

"They wished to slay me but the God of my fathers guarded me;

"They let me down into a pit and the Most High brought me up again;

"I was sold into slavery, and the Lord of all made me free;

"I was beset with hunger, and the Lord himself nourished me;

"I was alone, and God comforted me;

"I was sick and the Lord visited me;

"I was in prison, and my God showed favor unto me:

"In bonds, and he released me;

"Bitterly spoken against by the Egyptians and he delivered me;

"Envied by my fellow slaves and He exalted me;

"I struggled against a shameless woman, urging me to transgress with her, but the God of Israel my father, delivered me from the burning flame...;

"I remembered the words of my father ... I wept and prayed

unto the Lord, and I fasted ...;

"For God loveth him who in a den of wickedness combines fasting with chastity, rather than the man who in king's chambers combines luxury with license.

"Ye see, therefore, my children how great things patience worketh, and prayer with fasting.

"And wheresoever the Most High dwelleth, even though envy, or slavery, or slander befalleth a man, the Lord dwelleth in him, for the sake of his chastity, not only delivereth him from evil, but also exalteth him even as me. For in every way the man is lifted up, whether in deed or in word or in thought." (Testament of Joseph I;1-81, II:1-8)

Centuries later during His ministry, the Lord speaking of the judgment and who would sit on the King's right hand said:

"Come ye blessed of my Father, inherit the kingdom prepared for you from the foundation of the world: For I was an hungered, and ye gave me meat: I was thirsty, and ye gave me drink: I was a stranger, and ye took me in: Naked, and ye clothed me: I was sick, and ye visited me, I was in prison, and ye came unto me.

"Then shall the righteous answer him, saying, Lord, when saw we thee an hungered, and fed thee? or thirsty, and gave thee drink? When saw we thee a stranger, and took thee in, or naked, and clothed thee? Or when saw we thee sick, or in prison, and came unto thee?

"And the King shall answer and say unto them, Verily I say unto you, Inasmuch as ye have done it unto the least of these my brethren, ye have done it unto me." (Matt. 25:34-40)

Note that the Lord does not expect us to do things He has not already done for us, as Joseph so eloquently testified. And when we do these things "to the least of these my brethren" we live the higher law, that Jesus taught us, which is very much a part of a Zion Society; as is chastity, prayer, fasting, humility, patience and long suffering, characteristics of Joseph's life, even when he was in prison.

370

The Mosiac Dispensation Was A Preparatory Dispensation Due To Loss Of The Higher Law And The Melchizedek Priesthood Necessary For A Zion Society. However, The Higher Law And Priesthood, And Elements Of A Zion Society Were Returned To Earth During The Savior's Ministry and Dispensation, As The Examples Given Above and Below Illustrate.

After the Savior's resurrection, those entering the covenant through baptism soon lived in a society where they had all things in common, as this scripture depicts:

"Now when they heard this they were pricked in their heart, and said unto Peter, and to the rest of the apostles, Men and brethren, what shall we do? Then Peter, said unto them, repent and be baptized every one of you in the name of Jesus Christ for the remission of sins, and ye shall receive the gift of the Holy Ghost...

"Then they that gladly received his word were baptized, and the same day there were added unto them about three thousand souls. And they continued steadfastly in the apostles doctrine and fellowship, and in breaking of bread, and in prayers...

"And all that believed were together, and had all things in common: And sold their possessions and goods, and parted them to all men, as every man had need. And they continuing daily with one accord in the temple, and breaking bread from house to house, did eat their meat with gladness and singleness of heart, Praising God and having favour with all the people..." (Acts 2:37-47)

Note the "sufficient for the need" principle operable here.

Those with resources voluntarily gave them up so that others in the covenant would have their needs filled.

Alma, a western hemisphere prophet, speaking to those about to receive the baptismal covenant, in the process identified some characteristics of a Zion Society when he said:

"as ye are desirous to come into the fold of God, and to be called his people, and are willing to bear one another's burdens, that they might be light; Yea, and are willing to mourn with those that mourn; yea, and comfort those that stand in need of comfort, and to stand as witnesses of God at all times and in all things, and in all places that ye may be in, even until death, that ye may be redeemed of God and be numbered with those of the first resurrection, that ye may have eternal life--

"Now I say unto you, if this be the desire of your hearts, what have you against being baptized in the name of the Lord, as a witness before him that ye have entered into a covenant with him, that ye will serve him and keep his commandments, that he may pour out his Spirit more abundantly upon you?" (Mosiah 18:8-10)

Those entering the covenant through baptism in America shortly after the Savior's appearance to the people there, lived in harmony with one another and

"there were no contentions and disputations among them, and every man did deal justly one with another. And they had all things common among them; therefore there were not rich and poor, bond and free, but they were all made free, and partakers of the heavenly gift... There were no robbers, nor murderers, neither were there Lamanites, nor any manner of -ites; but they were in one, the children of Christ, and heirs to the kingdom of God." (4Ne. 1:2-3)

Unfortunately, such a Zion Society did not last long in either the eastern or western hemisphere after the Savior's resurrection, or in centuries past as in Alma's day, because its members reverted to behaviors of the natural man. The behaviors of the natural man must be discarded and replaced with behaviors related to sacrifice, service and consecration of self to a higher cause, by those entering a Zion Society as taught by the Savior and His prophets.

"For the natural man is an enemy to God, and has been from the fall of Adam, and will be, forever, and ever, unless he yields to the enticings of the Holy Spirit, and putteth off the natural man and becometh a saint through the atonement of Christ the Lord, and becometh as a child, submissive, meek, humble, patient, full of love, willing to submit to all things which the Lord seeth fit to inflict upon him, even as a child doth submit to his father." (Mosiah 3:19)

In summary, the provisions of the Abrahamic Covenant continued through Isaac and Jacob/Israel were intended to help establish a Zion Society by Israel's posterity, millennia ago, but after having been subjected to Egyptian rule for hundreds of years, the children of Israel were far from righteousness. After spending forty days on the mount and returning to the camps of Israel at Sinai's base and finding they had so soon fallen into sin, the Lord through Moses, withdrew the higher priesthood operative in the days of Enoch, Noah, Abraham, Isaac and Jacob, described above, and replaced it with a preparatory priesthood and a law of carnal commandments of which the Ten commandments are still a part. In our day the Lord explains:

"The power and the authority of the higher, or Melchizedek Priesthood is to hold the keys of all spiritual blessings of the church - To have the privilege of receiving the mysteries of the kingdom of heaven, to have the heavens opened unto them, ... and to enjoy the communion of God the Father, and Jesus the mediator of the new covenant." (D&C 107:18-19)

"And this greater priesthood [Melchizedek] administereth the gospel and holdeth the key of the mysteries of the kingdom, even the key of the knowledge of God. Therefore, in the ordinances thereof, the power of godliness is manifest. And without the ordinances thereof, and the authority of the priesthood, the power of godliness is not manifest unto men in the flesh. For without this no man can see the face of God, even the Father, and live. Now this Moses plainly taught to the children of Israel in the wilderness and sought diligently to sanctify his people that they might behold the face of God; But they hardened their hearts and could not endure his presence, therefore the Lord ... swore that they should not enter into his rest

373

while in the wilderness, which rest is the fulness of glory. Therefore he took Moses out of their midst, [translated Moses] and the Holy [Higher] Priesthood also; And the lesser priesthood continued, which priesthood holdeth the keys of the ministering of angels and the preparatory gospel..." (D&C 84:19-26, JST Exodus 32: 14, 33: 20, 34:1-2)

Since a Zion Society requires a fully operational higher or Melchizedek priesthood, it is understandable that the books of Leviticus, Numbers and Deuteronomy have little to say about a Zion Society. King David did have things to say about Zion in the book of Psalms, but it is Isaiah that has the most to say of the Old Testament prophets, and it is Isaiah that Book of Mormon prophets quote the most. Jeremiah, Joel, Micah and Zechariah have a few things to say as do Romans, Hebrews and the Book of Revelation, and they will be referenced also, but it is latter day revelation coupled with writings related to the scriptures which best illuminate the characteristics and purposes of a Zion Society.

Zion or Sion is mentioned in Deuteronomy 4:48, 2 Samuel 5:7, Psalms 2:6, 9:11, 14:7, 48:2, 50:2, 69:35, 76:2, 87:2, 102:13, 125:1, 128:5 and 132:13-16. From these scriptures we learn that the city of David, or Jerusalem was also called the city of Zion, that though the heathen shall rage the Lord God speaks of His son whom He anointed "my king upon my holy hill of Zion", that the Lord "dwelleth in Zion", that the salvation of Israel shall "come out of Zion"; after they have been gathered, and "Jacob shall rejoice, and Israel shall be glad."

We also learn that Zion, the city of God, the joy of the whole earth, shall be established forever, "that out of Zion, the perfection of beauty, God hath shined"; that "God will save Zion and will build the cities of Judah", that in Salem [Jerusalem] "is his tabernacle, and his dwelling place in Zion; that "he loveth the gates of Zion more than all the dwellings of Jacob ... and the highest himself shall establish her"; that Zion shall be built up when the Lord appears in His glory; that "they that trust in the Lord, shall be as Mount Zion, which cannot be removed but abideth for ever"; that "the Lord hath chosen Zion; he hath desired it for his habitation ... and will satisfy her poor with bread ... clothe her priests with salvation, and her saints shall shout aloud for joy." (See references listed second paragraph above)

Zion is mentioned in Jeremiah 3:14, 4:6, 8:19, 9:19, 26:18, 30:17, and 31:6. From these scriptures we learn that in the last days the Lord will gather Israel, one of a city and two of a family and bring them to Zion; that Zion is to be the standard; that the Lord is in Zion; that because of wickedness of Israel's people the Zion of Jeremiah and Micah's day "shall be plowed like a field and Jerusalem shall be become heaps and the mountain of the house as the high places of a forest; that in the last days Judah and Israel shall be gathered to their own lands and Christ shall reign over them, and they shall say "This is Zion"; that in the last days Israel shall be gathered and that Ephraim, one of the twelve tribes of Israel, has the right of the first born; that the Lord will make a new covenant with them, to be inscribed in the heart; and "that the watchman upon the mount Ephraim shall cry, Arise ye, and let us go up to Zion unto the Lord our God."

Zion is mentioned in Joel 2:32, and 3:14-17.

From these scriptures we learn that after declaring in the last days the Lord will pour out his Spirit upon all flesh, there will be those who will dream dreams and see visions,

"And it shall come to pass, that whosoever shall call on the name of the Lord shall be delivered; for in mount Zion and in Jerusalem shall be deliverance", as the Lord hath said, and in the remnant the Lord shall call"; that in the last days nations shall be at war, multitudes shall stand in the valley of decision as His Second Coming draws near:

"Multitudes, multitudes in the valley of decision; for the day of the Lord is near in the valley of decision.

"The sun and the moon shall be darkened and the stars shall

withhold their shining, And the Lord also shall roar out of Zion, and utter his voice from Jerusalem; and the heavens and the earth shall shake; but the Lord will be the hope of his people, and the strength of the children of Israel. So shall ye know that I am the Lord your God dwelling in Zion my holy mountain; then shall Jerusalem be holy, and there shall be no strangers pass through her anymore."

Zion is mentioned in Micah 3:10 and 4:7, and in Zechariah 8:2. From these scriptures we learn that the Lord shall reign in Zion and that in the last days Jerusalem shall be restored, the posterity of Judah shall be gathered and the Lord will bless his people beyond anything of the past.

References to Zion in the New Testament appear to be limited to those in Romans 11:26, Hebrews 12:22, and Revelations 14:1. From these scriptures we learn that

"all Israel shall be saved; as it is written, There shall come out of Sion the Deliverer, and shall turn away ungodliness from Jacob: For this is my covenant unto them, when I shall take away their sins"; that the Lord chasteneth those whom he loves, that exalted Saints belong to the Church of the Firstborn; and that they "come unto mount Sion, and unto the city of the living God, the heavenly Jerusalem, and to an innumerable company of angels, To the general assembly of the Church of the Firstborn, which are written in heaven, and to God the Judge of all, and to the spirits of just men made perfect, And to Jesus the mediator of the new covenant ..."; and that the Lamb of God, Jesus Christ shall yet "stand on the mount Sion, and with him an hundred forty and four thousand, having their Father's name written in their foreheads.".

Isaiah saw the establishment of Zion in the last days and he was much quoted by Book of Mormon prophets

During the life of Isaiah the prophet, the Lord declared the children of Israel were apostate, rebellious and corrupt, and only a small remnant were faithful. All were called to repentance through Isaiah, and to work righteousness. Their sacrifices and feasts were rejected by the Lord, but He declared later He would

"restore the judges as at the first, and thy counsellors as at the beginning; afterward thou shalt be called, the city of righteousness, the faithful city. Zion shall be redeemed with judgment, and her converts in righteousness."(Isaiah 1:26-27)

Isaiah saw the latter-day temple, the gathering of Israel, the Millennial judgment and peace

"...And it shall come to pass in the last days, that the mountain of the Lord's house shall be established in the tops of the mountains, and shall be exalted above the hills, and all nations shall flow unto it. And many people shall go and say, Come ye, and let us go up to the mountain of the Lord, to the house of the God of Jacob; and he will teach us of his ways, and we will walk in his paths; for out of Zion shall go forth the law; and the word of the Lord from Jerusalem." Isa 2:1-3, 2 Ne 12:3)

Judah and Jerusalem were punished for their disobedience. Her cities were likened to daughters:

"Because the daughters of Zion are haughty, and walk with stretched forth necks and wanton eyes, walking and mincing as they go, making a tinkling with their feet: Therefore the Lord will smite ... the daughters of Zion ... the Lord will take away ... there tinkling ornaments, their cauls, and their round tires like the moon, The chains, and the bracelets and the mufflers, the bonnets, the ornaments of the legs, and the headbands, and the tablets and the earrings The rings and nose jewels... Thy men shall fall by the sword, and thy mighty in war."(Isa 3:16-23, 2Ne 13:16-25)

But Zion and her daughters shall be redeemed in the Millennial day.

"In that day shall the branch of the Lord be beautiful and glorious, and the fruit of the earth shall be excellent and comely for them that are escaped of Israel ... he that is left in Zion, and he that remaineth in Jerusalem, shall be called holy ... When the Lord shall have washed away the filth of the daughters of Zion, and shall have purged the blood of Jerusalem from the midst thereof by the spirit of judgment, and by the spirit of burning. And the Lord shall create upon every dwelling place of mount Zion and upon her assemblies, a cloud and smoke by day, and the shining of a flaming fire by night..." (Isa 4:1-5, 2Ne 14:1-5)

Knowledge of God shall cover the earth during the Millennium. "... for the earth shall be full of knowledge of the Lord, as the waters cover the sea." (Isa 11:9) An ensign is to be raised and Israel gathered. In the Millennial day all men shall praise the Lord... "Behold God is my salvation; I will trust, and not be afraid, for the Lord JEHOVAH, is my strength and my song; he is become my salvation."(Isa 12:1-2)

Latter-day prophets have said that the destruction of Babylon or the world is a type of destruction to be at the Second Coming, in a day of wrath and vengeance, but Israel, the true believers in Messiah/Christ are to be gathered and enjoy Millennial rest. As Lucifer was cast out of heaven for rebellion, so will he be cast off the earth during the Millennium and Israel shall triumph over Babylon or the world. "What shall one then answer the messengers of the nation? That the Lord hath founded Zion, and the poor of his people shall trust in it." Isa 14:1-32, 2Ne 24:32)

Men shall transgress the law and break the everlasting covenant, at the Second Coming they that repent not shall be burned.

Immediately before that day, however,

"The earth shall reel to and fro like a drunkard, and shall be removed like a cottage ... in that day .. the Lord shall punish the host of the high ones, that are on high, and the kings of the earth upon the earth, And they shall be gathered together as prisoners are gathered in a pit, and shall be shut up in the prison, and after many days shall they be visited. Then the moon shall be confounded and the sun ashamed, when the Lord of hosts shall reign in mount Zion, and in Jerusalem and before his ancients gloriously." (Isa 24:1-23)

The Lord "hast been strength to the poor, a strength to the needy in his distress, a refuge from the storm ... in this mountain [mount Zion] shall the Lord of hosts make unto all people a feast of fat things, a feast of wines, well refined. He will "swallow up death in victory; and the Lord God will wipe away tears from all faces...And it shall be said in that day, Lo this is our God"[!] (Isa 25:1-14)

For those who fight against Zion, it shall "be unto them, even as unto a hungry man who dreameth, and behold, he eateth, but he awaketh, and his soul is empty; or like unto a thirsty man dreameth, and behold he drinketh; but he awaketh, and behold he is faint and his soul hath appetite: so shall the multitude of all the nations be, that fight against mount Zion." (JST Isa 29:1-8, 2Ne 27:3)

The Lord has waited for the day of restoration to bless scattered Israel with gathering and with his presence

..."for the Lord is a God of judgment; blessed are all they that wait on the Lord. For the people shall dwell in Zion at Jerusalem: thou shalt weep no more: he will be very gracious unto thee at the voice of thy cry; when he shall hear it, he will answer you." (Isa 30:18)

King Messiah, when He comes shall reign in righteousness. The land of Israel from which the covenant children were scattered was to be a wilderness until the day of restoration and gathering. But apostasy and wickedness precedes His Second Coming.

"The Lord ... filled with judgment and righteousness .... Look upon Zion, the city of our solemnities." (Isa 33:5,21) Zion and her stakes are to be perfected ..."For the Lord is our judge, the Lord is our lawgiver, the Lord is our king; he will save us." (v 22)

In the day of restoration the deserts "parched ground shall become a pool, the thirsty land springs of water ... And the ransomed of the Lord shall return and come to Zion with songs of everlasting joy upon their heads; they shall obtain joy and gladness, and sorrow and sighing shall flee away."(Isa 35:7-10)

"The grass withereth, the flower fadeth; but the word of our God shall stand forever O, Zion, that bringest good tidings, get thee up unto a high mountain O Jerusalem."(Isa 40:9)

"Hearken unto me, ye stout hearted, that are far from righteousness: I bring near my righteousness. It shall not be far off, and my salvation shall not tarry, and I will place salvation in Zion, for Israel is my glory," [sayeth the Lord.] (Isa 46:13)

Isaiah reiterated that in the last days the Lord shall comfort Zion and gather Israel. The redeemed shall come to Zion amid great joy.

"Look unto Abraham your father, and unto Sarah that bare you: for I called him alone, and blessed him and increased him. For the Lord shall comfort Zion: he will comfort all her waste places; and he will make her wilderness like Eden, and her desert like the garden of the Lord; joy and gladness shall be found therein, thanksgiving and the voice of melody ... the redeemed of the Lord shall return, and come with singing unto Zion; and everlasting joy and holiness shall be upon their heads; they shall obtain gladness and joy; and sorrow and mourning shall flee away.

[And the Lord sayeth] "unto Zion, Behold, Thou art my people.

"Awake, awake, put on thy strength, O Zion, put on thy beautiful garments O Jerusalem, the holy city ... Shake thyself from the dust, arise, ... loose thyself from the bonds of thy neck, O captive daughter of Zion." (Isa 51:1-23, 2 Ne 8:1-25)

"How beautiful upon the mountains are the feet of him that bringeth good tidings that publisheth peace; that bringeth good tidings of good, that publisheth salvation; that saith unto Zion, Thy God reigneth... Thy watchmen shall lift up the voice; with the voice together shall they sing for they shall see eye to eye, when the Lord shall bring Zion again." (Isa 52:1-15)

In the last days Zion and her stakes shall be established and enlarged, and Israel shall be gathered in mercy and tenderness and they shall triumph.

"Enlarge the place of thy tent ... lengthen thy cords, strengthen thy stakes ... and all thy children shall be taught of the Lord, and great shall be the peace of thy children, In righteousness shalt thou be established..." (Isa 54:1-17,3Ne 22:1-17)

All who keep the commandments shall be exalted. Strangers will join Israel and gather others to the house of the Lord in the last days. Though Israel is separated from God by iniquity, Messiah shall intercede, come to Zion in the last days, and redeem the repentant.

"And the Redeemer shall come to Zion, and unto them that turn from transgression in Jacob, said the Lord." (Isa 59:20)

In the last days Israel shall rise again as a mighty nation. Gentile people shall join with them and serve her - Zion shall be established and, over time, they shall dwell in celestial splendor.

"The sun shall be no more thy light by day: Neither for brightness shall the moon give light unto thee, but the Lord shall be unto thee an everlasting light, and thy God thy glory. Thy sun shall no more go down; neither shall thy moon withdraw itself; for the Lord shall be thine everlasting light, and the days of thy mourning shall be ended. Thy people also shall all be righteous; they shall inherit the land forever, the branch of my planting, the work of my hands, that I may be glorified...." (Isa 60:1-22)

Messiah comes to preach good tidings unto the meek. He was sent to bind up the brokenhearted, to proclaim liberty to the captives, and the opening of the prison to them that are bound;

"To proclaim the acceptable year of the Lord, and the day of vengeance of our God, to comfort all that mourn, To appoint unto them that mourn in Zion, to give unto them beauty for ashes, the oil of joy for mourning, the garment of praise for the spirit of heaviness, that they might be called trees of righteousness, the planting of the Lord, that he might be glorified." (Isa 61:1-11)

In the last days Israel shall be gathered, Zion shall be established, her watchmen shall teach about the Lord, the gospel standard is lifted and those of Israel living the covenant shall be redeemed.

"And they shall call them, The Holy people, The redeemed of the Lord..." (Isa 62:1-12)

Isaiah's record closes with a reaffirmation that the Second Coming is the year of the redeemed of the Lord, and they shall acknowledge him as their Father. The Lord's people will rejoice and triumph during the Millennium. Israel as a nation will be born in a day; the wicked shall be destroyed; the Gentiles shall hear the gospel and Zion shall flourish from the day of travail, as she brings forth her children. (Isa 66:1-24)

Nephi saw the establishment of a Zion Society in the latter-days

Just as Isaiah saw in vision the future of the Lord's covenant people Israel, and the establishment of a Zion Society in the last days, so did a number of Book of Mormon prophets beginning with Nephi, son of Lehi. He saw in vision the discovery and colonizing of America; the loss of many plain and precious parts of the Bible, the resultant state of Gentile apostasy, the restoration of the gospel, the coming forth of latter-day scripture, and the building up of a Zion Society. As part of this vision, Nephi also saw the Savior of mankind would visit Lehi's posterity in America and that Lehi's posterity had written scriptures containing plain and precious truths which were to come forth in the latter-days through the gift and power of the Lamb of God:

"And in them shall be written my gospel, saith the Lamb, and my rock and my salvation. And blessed are they who shall seek to bring forth my Zion at that day, for they shall have the gift and the power of the Holy Ghost; and if they endure unto the end they shall be lifted up at the last day, and shall be saved in the everlasting kingdom of the Lamb; and whoso shall publish peace, yea, tidings of great joy, how beautiful upon the mountains shall they be." (1Ne 1:35-37)

The people of Lehi had brought with them plates of brass which contained Israel's scriptures until the time of their departure, and these scriptures contained most or all the writings of Isaiah. Nephi, his brother Jacob and other prophets searched and pondered these scriptures, especially those Isaiah had written, and they quoted Isaiah extensively, as may be seen in some of the above notes.

But these American prophets had other things to say about a Zion Society not found in the writings of Isaiah. They knew, for example, that Messiah would be a light to the Gentiles, that at his resurrection the Savior would free the prisoners, and that Israel would be gathered with power in the last days. Though those who once knew of a Zion Society thought "The Lord hath forsaken me, and my Lord hath forgotten me," they would learn that they were not forgotten or forsaken by the Lord, but would be gathered first and the repentant among them would be redeemed. (1Ne 21:1-14) They also understood Israel was to be gathered, the repentant saved, the wicked would be burned as stubble, and that

"every nation which shall war against thee, O house of Israel, shall be turned one against another, and they shall fall into the pit which they digged to ensnare the people of the Lord. And all that fight against Zion shall be destroyed..." (1 Ne 22:1-14)

The Lord condemned priestcrafts saying:
"there shall be no priestcrafts; for behold, priestcrafts are that men preach and set themselves up for a light unto the world, that they may get gain and praise of the world; but they seek not the welfare of Zion. Behold, the Lord hath forbidden this thing; wherefore, the Lord God hath given a commandment that all men should have charity, which charity is love. And except they should have charity they were nothing. Wherefore if they should have charity they would not suffer

the laborer in Zion to perish. But the laborer in Zion shall labor for Zion; for if they labor for money they shall perish." (2Ne 26:29-31)

In the last days false teachings and doctrines are to give way to the truth, and the truth is the kingdom of the devil must shake and fall. To prevent his kingdom from falling the devil will rage in the hearts of men in the last days and

"stir them up to anger against that which is good. And others will he pacify, and lull them away into carnal security, that they will say: All is well in Zion; yea Zion prospereth, all is well - and thus the devil cheateth their souls, and leadeth them away carefully down to hell... wo be unto him that is at ease in Zion. Wo be unto him that crieth: All is well! Yea, wo unto him that hearkeneth unto the precepts of men, and denieth the power of God, and the gift of the Holy Ghost! ... wo unto all those who tremble, and are angry because of the truth of God... Cursed is he that putteth his trust in man, or maketh flesh his arm, or shall hearken unto the precepts of men, save their precepts shall be given by the power of the Holy Ghost."(2Ne 28:21-30)

Abinadi, another western hemisphere prophet who lived about 150 years before the Savior's birth, also had revealed to him many important concepts concerning the coming of the Savior and his mission on earth. His enemies imprisoned him and threatened to put him to death, which they eventually did; but not before Abinadi had delivered his messages which explained what Isaiah meant when he declared:

"How beautiful upon the mountains are the feet of him that bringeth good tidings; that bringeth good tidings of good that publisheth salvation; that saith unto Zion, Thy God reigneth. Thy watchmen shall lift up the voice; with the voice together shall they sing; for they shall see eye to eye when the Lord shall bring again Zion..." (Isa 52:7-10))

Speaking to the Nephites during His visit to the American continent, after His resurrection, the Lord said that Israel would be gathered from their long dispersion and He shall establish among them His Zion, when the Book of Mormon comes forth, the Gentiles are established as a free people in America, and they shall be saved if they believe and obey and that Israel shall build the New Jerusalem in America and the lost tribes shall return. (3Ne. 21:1-29)

After summarizing the gifts of the Spirit given to the faithful, advising us to lay hold upon every good gift, and reminding us that every good gift cometh of Christ, that we must have faith, hope and charity, else we cannot be saved in the kingdom of God; Moroni, in his final chapter, appealed to the posterity of Israel by saying:

"... awake, and arise from the dust, O Jerusalem; yea, and put on thy beautiful garments, O daughter of Zion; and strengthen thy stakes and enlarge thy borders forever, that thou mayest no more be confounded, that the covenants of the Eternal Father which he hath made unto thee, O house of Israel, may be fulfilled. Yea, come unto Christ and be perfected in him..." (Mor. 10:31-32)

Moroni closes his record and concludes his thoughts on these matters indicating he will meet those of us perfected in Christ at the pleasing bar of God, the Eternal Judge of the alive and the dead.

Summary
Purpose of a Zion Society

In summary, the purpose of a Zion Society is to establish an environment necessary for bringing about the perfection and eventual redemption of Israel, the true believers in Messiah/Christ, and return its members to the presence of God in a perfected, sanctified, glorified and exalted state.

Characteristics of a Zion Society

A Zion Society is a society where its people dwell in

righteousness, and are worthy of the presence of God; where the fear and glory of God rests upon the people; where the land, mountains and high places are blessed of Him and do flourish; where its people are of one heart and one mind, and there are no poor among them.

A Zion Society is a place of refuge, peace, safety and protection, where Satan has no power, where there will be no long separation between the spirit and the body we call death, but people are changed in the twinkling of an eye; where people live a higher law than the laws of man on earth; where those in the covenant have all things in common, making sure every man, woman and child's needs are met.

A Zion Society is a society where those entering the covenant through baptism are willing to bear one another's burdens that they may be light; where members are willing to mourn with those who mourn and comfort those that stand in need of comfort, and are willing to stand as witnesses of God at all times and in all places, that they may be redeemed of God, be numbered in the first resurrection and receive eternal life.

A Zion Society is a society in which there are no contentions and no disputations, where every person deals justly with one another; where there are no rich, no poor, where none are in bonds and are all free, where there are no robbers, murderers, and no priestcrafts, where false teachings give way to the truth, where all are the children of the Messiah/Christ, and are heirs to the kingdom of God.

A Zion Society is a society in which there is a fully operational higher or Melchizedek Priesthood, with all the powers, duties and responsibilities and blessings once held by such men as Enoch, Melchizedek, Abraham, Isaac, Israel, Joseph, Elijah and others; where the ultimate goal is to be ready for the return of the Messiah/Christ, who will usher in the Millennium, and upgrade the earth by making sure a knowledge of God is pervasive in the earth, and that this knowledge sweeps the earth as with a flood;

A Zion Society's stakes are to be strengthened, increased in number and their borders enlarged; as the society puts on her beautiful garments, and breaks forth out of obscurity for all the world to see, hear and abide by her messages; as Israel, the true believers in Messiah/Christ are gathered from all the world, in mercy and tenderness, and where the gathered have taken the Holy Ghost to be their guide.

A Zion Society is a society where the people have chosen the Lord's plan of salvation and exaltation and show that they love the Lord and one another by the words they speak and the deeds they do; where the people give tithes of all they have to the Lord's authorized servants, who are the keepers of the storehouse of God, appointed to receive tithes for the poor; after the same manner of Abraham, who **"paid unto Melchizedek tithes of all that he had, of all the riches which he possessed, which God had given him, more than which he had need."** (JST Gen 14:25-40)

A Zion Society is a society where leaders seek to establish righteousness, bring about and live in peace; and where the people are counseled to **go and do the works of Abraham, which includes living the "sufficient for the need" principle, by voluntarily** giving any excess financial and other resources to the Lord's authorized servants who use it for purposes approved of the Lord, including a storehouse with provisions for the poor and needy. **Ultimately tithing as we know it on our day, will be swallowed up in the grander principle of full consecration of ourselves, our talents and resources for the welfare of Zion and the Lord's cause.** Put another way, whereas the current minimum standard or guiding principle is defined as ten percent of income, the grander, guiding principle of full consecration is rooted in the "sufficient for the need", or "more than which he had need" principle. Individuals define for themselves, under the influence of the Spirit, what is sufficient for the need, and voluntarily gives the excess for the blessing of others, for welfare of Zion, and for the building of the kingdom of God on earth.

A Zion Society is a society in which selfishness, pride, hate, envy, jealousy, licentiousness, haughtiness, anger, self aggrandizement, and compulsion are replaced with selflessness, humility, love, generosity, compassion, patience, chastity, self control, personal righteousness and persuasion; and in which the lives of each member are in the process of being upgraded and improved through sacrifice, service and consecration of self to a higher cause.

A Zion Society is a society in which its members seek the welfare of Zion, by living the higher law as exemplified by the Savior's messages in the Sermon on the Mount, especially to be perfect as the Father or the Son are perfect, with the challenge to be as the Savior is, asking one self in every circumstance: "What would the Savior do in this situation?," and acting accordingly.

A Zion Society is a society in which its members seek to know the only true God and Messiah/Christ whom He sent, where such knowledge motivates one to do what must be done, in order to be or become as He is, thereby becoming heirs and joint heirs, ultimately receiving exaltation and eternal life.

A Zion Society is a society in which members practice what they preach, and in the process become perfect as the Savior is. This is the plan for us to follow which incorporates the principle of patterns. We are given patterns so we can duplicate the end result by following them, just as a seamstress follows a pattern which results in the dress she wants. So it is in our lives. We can inherit immortality and eternal life, which is God's plan for us, if we will follow the patterns that will help us develop Christ-like characteristics in our lives.

We now move to latter-day scripture which leads us to conclude that the Lord's pruning of the vineyard for the last time will result in a new world order patterned after a Zion Society like unto Enoch's City.

CHAPTER XIX

A ZION SOCIETY
PATTERNED AFTER PREVIOUS ZION SOCIETIES
IS TO BE THE NEW WORLD ORDER.
WHEN AND WHERE WILL SUCH A SOCIETY
BE BUILT AND WHO WILL BUILD IT?

The purposes and characteristics of a Zion Society as reported by previous prophets and as traced from Enoch through Noah, from Noah through Abraham, from Abraham through Moses, and from Moses through Messiah/Jesus Christ has just been discussed. We shall now discuss the emergence of a Zion Society as the New World Order in this the final dispensation, the dispensation of the fulness of times, just before Jehovah/Christ as Messiah, comes again, this time in all glory and majesty.

A New World Order is not likely to come through the United Nations, through the International Monetary Fund, through a Superpower imposing its will or political ideology on the rest of the world; or through a conglomerate of worldwide international corporations or banks with economic ideology or monetary profit as its bottom line motivating factor.

A New World Order has been prophesied to come in the last days before the Millennium through the establishment of a Zion Society with members who accept Messiah/Jesus Christ as their leader, role model and their God; members with clean hands and pure hearts, as the Psalmist has said, who have taken righteousness as their guiding principle. At His coming, the world as we know it, will pass away, the wicked burned as stubble and the righteous shall be caught up to meet Him. Indeed, He is the long awaited Messiah of the Jews and of the Christian world.

Thus far we have discussed [1] why another restoration of the Gospel was needed in the latter days, [2] identified elements essential to the restoration of God's plan for mankind which preceded its restoration; [3] the gospel's actual restoration; [4] the restoration of the temporal and spiritual priesthoods and the reestablishment of related ordinances; [5] the gathering together of scriptures written in previous dispensations has been discussed, alongside latter-day revelation and selected concepts set forth in them; [6] the building of latter-day temples, [7] the gathering, perfection and eventual redemption of Israel as foreshadowed in the scriptures; [8] and have described the characteristics and purposes of a Zion Society as set forth from Enoch through the time of Christ's first coming in the meridian of time.

We now turn our attention to the emergence of a New World Order in these last days after His resurrection and just before His return to usher in the Millennium.

Through latter-day scripture the Lord has carefully outlined how this new world order should be established, including its key elements. In truth, living according to the precepts that are laid out will prepare people to live in the presence of God, for these principles help them be of one mind and one heart with Him. These principles will also help mankind put the things of this world in proper perspective and focus on the eternal values set forth by the Lord. One must also consider that, given the prophecies of the future, and the fate of the unrepentant wicked, that keeping this council is of a similar magnitude as Noah's warning were to the people of his day.

[Section 6]

Revelation given to Joseph Smith His latter-day prophet and Oliver Cowdery, at Harmony, Pennsylvania in April 1829, before the Church was organized:

"Now, as you have asked, behold, I say unto you, keep my commandments, and seek to bring forth and establish the cause of Zion. Seek not for riches, but for wisdom, and behold, the mysteries of God shall be unfolded unto you, and then shall you be made rich. Behold, he that hath eternal life is rich". (D&C 6:6-7;11:6,)

The message pertaining to the bringing forth and establishment of Zion in D&C 6:6 was repeated to Joseph Smith and his brother Hyrum shortly after the restoration of the Aaronic Priesthood in Harmony, Pennsylvania. (11:6)

[Section 12]

A part of the same message in D&C 6:6 and 11:6 was repeated in May 1829 at Harmony, Pennsylvania, adding that those who have desires to bring forth and establish this work,

"shall be humble and full of love, having faith, hope and charity, being temperate in all things, whatsoever shall be entrusted to his care."(D&C 12:6-7)

[Section 14]

In June 1829 a revelation was given at Fayette, New York through Joseph Smith to David Whitmer, on the same subject:

"Seek to bring forth and establish my Zion. Keep my commandments in all things. And if you keep my commandments and endure to the end you shall have eternal life, which is the greatest of all gifts of God."(D&C 14:6)

[Section 21]

In a revelation to Joseph Smith April 6, 1830, as the Church was organized in Fayette, New York, the Lord said of Joseph Smith:

"Him have I inspired to move the cause of Zion in mighty power for good, and his diligence I know, and his prayers I have heard. Yea, his weeping for Zion I have seen, and I will cause that he shall mourn for her no longer; for his days of rejoicing are come unto the remission of his sins and the manifestation of my blessings upon his works." (D&C 21:7-8)

[Section 24]

To Joseph Smith the Lord gave this revelation at Harmony, Pennsylvania in July, 1830:

"And it shall be given thee in the very moment what thou shalt speak and write, and they shall hear it, or I will send unto them a cursing instead of a blessing. For thou shalt devote all thy service in Zion; and in this thou shalt have strength. Be patient in afflictions, for thou shalt have many; but endure them, for lo, I am with thee, even unto the end of thy days." (D&C 24:6-8)

[Section 28]

Through Joseph Smith to Oliver Cowdery in September, 1830 at Fayette, New York the Lord gave this revelation:

"And now, behold, I say unto you that it is not revealed, and no man knoweth where the city of Zion shall be built, but it shall be given hereafter. Behold, I say unto you that it shall be built on the borders of the Lamanites."(D&C 28:9)

[Section 35]

To Joseph Smith and Sidney Rigdon the Lord gave revelation at Fayette, New York in December 1830:

"Keep all the commandments and covenants by which ye are bound; and I will cause the heavens to shake for your good, and Satan shall tremble and Zion shall rejoice upon the hills and flourish." (D&C 35:24)

[Section 38]

Through Joseph Smith revelation was given at Fayette, New York January 2, 1831:

"Thus saith the Lord your God, even Jesus Christ, the Great I Am, Alpha and Omega ... I am the same which spake and the world was made, and all things came by me. I am the same which have taken the Zion of Enoch into mine own bosom ..."(D&C 38:1-4)

[Section 39]

Through Joseph Smith at Fayette, New York revelation was given to James Covill January 5, 1831:

"Thou art called to labor in my vineyard, and to build up my church, and to bring forth Zion, that it may rejoice upon the hills and flourish."(D&C 39:13)

[Section 45]

Revelation through Joseph Smith at Kirtland, Ohio, March 7,

1831:

"Wherefore I, the Lord, have said, gather ye out from the eastern lands, assemble ye yourselves together ye elders of my church; go ye forth into the western countries, call upon the inhabitants to repent, and inasmuch as they do repent, build up churches unto me. And with one heart and with one mind, gather up your riches that ye may purchase an inheritance which shall hereafter be appointed unto you.

"And it shall be called the New Jerusalem, a land of peace, a city of refuge, a place of safety for the saints of the Most High God. And the glory of the Lord shall be there, and the terror of the Lord also shall be there, insomuch that the wicked will not come unto it, and it shall be called Zion.

"And it shall come to pass among the wicked, that every man that will not take up his sword against his neighbor must needs flee unto Zion for safety. And there shall be gathered unto it out of every nation under heaven; and it shall be the only people that shall not be at war one with another. And it shall be said among the wicked; Let us not go up to battle against Zion, for the inhabitants of Zion are terrible; wherefore we cannot stand. And it shall come to pass that the righteous shall be gathered out from among all nations, and shall come to Zion, singing with songs of everlasting joy..." (D&C 45:64-71)

[Section 49]

Revelation through Joseph Smith to Sidney Rigdon, Parley P. Pratt and Leman Copely Kirtland Ohio, March 1831.

"...continue in steadfastness, looking forth for the heavens to be shaken, and the earth to tremble and to reel to and fro as a drunken man, and for the valleys to be exalted, and for the mountains to be made low, and for the rough places to become smooth - and all this when the angel shall sound his trumpet. But before the great day of the Lord shall come, Jacob shall flourish in the wilderness, and the Lamanites shall blossom as the rose. Zion shall flourish upon the hills and rejoice upon the mountains, and shall be assembled together unto the place which I have appointed." (D&C 49:23-25)

Doctrine and Covenants Sections 57 through 60 were given at the geographical location of Zion's future capital city in Jackson County, Missouri.

[Section 57]

Revelation given through Joseph Smith July 20, 1831 in Zion, Jackson County, Missouri.

"Wherefore, this is the land of promise, and the place for the city of Zion. And thus saith the Lord your God, if you will receive wisdom here is wisdom. Behold, the place which is now called Independence is the center place; and a spot for the temple is lying westward, upon a lot which is not far from the courthouse." (D&C 57:2-3)

[Section 58]

Revelation given through Joseph Smith August 1, 1831 in Zion, Jackson County, Missouri. The Lord foreshadowed much tribulation to come before the center place of Zion would be permanently secured:

"... blessed is he that keepeth my commandments, whether in life or in death; and he that is faithful in tribulation, the reward of the same is greater in the kingdom of heaven. Ye cannot behold with your natural eyes, for the present time, the design of your God concerning those things which shall come hereafter, and the glory which shall follow after much tribulation.

"For after much tribulation come the blessings. Wherefore the day cometh that ye shall be crowned with much glory, the hour is not yet, but the day is nigh at hand. Remember this, which I tell you before, that you may lay it to heart, and receive that which is to follow. Behold, verily I say unto you, for this cause I have sent you - that you might be obedient, and that your hearts might be prepared to bear testimony of the things which are to come. And also that you might be honored in laying the foundation, and in bearing record of the land which the Zion of God shall stand; And also that a feast of fat things, of wine on the lees, well refined, that the earth may know that the mouths of the prophets shall not fail; Yea a supper of the house of the Lord well prepared, unto which all nations shall be invited.

"First, the rich and the learned, and the wise and the noble; And after that cometh the day of my power; then shall the poor, the lame, and the blind, and the deaf, come in unto the marriage of the Lamb, and partake of the supper of the Lord, prepared for the great day to come. Behold, I, the Lord, have spoken it. And that the testimony might come from Zion, yea, from the mouth of the city of the heritage of God-" (v 1-13)

Even though they may have understood much tribulation lay ahead of them, they knew not that, as the Saints of God, they would be driven from the place designated as His center place for Zion. Under command of the Lord the Saints proceeded to establish Zion in Missouri. Martin Harris was to set the example for the church:

"in laying his moneys before the bishop of the church ... it is wisdom also that there should be lands purchased in Independence, for the place of the [bishop's] storehouse, and also for the house of printing." (v 34-37)

While some of the Saints were to be planted there in the geographical location of Zion's center and given an inheritance, "the residue of the elders of my church, the time has not yet come, for many years, for them to receive their inheritance in this land, except they desire it through the prayer of faith, only as it shall be appointed unto them of the Lord. For behold, they shall push the people together from the ends of the earth."(v 44-45)

Though the center place of Zion was identified, its actual occupation by most of the covenant people was and is to come later. For the foreseeable future most of the elders of the church were to be engaged in missionary work, that is, pushing the people together from the ends of the earth.

An agent [bishop] was to be appointed:

"by the voice of the church, unto the church in Ohio, to receive moneys to purchase lands in Zion. And I give unto my servant Sidney Rigdon a commandment, that he shall write a description of the land of Zion, and a statement of the will of God, as it shall be made known by the Spirit unto him; ...

"And let my servant Sidney Rigdon consecrate and dedicate this land and the spot for the temple unto the Lord..." (v 50-57, D&C 58;1-65)   **[Section 59]**

Revelation given through Joseph Smith in Zion, Jackson County, Missouri August 7, 1831.

"Behold, blessed, saith the Lord, are they who have come up unto this land with an eye single to my glory, according to my commandments. For these shall inherit the earth, and those that die shall rest from their labors, and their works shall follow them; and they shall receive a crown in the mansions of my Father, which I have prepared for them. Yea, blessed are they whose feet stand upon the land of Zion, who have obeyed my gospel; for they shall receive for their reward the good things of the earth, and it shall bring forth its strength. And they shall also be crowned with blessings from above .... and with revelations in their time - they that are faithful and diligent before me." (D&C 59:1-4)

[Section 62]

Relation through Joseph Smith at Chariton, Missouri August 13, 1831 while his party, returning to Ohio from the newly appointed land of Zion in Independence, Missouri, met another group bound for Zion.

"And now continue your journey. Assemble yourselves upon the land of Zion: and hold a meeting and rejoice together and offer a sacrament unto the Most High..." (D&C 62:4)

[Section 63]

Revelation to Joseph Smith in Kirtland, Ohio shortly after their return from the land of Zion in Missouri, late August 1831:

"And now, behold, this is the will of the Lord your God concerning his saints, that they should assemble themselves together unto the land of Zion, not in haste, lest there should be confusion, which bringeth pestilence. Behold the land of Zion - I the Lord, hold it in mine own hands; ... Wherefore the land of Zion shall not be obtained but by purchase or by blood, otherwise there is none inheritance for you. And if by purchase, behold ye are blessed; And if by blood, as you are forbidden to shed blood, lo, your enemies are upon you, and ye shall be scourged from city to city, and from synagogue to synagogue and but few shall stand to receive an inheritance... Wherefore, seeing that I the Lord, have decreed all these things upon the face of the earth, I will that my saints should be assembled upon the land of Zion;

"And that every man should take righteousness in his hands and faithfulness upon his loins, and lift a warning voice unto the inhabitants of the earth; and declare both by word and by flight that desolation shall come upon the wicked...

"And let all the moneys which can be spared... be sent up unto the land of Zion unto them whom I have appointed to receive... Behold I the Lord, will give unto my servant Joseph Smith Jun., power that he shall be enabled to discern by the Spirit those who shall go up unto the land of Zion, and those of my disciples who shall tarry...

"He that is faithful and endureth shall overcome the world. He that sendeth treasures unto the land of Zion shall receive an inheritance in this world, and his works shall follow him, and also a reward in the world to come.

"Yea, and blessed are the dead that die in the Lord, from henceforth, when the Lord shall come, and old things shall pass away, and all things become new, they shall rise from the dead and shall not die after, and shall receive an inheritance before the Lord, in the holy city.

"And he that liveth when the Lord shall come and hath kept

the faith, blessed is he; nevertheless, it is appointed unto him to die at the age of man. Wherefore, children shall grow up until they become old; old men shall die, but they shall be changed in the twinkling of an eye. Wherefore, for this cause preached the apostles unto the world the resurrection of the dead.

"These things are the things ye must look for; and, speaking after the manner of the Lord, they are now nigh at hand, and in a time to come, even in the day of the coming of the Son of Man. And until that hour there will be foolish virgins among the wise; and in that hour cometh an entire separation of the righteous and the wicked; and in that day will I send mine angels to pluck out the wicked and cast them into unquenchable fire." (D&C 63:24-54)

[Section 64]

Revelation given through Joseph Smith to the elders of the Church at Kirtland, Ohio, September 11, 1831:

"...I, the Lord, will not hold any guilty that shall go with an open heart up to the land of Zion; for I, the Lord, require the hearts of the children of men. Behold, now it is called today until the coming of the Son of Man, and verily it is a day of sacrifice, and a day for the tithing of my people; for he that is tithed shall not be burned at his coming. For after today cometh the burning--this is speaking after the manner of the Lord-   For verily I say, tomorrow all the proud and they that do wickedly shall be burned as stubble; and I will burn them up, for I am the Lord of Hosts; and I will not spare any that remain in Babylon. Wherefore, if ye believe me, ye will labor while it is called today." (v 22-25)

[When shall the Lord come? Now is called today. During tomorrow which follows today cometh the burning, "wherefore if you believe me, ye will labor while it is called today."]

Speaking to Bishop Newell K. Whitney and his assistant Sidney Gilbert:

..."Wherefore, as ye are agents, ye are on the Lord's errand, and whatever ye do according to the will of the Lord is the Lord's business, And he hath sent you to provide for his saints in these last days, that they may obtain inheritance in the land of Zion.

"Wherefore, be not weary in well-doing, for ye are laying the foundation of a great work. And out of small things proceedeth that which is great. Behold, the Lord requireth the heart and a willing mind; and the willing and obedient shall eat the good of the land of Zion in these last days. And the rebellious shall be cut off out of the land of Zion, and shall be sent away, and shall not inherit the land.

"... Behold, I, the Lord, have made my church in these last days like unto a judge sitting on a hill, or in a high place to judge the nations. For it shall come to pass that the inhabitants of Zion shall judge all things pertaining to Zion.

"...For, behold, I say unto you that Zion shall flourish, and the glory of the Lord shall be upon her. And she shall be an ensign unto the people, and there shall come unto her out of every nation under heaven. And the day shall come when the nations of the earth shall tremble because of her, and fear because of her terrible ones. The Lord hath spoken it. Amen."(D&C 64:29-43)

[Section 66]

Revelation given through Joseph Smith at Orange, Ohio October 25, 1831 at the request of William E. Mclellin:

"Tarry not many days in this place; go not up unto the land of Zion as yet; but inasmuch as you can send, send; otherwise, think not of thy property. Go unto the eastern lands, bear testimony in every place, unto every people and in their synagogues, reasoning with the people. Seek not to be cumbered. Forsake all unrighteousness... Keep these sayings, for they are true and faithful; and thou shalt magnify thine office, and push many people to Zion with songs of everlasting joy upon their heads." (D&C 66:6-11)

[Section 68]

Revelation given through Joseph Smith at Hiram, Ohio November 1831, at the request of four elders:

It was made clear that parents in Zion have the key

responsibility in teaching their children the gospel, and seeing to it that their children are baptized for the remission of sin when eight years old, and

"they shall also teach their children to pray and walk uprightly before the Lord;" [that] "the inhabitants of Zion shall observe the Sabbath day to keep it holy," and that God was not well pleased with the inhabitants of His newly formed Zion because "there are idlers among them; and their children are also growing up in wickedness; they also seek not earnestly the riches of eternity, but their eyes are full of greediness..." and declared such things "must be done away from among them." (D&C 68:25-35)

[Section 69]

Revelation given through Joseph Smith at Hiram, Ohio November, 1831 just after the preface of the Doctrine and Covenants was revealed:

"Zion shall be a seat and a place to receive" records of and a place to account for stewardships of the Lord's servants as they labor for the cause of Zion,

"obtaining all things which shall be for the good of the church, and for the rising generations that shall grow up on the land of Zion, to possess it from generation to generation, forever and ever, Amen." (D&C 69:1-8)

[Section 133]

Revelation given through Joseph Smith at Hiram, Ohio November 3, 1831 at a time when the elders of the Church desired to know more about the gathering and other things:

"Send forth the elders of my church unto the nations which are afar off; unto the islands of the sea; send forth unto foreign lands; call upon all nations, first upon the Gentiles and then upon the Jews. And behold and lo, this shall be their cry, and the voice of the Lord unto all people:

"Go ye forth unto the land of Zion, that the borders of my people may be enlarged, and that her stakes may be strengthened, and that Zion may go forth unto the regions round about.

"Yea, let the cry go forth among all people; Awake and arise and go forth to meet the Bridegroom; behold and lo, the Bridegroom cometh; go ye out to meet him. Prepare yourselves for the great day of the Lord.

"Watch therefore, for ye know neither the day nor the hour. Let them, therefore, who are among the Gentiles flee unto Zion. And let them who be of Judah flee unto Jerusalem, unto the mountains of the Lord's house.

"Hearken and hear, O ye inhabitants of the earth. Listen ye elders of my church together, and hear the voice of the Lord; for he calleth upon all men, and he commandeth all men everywhere to repent. For behold, the Lord God hath sent forth the angel crying through the midst of heaven, saying: Prepare ye the way of the Lord, and make his paths straight, for the hour of his coming is nigh--

"When the Lamb shall stand upon Mount Zion, and with him a hundred and forty-four thousand, having their names written on their foreheads. Wherefore, prepare ye for the coming of the Bridegroom; go ye, go ye out to meet him. For behold, he shall stand upon the mount of Olivet, and upon the mighty ocean, even the great deep, and upon the islands of the sea, and upon the land of Zion.

"And he shall utter his voice out of Zion, and he shall speak from Jerusalem, and his voice shall be heard among all people; And it shall be a voice as the voice of many waters, and as the voice of a great thunder, which shall break down the mountains, and the valleys shall not be found.

"He shall command the great deep, and it shall be driven back into the north countries, and the islands shall become one land; and the land of Jerusalem and the land of Zion shall be turned back into their own place, and the earth shall be like as it was in the days before it was divided.

"And the Lord, even the Savior, shall stand in the midst of his people, and shall reign over all flesh. And they who are in the north countries shall come in remembrance before the Lord; and their prophets shall hear his voice, and shall no longer stay themselves; and they shall smite the rocks and the ice shall flow down at their presence.

"And an highway shall be cast up in the midst of the great deep. Their enemies shall become a prey unto them. And in the barren deserts there shall come forth pools of living water; and the parched ground shall no longer be a thirsty land.

" And they shall bring forth their rich treasures unto the children of Ephraim, my servants. And the boundaries of the everlasting hills shall tremble at their presence. And there shall they fall down and be crowned with glory, even in Zion, by the hands of the servants of the Lord, even the children of Ephraim.

"And they shall be filled with songs of everlasting joy. Behold, this is the blessing of the everlasting God upon the tribes of Israel, and the richer blessing upon the head of Ephraim and his fellows. And they also of the tribe of Judah, after their pain, shall be sanctified in holiness before the Lord, to dwell in his presence day and night forever and ever." (D&C 133:8-35)

[Section 70]

As reported in Chapter XIII, outlines of, or amplifications to the law of consecration which are essential to every man and woman for exaltation, were introduced in November, 1831, in connection with the publication of the Book of Doctrine and Covenants, including "a sufficient for the need principle", with any excess acquired in the transaction of business to be given to the Lord's storehouse for the benefit of current and future generations of the inhabitants of Zion, according to the laws of the kingdom. No one in Zion is exempt from this law of stewardship and accountability, which is very much part of the law of consecration, meaning the "sufficient for the need" principle applies to all, including those who are appointed to administer spiritual things, as well as those appointed to administer temporal things, otherwise the abundance of the manifestations of the Spirit shall be withheld.

[Section 72]

About a month after the Lord's preface to the Doctrine and Covenants was given, several elders and members assembled to learn their duty and be further edified. Revelation given through Joseph Smith was received the same day December 4, 1831.

Speaking to the "high priests of my church to whom the kingdom and power have been given... it is expedient in me for a bishop to be appointed ... in this part of the Lord's vineyard ... it is required ... of every steward, to render an account of his stewardship, both in time and in eternity. For he who is faithful and wise in time is accounted worthy to inherit the mansions prepared for them of the father.

"... the elders of the church ... shall render an account of their stewardship unto the bishop, who shall be appointed of me in this part of my vineyard. These things shall be had on record, to be handed over unto the bishop in Zion. [Later a Presiding Bishop was appointed to oversee the fiduciary and other stewardship functions of local bishops]

"... verily I say unto you, my servant Newel K. Whitney is the man who shall be appointed and ordained unto this power... the duty of the bishop .. is verily this--

"To keep the Lord's storehouse; to receive funds of the church in this part of the vineyard; To take an account of the elders as before has been commanded; and to administer to their wants, who shall pay for that which they receive, inasmuch as they have wherewith to pay; That this also may be consecrated to the good of the church, to the poor and the needy.

"And he who hath not wherewith to pay, an account shall be taken and handed over to the bishop of Zion, who shall pay the debt out of that which the Lord shall put into his hands. And the labors of the faithful who labor in spiritual things, in administering the gospel and the things of the kingdom unto the church, and unto the world, shall answer the debt unto the bishop in Zion;

"Thus it cometh out of the church for according to the law every man that cometh up to Zion must lay all things before the bishop in Zion...

"A certificate from the judge or bishop in this part of the vineyard, unto the bishop in Zion, rendereth every man acceptable, and answereth all things, for an inheritance, and to be received as a wise steward and a faithful laborer; Otherwise he shall not be accepted of the bishop of Zion.

"... they that are appointed by the Holy Spirit to go up unto Zion, and they who are privileged to go up unto Zion--Let them carry up unto the bishop a certificate from three elders of the church, or a certificate from the bishop; Otherwise he who shall go up unto the land of Zion shall not be accounted as a wise steward." (D&C 72:1-26)

[Section 78]

Revelation given through Joseph Smith at Hiram, Ohio March 1832 regarding the establishment of a storehouse for the poor.

"... it must needs be that there be an organization of my people, in regulating and establishing the affairs of the storehouse for the poor of my people, both in this place and in Zion-- For a permanent and everlasting establishment and order unto my church, to advance the cause, which ye have espoused, to the salvation of man, and to the glory of your Father who is in heaven;

"That you may be equal in the bonds of heavenly things, yea, and earthly things also, for the obtaining of heavenly things. For if ye are not equal in earthly things ye cannot be equal in obtaining heavenly things; For if you will that I give unto you a place in the celestial world, you must prepare yourselves by doing the things which I have commanded you and required of you.

"... Wherefore, a commandment I give unto you, to prepare and organize yourselves by a bond or everlasting covenant that cannot be broken ... That through my providence, notwithstanding the tribulation which shall descend upon you, that the church may stand independent above all other creatures beneath the celestial world.

"That you may come up unto the crown prepared for you, and be made rulers over many kingdoms, saith the Lord God, the Holy One of Zion, who hath established the foundations of Adam-ondi-Aman; Who hath appointed Michael your prince, and established his feet, and set him upon high, and given unto him the keys of salvation under the counsel and direction of the Holy One, who is without beginning of days or end of life." (D&C 78:1-16)

[Section 82]

Revelation given to Joseph Smith in Jackson County, Missouri April 26, 1832. Joseph Smith had recently been sustained as President of the High Priesthood.

In this revelation the Lord set forth a number of principles which are important characteristics of a Zion Society such as: if we expect to be forgiven of our trespasses we must forgive the trespasses of others; where much is given much is required; the Lord is bound when we do what He says; Zion's destiny is for it to increase in beauty and holiness; and every man should seek the interest of his neighbor.

"...inasmuch as you have forgiven one another your trespasses, even so I, the Lord, forgive you; Nevertheless, there are those among you who have sinned exceedingly... For of him whom much is given much is required; and he who sins against the greater light shall receive the greater condemnation. Ye call upon my name for revelation, and I give them unto you; and inasmuch as ye keep not my sayings, which I give unto you, ye become transgressors; and justice and judgment are the penalty which is affixed unto my law. Therefore, what I say unto one I say unto all; Watch, for the adversary spreadeth his dominions, and darkness reigneth; And the anger of God kindleth against the inhabitants of the earth; and none doeth good, for all have gone out of the way.

"And now, verily I say unto you, I, the Lord, will not lay any sin to your charge; go your ways and sin no more; but unto that soul who sinneth shall the former sins return, saith the Lord your God. And again, I say unto you, I give unto you a new commandment, that you may understand my will concerning you; Or in other words, I give unto you directions how you may act before me, that it may turn to you for your salvation.

"I, the Lord, am bound when ye do what I say, but when ye do not what I say, ye have no promise." (v 1-10)

Bishops, counselors and others had been called. To these brethren: Edward Partidge, Newell K. Whitney, A. Sidney Gilbert, Sidney Rigdon, Joseph Smith, John Whitmer and Martin Harris the Lord said it was expedient that they should be:

"bound together by a bond and covenant which cannot be broken by transgression, except judgment shall immediately follow, in your several stewardships-

"To manage the affairs of the poor, and all things pertaining to the bishopric both in the land of Zion and in the land of Kirtland; for I have consecrated the land of Kirtland in mine own due time for the benefit of the saints of the Most High, and for a stake of Zion. For Zion must increase in beauty, and in holiness; her borders must be enlarged; her stakes must be strengthened; yea, verily, I say unto you, Zion must arise and put on her beautiful garments. Therefore, I give unto you this commandment, that ye bind yourselves by this covenant, and it shall be done according to the laws of the Lord. Behold, here is wisdom also in me for your good.

"And you are to be equal, or in other words, you are to have equal claims on the properties, for the benefit of managing the concerns of your stewardships, every man according to his wants, and his needs, inasmuch as his wants are just.

"And all this for the benefit of the church of the living God, that every man may improve his talent, that every man may gain other talents, yea even an hundred fold, to be cast into the Lord's storehouse to become the common property of the whole church-- Every man seeking the interest of his neighbor, and doing all things with an eye single to the glory of God.

"This order I have appointed to be an everlasting covenant unto you, and unto your successors, inasmuch as you sin not. And the soul that sins against this covenant, and hardeneth his heart against it, shall be dealt with according to the laws of my church, and shall be delivered over to the buffetings of Satan until the day of redemption. And now verily, I say unto you and this is wisdom, make yourselves friends with the mammon of unrighteousness, and they will not destroy you. For even yet the kingdom is yours, and shall be forever, if you fall not from your steadfastness." (D&C 82: 11-24)

Note that Lord's Zion Society is to increase in beauty and holiness; she is to arise and put on her beautiful garments; her borders enlarged and her stakes strengthened; that bishoprics in Zion have a responsibility to manage the affairs of the poor of their respective wards; that where members voluntarily bind themselves together to bear one another's burdens, and are willing to mourn with those that mourn, and comfort those that stand in need of comfort; they are to have equal claims on properties related to their respective stewardships, according to want and need assuming those wants and needs are just; so that every man may improve his talents as much as a hundred fold, with this excess being cast into the Lord's storehouse becoming common property administered by bishops to help neighbor's in need. Once the terms and conditions of a covenant set by the Lord are fulfilled by man, the Lord will not renege on His promises made in that covenant, but is bound to carry them out.

[Section 83]

A revelation concerning women and children, widows and orphans was received by Joseph Smith at Independence, Missouri April 30, 1832 as he sat in council with his brethren.

"... concerning women and children, those who belong to the church, who have lost their husbands or fathers: Women have claim on their husbands for their maintenance, until their husbands are taken; and if they are not found transgressors they shall have fellowship in the church. And if they are not faithful they shall not have fellowship in the church; yet they may remain upon their inheritances according to the laws of the land.

"All children have claim upon their parents for their maintenance until they are of age. And after that, they have claim upon the church, or in other words, upon the Lord's storehouse, if their parents have not wherewith to give them inheritances. And the storehouse shall be kept by the consecrations of the church; and widows and orphans shall be provided for, as also the poor." (D&C 83:1-6)

Note that in a Zion Society, children have first claim on their parents for their maintenance until they are of age; a women has first claim on her husband for maintenance until his death; but those children who have lost their fathers or are orphans and women who have lost their husbands have claim upon the church. The church is to provide for them and for the poor by way of the storehouse replenished by the consecrated contributions in money, time, talent and other resources.

[Section 84]

In a revelation on the priesthood given through and to Joseph Smith at Kirtland, Ohio September 22 and 23, 1832, and six elders who had united their hearts the Lord said that:

"his church, [was] established in the last days for the restoration of his people, as he has spoken by the mouth of his prophets, and for the gathering of his saints to stand upon Mount Zion, which shall be the city of New Jerusalem;... that the city of New Jerusalem shall be built by the gathering of the saints, beginning at this place, even the place of the temple, which temple shall be reared in this generation." (v 1-4)

After setting forth the priesthood from Moses back to Adam and the marvelous promises made to those who magnify their priesthood callings and sanctify themselves, as reported in Chapter XIII, the Lord reemphasized the importance of the oath and covenant of the priesthood to each holder of said priesthood saying:

"And the Father teacheth him of the covenant which he has renewed and confirmed upon you, which is confirmed upon you for your sakes, and not for your sakes only, but for the sake of the whole world. And the whole world lieth in sin, and groaneth under darkness and under the bondage of sin... because they come not unto me. For whoso cometh not unto me is under the bondage of sin. And whoso receiveth not my voice is not acquainted with my voice, and is not of me... the whole world groaneth under sin and darkness even now.

"And your minds in times past have been darkened because of unbelief and because you have treated lightly the things you have received--Which vanity and unbelief has brought the whole church under condemnation.

"And this condemnation resteth upon the children of Zion, even all. And they shall remain under this condemnation until they repent and remember the new covenant, even the Book of Mormon and the former commandments which I have given them, not only to say, but to do according to that which I have written--

"That they may bring forth fruit meet for their Father's kingdom; otherwise there remaineth a scourge and judgment to be poured out upon the children of Zion. For shall the children of the kingdom pollute my holy land? Verily, I say unto you, Nay. Verily, verily, I say unto you who now hear my words, which are my voice, blessed are ye inasmuch as you receive these things." (v 48-60)

The new covenant was confirmed upon the members especially the priesthood, not only for their sakes, but for the sake of the whole world, that all may be brought unto Christ. Of all the scriptures, the Book of Mormon bears witness of the divinity of Jesus Christ and His atonement, and describes with greater clarity His role in gathering, perfecting and redeeming Israel. But the children of Zion, or members in the covenant, were and are not using the Book of Mormon and the Doctrine and Covenants in word and deed as effectively as they should in bringing people to Christ.

The Lord therefore firmly chastised the children of Zion, especially the apostles, then and even now, for this failure, but the Lord said He would forgive them [us]

"with this commandment--that you remain steadfast in your minds in solemnity and the spirit of prayer, in bearing testimony to all the world of those things which are communicated to you.

"Therefore, go ye into all the world and unto whatsoever place ye cannot go ye shall send, that the testimony may go from you into all the world unto every creature. And as I said unto mine apostles, even so I say unto you, for you are mine apostles, even God's high priests; ye are they whom my Father hath given me; ye are my friends; Therefore, as I said unto mine apostles I say unto you again, that every soul who believeth on your words, and is baptized by water for the remission of sins, shall receive the Holy Ghost.

"And these signs shall follow them that believe-- In my name they shall do many wonderful works; In my name they shall cast out devils; In my name they shall heal the sick; In my name they shall open the eyes of the blind, and unstop the ears of the deaf; And the tongue of the dumb shall speak; And if any man shall administer poison unto them it shall not hurt them; and the poison of the serpent shall not have power to harm them.

"But a commandment I give unto them, that they shall not boast themselves of these things, neither speak them before the world; for these things are given unto you for your profit and for salvation. Verily, verily, I say unto you, they who believe not your words, and are not baptized in my name, for the remission of their sins, that they may receive the Holy Ghost, shall be damned, and shall not come into my Father's kingdom where my Father and I am. And this revelation and commandment, is in force from this very hour upon all the world, and the gospel is unto all who have not received it." (v 61-75)

From these verses we see that those who do not believe the words of the apostles and the missionaries whom they send, are not baptized for the remission of sins and therefore cannot receive the Holy Ghost with its cleansing and sanctifying power; and without these things they cannot enter the kingdom where the Father and the Son are.

"But, verily, I say unto all those to whom the kingdom has been given--from you it must be preached unto them, that they shall repent of their former evil works; for they are to be upbraided for their evil hearts of unbelief and your brethren in Zion for their rebellion against you at the time I sent you.

"And again I say unto you, my friends, for from henceforth I shall call you friends, it is expedient that I give unto you this commandment, that ye become even as my friends in days when I was with them, traveling to preach the gospel in my power; For I suffered them not to have purse or scrip, neither two coats. Behold, I send you out to prove the world, and the laborer is worthy of his hire.

"And any man that shall go and preach this gospel of the kingdom and fail not to continue faithful in all things, shall not be weary in mind, neither darkened, neither in body, nor joint; and a hair of his head shall not fall to the ground unnoticed. And they shall not go hungry, neither athirst."(v76-80)   Note that the Lord expects his missionaries to travel light, and not to be burdened with extra baggage or clothing, or to rely on money, but to let the Spirit guide them in their travels and they will be taken care of by people the Lord has inspired to help, or who, on their own, wanted to help.

"Therefore take no thought for the morrow, for what ye shall eat, or what ye shall drink, or wherewithal ye shall be clothed. For consider the lilies of the field, how they grow, they toil not, neither do they spin; and the kingdoms of the world in all their glory, are not arrayed like one of these. For your Father, who is heaven, knoweth that you have need of all these things. Therefore, let the morrow take thought for the things of itself.

"Neither take ye thought beforehand what ye shall say; but treasure up in your minds continually the words of life, and it shall be given you in the very hour that portion that shall be meted unto every man...

"Behold, I send you out to reprove the world of all their unrighteous deeds, and to teach them of a judgment which is to come. And whoso receiveth you, there I will be also, for I will go before your face, I will be on your right hand and on your left, and my Spirit shall be in your hearts, and mine angels round about you, to bear you up. Whoso receiveth you receiveth me; and the same will feed you, and clothe you and give you money. And he who feeds you, or clothes you, or gives you money, shall in no wise lose his reward." (v 81-90)

Note how the Lord ties in the work of these latter days to the work of His ministry. He issued the same counsel to His apostles today as he did during His ministry. And it requires much faith to go forward, as He has commanded. But faith not only is a first principle of the gospel, it is a pillar principle of a Zion Society. As Nephi son of Lehi once declared: "And I was led by the Spirit, not knowing beforehand the things I should do." (1Ne 4:6) Such is the faith needed for members of a Zion Society.

The Lord continued with His instruction indicating that those who take care of the missionaries are His disciples and when they do it, you may know they are His disciples. For those who reject the messages of the Gospel, the Lord set forth a procedure missionaries may follow, in bearing testimony of their rejection, to the Father.

Returning to the topic of earth's nations the Lord said:

"For I, the Almighty, have laid my hands upon the nations, to scourge them for their wickedness. And plagues shall go forth, and they shall not be taken from the earth until I have completed my work, which shall be cut short in righteousness-- Until all shall know me, who remain, even from the least unto the greatest, and shall be filled with knowledge of the Lord, and shall see eye to eye, and shall lift up their voice, and with a voice together sing this new song saying:

"The Lord hath brought again Zion, According to the election of grace,

> Which was brought to pass by the faith and covenant of their fathers

> The Lord hath redeemed his people, And Satan is bound and time is no longer,

> The Lord hath gathered all things in one.

> The Lord hath brought Zion from above.

> The Lord hath brought up Zion from beneath.

> The earth has travailed and brought forth her strength;

> And truth is established in her bowels;

> And the heavens have smiled upon her;

> And she is clothed with the glory of God;

> For he stands in the midst of his people.

> Glory, and honor, and power and might,

> Be ascribed to our God; for he is full of mercy, justice, grace and truth, and peace,

> Forever and ever, Amen." (v 96-102)

After describing conditions throughout the world and emphasizing the need for the Gospel to be proclaimed to its peoples, the Lord turned His attention to the interrelated perfecting principles of a Zion Society.

"And again, verily, verily, I say unto you, it is expedient that every man who goes forth to proclaim mine everlasting gospel, that inasmuch as they have families, and receive money by gift, that they should send it to them or make use of it for their benefit, as the Lord shall direct them, for thus it seemeth me good.

"And let all those who have not families, who receive money, send it unto the bishop in Zion, or unto the bishop in Ohio, that it may be consecrated for the bringing forth of the revelations and the printing thereof, and for establishing Zion. And if any man shall give unto any of you a coat, or a suit, take the old and cast it unto the poor, and go on your way rejoicing.

"And if any man among you be strong in the Spirit, let him

take with him, him that is weak, that he may be edified in all meekness, that he may become strong also. Therefore, take with you those who are ordained unto the lesser priesthood, and send them before you to make appointments, and to prepare the way, and to fill appointments that you yourselves are not able to fill. Behold, this is the way that mine apostles, in ancient days, built up my church unto me.

"Therefore, let every man stand in his own office, and labor in his own calling; and let not the head say unto the feet it hath no need of the feet; for without the feet how shall the body be able to stand? Also the body hath need of every member, that all may be edified together, that the system may be kept perfect." (v 103-110)

Note the "sufficient for the need" and the "one heart and one mind" principles operating for the purpose of building up Zion in these verses. Gifts of money to missionaries are not to be spent for personal enrichment, but to be sent to their families at home for their use, or for missionaries to use it for themselves if there is a need, as the Lord prompts them. Missionaries without families are to send gifts of money received by them to the bishop in Zion and/or in Ohio for the purpose of publishing and printing the Doctrine and Covenants sections received to date. Gifts of clothing such as a coat or a suit are to be used by the missionaries themselves and instead of throwing away their old clothes, they should give them to the poor and go away rejoicing.

Instead of two strong missionaries serving together as companions, the strong ones should take weaker ones of the lesser priesthood with them, that they may also be edified and they too may become strong. To accomplish goals, individual members may be assigned different roles, and should labor in their own offices and callings. However, whether leader or follower, the body of the church has need for every member and when members work together with one heart and one mind, all are edified together, and the system works perfectly.

414

More specific assignments followed:

"And behold, the high priests should travel, and also the elders, and also the lesser priests; but the deacons and teachers should be appointed to watch over the church, and to be standing ministers in the church. And the bishop, Newell K. Whitney, also should travel round about and among all the churches, searching after the poor, to administer to their wants by humbling the rich and the proud. He should also employ an agent to take charge and to do his secular business as he shall direct.

"Nevertheless, let the bishop go unto the city of New York, also to the city of Albany, and also to the city of Boston, and warn the people of those cities with the sound of the gospel with a loud voice of the desolation and utter abolishment which await them if they do reject these things. For if they do reject these things the hour of their judgment is nigh, and their house shall be left unto them desolate. Let him trust in me and he shall not be confounded; and a hair of the head shall not fall to the ground unnoticed.

"And verily I say unto you, the rest of my servants go ye forth as your circumstances may permit, in your several callings, unto the great and notable cities and villages, reproving the world in righteousness of all their unrighteous and ungodly deeds, setting forth clearly and understandingly the desolation of abomination in the last days. For with you saith the Lord Almighty, I will rend their kingdoms; I will not only shake the earth, but the starry heavens shall tremble. For I, the Lord, have put forth my hand to exert the powers of heaven; ye cannot see it now, yet in a little while and ye shall see it, and know that I am, and that I will come and reign with my people. I am Alpha and Omega, the beginning and the end, Amen." (v 111-120, D&C 84:1-120)

From these verses we learn that the Lord will hold people accountable for accepting or rejecting Jesus Christ as the Savior and Redeemer of the world and His Zion Society. He will hold people accountable for the way they treat the poor; for in a Zion Society there

415

are no poor among them. The rich and proud and their kingdoms who reject the Savior and His Zion Society will be shaken, will fall and become desolate, forsaken, abandoned, deserted and uninhabited; for in "a little while and ye shall see it, and know that I am, and that I will come and reign with my people;" saith the Lord. (D&C 84:120)

[Section 85]]

This revelation was given through Joseph Smith at Kirtland, Ohio November 27, 1832 and was contained on a letter to W. W. Phelps in Independence, Missouri, answering questions about those Saints who have moved to Zion, but had not received their inheritances according to the established order of the church. Among other things the Lord said that material inheritances in Zion are to be received through consecration and:

"It is the duty of the Lord's clerk, whom he has appointed to keep a history, and a general church record of all things that transpire in Zion, and of all those who consecrate properties, and receive inheritances from the bishop; And also their manner of life, their faith, and works; and also of the apostates who apostatize after receiving their inheritances.

"It is contrary to the will and commandment of God that those who receive not their inheritances by consecration, agreeable to his law, which he has given, that he may tithe his people, to prepare them against the day of vengeance and burning, should have their names enrolled with the people of God. Neither is their genealogy to be kept, or to be had where it may be found on any of the records or history of the church. Their names shall not be found, neither the names of the fathers, nor the names of the children written in the book of the law of God, saith the Lord of Hosts...

"And it shall come to pass that I, the Lord God, will send one mighty and strong holding the sceptre of power in his hand, clothed with light for a covering, whose mouth shall utter words, eternal words; while his bowels shall be a fountain of truth, to set in order the house of God, and to arrange by lot the inheritance of the saints

416

whose names are found, and the names of their fathers, and of their children, enrolled in the book of the law of God;...

"And all they who are not found written in the book of remembrance shall find none inheritance in that day... These things I say not of myself; therefore, as the Lord speaketh, he will also fulfill...

"And they who are of the High Priesthood, whose names are not found written in the book of the law, or that are found to have apostatized, or to have been cut off from the church, as well as the lesser priesthood, or the members, in that day shall not find an inheritance among the saints of the Most High.

"Therefore, it shall be done unto them as unto the children of the priests, as will be found recorded in the second chapter and sixty-first and second verses of Ezra." (D&C 85: 1-12)

The Lord seems to be saying that some members who initially received an inheritance in the land of Zion did not turn over all their resources to the pool of resources from which the bishop would draw for consecrated inheritances. The inheritances of those involved were therefore not consecrated and consequently their names, nor their children's names would be numbered among them or in their genealogies, or in the book of the law of God.

[Section 88]

In His great intercessory prayer given just before His death and resurrection the Lord had declared: "for this is life eternal that they might know thee the only true God and Jesus Christ whom thou hast sent." We learn more about them in Section 88 given in December 1832, when the Lord said He would

"send upon you another Comforter, even upon you my friends, that it may abide in your hearts, even the Holy Spirit of promise, which other Comforter is the same that I promised unto my disciples, as is recorded in the testimony of John. This Comforter is the promise which I give unto you of eternal life, even the glory of the celestial kingdom; Which glory is that of the church of the Firstborn,

417

even of God, the holiest of all, through Jesus Christ his Son--

"He that ascended up on high, as also he descended below all things, in that he comprehended all things, that he might be in all and through all things, the light of truth: Which truth shineth. This is the light of Christ. As also he is in the sun, and the light of the sun, and the power thereof by which it was made. As also he is in the moon, and is the light of the moon, and the power thereof by which it was made; And also the light of the stars, and the power thereof by which they were made; And the earth also, and the power thereof, even the earth upon which you stand.

"And the light which shineth which giveth you light, is through him who enlighteneth your eyes, which is the same light that quickeneth your understandings; Which light proceedeth forth from the presence of God to fill the immensity of space-- The light which is in all things, which giveth life to all things, which is the law by which all things are governed, even the power of God who sitteth upon his throne, which is in the bosom of eternity, who is in the midst of all things." (v 3-13)

Thus we see that the other Comforter is the assurance that they so receiving it shall inherit eternal life in the celestial kingdom; and that the light of Christ permeates the immensity of space; the sun, the moon and the stars, and gives life to all things; and He is also the light of truth. Members of the Zion Society in the last days were sometimes referred to as the first laborers in the last kingdom and were commanded to

"... assemble yourselves together, and organize yourselves, and prepare yourselves, and sanctify yourselves; yea, purify your hearts, and cleanse your hands and your feet before me, that I may make you clean; That I may testify unto your Father, and your God, and my God, that you are clean from the blood of this wicked generation; that I may fulfill this promise, this great and last promise, which I have made unto you, when I will. Also, I give unto you a commandment that ye shall continue in prayer and fasting from this time forth.

"And I give unto you a commandment that you shall teach one another the doctrine of the kingdom. Teach ye diligently and my grace shall attend you, that you may be instructed more perfectly in theory, in principle, in doctrine, in the law of the gospel, in all things that pertain unto the kingdom of God, that are expedient for you to understand; Of things both in heaven and in the earth, and under the earth; things which are, things which must shortly come to pass; things which are at home, things which are abroad; the wars and perplexities of the nations, and the judgments which are on the land; and a knowledge also of countries and of kingdoms--That ye may be prepared in all things when I shall send you again to magnify the calling whereunto I have called you, and the mission with which I have commissioned you." (v 74-80)

After discussing the resurrection and final judgment reported in Chapter XXI, the Lord returned to perfecting principles which are essential to His Zion Society:

"And as all have not faith, seek ye diligently and teach one another words of wisdom; yea, seek ye out of the best books words of wisdom; seek learning, even by study and also by faith. Organize yourselves; prepare every needful thing; and establish a house, even a house of prayer, a house of fasting, a house of faith, a house of learning, a house of glory, a house of order, a house of prayer, a house of God; That your incomings may be in the name of the Lord; that your outgoings may be in the name of the Lord; that all your salutations may be in the name of the Lord, with uplifted hands unto the most high.

"Therefore, cease from all your light speeches, from all laughter, from all your lustful desires, from all your pride and light-mindedness, and from all your wicked doings. Appoint among yourselves a teacher, and let not all be spokesmen at once; but let one speak at a time and let all listen unto his sayings, that when all have spoken that all may be edified of all, and that every man may have an equal privilege.

"See that ye love one another; cease to be covetous; learn to impart one to another as the gospel requires. Cease to be idle; cease to be unclean; cease to find fault one with another; cease to sleep longer than is needful; retire to thy bed early, that ye may not be weary; and arise early, that your bodies and your minds may be invigorated. And above all things, clothe yourselves with the bond of charity, as with a mantle, which is the bond of perfectness and peace. Pray always, that ye may not faint, until I come, Behold, and lo, I will come quickly, and receive you unto myself, Amen." (v 119-126)

The remaining fifteen verses of this section pertain to the order of the house prepared for the presidency of the school of the prophets, established for their instruction, setting forth the requirement that none shall be received therein, save he is clean from the blood of this generation.

Worthy of note is that while entrance into the covenant requires new members to be washed clean from their owns sins through the ordinance of baptism; entrance into the Lord's house to partake of other ordinances requires the member to be clean from the blood [and sins] of this generation. Later this washing ordinance would become part of the preparation of members being prepared for the endowment and sealing ordinances of the temple.

The ordinance of the washing of feet was instituted and is to be administered by the president or presiding elder of the church, after partaking the sacrament according to the pattern given in John's testimony Chapter 13. (D&C 88:1-141)

[Section 89]
Known as the Word of Wisdom this revelation was received in response to a prayer offered by Joseph Smith on the subject as he pondered the many uses of tobacco among the early Saints. It indeed is a word of wisdom to all who aspire to be part of Zion, "showing forth the order and will of God in the temporal salvation of all saints

in the last days," (v 2) who wish to identify with a Zion Society as the New World Order.

"Given for a principle with promise, adapted to the capacity of the weak and weakest of all saints, who are or can be called saints. Behold, verily, thus saith the Lord unto you; In consequence of evils and designs which do and will exist in the hearts of conspiring men in the last days, I have warned you, and forewarn you, by giving unto you this word of wisdom by revelation--

"That inasmuch as any man drinketh wine or strong drink among you, behold, it is not good, neither meet in the sight of your Father, only in assembling yourselves together to offer up your sacraments before him. And, behold, this should be wine, yea, pure wine of the grape of the vine, of your own make.

"And again strong drinks are not for the belly, but for the washing of your bodies. And again, tobacco is not for the body, neither for the belly, and is not good for man, but is an herb for bruises and all sick cattle, to be used with judgment and skill. And again, hot drinks are not for the body or belly.

"And again, verily I say unto you, all wholesome herbs God hath ordained for the constitution, nature and use of man- Every herb in the season thereof, and every fruit in the season thereof; and these to be used with prudence and thanksgiving.

"Yea, flesh also of beasts and of the fowls of the air, I, the Lord, have ordained for the use of man with thanksgiving; neverthe less they are to be used sparingly; And it is pleasing unto me that they ought not to be used, only in times of winter or of cold, or famine.

"All grain is ordained for the use of man and of beasts, to be the staff of life, not only for man but for the beasts of the field, and the fowls of heaven, and all wild animals, that run or creep on the earth; And these hath God made for the use of man only in times of famine and excess of hunger. All grain is good for the food of man; and also the fruit of the vine; that which yieldeth fruit, whether in the ground or above the ground-- Nevertheless, wheat for man, and corn for the ox, and oats for the horse, and rye for the fowls and for swine, and for all beasts of the field, and barley for all useful animals, and for mild drinks, as also other grain.

"And all saints who remember to keep and do these sayings, walking in obedience to the commandments, shall receive health in their navel and marrow to their bones; And shall find wisdom and great treasures of knowledge, even hidden treasures; And shall run and not be weary, and shall walk and not faint. And I, the Lord, give unto them a promise, that the destroying angel shall pass by them, as the children of Israel, and not slay them." (D&C 89:1-21)

Some time after this revelation was received in 1833, hot drinks were defined as tea and coffee, the use of which was widespread among members of the Church. Many of the most prominent priesthood holders in the Church used tobacco. They smoked it, chewed it, and snuffed it. The drinking of fermented wine and hard liquor was common among the early saints following the Church's organization in 1830. Journals kept by those living on the frontier where gardens and truck farming were non-existent indicate some individuals ate as much as nine pounds of red meat a day to sustain themselves in their vigorous activities.

It took time for this word of wisdom to take hold among the early saints. Those who lived the word of wisdom then, had only the word of the Lord's prophet as reasons to make this important change in their daily routines, diets and conduct. A hundred years later conspiring men in the 1930's and 1940's were still claiming that there was not a cough in a carload of a certain brand of cigarettes, if you smoked them. In others, medical doctors were used in tobacco advertisement endorsements, claiming their cigarettes were good for the user's T-zone. The T-zone depicted in advertisements was formed as an inverted T comprised of the head with its eyes, ears, nose and throat, and lower down with a crossbar extended across the chest where the lungs, heart and other vital organs are. After World War II medical research began to report the adverse affects of tobacco on humans and the most adversely affected areas were in that very inverted T-zone. Indeed, those who lived the word of wisdom by heeding the Lord's prophet were protected from the evils, designs and lies of conspiring men, which would have increased their chances of getting cancer many fold in some form; long before organizations like GASP came into existence.

The adverse affects of wines and liquor were identified much earlier and the plight of "winos" and "drunkards" was discussed and debated in secular society for generations, but it was not until the 1900's that substances in drugs like tobacco and alcohol were declared to be addictive. Once hooked, many were unable to give up the substance's use. Thousands of people who wanted to quit were and continue to be buried in early graves with their addictions, after having spent billions of dollars, having ruined untold numbers of marriages, and having destroyed thousands of families because of a detrimental habit they could not quit; a habit aided and abetted by conspiring and evil men who lie in wait to deceive.

While in milder form, the addictions caused by the use of tea and coffee are substantial, with many medical doctors routinely requesting their patients to cut down or eliminate their use in the interest of better health.

Recent medical research studies indicate that considerable consumption of grains which provides fiber is indeed good for man, and tends to confirm that the eating of meat in diets should be done sparingly.

[Section 90]

Revelation to Joseph Smith at Kirtland, Ohio March 8, 1833 continuing the establishment of the First Presidency and the ordination of counselors in the same March 18, 1833. In it the Lord blesses the First Presidency saying:

"thou art blessed from henceforth that bear the keys of this kingdom given unto you which kingdom is coming forth for the last time,". He identifies "Sidney Rigdon and Frederick G. Williams" as

Joseph Smith's counselors, declaring, "they are accounted equal with thee in holding the keys of this last kingdom; As also through your administration the keys of the school of the prophets, which I have commanded to be organized; That thereby they may be perfected in their ministry for the salvation of Zion, and of the nations of Israel, and of the Gentiles, as many as will believe;

"That through your administration they may receive the word, and through their administration the word may go forth unto the ends of the earth, unto the Gentiles first, and then, behold, and lo, they shall turn unto the Jews. And then cometh forth the day when the arm of the Lord shall be revealed in power in convincing the nations, the heathen nations, the house of Joseph, of the gospel of their salvation.

"For it shall come to pass in that day, that every man shall hear the fulness of the gospel in his own tongue, and in his own language, through those who are ordained unto this power, by the administration of the Comforter, shed forth upon them for the revelation of Jesus Christ...

"And when you have finished the translation of the prophets, you shall from henceforth preside over the church and the school; And from time to time, as shall be manifested by the Comforter, receive revelations to unfold the mysteries of the kingdom; And set in order the churches...

"And behold, verily I say unto you, that ye shall write this commandment, and say unto your brethren in Zion, in love greeting, that I have called you also to preside over Zion in mine own due time...that your brethren in Zion begin to repent, and the angels shall rejoice over them...verily... I the Lord will contend with Zion, and plead with her strong ones, and chasten her until she overcomes and is clean before me. For she shall not be removed out of her place. I, the Lord, have spoken it." (D&C 90:1-15,32-37)

Note that the school of the prophets, or apostles, was and is to perfect their ministry for the salvation of Zion, for the nations of Israel, for the Gentiles and for as many as may believe, that the gospel may be taken to the ends of the earth.

The First Presidency holds the keys to this last dispensation of time, they give direction to the Twelve Apostles, and in due time will preside over the Zion Society not only for church members, but for the whole earth.

[Section 92]

A select group of leaders: Joseph Smith the Prophet, Oliver Cowdery, Martin Harris, John Whitmer, Book of Mormon witnesses, Bishops Edward Partridge and Newell K. Whitney, Sidney Rigdon, member of the First Presidency, A. Sidney Gilbert, Bishop's agent, and W.W. Phelps Church printer, united together April 26, 1832 to manage the affairs of the poor, and all things pertaining to the bishopric both in the land of Zion and in the land of Kirtland. In essence this was a unit of the United Order. Eleven months later, March 15, 1833, Frederick G. Williams who had recently been appointed a counselor in the First Presidency, was admitted to the above noted group of the United Order. With his entry, all three members of the First Presidency Joseph Smith, Sidney Rigdon, and Frederick G. Williams, and all bishops appointed to date, were a select group indeed.

"Verily, thus saith the Lord, I give unto the united order, organized agreeable to the commandment previously given, a revelation and commandment concerning my servant Fredrick G. Williams, that ye shall receive him into the order. What I say unto one I say unto all. And again, I say unto my servant Frederick G. Williams, you shall be a lively member in this order, and inasmuch as you are faithful in keeping all former commandments you shall be blessed forever." (D&C 92:1-2)

[Section 93]

Revelation given through Joseph Smith at Kirtland, Ohio May 6, 1833

"And verily I say unto you, that it is my will that you should hasten to translate my scriptures, and to obtain a knowledge of history, and of countries, and of kingdoms, of laws of God, and man, and all this for the salvation of Zion." (D&C 93:53)

Joseph said that he had completed the translation and review of the New Testament on the 2nd of February 1833, no more to be opened until he arrived in Zion. He had intended to have this revised version of the scriptures published in Zion, at the printing house they had set up there, but before the printing could be organized, persecution arose which made the undertaking impracticable. Such was the unsettled state of the Church through the Prophet's remaining years. He wanted to go through the translation of the Scriptures again, perfecting points of doctrine which the Lord restrained him from giving in plainness and fullness at the time, [February 2, 1833].

He was martyred before that took place. (HC 1:324)

At this date, [1998] those portions contained in the Pearl of Great Price and at the end of the Church edition of the Old and New Testaments, 1979 and thereafter editions are the only authoritative portions available for examination. Thus the standard works of scripture for Zion at this date include the Old and New Testaments, which includes some of the Joseph Smith translations, the Book of Mormon, the Doctrine and Covenants and the Pearl of Great Price; and the official pronouncements of the prophets twice yearly in the ENSIGN.

[Section 94]
Revelation given through Joseph Smith at Kirtland, Ohio May 6, 1833.

"I say unto you my friends, a commandment I give unto you, that ye shall commence a work of laying out and preparing a beginning and foundation of the city of the stake of Zion, here in the land of Kirtland, beginning at my house." (D&C 94:1)

[Section 96]
Revelation given through Joseph Smith regarding the order of the City or Stake of Zion at Kirtland, Ohio June 4, 1833.

"it is expedient in me [the Lord] that this stake that I have set for the strength of Zion should be made strong. Therefore, let my servant [Bishop] Newel K. Whitney take charge of the place which is named among you, upon which I design to build mine holy house. And again, let it be divided into lots, according to wisdom, for the benefit of those who seek inheritances, as it shall be determined in council among you. Therefore, take heed that ye see to this matter, and that portion that is necessary to benefit mine order, for the purpose of bringing forth my word to the children of men. For behold, verily I say unto you, that is most expedient [appropriate] in me, that my word should go forth unto the children of men, for the purpose of subduing the hearts of the children of men for your good. Even so, Amen." (D&C 96:1-5)

The Lord seems to be saying that the establishment of a storehouse for the poor of His people, both in Kirtland, Ohio and in Independence, Missouri; spoken of in Section 78 dated March 1832, for a permanent and everlasting establishment and order unto the church, was part of the infrastructure He wanted laid, necessary to advance the cause of Zion and necessary to the salvation of men, and to the glory of their Father in heaven.

Previously, as plans were being made for the facility or headquarters building for the First Presidency, for the printing facility, and for the Temple, the Lord reminded them of the need to provide inheritances for those entering this united order which included a storehouse for the poor of my people:

"That you may be equal in the bonds of heavenly things, yea, and earthly things also, for the obtaining of heavenly things. For if ye are not equal in earthly things ye cannot be equal in obtaining heavenly things; For if you will that I give unto you a place in the celestial world, you must prepare yourselves by doing the things which I have commanded you and required of you." (D&C 78:5-7)

The Lord closes Section 96 by letting the brethren in the United Order know that John Johnson "whose offering I have accepted, and whose prayers I have heard, unto to whom I give a promise of eternal life inasmuch as he keepeth my commandments from henceforth--For he is a descendant of Joseph and a partaker of the blessings of the promise made unto the fathers-- Verily, I say unto you, it is expedient in me that he should become a member of the order, that he may assist in bringing forth my word unto the children of men. Therefore, ye shall ordain him unto this blessing, and he shall seek diligently to take away incumbrances that are upon the house named among you, and that he may dwell therein." (D&C 96:6-9, 1-9)

It appears the Lord is saying that established orders would provide the support necessary to sustain members of the order called to missionary service while they were away.

[Section 97]

"On the same day (July 23rd) while the brethren in Missouri were preparing to leave the county, through the violence of the mob, the cornerstones of the Lord's House were laid in Kirtland, after the order of the Holy Priesthood." (HC 1:400)

Section 97 was revelation given through Joseph Smith at Kirtland, Ohio August 2, 1833. Members of the Church in Missouri having been subjected to severe persecution were forced to sign an agreement to leave where the center place for Zion was to be in Jackson County on July 23, 1833. In the face of this adversity the Lord expressed His pleasure concerning a school that had been set up with the aid of Parley P. Pratt.

Though the Saints were being driven out the Lord assured those who observe their covenants that they are acceptable before Him, and reiterated:

"my will that a house should be built unto me in the land of Zion, like unto the pattern which I have given you. Yea, let it be built speedily, by the tithing of my people. Behold, this is the tithing and the sacrifice which, I the Lord, require at their hands, that there may be a house built unto me for the salvation of Zion.- For a place of

428

thanksgiving for all saints, and for a place of instruction for all those who are called to the work of the ministry in all their several callings and offices;

"That they may be perfected in the understanding of their ministry, in theory, in principle, and in doctrine, in all things pertaining to the kingdom of God on earth, the keys of which have been conferred upon you.

"And inasmuch as my people build a house unto me in the name of the Lord, and do not suffer any unclean things to come into it, that it may not be defiled, my glory shall rest upon it. Yea, and my presence shall be there, for I will come into it, and all the pure in heart that shall come into it shall see God...

"And now, behold, if Zion do these things, she shall prosper, and spread herself and become very glorious, very great, and very terrible. And the nations of the earth shall honor her, and shall say: Surely Zion is the city of our God, and surely Zion cannot fall, neither be moved out of her place, for God is there, and the hand of the Lord is there;

"And he hath sworn by the power of his might to be her salvation and her high tower. Therefore, verily, thus saith the Lord, let Zion rejoice, for this is Zion--THE PURE IN HEART; therefore, let Zion rejoice, while all the wicked shall mourn. For behold, and lo, vengeance cometh speedily upon the ungodly as the whirlwind; and who shall escape it?

"The Lord's scourge shall pass over by night and by day, and the report thereof shall vex all people; Yea, it shall not be stayed until the Lord come: For the indignation of the Lord is kindled against their abominations and all their wicked works. Nevertheless Zion shall escape if she observe to do all things whatsoever I have commanded her. But if she observe not to do whatsoever I have commanded her, I will visit her according to all her works, with sore affliction, with pestilence, with plague, with sword, with vengeance, with devouring fire.

"Nevertheless, let it be read this once to her ears, that I, the Lord have accepted of her offering; and if she sin no more none of these things shall come upon her; And I will bless her with blessings, and multiply a multiplicity of blessings upon her, and upon her generations forever and ever, saith the Lord your God." (97:1-28, HC 1:400-402)

Worthy of note is the thought that God holds Zion, as an entity, accountable for the collective things that her members do. Vengeance will come to those who ignore the commands of God. If the commands of God are obeyed, Zion, the pure in heart shall rejoice. If not, as an entity, she will be visited with sore affliction, with pestilence, with plague, with sword, and with devouring fire.

[Section 99]

In this section, reported in Chapter XIII, was an illustration the Lord expects bishops in Zion, especially those with a functioning United Order to care for an Elder's children while that Elder is away on missionary assignment.

[Section 100]

Revelation given to Joseph Smith and Sidney Rigdon at Perrysburg, New York October 12, 1833, in which they were to continue their journey and not worry about their families or Zion.

"And now I give unto you a word concerning Zion. Zion shall be redeemed, although she is chastened for a little season. [However] inasmuch as they keep my commandments they shall be saved. Therefore, let your hearts be comforted; for all things shall work together for the good to them that walk uprightly, and to the sanctification of the church. For I will raise up unto myself a pure people, that will serve me in righteousness." (D&C 100:12-16)

[Section 101]

Revelation given to Joseph Smith at Kirtland, Ohio December 16, 1833. Mobs had driven the Saints from their homes in Jackson County and some of them had tried to establish themselves in Van Buren county, Missouri but persecution followed them. The main body of the saints was in Clay county at that time. Threats of death against individual Saints and families were many. They had lost household furniture, clothing, livestock and other personal property and many of their crops had been destroyed.

In this revelation the Lord reaffirms the Saints were being chastened and afflicted because of their transgressions, but assured them His indignation would fall on those responsible in due time, that His people will be gathered and comforted, that Zion and her stakes will be established, that the Saints shall be blessed and rewarded, that the Saints should continue their gathering together, that the Lord established the Constitution of the United States and that the Saints are to petition for the redress of grievances according to the parable of the woman and the unjust judge. The nature of life during the Millennium is also set forth.

"And they that have been scattered shall be gathered. And all they who have mourned shall be comforted. And all they that have given their lives for my name shall be crowned. Therefore, let your hearts be comforted concerning Zion; for all flesh is in mine hands; be still and know that I am God.

"Zion shall not be moved out of her place, notwithstanding her children are scattered. They that remain, and are pure in heart, shall return, and come to their inheritances, they and their children, with songs of everlasting joy to build up the waste places of Zion--And all these things that the prophets might be fulfilled.

"And behold, there is none other place appointed than that which I have appointed; neither shall there be any other place appointed than that which I have appointed, for the work of the gathering of my saints--

"Until the day cometh when there is no more room for them; and then I have other places which I will appoint unto them, and they shall be called stakes, for the curtains or the strength of Zion. (v 13-21)

"... Behold, here is wisdom concerning the children of Zion,

431

even many, but not all, they were found transgressors, therefore they must be chastened---He that exalteth himself shall be abased, and he that abaseth himself shall be exalted. And now, I will show unto you a parable, that you may know my will concerning the redemption of Zion."[The Lord's parable of nobleman and the olive trees signifies the troubles and eventual redemption of Zion, see v 43-62]

"... Again, verily I say unto you I will show unto you wisdom in me concerning all the churches, inasmuch as they are willing to be guided in a right and proper way for their salvation--

"That the work of the gathering together of my saints may continue, that I may build them up unto my name upon holy places; for the time of harvest is come, and my word must needs be fulfilled.

"Therefore, I must gather together my people, according to the parable of the wheat and the tares, that the wheat may be secured in the garners to possess eternal life, and be crowned with celestial glory, when I shall come in the kingdom of my Father to reward every man according as his work shall be; While the tares shall be bound in bundles, and their bands made strong, that they may be burned with unquenchable fire.

"Therefore, a commandment I give unto all the churches, that they shall continue to gather together unto the places which I have appointed. Nevertheless, as I have said unto you in a former commandment, let not your gathering be in haste, nor by flight; but let all things be prepared before you. And in order that all things be prepared before you, observe the commandment which I have given concerning these things--

"Which saith, or teacheth, to purchase all the lands with money, which can be purchased for money, in the region round about the land which I have appointed to be the land of Zion, for the beginning of the gathering of my saints...if they will hearken unto this counsel they may buy lands and gather together upon them; and in this way they may establish Zion." (v 63-72)

"... Now unto what shall I liken the children of Zion? I will liken them unto the parable of the woman and the unjust judge, for men ought to pray and not be faint.."(v 81-91)

"Therefore, it is my will that my people should claim, and hold claim upon which I have appointed unto them, though they should not be permitted to dwell thereon. Nevertheless, I do not say they shall not dwell thereon; for inasmuch as they bring forth fruit and works meet for my kingdom they shall dwell thereon.

"... They shall build, and another shall not inherit it; they shall plant vineyards, and they shall eat the fruit thereof." (v 99-101; D&C 101:13-101)

[Section 103]

Revelation given through Joseph Smith at Kirtland, Ohio February 24, 1834 upon the arrival of Parley P Pratt and Lyman Wight who had come from Missouri to counsel with the Prophet as to the relief of the Saints there who had been driven from their lands.

Among other things The Lord said that His Saints

"were set up to be a light unto the world, and to be the saviors of men... I have decreed that your brethren which have been scattered shall return to the lands of their inheritances and shall build up the waste places of Zion. For after much tribulation, as I have said unto you in a former commandment, cometh the blessing.

"Behold, this is the blessing which I have promised after your tribulations, and the tribulations of your brethren--your redemption and the redemption of your brethren, even the restoration to the land of Zion, to be established, no more to be thrown down...

"Behold, I say unto you, the redemption of Zion must needs come by power; Therefore, I will raise up unto my people a man, who shall lead them like as Moses led the children of Israel. For ye are the children of Israel, and the seed of Abraham, and ye must needs be led out of bondage by power, and with an outstretched arm. And as your fathers were led at the first, even so shall the redemption of Zion be. Therefore let not your hearts faint, for I say not unto you as I said unto your fathers; Mine angel shall go up before you, but not my presence.

But I say unto you: Mine angels shall go up before you, and also my presence, and in time ye shall possess the goodly land."(v 9-20)

In the verses that followed the Lord reaffirmed the Saints were to gather to Zion in Missouri, even if that placed them in harms way; and "... Let no man be afraid to lay down his life for my sake; for whoso layeth down his life for my sake shall find it again..And whoso is not willing to lay down his life for my sake is not my disciple." (21-28)

Realizing that their numbers in Zion were few at this date, and that more were needed to strengthen Zion, a call for five hundred men to be organized in companies of twenties, fifties and hundreds was issued, but if that many could not be found to assemble three hundred, or even a hundred. Joseph Smith was to go with them as leader. Eventually this group was known as Zion's Camp. This Camp made the trip to Zion in Missouri. Several men of the Camp, having been tried and tested under adverse conditions, later became members of the twelve apostles in 1835 at the Lord's command through the Three Witnesses of the Book of Mormon.(v 29-40)

[Section 104]

The major theme of this revelation was to temporarily dissolve the United Order which had been set up in Kirtland and reorganize it. The properties as stewardships were to be divided among the members of the Order. However, some important concepts related to a Zion Society are also discussed here.

"Verily I say unto you my friends, I given unto you counsel, and a commandment, concerning all the property which belong to the order which I commanded to be organized and established, to be a united order, and an everlasting order for the benefit of my church, and for the salvation of men until I come--With promise immutable and unchangeable, that inasmuch as those whom I commanded are faithful they should be blessed with a multiplicity of blessings; But inasmuch as they were not faithful they were nigh unto cursings... It is wisdom in me, therefore, a commandment I give unto you, that ye shall organize yourselves and appoint every man his stewardship; That every man may give an account unto me of the stewardship which is appointed unto him.

"For it is expedient that I, the Lord should make every man accountable, as a steward over earthly things, which I have made and prepared for my creatures. I, the Lord stretched out the heavens, and built the earth, my very handiwork; and all things therein are mine. And it is my purpose to provide for my saints in mine own way; and behold this is the way that I, the Lord, have decreed to provide for my saints, that the poor shall be exalted, in that the rich are made low. For the earth is full, and there is enough and to spare; yea I prepared all things, and have given unto the children of men to be agents unto themselves.

"Therefore, if any man shall take of the abundance which I have made, and impart not his portion according to the law of my gospel, unto the poor and the needy he shall, with the wicked, lift up his eyes in hell, being in torment." (D&C 104:1,11-18)

The rest of this section declares the stewardships and blessings of the original order in Kirtland which was dissolved and two separate orders were established, the first to be called the United Order of the Stake of Zion, the City of Kirtland. And the other in Missouri was to be called the United Order of the City of Zion. Each would operate separately. Though they were in the process of reorganization, they were not to neglect their stewardships with regard to printing God's words or His scriptures, and the revelations given:

"For the purpose of building up my church and kingdom on the earth, and to prepare my people for the time when I shall dwell with them, which is nigh at hand.." (v 58-59)

The general treasuries of United Orders, as established, were to operate of the basis of common consent, and if those in the Order were to pay all their debts the Lord promised to deliver them from financial bondage. (D&C 104:60-86)

[Section 105]

Revelation given through Joseph Smith on Fishing River, Missouri June 22, 1834. Mob violence had increased and organized bodies from several counties had declared their intent to destroy the people, thereby frustrating plans to purchase lands in Zion and plant the people of Israel there.

"... Zion cannot be built up unless it is by the principles of the law of the celestial kingdom... my people must needs be chastened until they learn obedience, if it must needs be, by the things which they suffer...

"Therefore, in consequence of the transgressions of my people it is expedient in me that mine elders should wait a little season for the redemption of Zion--That they themselves may be prepared, and that my people may be taught more perfectly, and have experience, and know more perfectly, concerning their duty; and the things which I require at their hands.

"And this cannot be brought to pass until mine elders are endowed with power from on high. For behold, I have prepared a great endowment and blessing to be poured out upon them, inasmuch as they are faithful and continue in humility before me. Therefore it is expedient in me that mine elders should wait for a little season, for the redemption of Zion.

"For behold, I do not require at their hands to fight the battles of Zion; for, as I said in a former commandment; even so will I fulfill -- I will fight your battles.

"Talk not of judgments, neither boast of faith nor of mighty works, but carefully gather together, as much in one region as can be, consistently with the feelings of the people. And behold, I will give unto you favor and grace in their eyes, that you may rest in peace and safety...

"Now, behold, I say unto you, my friends, in this way you may find favor in the eyes of the people, until the army of Israel becomes very great. And I will soften the hearts of the people, as I did the heart of Pharaoh...

"first let my army become very great, and let it be sanctified before me, that it may become fair as the sun, and clear as the moon, and that her banners may be terrible unto all nations;

"That the kingdoms of this world may be constrained to acknowledge that the kingdom of Zion is in very deed the kingdom of our God and his Christ; therefore let us become subject unto her laws.

" Verily I say unto you, it is expedient in me that the first elders of my church should receive their endowment from on high in my house, which I have commanded to be built unto my name in the land of Kirtland. And let those commandments which I have given concerning Zion and her law be executed and fulfilled after her redemption.

"There has been a day of calling, but the time has come for a day of choosing; and let those be chosen that are worthy. And it shall be manifest unto my servant, by the voice of the Spirit, those that are chosen; and they shall be sanctified; And inasmuch as they follow the counsel they receive, they shall have power after many days to accomplish all things pertaining to Zion."
(D&C 105:5-37)

[Section 107]

In a revelation on the priesthood given to Joseph Smith at Kirtland, Ohio, March 28, 1835, the functions of priesthood quorums, high councils and the office of Bishop in Zion were set forth.

"The Twelve [Apostles] are a Traveling Presiding High Council to officiate in the name of the Lord under the direction of the Presidency of the Church.

"... The standing high councils, at the stakes of Zion, form a quorum equal in authority in the affairs of the church, in all their decisions, to the quorum of presidency, or the traveling high council. The high council in Zion form a quorum equal in authority in the affairs of the church, in all their decisions, to the councils of the

437

Twelve at the stakes of Zion.

...."for the office of a bishop is in administering temporal things; Nevertheless a bishop must be from the High Priesthood...

may be set apart unto the ministering of temporal things having a knowledge of them by the Spirit of truth; And also to be a judge in Israel, to do the business of the church ... by the assistance of two counselors...

"... This is the duty of a bishop... he shall be a judge even a common judge among the inhabitants of Zion, or in a stake of Zion... where he shall be set apart unto this ministry, until the borders of Zion are enlarged and it becomes necessary to have other bishops or judges in Zion or elsewhere."

The Lord introduced an appeal process which members may use if they are not satisfied with decisions at the local level; set forth a number of offices in the church and described their responsibilities and counseled all to learn their respective duties and act in the office to which he is appointed with all diligence.

The First Presidency and the Quorum of Twelve constitute the highest court in the Church. The Lord set forth the number and the leadership of the deacons, teachers and priests quorums of the Aaronic Priesthood; and the number and leadership of the elders, high priests and seventy's quorums.

With reference to the Seventy the Lord said the Seventy were to have seven presidents one for each of seven quorums with the seventh president to preside over the other six.

"...these Seventy are to be traveling ministers, unto the Gentiles first and also unto the Jews. Whereas other officers of the church, who belong not unto the Twelve, neither to the Seventy, are not under the responsibility to travel among all nations. but are to travel as their circumstances shall allow, notwithstanding they may hold as high and responsible offices in the church.

"... the duty of the president of the office of the High Priesthood is to preside over the whole church, and to be like unto

Moses-- Behold, here is wisdom; yea, to be a seer, a revelator, a translator, and a prophet, having all the gifts of God which he bestows upon the head of the church. Wherefore, now let every man learn his duty, and to act in the office in which he is appointed in all diligence. He that is slothful shall not be counted worthy to stand, and he that learns not his duty and shows himself not approved, shall not be counted worthy to stand." (D&C 107: 33-100)

[Section 109]

In a prayer given at the dedication of the Kirtland Temple revealed to Joseph Smith, March 27, 1836:

"O Jehovah, have mercy on this people ... Put upon thy servants the testimony of the covenant ... And whatsoever city thy servants shall enter, and the people of that city receive their testimony, let thy peace and thy salvation be upon that city; that they may gather out of that city the righteous; that they may come forth to Zion or to her stakes, the places of thine appointment, with songs of everlasting joy.

"... Have mercy O Lord upon the wicked mob, who have driven thy people, that they may cease to spoil, that they may repent of their sins if repentance is to be found; But if they will not; make bare thine arm, O Lord, and redeem that which thou didst appoint a Zion unto thy people.

"... Have mercy O Lord, upon the nations of the earth; have mercy upon the rulers of our land; may those principles, which were so honorably and nobly defended, namely the Constitution of our land, by our fathers, be established forever.

"Remember the kings, the princes, the nobles, and the great ones of the earth, and all people, and the churches, all the poor, the needy, and afflicted ones of the earth; That their hearts may be softened when thy servants shall bear testimony of thy name...

"That from among all these thy servants, the sons of Jacob, may gather out the righteous to build a holy city to thy name, as thou hast commanded them.

"We ask thee to appoint unto Zion other stakes beside this one which thou hast appointed, that the gathering of thy people may roll on to great power and majesty, that thy work may be cut short in righteousness." (D&C 109:34-59)

[Section 111]

Heavily in debt due to their labors in the ministry Joseph Smith, the Prophet, Sidney Rigdon, Hyrum Smith and Oliver Cowdery traveled to Salem, Massachusetts from Kirtland, Ohio to investigate claims that a large amount of money would be made available to them. They transacted some Church business and preached the gospel along the way. Upon arrival no money was made available to them. While in Salem, Massachusetts the Lord spoke to them through Joseph Smith August 6, 1836 saying:

"I, the Lord your God am not displeased with your coming this journey, notwithstanding your follies. I have much treasure in this city for you, for the benefit of Zion and many people in this city, whom I will gather out in due time for the benefit of Zion through your instrumentality.

"... Concern not yourselves about your debts, for I will give you power to pay them. Concern not yourselves about Zion, for I will deal mercifully with her." (D&C 111:1-11)

While they had come for badly needed money, the Lord informed them the real treasure was in the souls of men and women there, who would soon join them in the cause of Zion.

[Section 113]

Answering certain questions concerning the writings of Isaiah the Prophet Joseph Smith said in March 1838:

"'Questions by Elias Higbee: What is meant by the command in Isaiah, 52nd chapter, 1st verse, which saith: Put on thy strength, O Zion- and what people had Isaiah reference to?

"He had reference to those whom God should call in the last days, who should hold the power of priesthood to bring again Zion, and the redemption of Israel, and to put on her strength is to put on the authority of the priesthood which she, Zion, has a right to by lineage; also to return to that power which she had lost.

"What are we to understand by Zion loosing herself from the bands of her neck; second verse? We are to understand that the scattered remnants are exhorted to return to the Lord from whence they have fallen; which if they do, the promise of the Lord is that he will speak to them, or give them revelation. See the 6th, 7th and 8th verses. The bands of her neck are the curses of God upon her, or the remnants of Israel in their scattered condition among the Gentiles." (D&C 113:7-10)

[Section 115]

In revelation given through Joseph Smith at Far West, Missouri April 26, 1838, the Lord linked His Church to Zion in the last days and called upon every member to shine forth as an example, to gather to Zion which will be a defense and a refuge against the storms of life and of the wrath of God in these words:

"Verily, thus saith the Lord unto you, my servant Joseph Smith Jun., ...And also unto my faithful servants who are of the high council of my church in Zion, for thus it shall be called, and unto all elders and people of my Church of Jesus Christ of Latter-day Saints, scattered abroad in all the world; For thus shall my church be called in the last days, even The Church of Jesus Christ of Latter-day Saints. Verily I say unto you all: Arise and shine forth, that thy light may be a standard for the nations; And that the gathering together upon the land of Zion, and upon her stakes, may be a defense and a refuge from the storm, and from wrath when it shall be poured out without mixture upon the whole earth." (v 1-6)

Continuing, the Lord intended for Far West to be a holy and consecrated land to Him. He commanded the Saints to build a house at Far West, for a gathering together of His Saints to worship Him, and that other stakes be formed in the regions round about, but persecution and intolerance forced them to delay and subsequently abandon these plans, because they were forced out of Missouri before it could be done. However, they were able to begin the foundation which stands today. Closing this revelation the Lord reaffirmed that Joseph Smith held the keys of the kingdom of God on earth:

"For behold, I will be with him, and I will sanctify him before the people; for unto him have I given the keys of this kingdom and ministry." (v 7-19; D&C 115:1-19)

[Sections 119 and 120]

Revelation given through Joseph Smith July 8, 1838 at Far West, Missouri.

"Verily, thus saith the Lord, I require all their surplus property to be put into the hands of the bishop of my church in Zion, For the building of mine house, and for the laying of the foundation of Zion and for the priesthood, and for the debts of the Presidency of my Church.

"And this shall be the beginning of the tithing of my people. And after that, those who have thus been tithed shall pay one-tenth of all their interest annually, and this shall be a standing law unto them forever, for my holy priesthood, saith the Lord... all those who gather unto the land of Zion shall be tithed of their surplus properties... by this law [they] sanctify the land of Zion unto me... and this shall be an ensample unto all the stakes of Zion..."(D&C 119:1-7)

"Verily, thus saith the Lord, the time is now come, that it [the properties tithed named in Section 119] shall be disposed of by a council, composed of the First Presidency of my Church, and the bishop and his council, and by my high council; and by mine own voice unto them, saith the Lord." (D&C 120:1; HC 3:44)

Thus we see the law of tithing is to be observed in Zion, and the land of Zion is sanctified thereby. At the time of this revelation the term tithing had meant not just one tenth, but all free will offerings or contributions to the Church. Previously given to the membership, but mainly entered into by the leading elders, was the law of consecration and stewardship of property. The Saints were to pay their surplus property and then give, as tithing, one tenth of their interest annually.

Failure on the part of many of the early participants to abide by this covenant of consecration and stewardship of property resulted in the Lord's withdrawal of it for a time. In its place the Lord gave the current law of tithing to the whole Church which calls for contributions of one-tenth of their interest annually.

Ultimately, however, living the law of consecration and stewardship of property may well be encouraged or required by some or all of the Saints in the future, as the Gospel roles forth and fills the whole earth.

The Lord's covenant people early in this dispensation were compelled to leave Missouri, the land designated by the Lord as the center place of Zion because of persecution, illegal procedures and an exterminating order issued by Missouri Governor Lilburn W. Boggs. The Saints acquired a swampy area containing the former village of Commerce, Illinois on the Mississippi River. A little more than two years later the Saints had transformed the swamp into a beautiful city called Nauvoo, and here the headquarters of the Church had been established.

[Section 124]

Here also the Lord commanded through a revelation to Joseph Smith given at Nauvoo, Illinois, January 19, 1841 that a solemn proclamation of the gospel be made to the President the United States, and to governors and rulers of nations, declaring in part:.

"I say unto you, that you are now called immediately to make a solemn proclamation of my gospel, and of this stake which I have planted to be a cornerstone of Zion,...

"This proclamation shall be made to the kings of the world, to the four corners thereof, to the honorable president-elect, and the high-minded governors of the nation in which you live, and to all the nations of the earth scattered abroad. Let it be written in the spirit of meekness and by the power of the Holy Ghost, which shall be in you at the time of the writing of the same; For it shall be given you by the Holy Ghost to know my will concerning those kings and authorities, even what shall befall them in a time to come. For behold, I am about to call upon them to give heed to the light and glory of Zion, for the set time has come to favor her...

"I will visit and soften their hearts, many of them for your good, that ye may find grace in their eyes, that they may come to the light of truth, and the Gentiles to the exaltation or lifting up of Zion. For the day of my visitation cometh speedily, in an hour ye think not of; and where shall be the safety of my people, and refuge for those who shall be left of them? Awake, O kings of the earth! Come ye, O come ye, with your gold and your silver, to the help of my daughters of Zion." (v 2-11)

In addition to Joseph Smith, others had also been called to help lay the foundation of Zion including Hyrum Smith, whom the Lord loves "for the integrity of his heart", William Law, other authorities and "a high council, for the corner-stone of Zion." They were to build a house in which strangers could lodge, a healthful and holy house. (v 12-25)

Zion was also to be a place of refuge and a place to do baptisms for the dead.

"For it is ordained that in Zion, and in her stakes, and in Jerusalem, those places which I have appointed for refuge, shall be places for your baptisms for your dead". (v 36,118,131)

After discussing at length the Temple where ordinance work for both the living and the dead is performed, the Lord said He

"will save all those of your brethren who have been pure in heart, and have been slain in the land of Missouri" (v 55) As He discussed the boarding house for visiting strangers which the Saints were to build, the Lord indicated Joseph Smith and his house was to have place therein, from generation to generation:

"For this anointing have I put upon his head, that his blessing shall also be put upon the head of his posterity after him. And as I said unto Abraham concerning the kindreds of the earth, even so I say unto my servant Joseph; In thee and in thy seed shall the kindred of the earth be blessed. therefore, let my servant Joseph and his seed after him have place in that house, from generation to generation, forever and ever, saith the Lord. And let the name of that house be called Nauvoo House; and let it be a delightful habitation for man, and a resting-place for the weary traveler, that he may contemplate the glory of Zion, and the glory of this, the corner-stone thereof; That he may receive also the counsel from those whom I have set to be as plants of renown, and as watchmen upon her walls." (v 56-61)

A quorum presidency was established to build the house and shares of stock were to be sold for the same. Individuals were invited, by name, to buy stock and were promised certain blessings by the Lord if they did. (v 62-122) Unfortunately Joseph Smith was martyred before such a facility was completed.

[Section 136]

Through Brigham Young at Winter Quarters of the Camp of Israel after the martyrdom of Joseph Smith and his brother Hyrum, and after the Saints had been driven from Nauvoo came this revelation, January 14, 1847.

..."Let all the people of the Church of Jesus Christ of Latter-day Saints, and those who journey with them, be organized into companies, with a covenant and promise to keep all the commandments and statutes of the Lord our God. Let the companies be organized with captains of hundreds...fifties... tens, with a president and two counselors at their head, under the direction of the Twelve Apostles. And this shall be their covenant:

..." Let every man use all his influence and property to remove this people to the place where the Lord shall locate a stake of Zion. And if ye do this with a pure heart, in all faithfulness, ye shall be blessed:... And let my servants that have been appointed go and teach this, my will, to the saints, that they may be ready to go to a land of peace. Go thy way and do as I have told you, and fear not your enemies; for they shall not have power to stop my work. Zion shall be redeemed in mine own due time.

"... I am he who led the children of Israel out of the land of Egypt; and my arm is stretched out in the last days to save my people... My people must be tried in all things, that they may be prepared to receive the glory that I have for them, even the glory of Zion; and he that will not bear chastisement is not worthy of my kingdom.

"Let him that is ignorant learn wisdom by humbling himself, and calling upon the Lord his God, that his eyes may be opened that he may see, and his ears opened that he may hear. For my Spirit is sent forth into the world to enlighten the humble and contrite, and to the condemnation of the ungodly. Thy brethren have rejected you and your testimony, even the nation that has driven you out;

"And now cometh the day of their calamity, even the days of sorrow, like a woman that is taken in travail, and their sorrow shall be great unless they speedily repent, yea, very speedily. For they killed the prophets, and them that were sent among them; and they have shed innocent blood, which crieth from the ground against them.

"Therefore marvel not at these things for ye are not yet pure; ye can not yet bear my glory; but ye shall behold it if ye are faithful in keeping all my words that I have given you, from the days of Adam to Abraham, from Abraham to Moses, and from Moses to Jesus and his apostles, and from Jesus and his apostles to Joseph Smith whom I did call upon by mine angels, my ministering servants, and by mine own voice out of the heavens, to bring forth my work; Which foundation he did lay, and was faithful; and I took him to myself. Many have marveled because of his death; but it was needful that he should seal his testimony with his blood, that he might be honored and the wicked might be condemned."
(D&C 136:1-42)

SUMMARY

Moses led the children of Israel out of Egypt, from a land ripe in iniquity where they were held against their will, to the land promised to Abraham's and Israel's posterity. There they would occupy houses they did not build, and eat from vineyards they did not plant etc. in a land originally in the hands of Melchizedek, the great high priest, king of Salem and the prince of peace.

This land was promised to Abraham, Isaac and Israel whose posterity would occupy it in due time, but in Moses' day it was occupied by iniquitous people. In like manner did the Lord lead His covenant people Israel in these last days.

Just as the children of Israel were thrust or forced out of Egypt at the last by the Pharaoh, so were the Lord's covenant people thrust or forced out of Nauvoo. And just as the children of Israel were led by Moses, so were the Lord's covenant people in these last days led by their own Moses: Brigham Young.

Just as the children of Israel were not allowed to occupy the lands of their inheritance for a season because they were not yet spiritually pure, so are the Lord's covenant people in these last days prevented by their enemies from occupying their promised land of Zion in Missouri because they are not yet spiritually pure.

Just as the privilege of occupying the promised land in Moses' day was given to a future generation, so will the privilege of occupying Zion in America in our day be given to a future generation/s.

Just as the children of Israel lived in the wilderness preparatory to entering their land of inheritance, so are His covenant people Israel, the true believers in Messiah/Christ, who are being gathered spiritually; now live in a worldly wilderness in these last days, while their land of inheritance or Zion Society is being built first spiritually and then geographically.

The pure in heart, serving in righteousness will inherit both

447

the spiritual and geographical Zion of our day. There they will live with their God, who will come, not of humble birth as a babe this time, but as King of Kings and Lord of Lords to rule and reign in all glory and majesty. He will claim his people. We will recognize Him, not only as King of Kings and Lord of Lords, but as our elder brother whom we had known and loved in the pre-mortal world. He was our counselor, confidant, our Lord and our God who is now returning to an upgraded earth worthy of Him.

The purposes and characteristics of Zion Society in previous dispensations were set forth in Chapter XVIII. We now answer more directly the questions: when will a Zion Society be built in the last days and who will build it, spiritually and geographically?

The building of a Zion Society or a united one world order in these last days, with the work and glory of God as its purpose; based on the teachings, earth life, and mission of Jesus Christ, as enunciated by previous prophets, began when God the Eternal Father and His Son Jesus Christ appeared to Joseph Smith in 1820.

Over the next fourteen years the Lord simultaneously restored and made operational His Gospel with power, authority, ordinances and processes as they were in previous dispensations, for the purpose of [1] gathering scattered Israel and the true believers in Messiah/Christ, [2] perfecting the lives of those entering the covenant sufficient for salvation, exaltation and eternal life, and [3] redeeming the dead who accept vicarious work done for them, and who accept Jesus Christ's atonement.

Those who enter the covenant and keep its provisions become part of the Zion Society and commit themselves to help gather Israel, help perfect the Society's members and help redeem it's and all the world's kindred dead.

It is like living in a house while building it and watching it take shape, under the leadership of the master builder who is instructing us from heaven.

At the beginning of this chapter we offered an opinion that it is unlikely that a united one world society will emerge through the United Nations, a Super power, the International Monetary Fund or through a conglomeration of banks. Instead, such a society, a united one world Zion Society, will emerge with Messiah/Christ at its head.

This is not to say that one or all the above organizations will not play significant roles in bringing a Zion Society about. The United Nations Charter sets forth many admirable characteristics and programs which relate to a united one world Zion Society and so do some of the efforts of the International Monetary Fund, and the charitable acts of many individuals, groups and governments.

One such government emerging with elements of a Zion Society is located in Southern Africa, the Republic of Botswana. With its own resources derived from the sale of diamonds and cattle, the country has increased life expectancy of its people from forty years to sixty-five years of age in the three decades since gaining independence in 1966.

Building new roads, schools, colleges, universities, medical clinics, hospitals, creating the infrastructure for its cities and towns, constructing housing for their people at a rapid pace since independence, Botswana's democratically elected leaders have chosen to invest in its people rather than line their own pockets with money. The results are striking. There is economic electricity in the air. Their people are industrious, its telecommunications network is the best of twelve Southern Africa nations, and its currency, the Pula, is the strongest in Africa. Garbage is collected twice a week, in its capitol city Gaborone, citizens drink water from the tap because it is clean and pure. A state of the art slaughter house handling up to 1800 animals a day operates in downtown Lobatse, with no flies, no smell and no noise. Only Argentina exports more beef than Botswana.

Currently some 700 of Botswana's people are in the United States pursuing graduate degrees on all expenses paid, full ride scholarships, paid for by the Botswana government Students make a commitment to return home on completion of their studies to uplift and improve Botswana's people and the quality of their life. Of the 1,200 who have completed this program to date, all have returned home to Botswana and are functoning in responsible positions in business, industry and government.

Mmega, a Botswana newspaper, reported in January, 1997,

the government had just released its Task Group's Long Term Vision for Botswana.

Goals include:

to build

1. a prosperous, productive and innovative society,
2. a just and caring society,
3. an educated and informed society,
4. an open, democratic and accountable society, and
5. a moral, ethical and tolerant society.

The report sees the nation transforming itself into an industrialized and information society, setting the highest possible standards for vocational, technical and academic excellence.

They concluded that

"A moral and ethically upright, educated society... should be matched by a leadership of the same quality."

Botswana is certainly moving in the right direction and there is much to emulate.

Ultimately, however, Botswana's society and all others will be replaced with a Zion Society, with the purposes and characteristics summarized in Chapter XVIII, and with two world headquarter cities, one in Jerusalem and one in Jackson County, Missouri, under the general leadership of 144,000 high priests, 12,000 from each of the tribes of Israel, as we have learned from latter-day scripture and from the Book of Revelation.

A Zion Society is part of God's plan for preparing His people to enter His presence. For this to happen, they must enter the covenant, be tried and tested, gain experience, make choices and demonstrate that they will lean upon the arm of the Lord, and not be carried away by their desires for the temporal things of this earth, A Zion Society is also concerned with the gathering, perfection, and eventual redemption of the dead who died without a knowledge of Messiah/Christ and His saving ordinances.

Chapter XX elaborates on the saving and exalting ordinances of the temple done by the living for the blessing of the dead.

CHAPTER XX

PERFECTION AND REDEMPTION OF THE LIVING AND THE DEAD ARE INTEGRAL PARTS OF A ZION SOCIETY

Perfection and redemption of the living and the dead are integral parts of a Zion Society and are inextricably connected to covenants and ordinances performed in temples of the Lord. From the Church's commencement in this dispensation the Lord has placed top priority on building structures worthy of the ordinances and covenants entered into there.

Organized in Fayette, New York April 6, 1830, the Church's headquarters was moved to Kirtland, Ohio in February 1831 just ten months later, where the New York and other converts were counseled to gather. Barely were many able to find or build temporary lodging in the Kirtland area, when a large party of Elders under the leadership of Joseph Smith pushed on to Jackson County, Missouri nearly a thousand miles further west, arriving in mid-July 1831. On August 3rd, the spot for a temple was dedicated as indicated by the Lord through revelation:

"Behold, the place which is now called Independence is the center place; and the spot for the temple is lying westward, upon a lot which is not far from the Courthouse." (D&C 57:3) The Jackson County Courthouse was erected just four years earlier in 1827 to serve a new and growing Missouri County.

Many new church members arriving in Kirtland, Ohio moved on to Jackson County, Missouri, including the poor from Colesville, New York. Some of the arriving Saints were planted in Jackson County, Missouri while others including Joseph Smith returned to Kirtland a few weeks later, to oversee the movement of other arriving members on to Missouri from Ohio. A plat of the City of Zion was drawn up June 25, 1833 to serve a population of 15 to 20,000 people, including twelve temples. A description of the first House of the Lord or Temple to be built in Zion in this dispensation was set forth.

Simultaneously, a House of the Lord was planned for Kirtland, Ohio and construction was begun June 5th. The cornerstone was laid July 23, 1833 and the building was finished in 1836. Dedication meetings were begun in March. A dedicatory prayer was offered March 27, 1836 as reported in Chapter XIV. Heavenly messengers visited the temple April 3, 1836 returning priesthood keys to earth, and the Savior Himself appeared and accepted the Kirtland Temple as His house, also reported in Chapter XIV.

Intense persecution prevented the Jackson County Saints from starting construction of a temple in the New Jerusalem to be, necessitating they move from the county. Mob violence in late October, 1833 forced the Saints to move from Jackson County to the more friendly Clay, Davies and Caldwell Counties, but those who attempted to settle in Van Buren and Lafayette Counties were soon expelled. The residents of Clay, Davies and Caldwell Counties, who arrived there before the Latter-day Saints, soon turned hostile and forced the Saints to move from the state of Missouri.

A temple site in Far West, Missouri was identified in 1837, but its construction was postponed due to persecution and hostility. However, cornerstones were laid July 4, 1838, enabling the apostles to fulfill a prophecy concerning their departure for foreign missions.

In the meantime the purposes of the Kirtland Temple were fulfilled when Moses appeared there and conferred the keys of the gathering of Israel upon Joseph Smith; Elias appeared and conferred the keys of the gospel of Abraham which contained higher laws than the law of Moses, laws essential to the perfection and exaltation of men and women; and Elijah the prophet, appeared and conferred keys to the sealing power also upon Joseph Smith.

These three heavenly messengers, who once lived on earth, restored priesthood keys. Their appearance also foreshadowed what was later enunciated as the mission of the Church: 1) To preach the Gospel to every nation, kindred, tongue and people, that is, to gather

452

Israel, the true believers in Messiah/Christ, from wherever they are; 2) To reestablish the gospel of Abraham which contains the principles necessary to perfect the lives of those entering the covenant, that is, to perfect the Saints, thereby making it possible for them to become perfect as our Father in Heaven and Jesus Christ are perfect and become worthy of exaltation as an heir in the Father's kingdom; and 3) To redeem the dead through ordinances performed in their behalf and ultimately to seal family members, husbands to wives, parents to children, and children to parents for time and for all eternity, using the sealing power held by Elijah the prophet. The Savior also appeared and accepted the Kirtland Temple as His house as long as it remained unpolluted.

After serving its purposes as a place to restore higher priesthood keys and a place for the Savior to visit as His house, enemies of the Church soon seized the new temple and polluted it in various ways. By 1837 Joseph Smith and most of the Church leaders were on missions or in Missouri. Joseph Smith incurred the wrath of local government officers as he and others tried to assist the suffering Saints in Missouri being forced from their homes, and was imprisoned in the Liberty Jail. While so detained, Joseph Smith received some of the most beautiful and important revelations pertaining to the use of priesthood power, Sections 121, 122, and 123..

Joseph Smith and his brethren were allowed to leave or escape from the Liberty Jail. The Church leadership decided to locate the main body of the Saints in what was then Commerce, Illinois east of the Mississippi River, after the Governor of Missouri issued an extermination order forcing the Saints to leave the State.

Though driven from the State of Missouri in 1839, by 1841 the Saints had drained the swamps of Commerce, Illinois on a bend in the Mississippi River, built many homes and buildings, and renamed it Nauvoo the beautiful. Here the headquarters of the Church was established and here was a place where the Lord wanted a temple built. An article in the Times and Seasons referred to by Joseph Smith in a letter he sent to the Twelve in England, in October, 1840 said plans had been announced to build

"a temple for the worship of our God in this place. Preparations now making; every tenth day is devoted by the brethren for quarrying rock, etc... It is expected to be considerably larger than the one in Kirtland, and on a more magnificent scale... I presume the doctrine of 'baptism for the dead' has ere reached your ears, and may have raised some inquiries in your minds respecting the same... I would say that it was certainly practiced by the ancient churches; and St. Paul endeavors to prove the doctrine of the resurrection from the same... I first mentioned the doctrine in public when preaching the funeral sermon of Brother Seymour Brunson, and since then given general instructions in the Church on the subject. The Saints have the privilege of being baptized for some of their relatives who are dead, whom they believe would have embraced the Gospel, if they had been privileged with hearing it, and who have received the Gospel in the spirit, through the instrumentality of those who have been commissioned to preach to them while in prison." (HC 4:229-231)

[Section 124]

Three months later, January 19, 1841, following the announcement a temple would be built in Nauvoo, a revelation was received which set forth the urgency of completing the building right away. Individual brethren were called upon to lead the effort and members and others were to join together and build the temple. This temple was a high priority project, and failure to build it in a timely fashion would bring condemnation on the Church and its members as can be seen in the Lord's language.

"Come ye, with all your gold, and your silver, and your precious stones, and with all your antiquities; and with all who have knowledge of antiquities, that will come, may come, and bring the box-tree, the fir-tree, and the pine-tree, together with all the precious trees of the earth; And with iron, with copper, and with brass, and

454

with zinc, and with all your precious things of the earth; and build a house to my name, for the Most High to dwell therein.

"For there is not a place found on earth that he may come to and restore again that which was lost unto you, or which he hath taken away, even the fulness of the priesthood. For a baptismal font there is not upon the earth, that they, my saints, may be baptized for those who are dead--For this ordinance belongeth to my house, and cannot be acceptable to me, only, in the days of your poverty, wherein ye are not able to build a house unto me." (v 26-30)

In describing the purposes of a temple, the Lord led off with the ordinance of baptism for the dead and the priesthood necessary for it. The Apostle Paul alluded to the importance of this ordinance when he asked,

"Else what shall they do which are baptized for the dead, if the dead rise not at all"? why are they then baptized for the dead?" (I Cor. 15:29)

As was revealed and made clear in this dispensation, the dead will rise, yea,"even all", and each will be judged according to that which they received and lived by. The Lord indicates baptism for the dead was and is a temple ordinance. Therefore, at some point in the past history of some temples, such ordinances were performed. However, because of the initial poverty of the Saints in our day, He accepted the performance of baptisms for the dead outside a temple for a very limited duration, about a year. Initially these ordinances were performed in the Mississippi River, but the ordinances were not recorded or officially witnessed and eventually had to be done over again. Through revelation the Lord sought to emphasize the sanctity of this ordinance, to get it moved from rivers and ponds to His house, to make certain all such ordinances were officially recorded and witnessed and to focus individual member's efforts on their forebears.

"But behold, at the end of this appointment your baptisms for your dead shall not be acceptable unto me; and if you do not these things at the end of the appointment ye shall be rejected as a church,

455

with your dead, saith the Lord your God.

"For verily I say unto you, that after you have had sufficient time to build a house to me, wherein the ordinance of baptizing for the dead belongeth, and for which the same was instituted from before the foundation of the world, your baptisms for the dead cannot be acceptable to me; For therein are the keys of the holy priesthood ordained, that you may receive honor and glory.

"And after this time, your baptisms for the dead, by those who are scattered abroad, are not acceptable unto me, saith the Lord. For it is ordained that in Zion, and in her stakes, and in Jerusalem, those places which I have appointed for refuge, shall be the places for your baptisms for your dead." (v 32-35)

Other ordinances were also to be performed in temples including washings, anointings and solemn assemblies. For these purposes was a portable tabernacle built in the wilderness by Moses, and a more permanent temple was later built in Jerusalem in the promised land.

"And again, verily I say unto you, how shall your washings be acceptable unto me, except ye perform them in a house which you have built in my name? For, for this cause I commanded Moses that he should build a tabernacle, that they should bear it with them in the wilderness, and to build a house in the land of promise [Jerusalem], that those ordinances might be revealed which had been hid from before the world was.

"Therefore, verily I say unto you, that your anointings and your washings, and your baptisms for the dead, and your solemn assemblies, ... are ordained by the ordinance of my holy house which my people are always commanded to build unto my holy name. And verily I say unto you, let this house be built unto my name, that I may reveal mine ordinances unto my people; For I deign to reveal unto my church things which have been kept hid from before the foundation of the world, things that pertain to the dispensation of the fulness of times.

456

"And I will show unto my servant Joseph all things pertaining to this house, and the priesthood thereof, and the place whereon it shall be built... If ye labor with all your might, I will consecrate that spot that it shall be made holy." v 36-42)

As mentioned previously, these ordinances for the dead were performed in the Lord's holy temples in the past, but the major portion of this work has been left to the dispensation of the fulness of times, our dispensation. So the Lord counseled His anointed servants to proceed to build such a temple with all deliberate speed.

Realizing some would not work earnestly to build this temple, thinking that the real temple was to be built in Missouri, the Lord used a part of this revelation to address that concern, and admonished the Saints to build this temple with all their might even if it were a temporary structure, like in the days of Moses.

"Verily, verily, I say unto you, that when I give a commandment to any of the sons of men to do a work unto my name, and those sons of men go with all their might and with all they have to perform that work, and cease not their diligence, and their enemies come upon them and hinder them from performing that work, behold, it behooveth me to require that work no more at the hands of those sons of men, but to accept of their offerings...

"Therefore for this cause I have accepted the offerings of those whom I commanded to build up a city and a house unto my name, in Jackson county, Missouri, and were hindered by their enemies, saith the Lord your God. And this I make an example unto you, for your consolation concerning all those who have been commanded to do a work and have been hindered by the hands of their enemies, and by oppression, saith the Lord your God. For I am the Lord your God, and will save all those of your brethren who have been pure in heart, and have been slain in the land of Missouri, saith the Lord.

"And again, verily I say unto you, I command you again to build a house to my name, even in this place, that you may prove

457

yourselves unto me that ye are faithful in all things, whatsoever I command you, that I may bless you, and crown you with honor, immortality and eternal life." (v 49-55)

Three months following the revelations in Section 124, on April 6, 1841, the first day of the twelfth year of the Church of Jesus Christ of Latter-day Saints, four cornerstones were laid for the Temple, the first by the First Presidency, the second by the President of the High Priesthood, the third superintended by the Nauvoo Stake High Council with a pronouncement from Elias Higbee and the fourth by the Bishops, with a pronouncement from Bishop Newell K. Whitney.(HC 4:330)

Responding to the urgency for a place to do baptisms for the dead, the Brethren built a baptismal font in the center of the basement room, under the main hall of the Temple made of pine timber 12 by 16 feet, oval shaped with a basin four feet deep. It stood on the backs of twelve oxen four on each side and two on each end, their heads, shoulders and forelegs projecting out from under the font, also carved from pine timber. The lumber to build interior and exterior portions of the Temple was brought down the Mississippi River from Wisconsin and the water for the font was supplied by a well.

"This font was built for the baptisms for the dead until the Temple shall be finished, when a more durable one will supply its place." The font was dedicated for use November 8, 1841 by Brigham Young and its use was begun November 21st. (HC 4:446)

News that baptisms for the dead were being performed in this Nauvoo, Illinois temple baptistery reached Connecticut in 1842 and was reported by a Reverend Badger and published in the Norwalk Gazette weekly, August 17th.

He reported that every man must work on the temple every tenth day, and told of a baptistery standing on the backs of twelve oxen where baptisms were performed not only for the living but for the dead. He said that individuals are instructed that they can get their friends out of perdition by being baptized on their account.

"I saw one old man, who had been baptized thirteen times for his deceased children, because they were not Mormons, and heard of another about eighty years old who was baptized for George Washington, and Lafayette, and then for Thomas Jefferson, and then applied in behalf of Andrew Jackson, but they told him the general wasn't dead yet, so he waits awhile." (Norwalk Gazette weekly, August 17, 1842]

Later, individual member's focus in doing baptisms for the dead was clarified to be primarily for his/her direct forebears, their extended families and collateral lines, in keeping with the words of Malachi stating that Elijah was sent to

"plant in the hearts of the children the promises made to the fathers, and the hearts of children shall turn to their fathers. If it were not so, the whole earth would be utterly wasted at his coming." (JSH 1:39)

Elijah was the last prophet in the Northern Kingdom of Israel to have the sealing power before the ten tribes led by Ephraim's posterity abandoned the worship of the only true God in favor of Baal. Elijah demonstrated this sealing power transcended the powers of this earth when he used it to control the elements by calling down fire from heaven; by preventing rain for three and a half years until he called for it; by miraculously extending the widow's meal and cruse of oil as she and her son were preparing to die for want of bread; and by raising a young boy from the dead. (1Kgs 17 thru 2Kgs 2)

These powers were used by Elijah in a last ditch effort to show Israel that Baal was powerless to redeem them. As Malachi indicates the Second Coming of the Savior will be a great day for the righteous and obedient, because they welcome the return of their redeemer and salvation from the wilderness of the world. It will be a dreadful day for the non-believers and unrepentant because they will come to know the folly of their ways and face the consequences of their disobedience.

The term "fathers" is used in two ways. In the same way

459

Abraham went to the "fathers" to obtain the priesthood, Malachi refers to the children remembering the promises of eternal life made by the "fathers" or "patriarchs". To activate these promises, then, the hearts of the "children" must turn to their "fathers" to link themselves with their eternal family.

Section 127

In an inspired letter from Joseph Smith to the Latter-day Saints dated September 1, 1842 at Nauvoo, Illinois the Lord again calls attention to the temple and the work to be done for the dead there. These impressions were coming on the prophets mind even though he was in partial seclusion or hiding because enemies of the Church wanted it and its leader destroyed. He was not unlike the Apostle Paul in this regard.

"... And again, verily thus saith the Lord: let the work of my temple, and all the works which I have appointed unto you, be continued on and not cease; and let your diligence, and your perseverance, and patience, and your works be redoubled, and you shall in no wise lose your reward, saith the Lord of Hosts. And if they persecute you, so persecuted they the prophets and righteous men that were before you. For all this there is a reward in heaven.

"And again, I give unto you a word in relation to the baptism for your dead. Verily, thus saith the Lord unto you concerning your dead: When any of you are baptized for your dead, let there be a recorder, and let him be eye-witness of your baptisms; let him hear with his ears, that he may testify of a truth, saith the Lord; That in all your recordings it may be recorded in heaven; whatsoever you bind on earth may be bound in heaven; whatsoever you loose on earth may be loosed in heaven;

"For I am about to restore many things to the earth, pertaining to the priesthood, saith the Lord of Hosts. And again, let all the records be had in order, that they may be put in the archives of my holy temple, to be held in remembrance from generation to generation, saith the Lord of Hosts.

"I will say to all the saints, that I desired, with exceedingly great desire, to have addressed them from the stand on the subject of baptism for the dead, on the following Sabbath. But inasmuch as it is out of my power to do so, I will write the word of the Lord from time to time on that subject, and send it to you by mail, as well as many other things.

"I now close my letter for the present, for the want of more time; for the enemy is on the alert, and as the Savior said, the prince of the world cometh, but he hath nothing in me. Behold, my prayer to God is that you may be saved. And I subscribe myself your servant in the Lord, prophet and seer of the Church of Jesus Christ of Latter-day Saints." (D&C 127:4-12; HC 5:142-144)

Section 128

Further directions concerning baptisms for the dead were received by the Church just five days later in an epistle from the Prophet Joseph Smith, at Nauvoo, Illinois, dated September 6, 1842.

"I now resume the subject of the baptism for the dead, as that subject seems to occupy my mind, and press itself upon my feelings the strongest, since I have been pursued by my enemies. I write a few words of revelation to you concerning a recorder... it would be very difficult for one recorder to be present at all times ... To obviate this difficulty, there can be a recorder appointed in each ward of the city ... naming also some three individuals that are present ... that in the mouth of three witnesses every word may be established. Then let there be a general recorder, to whom all other records can be handed, being attended with certificates ... certifying that the record they made is true. Then the general church recorder can enter the record on the general church book with the certificates and all the attending witnesses.

"...You may think this order of things to be very particular; but ... it is only to answer the will of God, by conforming to the ordinance and preparation that the Lord ordained and prepared before the foundation of the world, for the salvation of the dead who should die

461

without a knowledge of the gospel.

"And further, I want you to remember that John the Revelator was contemplating this very subject in relation to the dead, when he declared... 'And I saw the dead, small and great, stand before God; and the books were opened, and another book was opened, which is the book of life; and the dead were judged out of those things which were written in the books, according to their works.'[Rev.20:12]

"You will discover in this quotation that the books were opened; and another book was opened, which was the book of life; but the dead were judged out of those things which were written in the books, according to their works; consequently, the books spoken of must be the books which contained the record of their works, and refer to the records which are kept on the earth. And the book which was the book of life is the record which is kept in heaven; the principle agreeing precisely with the doctrine which is commanded you in the revelation contained in the letter which I wrote to you previous to my leaving my place - - that in all your recordings it may be recorded in heaven.

"Now, the nature of this ordinance consists in the power of the priesthood, by the revelation of Jesus Christ, wherein it is granted that whatsoever you bind on earth shall be bound in heaven, and whatsoever you loose on earth shall be loosed in heaven. Or, in other words, taking a different view of the translation, whatsoever you record on earth shall be recorded in heaven, and whatsoever you do not record on earth shall not be recorded in heaven; for out of the books shall your dead be judged, according to their own works, whether they themselves have attended to the ordinances in their own propia persona, or by the means of their own agents, according to the ordinance which God has prepared for their salvation from before the foundation of the world, according to the records which they have kept concerning the dead.

"It may seem to some to be a very bold doctrine that we talk of-- a power which records or binds on earth and binds in heaven.

462

Nevertheless, in all ages of the world, whenever the Lord has given a dispensation of the priesthood to any man by actual revelation, or any set of men, this power has always been given. Hence, whatsoever those men did in authority, in the name of the Lord, and did it truly and faithfully, and kept a proper and faithful record of the same, it became a law on earth and in heaven, and could not be annulled, according to the decrees of the great Jehovah." (v 1-9)

Referencing the New Testament book of Matthew, and Paul's letters to the Corinthians, Joseph Smith continues:

"'And I say also unto thee, That thou art Peter, and upon this rock I will build my church; and the gates of hell shall not prevail against it. And I will give unto thee the keys of the kingdom of heaven: and whatsoever thou shalt bind on earth shall be bound in heaven; and whatsoever thou shalt loose on earth shall be loosed in heaven.' (Matt. 16:18-19)

"Now the great and grand secret of the whole matter, and the summum bonum of the whole subject that is lying before us, consists of obtaining the powers of the Holy Priesthood. For him to whom these keys are given there is no difficulty in obtaining a knowledge of facts in relation to the salvation of the children of men, both as well for the dead as for the living. Herein is the glory and honor, and immortality and eternal life-- The ordinance of baptism by water, to be immersed therein in order to answer to the likeness of the dead, that one principle might accord with the other; to be impressed in the water and come forth out of the water is in the likeness of the resurrection of the dead coming forth out of their graves; hence this ordinance was instituted to form a relationship with the ordinance of baptism of the dead, being in likeness of the dead.

"Consequently, the baptismal font was instituted as a similitude of the grave, and was commanded to be in a place underneath where the living are wont to assemble, to show forth the living and the dead, and that all things may have their likeness, and that they may accord one with another--- that which is earthly

463

conforming to that which is heavenly as Paul hath declared,..." (v 10-13, I Cor 15:46-48)

"And now, my dearly beloved brethren and sisters, let me assure you that these are principles in relation to the dead and the living that cannot be lightly passed over, as pertaining to our salvation. For their salvation is necessary to our salvation, as Paul says concerning the fathers -- that they without us cannot be made perfect-- neither can we without our dead be made perfect.

"... the earth will be smitten with a curse unless there is a welding link of some kind or other between the fathers and the children... for it is necessary in the ushering in of the dispensation of the fulness of times ... that a whole and complete and perfect union, and welding together of dispensations, and keys, and powers, and glories should take place, and be revealed from the days of Adam even to the present time. And not only this, but those things which never have been revealed from the foundation of the world, but have been kept hid from the wise and prudent, shall be revealed unto babes and sucklings in this the dispensation of the fulness of times.

" Now, what do we hear in the gospel which we have received? A voice of gladness! A voice of mercy from heaven; and a voice of truth out of the earth; glad tidings for the dead; a voice of gladness for the living and the dead; glad tidings of great joy. How beautiful upon the mountains are the feet of those that bring glad tidings of good things, and that say unto Zion: Behold, thy God reigneth! As the dews of Carmel, so shall the knowledge of God descend upon them!

And again, what do we hear? Glad tidings from Cumorah! Moroni, an angel from heaven, declaring the fulfillment of the prophets-- the book to be revealed. A voice of the Lord in the wilderness of Fayette, Seneca county, declaring the three witnesses of the book!... The voice of Peter, James and John in the wilderness between Harmony, Susquehanna county, and Colesville, Broome county, on the Susquehanna river, declaring themselves as possessing the keys of the kingdom, and of the dispensation of the fulness of times! ...

"And the voice of Michael, the archangel; the voice of Gabriel, and of Raphael, and of divers angels, from Michael to Adam down to the present time, all declaring their dispensations, their rights, their keys, their honors, their majesty, their glory, and the power of their priesthood; giving line upon line, precept upon precept; here a little and there a little; giving us consolation by holding forth that which is to come, confirming our hope! ...

"Let your hearts rejoice, and be exceedingly glad. Let the earth break forth into singing. Let the dead speak forth anthems of eternal praise to the King Immanuel, who hath ordained before the world was, that which would enable us to redeem them out of their prison; for the prisoners shall go free. Let the mountains shout for joy, and all ye valleys cry aloud; and all ye seas and dry lands tell the wonders of your Eternal King! And ye rivers, and brooks and rills, flow down with gladness. Let the woods and all the trees of the field praise the Lord; and ye rocks weep for joy! And let the sun, moon, and the morning stars sing together and let all the sons of God shout for joy!

"And let the eternal creations declare his name forever and ever! And again I say, how glorious is the voice we hear from heaven, proclaiming in our ears, glory, and salvation, and honor, and immortality, and eternal life; kingdoms, principalities, and powers!

"Behold, the great day of the Lord is at hand; and who can abide the day of his coming, and who can stand as he appeareth? For he is like a refiner's fire and like fuller's soap; and he shall sit as a refiner and purifier of silver, and he shall purify the sons of Levi, and purge them as gold and silver, that they may offer unto the Lord an offering in righteousness.

"Let us therefore, as a church and a people, and as Latter-day Saints, offer unto the Lord an offering in righteousness; and let us present in his holy temple, when it is finished, a book containing the record of our dead, which shall be worthy of all acceptation ..." (D&C

128:14-25)

Section 130

Inspired items of instruction given by Joseph Smith, at Ramus, Illinois, April 3, 1843 included declarations that the Father and the Son may appear personally to man; that angels reside in a celestial sphere; that when the earth is upgraded and celestialized, it will be a great Urim and Thummim; that a white stone is given to all who enter the celestial world; that the time of the Second Coming is withheld from the prophet; that intelligence gained in this life rises with us in the resurrection; that all blessings come by obedience to law; and that the Father and the Son have bodies of flesh and bones just as has been promised to all who rise in the resurrection.

More specifically,

"When the Savior shall appear we shall see him as he is. We shall see that he is a man like ourselves. And that same sociality which exists among us here will exist among us there, only it will be coupled with eternal glory, which glory we do not now enjoy.

"John 14:23-- The appearing of the Father and the Son, in that verse, is a personal appearance; and the idea that the Father and the Son dwell in a man's heart is an old sectarian notion, and is false.

"In answer to the question--Is not the reckoning of God's time, angel's time, prophet's time and man's time, according to the planet on which they reside? I answer, Yes. But there are no angels who minister to this earth but those who do belong or have belonged to it. The angels do not reside on a planet like this earth; But they reside in the presence of God, on a globe like a sea of glass and fire, where all things for their glory are manifest, past, present, and future, and are continually before the Lord. The place where God resides is a great Urim and Thummim.

"This earth, in its sanctified and immortal state, will be made like unto crystal and will be a great Urim and Thummim to the inhabitants who dwell thereon, whereby all things pertaining to an inferior kingdom, or all kingdoms of a lower order, will be manifest to those who dwell on it; and this earth will be Christ's.

"Then the white stone mentioned in Revelation 2:17, will become a Urim and Thummim to each individual who receives one, whereby, things pertaining to a higher order of kingdoms will be made known; And a white stone is given to each of those who come into the celestial kingdom, whereon is a new name written, which no man knoweth save he that receiveth it. The new name is the key word.

"...Whatever principle of intelligence we attain unto in this life, it will rise with us in the resurrection. And if a person gains more knowledge and intelligence in this life through his diligence and obedience than another, he will have so much the advantage in the world to come. There is a law, irrevocably decreed in heaven before the foundation of this world, upon which all blessings are predicated-- And when we obtain any blessing from God, it is by obedience to that law upon which it is predicated.

"The Father has a body of flesh and bones as tangible as man's; the Son also; but the Holy Ghost is a personage of Spirit. Were it not so, the Holy Ghost could not dwell in us. A man may receive the Holy Ghost, and it may descend upon him and not tarry with him." (D&C 130:1-11,18-23; HC 5:323-325)

Section 131

Instructions given by Joseph Smith through inspiration at Ramus, Illinois May 16, 1843, declare that celestial marriage is essential to exaltation in the highest heaven. More specifically,

"In the celestial glory there are three heavens or degrees; And in order to obtain the highest, a man must enter into the order of the priesthood [meaning the new and everlasting covenant of marriage]; And if he does not, he cannot obtain it. He may enter into the other, but that is the end of his kingdom; he cannot have an increase." (D&C 131:1-4;HC 5:392-393)

Section 132

467

More revelation relating to the new and everlasting covenant including the eternity of the marriage covenant was recorded at Nauvoo, Illinois July 12, 1843; although historical records indicate the doctrines and principles involved, including the plurality of wives, had been known by the Prophet Joseph Smith since 1831.

In this revelation we learn that exaltation is gained through the new and everlasting covenant; what the terms and conditions of that covenant are; and that celestial marriage and a continuation of the family unit enable men to become gods. We also learn about the strait and narrow way that leads to eternal lives; that there is a law given relative to blasphemy against the Holy Ghost; that promises of eternal increase and exaltation have been made to prophets and saints in all ages; that Joseph Smith was given the power to bind on earth and in heaven and that the Lord sealed upon him his exaltation. In addition, Emma Smith was counseled to be faithful and true and laws governing the plurality of wives were set forth.

More specifically,

"... prepare thy heart to receive and obey the instructions which I am about to give you... I reveal unto you a new and everlasting covenant... for all who will have a blessing at my hands shall abide the law which was appointed for that blessing, and the conditions thereof, as were instituted from before the foundation of the world.

"... the new and everlasting covenant ... was instituted for the fulness of my glory; and he that receiveth a fulness thereof must and shall abide the law... the conditions of this law are these: All covenants, contracts, bonds, obligations, oaths, vows, performances, connections, associations, or expectations, that are not made and entered into and sealed by the Holy Spirit of promise, of him who is anointed,... whom I have appointed on the earth to hold this power ... are of no efficacy, virtue or force in and after the resurrection from the dead; for all contracts that are not made unto this end have an end when men are dead.

"Behold, mine house is a house of order, saith the Lord God, and not a house of confusion. Will I accept of an offering, saith the Lord, that is not made in my name? Or will I receive at your hands that which I have not appointed? And will I appoint unto you, saith the Lord, except it be by law, even as I and my Father ordained unto you, before the world was?

"I am the Lord thy God, and I give unto you this commandment-- that no man shall come unto the Father but by me or by my word, which is my law, saith the Lord. And everything that is in the world, whether it be ordained of men, by thrones, or principalities, or powers, or things of name, whatsoever they may be, that are not by me or by my word, saith the Lord, shall be thrown down, and shall not remain after men are dead, neither in nor after the resurrection, saith the Lord your God. For whatsoever things remain are by me; and whatsoever things are not by me shall be shaken and destroyed.

"Therefore, if a man marry him a wife in the world, and he marry her not by me nor by my word, and he covenant with her so long as he is in the world, and she with him, their covenant and marriage are not of force when they are dead, and when they are out of the world. [On the other hand]

"... verily I say unto you if a man marry a wife by my word, which is my law, and by the new and everlasting covenant, and it is sealed unto them by the Holy Spirit of promise, by whom I have appointed this power and the keys of this priesthood; it shall be said unto them-- Ye shall come forth in the first resurrection; and if it be after the first resurrection; in the next resurrection; and shall inherit thrones, kingdoms, principalities and powers, dominions, all heights and depths--then shall it be written in the Lamb's Book of Life, that he shall commit no murder whereby to shed innocent blood, and if ye abide in my covenant, and commit no murder whereby to shed innocent blood, it shall be done unto them in all things whatsoever my servant hath put upon them, in time and through all eternity; and shall be in full force when they are out of the world; and they shall pass by the angels, and the gods, which are set there, to their exaltation and glory in all things, as hath been sealed upon their heads, which glory shall be a fulness and a continuation of the seeds forever and ever.

"Then shall they be gods; because they have no end; therefore shall they be from everlasting to everlasting, because they continue; then shall they be above all, because all things are subject unto them. Then shall they be gods, because they have all power, and the angels are subject unto them. Verily, verily, I say unto you, except ye abide my law you cannot attain to this glory.

"...This is eternal lives-- to know the only wise and true God, and Jesus Christ whom he hath sent. I am he, Receive ye, therefore, my law." (v 4-15, 19-24)

The Lord also said that those who choose not marry for time and for all eternity when the opportunity is available through one having authority, and are otherwise worthy,

"... are appointed angels in heaven, which angels are ministering servants, to minister for those who are worthy of a far more, and an exceeding, and eternal weight of glory. For these angels did not abide my law; therefore, they cannot be enlarged, but remain separately and singly, without exaltation, in their saved condition, to all eternity; and from henceforth are not gods, but are angels of God forever and ever." (v 16-17)

Section 137
See Chapter XIV

At a prayer meeting in the assembly room over a store six apostles received their endowments and further instructions in the Priesthood, December 1, 1843 in the presence of a group of thirty-five. (HC 6:98) However, administration of this ordinance did not begin until after endowment rooms were completed in the Temple, December 10, 1845.

After Joseph Smith was martyred June 27th, work on the Temple had resumed in August, 1844. The capstone was laid in May, 1845, construction of a more permanent baptismal font was begun in June, and the building was sufficiently finished to begin its use for general conference in October, 1845.(HC 7:456)

Endowment ordinances for both men and women were begun December 10, 1845, with Church leaders working essentially night and day to accommodate those wishing to receive them. An altar was completed and used for the first time to seal husbands and wives together for time and for all eternity January 7, 1846. (HC 7:566) Thousands of Saints were endowed in the Nauvoo Temple and sealed to their spouses for time and for all eternity, just prior to their forced exodus to the west, including many forebears of the author: destination the Salt Lake Valley, soon to be Utah Territory.

Crossing the Mississippi River by the departing Saints began in early February. Brigham Young, President of the Quorum of Twelve Apostles, his family and others crossed the river February 15, 1846 to take charge of the Camp of Israel in its journey west.

Not only did the early Latter-day Saints gather the honest in heart with great vigor, they built the Nauvoo Temple with that same vigor, so that the upgrade, perfection and eventual redemption of all entering the covenant might be realized, even though they knew that the Temple would soon be in the hands of their enemies, which it was. Fire burned the roof as the Saints departed for the west, and the entire building was destroyed by fire in November, 1848. (HC 7:581, 617n, 618n)

About four days after their arrival in the Salt Lake Valley July 24, 1847, Brigham Young pushed his cane into the ground and declared, here we will build a temple to our God. However, temples were completed in St, George, Manti, and Logan, Utah before the Salt Lake Temple's completion in 1893. Some fifteen years after the Salt Lake Temple's completion, the then Prophet and President of the Church, Joseph F. Smith, received a revelation which greatly increased our understanding of the great work for the dead done in Temples.

[Section 138]

Concerning a vision given to him in Salt Lake City, Utah, on October 3, 1918 the Prophet and President of the Church of Jesus Christ of Latter-day Saints, Joseph F. Smith said:

"On the third of October, in the year nineteen hundred and eighteen, I sat in my room pondering over the scriptures; And reflecting upon the great atoning sacrifice that was made by the Son of God for the redemption of the world; And the great and wonderful love made manifest by the Father and the Son in the coming of the Redeemer into the world; That through the atonement, and by obedience to the principles of the gospel, mankind might be saved.

"While I was thus engaged, my mind reverted to the writings of the apostle Peter, to the primitive saints scattered abroad throughout Pontus, Galatia, Cappadocia, and other parts of Asia, where the gospel had been preached after the crucifixion of the Lord.

"I opened the Bible and read the third and fourth chapters of the first epistle of Peter, and as I read I was greatly impressed, more than I had ever been before, with the following passages:

"For Christ also hath once suffered for sins, the just for the unjust, that he might bring us to God, being put to death in the flesh, but being quickened by the Spirit; By which also he went and preached unto the spirits in prison; Which sometime were disobedient, when once the long-suffering of God waited in the days of Noah, while the ark was a preparing, wherein few, that is, eight souls were saved by water." (1 Peter 3:18-20)

"For for this cause was the gospel preached also to them that are dead, that they might be judged according to men in the flesh, but live according to God in the spirit." (1 Peter 4:6)

"As I pondered over these things which are written, the eyes of my understanding were opened, and the Spirit of the Lord rested upon me, and I saw the hosts of the dead, both small and great. And there were gathered together in one place an innumerable company of the spirits of the just, who had been faithful in the testimony of Jesus while they lived in mortality; And who had offered sacrifice in the similitude of the great sacrifice of the Son of God, and had suffered tribulation in their Redeemer's name.

"All these departed the mortal life, firm in the hope of a glorious resurrection, through the grace of God the Father and his Only Begotten Son, Jesus Christ. I beheld that they were filled with joy and gladness, and were rejoicing together because the day of their deliverance was at hand.

"They were assembled awaiting the advent of the Son of God into the spirit world, to declare their redemption from the hands of death. Their sleeping dust was to be restored unto its perfect frame, bone to his bone, and the sinews and the flesh upon them, the spirit and the body to be united never again to be divided, that they might receive a fulness of joy.

"While this vast multitude waited and conversed, rejoicing in the hour of their deliverance from the chains of death, the Son of God appeared, declaring liberty to the captives who had been faithful; And there he preached to them the everlasting gospel, the doctrine of the resurrection and the redemption of mankind from the fall, and from individual sins on condition of repentance.

"But unto the wicked he did not go, and among the ungodly and the unrepentant who had denied themselves while in the flesh, his voice was not raised; Neither did the rebellious who rejected the testimonies and the warnings of the ancient prophets behold his presence, nor looked upon his face.

"Where these were darkness reigned, but among the righteous there was peace; And the saints rejoiced in their redemption, and bowed the knee and acknowledged the Son of God as their Redeemer and Deliverer from death and the chains of hell. Their countenances shown, and the radiance from the presence of the Lord rested upon them, and they sang praises unto his holy name.

"I marveled, for I understood that the Savior spent about three years in his ministry among the Jews and those of the house of Israel, endeavoring to teach them the everlasting gospel and call them unto repentance; And yet, notwithstanding his mighty works, and miracles, and proclamation of the truth, in great power and authority, they were but few who hearkened to his voice and rejoiced in his presence, and received salvation at his hands.

"But his ministry among those who were dead was limited to the brief time intervening between the crucifixion and his resurrection; And I wondered at the words of Peter--wherein he said that the Son of God preached unto the spirits in prison, who sometimes were disobedient, when once the long-suffering of God waited in the days of Noah-- and how it was possible for him to preach to those spirits and perform the necessary labor among them in so short a time.

"And as I wondered, my eyes were opened, and my understanding quickened, and I perceived that the Lord went not in person among the wicked and the disobedient who had rejected the truth, to teach them; But behold, from among the righteous, he organized his forces and appointed messengers, clothed with power and authority, and commissioned them to go forth and carry the light of the gospel to them that were in darkness, even to all the spirits of men; and thus was the gospel preached to the dead.

"And the chosen messengers went forth to declare the acceptable day of the Lord and proclaim liberty to the captives who were bound, even unto all who would repent of their sins and receive the gospel. Thus was the gospel preached to those who had died in their sins, without a knowledge of the truth, or in transgression, having rejected the prophets.

"These were taught faith in God, repentance from sin, vicarious baptism for the remission of sins, the gift of the Holy Ghost by the laying on of hands, And all other principles of the gospel that were necessary for them to know in order to qualify themselves that they might be judged according to men on the flesh, but live according to God in the spirit.

"And so it was made known among the dead, both small and great, the unrighteous as well as the faithful, that redemption had been wrought through the sacrifice of the Son of God upon the cross. Thus was it made known that our Redeemer spent his time during his sojourn in the world of spirits, instructing and preparing the faithful spirits of the prophets who had testified of him in the flesh; That they might carry the message of redemption unto all the dead, unto whom he could not go personally, because of their rebellion and transgression, that they through the ministration of his servants might also hear his words.

"Among the great and mighty ones who were assembled in this vast congregation of the righteous were Father Adam, the Ancient of Days and father of all, And our glorious Mother Eve, with many of her faithful daughters who had lived through the ages and worshiped the true and living God. Abel, the first martyr, was there, and his brother Seth, one of the mighty ones, who was in the express image of his father, Adam.

"Noah, who gave warning of the flood, Shem, the great high priest; Abraham, the father of the faithful; Isaac, Jacob, and Moses, the great law-giver of Israel; And Isaiah, who declared by prophecy that the Redeemer was anointed to bind up the broken-hearted, to proclaim liberty to the captives, and the opening of the prison to them that were bound, were also there,

"Moreover, Ezekiel, who was shown in vision the great valley of dry bones, which were to be clothed upon with flesh, to come forth again in the resurrection of the dead, living souls; Daniel, who foresaw and foretold the establishment of the kingdom of God in the latter days, never again to be destroyed nor given to other people; Elias, who was with Moses on the Mount of Transfiguration; And Malachi, the prophet who testified of the coming of Elijah-- of whom also Moroni spake to the Prophet Joseph Smith, declaring that he

475

should come before the ushering in of the great and dreadful day of the Lord--were also there.

"The Prophet Elijah was to plant in the hearts of the children the promises made to their fathers, Foreshadowing the great work to be done in the dispensation of the fulness of times, for the redemption of the dead, and the sealing of the children to their parents, lest the whole earth be smitten with a curse and utterly wasted at his coming. All these and many more, even the prophets who dwelt among the Nephites and testified of the coming of the Son of God, mingled in the vast assembly and waited for their deliverance, For the dead had looked upon the long absence of their spirits from their bodies as a bondage.

"These the Lord taught, and gave them power to come forth, after the resurrection from the dead, to enter into his Father's kingdom, there to be crowned with immortality and eternal life, And continue thenceforth their labor as had been promised by the Lord, and be partakers of all blessings which were held in reserve for them that love him.

"The Prophet Joseph Smith, and my father, Hyrum Smith, Brigham Young, John Taylor, Wilford Woodruff, and other choice spirits who were reserved to come forth in the fulness of times to take part in laying the foundations of the great latter-day work, including the building of temples and the performance of ordinances therein for the redemption of the dead, were also in the spirit world.

"I observed that they were also among the noble and great ones who were chosen in the beginning to be rulers in the Church of God. Even before they were born, they, with many others, received their first lessons in the world of spirits and were prepared to come forth in the due time of the Lord to labor in his vineyard for the salvation of the souls of men.

"I beheld that the faithful elders of this dispensation, when they depart from mortal life, continue their labors in the preaching of the gospel of repentance and redemption, through the sacrifice of the

Only Begotten Son of God, among those who are in darkness and under the bondage of sin in the great world of the spirits of the dead.

"The dead who repent will be redeemed, through obedience to the ordinances of the house of God, And after they have paid the penalty of their transgression, and are washed clean, shall receive a reward according to their works, for they are heirs of salvation.

"Thus was the vision of the redemption of the dead revealed to me, and I bear record and know that this record is true, through the blessing of our Lord and Savior Jesus Christ, even so, Amen." (D&C 138:1-60)

Summary

Though [1] efforts to build a Temple in the New Jerusalem and in Far West, Missouri were temporarily frustrated,[2] the Temple in Kirtland, Ohio, later polluted by enemies of the Church, and [3] the Nauvoo Temple forcibly abandoned, polluted and burned after a few months use, other Temples were built after the Saints arrival in the west. These and other temples have taken their places and work for the living and the dead continues.

The Kirtland Temple served as the place for the Lord to restore priesthood keys essential to the mission of the Church through Moses, Elias and Elijah, keys to gathering Israel, perfecting the Saints and redeeming the dead. The Nauvoo Temple served as a place where early Latter-day Saints could enter additional covenants with the Lord, before their great trek west to the Salt Lake Valley, giving strength, courage and resolve to endure the hardships, suffering and death which was so much a part of those families who successfully made it into the tops of the mountains. The Nauvoo Temple was a place where they began doing baptisms for their kindred dead, and a place where husbands and wives were washed, anointed, endowed and sealed for time and for all eternity, again prior to their departure and the trials that lay ahead.

Temple building continues as high priority projects, for the Lord's covenant people, with the current prophet, seer and revelator leading the way. Brigham Young poked his cane into the ground and declared just four days after arriving in the valley in July 1847, here we will build a temple to our God, where the Salt Lake Temple now stands, and that temple was built to last through the Millennium. Other temples have followed with nearly eighty of them in service throughout the world at the time of this writing, with the expectation there will be one hundred of them operating or under construction by the year 2000. The building of temples in the New Jerusalem and the rebuilding of the temple in the Old Jerusalem lies ahead in the not too distant future.

Missionaries sent forth in most parts of the world are washed, anointed and endowed in Temples prior to their departure to gather Israel, the true believers in Messiah/Christ. Adults serious about perfecting their lives cannot be fully placed on the road to perfection without the covenants implicit in the endowment, nor can members be made perfect without their dead. We are given to understand that while temple ordinances for the living are indispensable functions of temples, the vast majority of temple work in the twentieth century and on into the Millennium will be by proxy for the dead.

Husbands and wives cannot have claim on each other and on their children throughout all eternity, without the sealing ordinances of the temple. Sealing ordinances are essential to being exalted and being crowned with glory, immortality, eternal life and entrance into the highest degree of the celestial kingdom. Little wonder then that the Lord placed and continues to place high priority on the building of temples as part of a Zion Society, and the work that takes place there.

We have discussed God's plan to redeem all of His children through the use of Priesthood sealing power, which binds in heaven what is bound on earth..Our focus shifts to signs of the second coming, His actual return, the Millennial reign of Messiah/Christ and the final judgment.

CHAPTER XXI

SIGNS OF AND HIS SECOND COMING,
THE MILLENNIAL REIGN OF MESSIAH/CHRIST
THE FINAL JUDGMENT

SIGNS OF AND HIS SECOND COMING

From the prophet Amos we learn that:

"Surely the Lord God will do nothing, but he revealeth his counsel [secret] unto his servants the prophets." (Amos 3:7)

Indeed, the prophets have said much concerning the second coming of Messiah, or the Messiah/Christ. The Lord God has revealed these signs even to prophets who lived before his first coming including Enoch, Job, King David, Isaiah, Daniel, Zechariah and Malachi. Mormon, a western hemisphere prophet, knew much concerning the Lord's second coming, as did Jesus' apostles after His ascension. They recorded what they knew.

For example, Enoch was shown the end from the beginning and was informed his city of Zion would be taken to heaven, before it happened. Enoch's city is scheduled to return to earth and become a sister to the Savior's own city of Zion, called the New Jerusalem:

"And righteousness shall I send down out of heaven; and truth will I send forth out of the earth, to bear testimony of Mine Only Begotten; his resurrection from the dead; yea and also the resurrection of all men; and righteousness and truth will I cause to sweep the earth as with a flood, to gather mine elect from the four quarters of the earth unto a place which I shall prepare, an Holy City, that my people may gird up their loins, and be looking forth for the time of my coming; for there shall be my tabernacle, and it shall be called Zion, a New Jerusalem. And the Lord said unto Enoch: Then shalt thou and all thy city meet them there, and we will receive them into our bosom, and they shall see us and we will fall upon their necks, and they shall fall upon our necks, and we will kiss each other. And there shall be mine abode, and it shall be called Zion, which shall come forth out of all the creations which I have made; and for a space of a thousand years the earth shall rest. And it came to pass that Enoch saw the day of the coming of the Son of Man, in the last days, to dwell on earth in righteousness for space of a thousand years.

"But before that day he saw great tribulations among the wicked; and he also saw the sea, that it was troubled, and men's hearts failing them, looking forth with fear for the judgments of the Almighty God, which should come upon the wicked." (Moses 7:62-66)

[From Job]

"For I know that my Redeemer lives, and that he shall stand at the latter days upon the earth." (Job 19:25)

[From Psalms]

"When the Lord shall build up Zion, he shall appear in his glory." (Psalms 102:16)

[From Isaiah]

"And it shall come to pass in the last days, that the mountain of the Lord's house shall be established in the top of the mountains, and shall be exalted above the hills; and all nations shall flow unto it. And many people shall go and say, Come ye, let us go up to the mountain of the Lord; to the house of Jacob; and he will teach us in his ways, and we will walk in his paths; for out of Zion shall go forth the law, and the word of the Lord from Jerusalem.

"And he shall judge among the nations, and shall rebuke many people; and they shall beat their swords into plowshares, and their spears into pruninghooks; nation shall not lift up sword against nation, neither shall they learn war any more.

"...The lofty looks of man shall be humbled, [and bowed down] and the haughtiness of man shall be bowed down, [and made low] and the Lord alone shall be exalted in that day." (Isa. 2:2-4,11,17; 2Ne 12:2-4,11,17)

"Comfort ye, comfort ye my people, saith your God. Speak ye comfortably to Jerusalem, and cry unto her, that her warfare is accomplished, that her iniquity is pardoned: for she hath received of the Lord's hand for all her sins. The voice of him that crieth in the wilderness, Prepare ye the way of the Lord, make straight in the desert a highway for our God. Every valley shall be exalted, and every mountain and hill shall be made low: and the crooked shall be made straight and the rough places plain: And the glory of the Lord shall be revealed, and all flesh shall see it together, for the mouth of the Lord hath spoken it. " (Isa. 40:2-5)

"...there is no God, else beside me: a just God and a Savior; there is none beside me. Look unto me and be ye saved... I have sworn by myself the word is gone out of my mouth in righteousness, and shall not return, That unto me every knee shall bow, and every tongue shall swear."(Isa.45:21-23; D&C 88:104)

"And I will make all my mountains a way, and my highways shall be exalted." (49:11; 1Ne 21:11)

"How beautiful upon the mountains are the feet of him that bringeth good tidings, that publisheth peace; that bringeth good tidings of good, that publisheth salvation; that saith unto Zion, Thy God reigneth! Thy watchmen shall lift up the voice; with the voice together shall they sing: for they shall see eye to eye, when the Lord shall bringeth again Zion. Break forth into joy, sing together ye waste places of Jerusalem: for the Lord hath comforted his people, he hath redeemed Jerusalem. The Lord hath made bare his arm in the eyes of all the nations; and all the ends of the earth shall see the salvation of our God." (Isa. 52:7-10)

"Who is this that cometh... with dyed garments... that is glorious in his apparel, traveling in the greatness of his strength?.. Wherefore art thou red in thine apparel, and thy garments like him that treadeth in the winefat? I have trodden the winepress alone; and of the people there was none with me: and their blood shall be sprinkled upon my garments, and will stain my raiment." (Isa. 63:2-4;

481

D&C 133:46)

[From Daniel]

"I saw in the night visions, and, behold, one like the Son of man came with the clouds of heaven, and came to the Ancient of days, and they brought him near before him. And there was given him dominion, and glory, and a kingdom, that all people, nations, and languages, should serve him; his dominion is an everlasting dominion, which shall not pass away, and his kingdom that which shall not be destroyed." (Daniel 7:13-14; Matt 26:64; Luke 21:25-28)

[From Zechariah]

"And it shall come to pass in that day, that I will seek to destroy the nations that come against Jerusalem. And I will pour upon the house of David, and upon the inhabitants of Jerusalem, the spirit of grace and of supplications: and they shall look upon me whom they have pierced, and they shall mourn for him, as one mourneth for his only son, and shall be in bitterness for him, that is in the bitterness for his firstborn.

"... And one shall say unto him, What are these wounds in thine hands? Then he shall answer, Those with which I was wounded in the house of my friends." (Zech 12:10, 13:6; D&C 45:51)

[From Malachi]

"But who shall abide the day of his coming? and who shall stand when he appeareth? for he is like a refiner's fire and like fullers' soap." (Mal 3:2; 3Ne 24:2)

[From Matthew]

"For the Son of man shall come in the glory of his Father with his angels; and then shall he reward every man according to his works." (Matt 16:27, 25:31)

[From Acts]

"Ye men of Galilee, why stand ye gazing up into heaven? this same Jesus, which is taken up from you into heaven, shall so come in like manner as ye have seen him go into heaven." (Acts 1:11)

[From Corinthians]

"For as in Adam all die, even so in Christ shall all be made alive. But every man in his own order: Christ the firstfruits; afterward they that are Christ's at his coming. Then cometh the end, when he shall have delivered up the kingdom to God, even the Father; when he shall have put down all rule and all authority and power. For he must reign, till he hath put all enemies under his feet. The last enemy that shall be destroyed is death."(I Cor 15:22-26)

[From I Thessalonians]

"For the Lord himself shall descend from heaven with a shout, with the voice of the archangel, and with the trump of God; and the dead in Christ shall rise first: Then we which are alive and remain shall be caught up together with them in the clouds, to meet the Lord in the air; and so shall we ever be with the Lord." (I Thess 4:16-17)

[II Thessalonians]

"... rest with us, when the Lord Jesus shall be revealed from heaven with his mighty angels, In flaming fire taking vengeance on them that know not God, and that obey not the gospel of our Lord Jesus Christ; ... When he shall come to be glorified in his saints, and be admired in all them that believe." (2Thes 1:7-9)

[From 2 Peter]

"But the day of the Lord will come as a thief in the night; in the which the heavens shall pass away with a great noise, and the elements shall melt with fervent heat, the earth also and the works that are therein shall be burned up... Looking for and hasting unto the coming of the day of God, wherein the heavens being on fire shall be dissolved, and the elements shall melt with fervent heat? Nevertheless we, according to his promise, look for new heavens and a new earth; wherein dwelleth righteousness. Wherefore, beloved, seeing that ye look for such things, be diligent that ye may be found of him, in peace, without spot and blameless." (2 Pet 3:10-14)

[From Jude]

"And Enoch also, the seventh from Adam prophesied of these, saying, Behold, the Lord cometh with ten thousands of his saints."

(Jude 1:14)

[From Revelation]

"The Revelation of Jesus Christ which God gave unto ... his servant John: Who bare record of the word of God and of the testimony of Jesus Christ, and of all things that he saw. ... Jesus Christ, ... is the faithful witness, and the first begotten of the dead, and the prince of the kings of the earth. Unto him that loved us, and washed us from our sins in his own blood, And made us kings and priests unto God and his Father; to him be glory and dominion forever and ever, Amen.

"Behold, he cometh with clouds; and every eye shall see him, and they also which pierced him; and all kindreds of the earth shall wail because of him." (Rev 1:1-7)

"For the great day of his wrath is come; and who shall be able to stand?" (Rev 6:17)

"And when he had opened the seventh seal, there was silence in heaven about the space of half an hour." (Rev 8:1)

From the Book of Mormon and the
Translation of Matthew through Joseph Smith

Shortly after His resurrection and ascension to heaven, the Savior of the world visited His covenant people in America, descendants of Israel through Joseph, Ephraim and Manasseh and commanded them to add to their scriptures. They had left Jerusalem before the days of Malachi.

"And it came to pass that he commanded them that they should write the words which the Father had given unto Malachi... Thus said the Father unto Malachi- Behold, I will send my messenger, and he shall prepare the way before me, and the Lord whom ye seek shall suddenly come to his temple, even the messenger of the covenant, whom you delight in, behold, he shall come, saith the Lord of Hosts...

"Behold, I will send you Elijah the prophet before the coming of the great and dreadful day of the Lord; And he shall turn the hearts of the fathers to the children, and the hearts of the children to their fathers, lest I come and smite the earth with a curse." (3Ne 24:1-2; 25:5)

After commanding the Nephites to call the Church in His name, Jesus said, His mission and atonement constitute the gospel and added: "...I came into the world to do the will of my Father, because my Father sent me. And my Father sent me that I might be lifted up upon the cross; and after that I had been lifted up upon the cross, that I might draw all men unto me, that as I have been lifted up by men even so should men be lifted up by the Father, to stand before me, to be judged of their works, whether they be good or whether they be evil--

"And for this cause have I been lifted up; therefore, according to the power of the Father I will draw all men unto me, that they may be judged according to their works. And it shall come to pass, that whoso repenteth and is baptized in my name shall be filled, and if he endureth to the end, behold, him will I hold guiltless before my Father at the day when I shall stand to judge the world. And he that endureth not unto the end, the same is he that is also hewn down and cast into the fire, from whence they can no more return, because of the justice of the Father..."(3Ne 27:13-17)

The Savior then commanded all men to repent and be baptized that they may be sanctified by the Holy Ghost, and rhetorically asked: "what manner of men ought ye to be? Verily I say unto you, even as I am." (3Ne 27:18-27)

[From Mormon]

Describing the signs of the Lord's coming in the latter-days when the Nephite record, i. e. the Book of Mormon, would come forth, Mormon declared:

"it shall come in a day when it shall be said that miracles are done away, and it shall come even as if one should speak from the dead... Yea, it shall come in a day when the power of God shall be denied, and churches become defiled and be lifted up in the pride of

485

their hearts...

"Yea, it shall come in a day when there shall be heard of fires, and tempests, and vapors of smoke in foreign lands; And there shall also be heard of wars, and rumors of wars, and earthquakes in divers places. Yea, it shall come in a day when there shall be great pollutions upon the face of the earth; there shall be murders, and robbing, and lying, and deceivings, and whoredoms, and all manner of abominations; when there shall be many who will say, do this, or do that, and it mattereth not, for the Lord will uphold such in the last day. But wo unto such, for they are in the gall of bitterness and in the bonds of iniquity..." (Mormon 8:26-32)

[From JST Matthew]

"... if any man shall say unto you, Lo, here is Christ, or there, believe it not; For in those days shall also arise false Christs, and false prophets, and shall show great signs and wonders, insomuch, that, if possible, they shall deceive the very elect, who are the elect according to the covenant. Behold, I speak these things to you for the elect's sake; and you also shall hear wars, and rumors of war; see that ye be not troubled, for all I have told you must come to pass, but the end is not yet...

"For as the light of the morning cometh out of the east, and shineth unto the west, and covereth the whole earth, so shall also the coming of the Son of Man be... And they [mine elect] shall hear of wars and rumors of wars. Behold, I speak for mine elect's sake: for nation shall rise against nation, and kingdom against kingdom; there shall be famines, and pestilences, and earthquakes, in diverse places. And again, because iniquity shall abound, the love of men shall wax cold; but he that shall not be overcome the same shall be saved. And again, this Gospel of the Kingdom shall be preached in all the world, for a witness unto all nations, and then shall the end come, or the destruction of the world.

"And immediately after the tribulation of those days, the sun shall be darkened, and the moon shall not give her light, and the stars shall fall from heaven, and the powers of heaven shall be shaken... Although, the days will come, that heaven and earth shall pass away, yet my words shall not pass away, but all shall be fulfilled.

"... after the tribulation of those days, and the powers of the heavens shall be shaken, then shall appear the sign of the Son of Man in heaven, and then shall all the tribes of the earth mourn, and they shall see the Son of Man coming in the clouds of heaven with power and great glory; And whoso treasureth up my word, shall not be deceived, for the Son of Man shall come, and he shall send his angels before him with the great sound of a trumpet, and they shall gather together the remainder of his elect from the four winds, from one end of heaven to the other... So ... mine elect, when they shall see all these things, they shall know that he is near, even at the doors; But of that day, and hour, no man knoweth; no not the angels of God in heaven, but my Father only." (JST Matt 24:21-40)

From the Doctrine and Covenants
through Joseph Smith

From the many, many references to the second coming in latter-day scripture we learn that Elijah was to come and did come prior to the Lord's second coming; that the Lord's coming is nigh at hand; that He decides when he will come in judgment, in His own due time; that He will come quickly and suddenly appear at His temple; that no man knoweth the hour and day of His coming; that it will be in an hour when ye think not, likened to the coming of a thief in the night; that He will not come in the form of a woman; that He will reveal himself from heaven with power and great glory; that the Lord will be ruler when He comes and that there will be no laws but His laws at His coming; that the Twelve apostles who were with Him in His ministry at Jerusalem will stand at His right hand in the day of His coming in a pillar of fire; that He will come in clouds of glory and the poor who are pure in heart shall see His coming; that those with clean hands and a pure heart, including the elect, shall abide the day of His coming and all should pray to abide the day of His coming;

that His people shall be redeemed and reign with Him on earth; that blessed is he who lives at His coming; that His righteous saints will be caught up to meet the Lord, shall see Him and be crowned by Him; that some of the dead are to rise when the Lord comes, all the rest will rise during the Millennium; that the Savior shall stand in the midst of His people and reign over all flesh; that all nations shall tremble at His coming; that the unrepentant will be destroyed by the brightness of the Lord's coming and will be consumed in fire; that he who is tithed shall not be burned at His coming.

Counseling all flesh, He declared: that he who fears the Lord will look for the signs of His coming; that His servants will have lamps and oil ready for the coming of the Bridegroom; and that His servants are to cry repentance, preparing the way of the Lord for the second coming.

What are some of the signs of His coming?

[From Section 29]

"the hour is nigh and the day soon at hand when the earth is ripe; and all the proud and they that do wickedly shall be as stubble; and I will burn them up, saith the Lord of Hosts; that wickedness shall not be upon the earth; For the hour is nigh, and that which was spoken by mine apostles, might be fulfilled... For I will reveal myself from heaven with power and great glory, with all the hosts thereof, and dwell in righteousness with men on earth a thousand years, and the wicked shall not stand....

"For a trump shall sound both long and loud, even as upon Mount Sinai, and all the earth shall quake, and they shall come forth-- yea, even the dead which died in me, to receive a crown of righteousness and to be clothed upon, even as I am, to be with me, that we may be one.

But, behold, I say unto you that before this great day shall the sun be darkened, and the moon shall be turned into blood, and the stars shall fall from heaven, and there shall be greater signs in heaven above and in the earth beneath; And there shall be weeping and wailing among the hosts of men; And there shall be a great hailstorm sent forth to destroy the crops of the earth.

And it shall come to pass, because of the wickedness of the world, that I will take vengeance upon the wicked, for they will not repent; for the cup of mine indignation is full; for behold, my blood shall not cleanse them if they hear it not. Wherefore, I the Lord God will send forth flies upon the face of the earth, which shall take hold of the inhabitants thereof, and shall eat their flesh, and shall cause maggots to come in upon them; And their tongues shall be stayed that they shall not utter against me; and their flesh shall fall from off their bones, and their eyes from their sockets; And it shall come to pass that the beasts of the forest and fowls of the air shall devour them up.

"And the great and abominable church which is the whore of all the earth, shall be cast down by devouring fire, according as it is spoken by the mouth of Ezekiel the prophet, who spoke of these things, which have not come to pass but surely must, as I live, for abominations shall not reign." (D&C 29:9-21)

[From Section 34]

"For behold, verily, verily, I say unto you, the time is soon at hand that I shall come in a cloud with power and great glory. And it shall be a great day at the time of my coming, for all nations shall tremble. But before that great day shall come the sun shall be darkened, and the moon be turned to blood, and the stars shall refuse their shining, and some shall fall, and great destructions await the wicked." (D&C 34:7-9)

[From Section 43]

"... hearken ye elders of my church whom I have appointed: Ye are not sent forth to be taught, but to teach the children of men the things which I have put into your hands by the power of my Spirit... and ye shall be endowed with power that ye may give even as I have spoken. Hearken ye, for behold, the great day of the Lord is nigh at hand. For the day cometh that the Lord shall utter his voice out of heaven; the heavens shall shake and the earth shall tremble, and the trump of God shall sound both long and loud, and shall say to the sleeping nations: Ye saints arise and live; ye sinners stay and sleep until I shall call again... Prepare yourselves for the great day of the Lord... How oft have I called upon you by the mouth of my servants, and by the ministering of angels, and by mine own voice, and by the voice of thunderings, and by the voice of lightnings, ... tempests, ... earthquakes,... great hailstorms, ... famines, ... and pestilences of every kind, and by the great sound of a trump... Behold, the day has come, when the cup of the wrath of mine indignation is full...

"Wherefore, labor ye, labor ye in my vineyard for the last time-- for the last time call upon the inhabitants of the earth. For in mine own due time will I come upon the earth in judgment, and my people shall be redeemed and shall reign with me on earth. For the great Millennium of which I have spoken by the mouth of my prophets shall come." (D&C 43:15-18,25-30)

[From Section 45]

Revelation given through Joseph Smith at Kirtland, Ohio, March 7, 1831 declares with solemnity that Christ is our advocate with the Father; the gospel is the messenger to prepare the way before the Lord; that Enoch and his brethren were received by the Lord himself.(v 15) He then set forth some of the signs of His Second Coming:

"...I will [said the Lord] speak unto you and prophecy, as unto men in days of old. And I will show it plainly as I showed it unto my disciples as I stood before them in the flesh, and spake unto them, saying: As ye have asked of me concerning the signs of my coming, in the day when I shall come in my glory in the clouds of heaven, to fulfill the promises that I have made unto your fathers,

"For as ye have looked upon the long absence of your spirits from your bodies to be a bondage, I will show unto you how the day of redemption shall come, and also the restoration of the scattered Israel...

"Ye say that ye know that the end of the world cometh; ye say also that ye know that the heavens and the earth shall pass away; And in this ye say truly, for so it is; but these things which I have told you shall not pass away until all shall be fulfilled. And this I have told you concerning Jerusalem; and when that day shall come, shall a remnant be scattered among all nations; But they shall be gathered again; but they shall remain until the times of the Gentiles be fulfilled.

"And in that day shall be heard wars and rumors of wars, and the whole earth shall be in commotion, and men's hearts shall fail them, and they shall say that Christ delayeth his coming until the end of the earth. And the love of men shall wax cold, and iniquity shall abound.

"And when the times of the Gentiles is come in, a light shall break forth among them that sit in darkness, and it shall be the fulness of my gospel; But they receive it not; for they perceive not the light, and they turn their hearts from me because of the precepts of men. And in that generation shall the times of the Gentiles be fulfilled.

"And there shall be men standing in that generation, that shall not pass until they see an over-flowing scourge; for a desolating sickness shall cover the land. But my disciples shall stand in holy places, and shall not be moved; but among the wicked, men shall lift up their voices and curse God and die.

"And there shall be earthquakes also in divers places, and many desolations; yet men will harden their hearts against me, and they will take up the sword, one against another. And now, when I the Lord had spoken these words unto my disciples, they were troubled. And I said unto them, be not troubled, for, when all these things shall come to pass, ye may know that the promises which have been made unto you shall be fulfilled.

"And when the light shall begin to break forth, it shall be with them like unto a parable which I will show you--Ye look and behold the fig trees, and ye see them with your eyes, and ye say when they begin to shoot forth, and their leaves are yet tender, that summer is nigh at hand; Even so it shall be in that day when ye shall see all these things, then shall they know that the hour is nigh.

"And it shall come to pass that he that feareth me shall be looking forth for the great day of the Lord to come, even so for the signs of the coming of the Son of Man.

"And they shall see signs and wonders, for they shall be shown forth in the heavens above, and in the earth beneath. And they shall behold blood, and fire and vapors of smoke. And before the day of the Lord shall come, the sun shall be darkened, and the moon be turned into blood, and the stars fall from heaven. And the remnant shall be gathered unto this place;

"And then shall they look for me, and, behold, I will come; and they shall see me in the clouds of heaven, clothed with power and great glory; with all the holy angels; and he that watches not for me shall be cut off.

"But before the arm of the Lord shall fall, an angel shall sound his trump, and the saints that have slept shall come forth to meet me in the cloud.

"Wherefore, if ye have slept in peace blessed are you; for as you now behold me and know that I am, even so shall ye come unto me and your souls shall live, and your redemption shall be perfected; and the saints shall come forth from the four quarters of the earth. Then shall the arm of the Lord fall upon all nations.

"And then shall the Lord set his foot upon this mount, and it shall cleave in twain, and the earth shall tremble, and reel to and fro, and the heavens shall also shake. And the Lord shall utter his voice, and all the ends of the earth shall hear it; and the nations of the earth shall mourn, and they that have laughed shall see their folly. And calamity shall cover the mocker, and the scorner shall be consumed; and they that have watched for iniquity shall be hewn down and cast into the fire.

"And then shall the Jews look upon me and say: What are these wounds in thine hands and in thy feet? Then shall they know that I am the Lord; for I will say unto them: These wounds are the wounds with which I was wounded in the house of my friends. I am he who was lifted up. I am Jesus that was crucified. I am the Son of God. And then shall they weep because of their iniquities; then shall they lament because they persecuted their king.

"And then shall the heathen nations be redeemed, and they that knew no law shall have part in the first resurrection; and it shall be tolerable for them. And Satan shall be bound, that he shall have no place in the hearts of the children of men.

"And at that day, when I shall come in my glory, shall the parable be fulfilled which I spake concerning the ten virgins. For they that are wise and have received the truth, and have taken the Holy Spirit for their guide, and have not been deceived--verily I say unto you, they shall not be hewn down and cast into the fire, but shall abide the day. And the earth shall be given unto them for an inheritance; and they shall multiply and wax strong, and their children shall grow up without sin unto salvation. For the Lord shall be in their midst, and his glory shall be upon them, and he will be their king and their lawgiver." (D&C 45:15-59)

Section 116

"Spring Hill is named by the Lord Adam-ondi-Ahman, because said he, it is the place where Adam shall come to visit his people, or the Ancient of Days shall sit, as spoken of by Daniel the Prophet." (D&C 116:1)

Section 133

An inquiry of the Lord was made by Joseph Smith at Hiram Ohio, in behalf of many Elders for more information about the gathering, perfection and redemption of Israel. An answer came on November 3, 1831 in which the saints were commanded to prepare for the Second Coming, to flee from Babylon, to come to Zion, and prepare for the great day of the Lord.

They were informed that the Savior will stand on Mount Zion; that the continents will become one land; that the lost tribes of Israel shall return; that the gospel was restored through Joseph Smith to be preached to all the world; that the Lord shall come down in vengeance upon the wicked; and that the gospel is to be sent forth to save the saints and for the destruction of the wicked.

In the process the Lord revealed more vividly some of the signs of his Second Coming and some things to transpire at His coming.

"For behold, the Lord God hath sent forth the angel crying through the midst of heaven, saying: Prepare ye the way of the Lord, and make his paths straight, for the hour of his coming is nigh--When the Lamb shall stand upon Mount Zion, and with him a hundred and forty-four thousand having his Father's name written on their foreheads.

"Wherefore, prepare ye for the coming of the Bridegroom; go ye, go ye out to meet him. For behold, he shall stand upon the mount of Olivet, and upon the great deep, and upon the islands of the sea, and upon the land of Zion. And he shall utter his voice out of Zion, and he shall speak from Jerusalem, and his voice shall be heard among all people;

"And it shall be a voice as the voice of many waters, and as the voice of a great thunder, which shall break down the mountains, and the valleys shall not be found. He shall command the great deep, and it shall be driven back into the north countries, and the islands shall become one land;

"And the land of Jerusalem and the land of Zion shall be turned back into their own place, and the earth shall be like as it was in the days before it was divided. And the Lord, even the Savior, shall stand in the midst of his people, and shall reign over all flesh.

"And they who are in the north countries shall come in remembrance before the Lord; and their prophets shall hear his voice, and shall no longer stay themselves; and they shall smite the rocks, and the ice shall flow down at their presence. And an highway shall be cast up in the midst of the great deep. Their enemies shall become a prey unto them.

"And in the barren deserts there shall come forth pools of living water; and the parched ground shall no longer be a thirsty land. And they shall bring forth their rich treasures unto the children of Ephraim, my servants. And the boundaries of the everlasting hills shall tremble at their presence. And there shall they fall down and be crowned with glory, even in Zion, by the hands of the servants of the Lord, even the children of Ephraim. And they shall be filled with songs of everlasting joy.

"Behold, this is the blessing of the everlasting God upon the tribes of Israel, and the richer blessing upon the head of Ephraim and his fellows. And they also of the tribe of Judah, after their pain, shall be sanctified in holiness, before the Lord, to dwell in his presence day and night, forever and ever.

"...And this gospel shall be preached unto every nation, kindred, tongue and people. And the servants of God shall go forth, saying with a loud voice; Fear God and give glory to him, for the hour of his judgment is come...

"for the presence of the Lord shall be as the melting fire that burneth, and as the fire which causeth the waters to boil. O Lord, thou shalt come down to make thy name known to thine adversaries, and all nations shall tremble at thy presence...Yea when thou comest down, and the mountains flow down at thy presence, thou shalt meet him who rejoiceth and worketh righteousness, who remembereth thee in thy ways.

"For since the beginning of the world have not men heard nor perceived by the ear, neither hath any eye seen, O God, besides thee, how great things thou hast prepared for him that waiteth for thee.

"And it shall be said: Who is this that cometh down from God in heaven with dyed garments; yea, from the regions which are not known, clothed in his glorious apparel, traveling in the greatness of his strength? And he shall say; I am he who spake in righteousness, mighty to save. And the Lord shall be red in his apparel and his garments like him that treadeth in the wine-vat. And so great shall be the glory of his presence that the sun shall hide his face in shame, and the moon shall withhold its light, and the stars shall be hurled from their places.

" And his voice shall be heard: I have trodden the wine-press alone, and have brought judgment upon all people; and none were with me; And I have trampled them in my fury, and I have tread upon them in mine anger, and their blood have I sprinkled upon my garments, and stained all my raiment; for this was the day of vengeance which was in mine heart.

"And now the year of my redemption is come; and they shall mention the loving kindness of their Lord, and all that he has bestowed upon them according to his kindness forever and ever. In all their afflictions he was afflicted. And the angel of his presence saved them; and in his love, and in his pity, he redeemed them, and bore them, and carried them all the days of old;

"Yea, and Enoch also, and they who were with him; the prophets who were before him; and Noah also, and they who were before him; and Moses also, and they who were before him; And from Moses to Elijah, and from Elijah to John, who were with Christ in his resurrection, and the holy apostles, with Abraham, Isaac and Jacob, shall be in the presence of the Lamb.

"And the graves of the saints shall be opened; and they shall come forth and stand on the right hand of the Lamb, when he shall stand upon Mount Zion, and upon the holy city, the New Jerusalem; and they shall sing the song of the Lamb, day and night forever and ever. And for this cause, that men might be made partakers of the glories which were to be revealed, the Lord sent forth the fulness of his gospel, his everlasting covenant, reasoning in plainness and simplicity--

"...unto him that repenteth and sanctifieth himself before the Lord shall be given eternal life. And upon them that hearken not to the voice of the Lord shall be fulfilled that which was written by the prophet Moses, that they should be cut off from among the people.

"And also that which was written by the prophet Malachi: For behold, the day cometh that shall burn as an oven, and all the proud, yea, and all that do wickedly, shall be as stubble, and the day cometh shall burn them up, saith the Lord of hosts, that it shall leave them neither root or branch... for ye obeyed not my voice when I called to you out of the heavens; ye believed not my servants, and when they were sent unto you ye received them not..." (D&C 133:17-71; HC 1:229-234)

[From Section 49]

"...verily, I say unto you, that the Son of Man cometh not in the form of a woman, neither of a man traveling on the earth. Wherefore, be not deceived, but continue in steadfastness, looking forth for the heavens to be shaken, and the earth to tremble and to reel to and fro as a drunken man, and for the valleys to be exalted, and for the mountains to be made low, and for the rough places to become smooth-- and all this when the angel shall sound his trumpet." (D&C 49:22-23)

[From Section 63]

"He that is faithful and endureth shall overcome the world... And he that liveth when the Lord shall come, and hath kept the faith, blessed is he; nevertheless, it is appointed to him to die at the age of man... old men shall die; but they shall be changed in the twinkling of an eye. Wherefore, for this cause preached the apostles unto the world the resurrection of the dead. These things are the things that ye must look for; and speaking after the manner of the Lord, they are nigh at hand, and in a time to come, even the day of the coming of the Son of Man. And until that hour there shall be foolish virgins among the wise; and at that hour cometh an entire separation of the righteous and the wicked; and in that day will I send mine angels to pluck out the wicked and cast them into unquenchable fire." (D&C 63:51-54)

ULTIMATELY MOST OF ADAM AND EVE'S POSTERITY WILL BE JUDGED ACCORDING TO THEIR WORKS

AND REWARDED WITH A DEGREE OF GLORY, CELESTIAL, TERRESTRIAL OR TELESTIAL AS PART OF THE FINAL JUDGMENT

Section 76

To put the Second Coming, the Millennial Reign of Messiah/Christ and the Final Judgment in context one first must understand [1] the grand council in heaven before the world was, [2] who was there, [3] the plan offered, [4] the acceptance of the plan, [5] the choice of one to implement the plan, [6] the rejection of the Son of Morning's processes of implementation, [7] the rebellion of Satan variously called Lucifer, the Son of the Morning, or the Devil-- who took one third of the hosts of heaven with him; [8] the war in heaven; [9] the blessings that came to those who aligned themselves with Jehovah; and [10] His way of implementing the Father's plan which was accepted; and [11] the denial of blessings to those who rebelled, along with Satan, and the influence they have had on those who are born, who live and die on this earth.

In the language used in the Proclamation of the Family, revealed in 1995:

"In the pre-mortal realm, spirit sons and daughters knew and worshiped God as their Eternal Father and accepted His plan by which His children could obtain a physical body and gain earthly experience to progress toward perfection and ultimately realize his or her divine destiny as an heir of eternal life. The divine plan of happiness enables family relationships to be perpetuated beyond the grave. Sacred ordinances and covenants available in holy temples make it possible for individuals to return to the presence of God and for families to be united eternally." (Proclamation of the Family, 1995)

With the writings of previous prophets in mind the Lord revealed through Joseph Smith and Sidney Rigdon February 16, 1832 at Hiram Ohio, important information about Satan and his role in the

498

world as part of Section 76 previously reported.

In explanation pertaining to the resurrection of the just and the unjust, Joseph and Sidney said the Savior, "touched the eyes of our understandings and they were opened, and the glory of the Lord shown round about. And we beheld the glory of the Son on the right hand of the Father, and received of his fulness; And saw the holy angels, and them who are sanctified before his throne, worshipping God, and the Lamb, who worship him forever and ever.

"And now, after the many testimonies which have been given of him, this is the testimony last of all that we give of him; That he lives! For we saw him, even on the right hand of God; and we heard the voice bearing record that he is the Only Begotten of the Father-- That by him, and through him and of him, the worlds are and were created, and the inhabitants thereof are begotten sons and daughters of God." (D&C 76: 19-24)

In sharp contrast, they were shown also

"that an angel of God who was in authority in the presence of God, who rebelled against the Only Begotten Son whom the Father loved and who was in the bosom of the Father, was thrust down from the presence of God and the Son, And was called Perdition, the heavens wept over him -- he was Lucifer, a son of the morning. And we beheld, and lo, he is fallen! is fallen, even a son of the morning!

"And while we were yet in the Spirit, the Lord commanded us that we should write the vision; for we beheld Satan, that old serpent, even the devil, who rebelled against God, and sought to take the kingdom of God and his Christ-- Wherefore, he maketh war with the saints of God, and encompasseth them round about. And we saw a vision of the sufferings of those with whom he made war and overcame, for thus came the voice of the Lord unto us;

"Thus saith the Lord concerning all those who know my power, and have been made partakers thereof, and suffered themselves through the power of the devil to be overcome, and to deny the truth and defy my power--They are they who are the sons of perdition, of whom I say that it would have been better for them never to have been born; For they are vessels of wrath, doomed to suffer the wrath of God, with the devil and his angels in eternity; Concerning whom I have said there is no forgiveness in this world nor in the world to come--

"Having denied the Holy Spirit after having received it, and having denied the Only Begotten Son of the Father, having crucified him unto themselves and put him to an open shame. These are they who shall go away into the lake of fire and brimstone, with the devil and his angels--And the only ones [for] whom the second death shall have any power. Yea, verily, the only ones who shall not be redeemed in the due time of the Lord, after the sufferings of his wrath." (v 25-38)

Having defined the condition of a relative few who will have no forgiveness for what they have done in this life, the Lord declared:

"... all the rest shall be brought forth by the resurrection of the dead, through the triumph and the glory of the Lamb, who was slain, who was in the bosom of the Father before the world was made.

"And this is the gospel, the glad tidings, which the voice out of the heavens bore record unto us--That he came into the world, even Jesus, to be crucified for the sins of the world, and to bear the sins of the world, and to sanctify the world, and to cleanse it from all unrighteousness; That through him all might be saved whom the Father had put into his power and made by him; Who glorifies the Father, and saves all the works of his hands, except the sons of perdition who deny the Son after the Father has revealed him." (v 39-43)

THE RESURRECTION OF THE JUST

While in His ministry on earth Jesus said to His disciples, in my Father's house are many mansions, if it were not so I would have told you, I go to prepare a place for you. In the revelation that follows,

He likens His mansions to kingdoms of glory, and spells out who will inherit which glory, based on performance.

"And again we bear record--- for we saw and heard, and this is the testimony of the gospel of Christ concerning them who shall come forth in the resurrection of the just--

"They are they who received the testimony of Jesus, and believed on his name and were baptized after the manner of his burial, being buried in the water in his name, and this according to the commandments which he has given--That by keeping the commandments they might be washed and cleansed from all their sins, and receive the Holy Spirit by the laying on of the hands of him who is ordained and sealed unto this power; And who overcome by faith and are sealed by the Holy Spirit of promise, which the Father sheds forth upon all those who are just and true.

"They are they who are of the church of the Firstborn. They are they into whose hands the Father has given all things-- They are they who are priests and kings, who have received of his fulness, and his glory; And are priests of the Most High, after the order of Melchizedek, which was after the order of Enoch, which was after the order of the Only Begotten Son. Wherefore, as it is written, they are gods, even the sons of God--

"Wherefore, all things are theirs, whether life or death, or things present, or things to come, all are theirs and they are Christ's and Christ is God's. And they shall overcome all things. Wherefore, let no man glory in man, but rather let him glory in God, who shall subdue all enemies under his feet. These shall dwell in the presence of God and his Christ forever and ever.

"These are they whom he shall bring with him, when he shall come in the clouds of heaven to reign on the earth over his people. These are they who shall have part in the first resurrection. These are they who shall come forth in the resurrection of the just.

"These are they who are come unto Mount Zion, and unto the city of the living God, the heavenly place, the holiest of all. These are they who have come to an innumerable company of angels, to the general assembly and church of Enoch, and of the Firstborn. These are they whose names are written in heaven, where God and Christ are the judge of all.

"These are they who are just men made perfect through Jesus the mediator of the new covenant, who wrought out this perfect atonement through the shedding of his own blood. These are they whose bodies are celestial, whose glory is that of the sun, even the glory of God, the highest of all, whose glory the sun of the firmament is written of as being typical."(v 51-70)

Identifying those who will inherit a glory of God that differs as does the glory of the sun to the earth's moon, called the terrestrial glory, Joseph and Sidney continue:

"And again, we saw the terrestrial world, and behold and lo, these are they who are of the terrestrial, whose glory differs from that of the church of the Firstborn who have received of the fulness of the Father, even as that of the moon differs from the sun in the firmament.

"Behold, these are they who died without law; And also they who are the spirits of men kept in prison, whom the Son visited, and preached the gospel unto them, that they might be judged according to men in the flesh; Who received not the testimony of Jesus in the flesh, but afterwards received it.

"These are they who are honorable men of the earth, who were blinded by the craftiness of men. These are they who receive of his glory, but not of his fulness. These are they who receive the presence of the Son, but not of the fulness of the Father. Wherefore, they are bodies terrestrial, and not bodies celestial, and differ in glory as the moon differs from the sun.

"These are they who are not valiant in the testimony of Jesus; wherefore, they obtain not the crown over the kingdom of our God. And now this is the end of the vision which we saw of the terrestrial, that the Lord commanded us to write while we were yet in the Spirit."

(v 71-80)

Describing the third kingdom or degree of glory which differs from the second as the moon does from the stars, Joseph and Sidney continue:

"And again, we saw the glory of the telestial, which glory is that of the lesser, even as the glory of the stars differs from that of the glory of the moon in the firmament. These are they who received not the gospel of Christ, neither the testimony of Jesus. These are they who deny not the Holy Ghost.

"These are they who shall not be redeemed from the devil until the last resurrection, until the Lord, even Christ the Lamb, shall have finished his work. These are they who receive not of the fulness in the eternal world, but of the Holy Spirit through the ministration of the terrestrial; And the terrestrial through the ministration of the celestial.

"And also the telestial receive it of the administering of angels who are appointed to minister for them, or who are appointed to be ministering spirits for them; for they shall be heirs of salvation. And thus we saw in the heavenly vision, the glory of the telestial, which surpasses all understanding. And no man knows it except him to whom God has revealed it." (v 81-90)

Again comparing the three degrees of glory Joseph and Sidney wrote with inspiration:

"And thus we saw the glory of the terrestrial which excels in all things the glory of the telestial, even in glory, and in power, and in might, and in dominion.

"And thus we saw the glory of the celestial, which excels in all things-- where God, even the Father, reigns upon his throne forever and ever. Before whose throne all things bow in humble reverence, and give him glory forever and ever.

"They who dwell in his presence are the church of the Firstborn, and they see as they are seen, and know as they are known, having received of his fulness and of his grace; And he makes them equal in power and in might, and in dominion.

"And the glory of the celestial is one, even as the glory of the sun is one. And the glory of the terrestrial is one, even as the glory of the moon is one. And the glory of the telestial is one, even as the glory of the stars is one; for as one star differs from another star in glory, even so differs one from another in glory in the telestial world;

"... These are they who ... received not the gospel, neither the testimony of Jesus, neither the prophets; neither the everlasting covenant. Last of all, these all are they who will not be gathered with the saints, to be caught up unto the church of the Firstborn, and received into the cloud.

"These are they who are liars, and sorcerers, and adulterers, and whore-mongers, and whosoever loves and makes a lie. These are they who suffer the wrath of God on earth. These are they who suffer the vengeance of eternal fire. These are they who are cast down to hell and suffer the wrath of the Almighty God, until the fulness of times, when Christ shall have subdued all enemies under his feet, and shall have perfected his work;

"When he shall deliver up the kingdom, and present it unto the Father, spotless, saying: I have overcome and have trodden the wine-press alone, even the wine-press of the fierceness of the wrath of Almighty God. Then shall he be crowned with the crown of his glory, to sit on the throne of his power to reign forever and ever." (v 91-108)

Those who inherit the telestial glory will eventually be redeemed after suffering the wrath of God and their numbers will be

"innumerable as the stars in the firmament of heaven, or as the sand upon the seashore", and they too "shall bow the knee, and every tongue confess to him who sits upon the throne forever and ever; for they shall be judged according to their works, and every man shall receive according to his own works, his own dominion, in the mansions which are prepared; And they shall be servants of the Most High; but where God and Christ dwell they cannot come, worlds without end. This is the end of the vision which we saw, which we were commanded to write while we were yet in the Spirit." (v 109-113)

But there were other things Joseph Smith and Sidney Rigdon were shown concerning the mysteries of the kingdom and the marvelous works of the Lord which they were commanded not to write or utter, which can only be seen, heard or understood by the power of the Holy Spirit. (v 114-119, D&C 76:1-119)

[From Section 63]

In August 1831 the Lord had said through Joseph Smith that "this is a day of warning and not a day of many words. For I, the Lord, am not to be mocked in the last days. Behold, I am from above, and my power lieth beneath, I am over all, and in all, and through all, and search all things, and the day cometh that all things shall be subject unto me. Behold, I am Alpha and Omega, even Jesus Christ, Wherefore, let all men beware how they take my name upon their lips... Remember that that which cometh from above is sacred and must be spoken with care, and by constraint of the Spirit..." (D&C 63:58-64)

THE EARTH WILL BE UPGRADED FROM IT'S TELESTIAL TO A TERRESTRIAL KINGDOM DURING THE MILLENNIUM AND UPGRADED AGAIN TO A CELESTIAL KINGDOM AT, OR, BEFORE THE FINAL JUDGMENT

[From Section 88]

Nine months later in December 1832, the Lord set forth with remarkable clarity and understandability as presented above, that there are three degrees of glory which men may inherit, the celestial, terrestrial and telestial glories, and set forth in general terms the criteria He will use in judging which glory each of His children will inherit, and declared that those judged worthily of and ready for a celestial glory may one day dwell in the presence of God and inherit all that He hath.

Declaring the urgent need for all who have received His voice of warning, and have entered the covenant, to warn his neighbor, the Lord added more specificity to the signs of His coming and the sequence of some events in these words revealed as part of Section 88:

The Lord said that resurrection of the dead comes through the redemption and that:

"the spirit and the body are the soul of man. And the resurrection from the dead is the redemption of the soul. And the redemption of the soul is through him that quickeneth all things, in whose bosom it is decreed that the poor and the meek of the earth shall inherit it." (v 15-17)

Enoch saw in vision the polluted earth, of our day, but that it would not always be that way. It would be cleansed, upgraded and sanctified and made ready for those who will inherit it including the poor and the meek:

"Therefore, it [the earth] must needs be sanctified from all unrighteousness, that it may be prepared for its celestial glory; for after it hath filled the measure of its creation, it shall be crowned with glory, even with the presence of God the Father; that bodies who are of the celestial kingdom may possess it forever and ever; for, for this intent was it made and created, and for this intent are they sanctified.

"And they who are not sanctified through the law which I have given unto you, even the law of Christ, must inherit another kingdom, even that of a terrestrial kingdom, or that of a telestial kingdom. For he who is not able to abide the law of a celestial kingdom cannot abide a celestial glory. And he who cannot abide a terrestrial kingdom, cannot abide a terrestrial glory. And he who cannot abide the law of a telestial kingdom cannot abide a telestial glory; therefore he is not meet for a kingdom of glory. Therefore he must abide a kingdom which is not a kingdom of glory." (v 14-24)

Thus we see that most of the posterity of Adam and Eve will inherit kingdoms of glory that is, the celestial, terrestrial or telestial kingdom as noted earlier. Still others will inherit a kingdom without glory. But the earth, however, is scheduled to abide the law of a celestial kingdom, so those who cannot abide the law of the celestial kingdom after the resurrection will be removed to another place in the universe:

"And again, verily I say unto you, the earth abideth the law of the celestial kingdom, for it filleth the measure of its creation, and transgresseth not the law-- Wherefore it shall be sanctified; yea, notwithstanding it shall die, it shall be quickened again, and shall abide the power by which it is quickened, and the righteous shall inherit it." (v 25-26)

Just as all flesh shall die and be quickened or resurrected, so will the earth itself die and be quickened or resurrected; and just as man is to be baptized with water to be cleansed and sanctified by the Holy Ghost, the baptism of fire, so was the earth baptized with water and is to be sanctified by fire to cleanse it from all unrighteousness.

Adding specificity to the resurrection, the Lord said that though our bodies may have been old and decrepit at death, they will be resurrected with the spirit with which it was laid down. Those who lived righteous lives and were spiritual giants on earth will be resurrected with that same spirit, and those who were far from righteous at death will be resurrected in that same state receiving celestial, terrestrial and telestial bodies, with some receiving bodies of no degree of glory because they did not receive that gift from God:

"For notwithstanding they die, they also shall rise again, a spiritual body. They who are of a celestial spirit shall receive the same body which was a natural body ; even ye shall receive your bodies, and your glory shall be that glory by which your bodies are quickened. Ye who are quickened by a portion of the celestial glory shall then receive of the same, even a fulness, And they who are quickened by a portion of the terrestrial glory shall then receive of the same, even a fulness. And also they who are quickened by a portion of the telestial glory shall them receive of the same, even a fulness.

"And they who remain shall also be quickened; nevertheless, they shall return again to their own place, to enjoy that which they are willing to receive, because they were not willing to enjoy that which they might have received. For what doth it profit a man if a gift is bestowed upon him, and he receive not the gift? Behold, he rejoices not in that which is given unto him, neither rejoices in him who is the giver of the gift." (v 27-33)

The Lord had said that obedience to celestial, terrestrial to telestial law prepares people for those respective kingdoms and glories and continued His instruction by saying that those who will to abide in sin remain filthy still; that all kingdoms are governed by law; that God hath given a law unto all things; and that man shall comprehend even God. He also gave the parable of the man sending servants into the field and visiting them in turn; declared that those who draw near unto the Lord shall see His face; and counseled members to sanctify themselves and teach one another the doctrines of the kingdom as reported in Chapter XIII. (v 34-80)

Shifting emphasis the Lord returned to the topic of every member's responsibility to warn his neighbor, to help gather Israel, help perfect and help redeem them through the atonement of Christ, under the canopy of a Zion Society.

"Behold, I sent you out to testify and warn the people, and it becometh every man who hath been warned to warn his neighbor. Therefore, they are left without excuse, and their sins are upon their own heads. He that seeketh me early shall find me, and shall not be forsaken. Therefore tarry ye, and labor diligently, that you may be perfected in your ministry to go forth among the Gentiles for the last time, as many as the mouth of the Lord shall name, to bind up the law and seal up the testimony, and to prepare the saints for the hour of judgment which is to come...

"entangle not yourselves in sin, but let your hands be clean, until the Lord comes. For not many days hence and the earth shall tremble and reel to and fro as a drunken man; and the sun shall hide his face, and shall refuse to give light; and the moon shall be bathed in blood; and the stars shall become exceedingly angry, and shall cast themselves down as a fig that falleth from off a fig-tree.

"And after your testimony cometh wrath and indignation upon the people. For after your testimony cometh the testimony of earthquakes, that shall cause groaning in the midst of her, and men shall not be able to stand. And also cometh the testimony of the voice of thunderings, and the voice of lightnings, and the voice of tempests, and the voice of the waves of the sea heaving themselves beyond their bounds. And all things shall be in commotion; and surely, men's hearts shall fail them; for fear shall come upon all people.

"And angels shall fly through the midst of heaven, crying with a loud voice, sounding the trump of God, saying: Prepare ye, prepare ye, O inhabitants of the earth; for the judgment of our God is come. Behold, and lo, the Bridegroom cometh; go ye out to meet him. And immediately there shall appear a great sign in heaven, and all people shall see it together.

"And another angel shall sound his trump, saying: That great church, the mother of abominations, that made all nations drink of the wine of the wrath of her fornication, that persecuteth the saints of God, that shed their blood--she who sitteth upon the many waters, and upon the isles of the sea--behold, she is the tares of the earth; she is bound in bundles; her bands are made strong, no man can loose them; therefore, she is made ready to be burned. And he shall sound his trump both long and loud, and all nations shall hear it.

"And there shall be silence in heaven for the space of half an hour; and immediately after shall the curtain of heaven be unfolded, as a scroll is unfolded after it is rolled up, and the face of the Lord shall be unveiled; And the saints that are upon the earth, who are alive, shall be quickened and be caught up to meet him. And they who have slept in their graves shall come forth, for their graves shall be opened; and they also shall be caught up to meet him in the midst of the pillar of heaven-- They are Christ's, the first fruits, they who shall descend with him first, and they who are on the earth and in their graves, who are first caught up to meet him; and all this by the voice of the sounding of the trump of the angel of God.

"And after this another angel shall sound, which is the second trump; and then cometh the redemption of those who are Christ's at his coming; who have received their part in that prison which was prepared for them; that they might receive the gospel, and be judged according to men in the flesh.

"And again, another trump shall sound, which is the third trump; and then come the spirits of men who are to be judged, and are found under condemnation; And these are the rest of the dead; and they live not again until the thousand years are ended, neither again, until the end of the earth.

"And another trump shall sound, which is the fourth trump, saying: There are found among those who are to remain until that great and last day, even the end, who shall remain filthy still.

"And another trump shall sound, which is the fifth trump, which is the fifth angel who committeth the everlasting gospel-- flying through the midst of heaven, unto all nations, kindreds, tongues and people; And this shall be the sound of his trump, saying to all people, both in heaven and in earth, and that are under the earth-- for every ear shall hear it, and every knee shall bow, and every tongue shall confess, while they hear the sound of the trump, saying: Fear God, and give glory to him who sitteth upon the throne forever and ever; for the hour of his judgment is come.

"And again, another angel shall sound his trump, which is the sixth trump, saying: She is fallen who made all nations drink of the wine of the wrath of her fornication; she is fallen, is fallen!

"And again, another angel shall sound his trump, which is the seventh angel, saying: It is finished, it is finished! The Lamb of God hath overcome and trodden the wine-press alone, even the wine-press of the fierceness of the wrath of Almighty God.

"And then shall the angels be crowned with the glory of his might, and the saints shall be filled with his glory, and receive their inheritance and be made equal with him.

And then shall the first angel again sound his trump in the ears of all living, and reveal the secret acts of men, and the mighty works of God in the first thousand years. And then shall the second angel sound his trump, and reveal the secret acts of men, and the thoughts and intents of their hearts, and the mighty works of God in the second thousand years-- And so on until the seventh angel shall sound his trump; and he shall stand forth upon the land and upon the sea, and swear in the name of him who sitteth upon the throne, that there shall be time no longer; and Satan shall be bound, that old serpent, who is called the devil, and shall not be loosed for a thousand years.

"And then he shall be loosed for a little season, that he may gather together his armies. And Michael the seventh angel, even the archangel, shall gather together his armies, even the hosts of heaven. And the devil shall gather together his armies; even the hosts of hell, and shall come up to battle against Michael and his armies.

"And then cometh the battle of the great God; and the devil and his armies shall be cast away into their own place, that they shall not have power over the saints any more at all. For Michael shall fight their battles, and shall overcome him who seeketh the throne of him who sitteth upon the throne, even the Lamb. This is the glory of God, and the sanctified; and they shall not anymore see death." (D&C 88:81-116)

In Doctrine and Covenants Sections 97, 101, 104, 106, and 130 we learn that the Lord's scourge will not be stayed until he comes; that all flesh shall see the Lord; that corruptible things will be consumed at His coming; that all things will be revealed at His coming; that the saints are to be crowned at His coming; that the scriptures are published to prepare people for the time when the Lord will dwell with them; that the Lord will come as a thief in the night;

that when the Savior appears, we shall see He is a man like ourselves; and that He and the Father have bodies of flesh and bone as tangible as man's.

THE MILLENNIAL REIGN OF MESSIAH/CHRIST

We have written that establishment of a Zion Society is for the purpose of gathering, perfecting and eventually redeeming Israel, the true believers of Messiah/Christ, and returning them to the presence of God the Father.

Returning mortals to the presence of the Father requires they be ready and worthy of His presence. Thus, perfecting the members of the covenant requires there be a place, standard, program and process to bring about this perfection and return to God.

A Zion Society is the place, the teachings of the Savior, as revealed personally and through His authorized servants, functioning as prophets, seers, and revelators, is the standard and program; and service to the Lord God and fellow beings, putting into practice the teachings of the Savior, is the process whereby perfection comes.

A Zion Society as the place, the teachings of the Savior as the standard and program, and service to the Lord God and fellow beings as the process; enables all to keep the two great commandments upon which the law and prophets are attached: to love the Lord thy God, with all thy heart, with all thy soul, might, mind and strength and to love thy neighbor as thyself.

Though those caught up to meet the Savior when He comes to usher in the Millennium, and those He brings with Him, are worthy enough to dwell in a terrestrial world and in the presence of the Savior, they are not yet perfect as He or the Father is perfect. They are not yet perfected sufficient to dwell in the presence of the Father. The earth also, while cleansed and upgraded to a terrestrial glory is not yet perfected and ready as a dwelling place of the Father.

One purpose of the Millennium, then, appears to be to perfect and make ready those who have not yet had a chance to know the true God and Jesus Christ whom He sent. They need to be introduced to the covenant, its teachings and principles, in the world of disembodied spirits, if they already have lived their mortal lives, enabling them to enter that covenant if they choose to do so. Those persons born during the Millennium will also need to be introduced to and enter the covenant if they choose to do so.

Baptism is a temporal ordinance performed by those in mortality and is a requirement for entrance into the kingdom of heaven. This ordinance is performed vicariously in temples for those who have already lived in mortality. Billions of souls who never knew the Father will be introduced to Him, His Son and the covenant during the Millennium.

Those already in the covenant serve as missionaries to those awaiting resurrection and to those on earth born during the Millennium. By the end of the Millennium every person whoever lived will have been introduced to the covenant, its teachings and principles and will have been given an opportunity to enter it, put its principles into practice and perfect their lives.

Another purpose of the Millennium appears to be to ready the inheritances of those being resurrected, [in my Father's house are many mansions, I go to prepare a place for you] to prepare and operate temples worldwide for those entering the covenant, and to subdue the earth and make it celestial, ready and worthy of a dwelling place for the Father. It appears that the work of the Millennium is both temporal and spiritual and that the powers of the Melchizedek priesthood will be utilized to remove mountains, turn waters out of their course etc. as necessary to subdue the earth.

THE MILLENNIUM AND THE FINAL JUDGMENT

While there is a final judgment, there are also several intermediate judgments. For example: there was an intermediate

513

judgment which allowed Heavenly Father's spirit children to come to earth, receive a body, and with their agency, gain experience. Another intermediate judgment occurs when a person enters the covenant and remains worthy to come forth in the first resurrection, either from the grave or by being caught up to meet Him, to be with Him during His Millennial reign.

The Savior's authorized servants have known from the days of Adam that the process of gathering, perfection and redemption of the true believers of Messiah/Christ would reach its zenith during His return, when He ushers in the Millennium and reigns for a thousand years, prior to the final judgment.

Enoch caught glimpses of and reported it as contained in the writings of Moses already described, as did Isaiah, Ezekiel, Daniel, Hosea, Joel, Micah, Zechariah, Matthew, John the Beloved, Nephi and Joseph Smith in their own writings.

From Isaiah 2:4 reiterated in Micah 4:3

"...for out of Zion shall go forth the law, and the word of the Lord from Jerusalem. And he shall judge among the nations, and shall rebuke many people; and they shall beat their swords into plowshares, and their spears into pruninghooks; nation shall not lift up sword against nation, neither shall they learn war any more."

Isaiah also said that in that day the earth shall be full of the knowledge of the Lord and that the people would see the glory of the Lord and that a new heaven and a new earth would result from His coming. (Isa.11:9, 35:2,65:17)

In addition to testifying as to the reality of the resurrection in his vision of the valley of dry bones, Ezekiel declared there would be but one shepherd and that the desolate land would become like the garden of Eden. (Ez. 34:23, 36:35)

Daniel reported something of the Millennium by saying the Son of Man or the Savior drew near to the Ancient of Days, and there was given to the Savior dominion, glory and a kingdom that all peoples, nations and languages should serve Him the Lord, and that

His kingdom would never be destroyed. (Dan. 7:14)

Hosea said the people would lie down safely; Joel and Zechariah said the Lord would dwell in Zion. (Ho. 2:18; Joel 3:17; Ze. 2:10)

Matthew said that the Son of Man will come to his kingdom with glory; (Matt. 16:28, 25:31) and that

"the days will come, that heaven and earth shall pass away; yet my words shall not pass away, but all shall be fulfilled. ... after the tribulation of those days, and the powers of heaven shall be shaken, then shall appear the sign of the Son of Man in heaven, and then shall all the tribes of the earth mourn; and they shall see the Son of Man coming in clouds of heaven with power and great glory; And whoso treasureth up my word, shall not be deceived, for the Son of Man shall come, and he shall send his angels before him with the great sound of a trumpet, and they shall gather together the remainder of his elect from the four winds, from one end of heaven to the other.(JST Matt.1:35-37)

John the Beloved, in the Book of Revelation, declared that Satan would be bound during the Millennium, that the Saints shall then live and reign with Christ for a thousand years, and that the dead will stand before God and be judged out of the books according to their works. (Rev. 20:2-5)

Nephi declared that Satan would be bound and have no power during the Millennium because of the righteousness of the people, and that during that period all things previously sealed shall be revealed. (1Ne. 22:26; 2Ne. 30:18)

Concerning the Millennium the Savior in part declared through Joseph Smith that the Lord will dwell on earth a thousand years; that the Lord's people will reign with him; that the Millennium was prophesied by the Lord's servants; that Satan would be bound during this period and loosed again at the end for a little season; that the righteous will not die a death as we know it, but will be changed in the twinkling of an eye; that the earth, as we know it, will pass away as by fire; that the wicked will go into unquenchable fire until the judgment; that the children of those who abide the Lord's coming will grow up without sin; that they all will grow old during the Millennium; that old men will also be changed in the twinkling of an eye; that in the beginning of the seventh thousand years the Lord will sanctify and make holy the earth; that those under condemnation will live not again until the thousand years are ended. (D&C 29:11; 29:22; 43:29-33; 45:58; 63:51; 77:12; 84:98-102; 88:101)

Section 101

Set forth as part of Section 101 given December 16, 1833 is a glimpse of the ushering in of, and character of life during the Millennium. After specifying the saints were to gather to existing stakes of Zion, and if there were not enough room for them there, other stakes would be created, the Lord said:

"Behold, it is my will, that all they who call on my name, and worship me according to mine everlasting gospel, should gather together and stand in holy places; And prepare for the revelation which is to come, when the veil of the covering of my temple, in my tabernacle, which hideth the earth, shall be taken off, and all flesh shall see me together. And every corruptible thing, both of man, or of the beasts of the field, or of the fowls of the heavens, or of the fish of the sea, that dwells upon all the face of the earth, shall be consumed;

"And also that of element shall melt with fervent heat; and all things shall become new, that my knowledge and glory may dwell upon all the earth. And in that day the enmity of man, and the enmity of beasts, yea, the enmity of all flesh, shall cease from before my face. And in that day whatsoever any man shall ask it shall be given unto him. And in that day Satan shall not have power to tempt any man. And there shall be no sorrow because there is no death.

"In that day an infant shall not die until he is old; and his life shall be as the age of a tree; And when he dies he shall not sleep, that is to say in the earth, but shall be changed in the twinkling of an eye, and shall be caught up, and his rest shall be glorious." (v 22-31)

Worthy of note is that all corruption and corrupted things of man, beasts and fowls will be consumed. Animosity, bitterness, hatred, hostility and rancor shall cease, carnivorous animals will no longer prey on other animals for food, and all will live together in the refuge of a peaceful and safe Zion Society under the leadership of Messiah. During the Millennium,

"... when the Lord shall come, he shall reveal all things-- Things most precious, things that are above, things that are beneath, things that are in the earth, and upon the earth, and in heaven. And all they who suffer persecution for my name, and endure in faith, though they be called to lay down their lives for my sake yet shall they partake of all this glory. Wherefore, fear not even unto death; for in this world your joy is not full, but in me your joy is full. Therefore, care not for the body, neither for the life of the body; but care for the soul, and for the life of the soul. And seek the face of the Lord always, that in patience ye may possess your souls, and ye shall have eternal life." (v 32-38)

EPILOGUE

SUMMARY AND OBSERVATIONS

As this book is brought to a close, reference is made to Daniel in the Old Testament, whose book is considered to contain significant revelatory material. Reference is also made to the words of Joseph Smith, seer, revelator and prophet of the dispensation of the fulness of times, as he explained the rise of The Church of Jesus Christ of Latter-day Saints in these last days.

Daniel was taken captive as the southern kingdom of Judah fell in 587 B.C. and most of his people, the Jews, were forcibly moved to Babylon by King Nebuchadnezzar. Daniel was given the name of Beltshazzar and was selected to be a servant in the king's court. He refused the king's meat in deference to the God of Abraham, Isaac and Jacob/Israel and as a result was thrown into a den of lions, but his life was protected and preserved by the power of God. From his book, the Book of Daniel, we are taught the important duty of being true to the God of Israel at all cost, and informed of the transcendent blessings of being faithful. Included in his blessings was the power to interpret dreams and to read strange writings on walls. He and his companions were given wisdom in consequence of their abstinence from wine; they were delivered from the fiery furnace; Daniel interpreted the handwriting on the wall and survived being cast into the den of lions. In each case deliverance came through God's blessing because of their faithfulness.

Of major significance is Daniel's interpretation of the kings dream in which the kingdom of God in the last days, or the new world order, is depicted as a little stone that is cut out of a mountain, without hands, which is to roll forth until it fills the whole earth. From Isaiah we learn that the mountain of the Lord's house in the last days is to be established in the tops of the mountains and all nations shall flow unto it.

The prophetic visions of Daniel reported in Chapter 7 present a succession of world monarchies or powers, the last of which will severely persecute those in the covenant. Using the symbolism of beasts Daniel shows how, at the end, the kingdoms of the world collapse and give place to the kingdom of God or the new world order, with Christ at its head, referred to as the Son of Man. The Son of Man stands before the Ancient of Days to receive power and glory. The Doctrine and Covenants Section 116 identifies Adam, who is also known as Michael, as the Ancient of Days. Daniel also testifies of mankind's resurrection in Chapter 12. Prior to the ultimate outcome, however, the covenant people of God will face great tribulation and persecution, and the world will be in commotion, but they will survive it while the wicked will not. (BD p. 652-3)

Prior to the Messiah/Christ's return or at His coming, it has been prophesied that the sun will be darkened, the moon turned to blood, the stars will lose their shining and appear to fall from the sky.

No one knows how this will come about, but we do know [1] that the result will be a new heaven and a new earth, [2] that these events will be glorious for the righteous and calamitous for the unrighteous, [3] that the world as we know it today shall pass away, [4] that the city of Enoch will return and take its place as a sister city to the New Jerusalem, [5] that the inhabitants of these two cities will be living the higher laws a Zion Society, which has become a united one world society, [6] that the earth is not a place of inheritance for the unrepentant wicked, [7] that the earth will return to what it was like in the days before it was divided, [8] that there will not be a long period of separation of spirit and body of human beings at death, for they will be changed in the twinkling of an eye, and [9] that animals will no longer rely on one another's flesh for food.

A number of scenarios might satisfy the conditions prophesied: the darkened sun, a blood-red moon, the loss of sparkle in stars and the earth's reeling to and fro as a drunken man, such as a nuclear war, the sudden appearance of a spheroid large enough to interfere with the rotation of the earth around its axis, and/or the return of Enoch's city, the battle of Armageddon etc. Whatever the scenario, the ultimate result will be an upgrade of the earth to a place of higher order. It will come through the wicked destroying each other, or the exercise of the powers of God directly by Himself, or by His authorized servants, or through a combination of all of these.

With reference to Enoch's city of Zion, prophesied to return and become a sister city of the New Jerusalem, the inhabitants of both cities are to fall on one other's necks and kiss each other. No one knows how large Enoch's city was, whether its people begot posterity during its long absence from this earth, whether they departed solely as individuals without real estate, or whether part of the earth departed with them.

These observations are made simply to sensitize readers to the notion that events surrounding the return of the Savior are of gigantic magnitude, and proportion, and will permeate everything. The earth, as we know it, will pass away. It will be replaced by a new heaven and a new earth, with flora and fauna and mankind whose relationships to one another are changed, and death as we know it shall not exist. The earth itself will be a different earth, worthy of the presence of the Son of God during the Millennium, and worthy of the presence of God the Father, after the Final Judgment, when it becomes a celestial kingdom of glory.

But, as our old sun refuses to give its light, as prophesied, <u>we do know that light is to be replaced by the light of Messiah/Christ</u>, as He comes in glory and majesty, with a brightness beyond description; a light brighter than at noonday. Whether the changes to be wrought will be the result of cataclysmic events like those mentioned or by the Savior Himself, no one knows, but He has the power to do it in any way He chooses.

It will be during and following these events that the earth is to be upgraded from a telestial to a terrestrial world, with light furnished by its Savior, brighter and perhaps hotter than before. His very presence may be sufficient to cause the elements to melt with fervent heat, hot enough to ignite all corrupted, combustible things resulting in massive fire, necessary to cleanse the earth. In the process all the proud and all that do wickedly are to be burned as stubble. Satan and his cohorts will flee into darkness, or will be cast there, because they cannot stand the light of Messiah/Christ and cannot bear His presence on earth. There Satan will be bound not to be loosed again for a thousand years.

It is true that the most wicked of the earth's inhabitants are to be burned as stubble, while the righteous are to be caught up to meet Him when He comes. However, this does not mean all who are caught up to meet Him are limited to those who have entered the covenant and have kept its provisions.

Those who are living a celestial law while on earth will be caught up to meet Him when the Savior comes. They and those who previously lived the celestial law before death, whom the Savior will bring with Him, will play key roles in governing the Zion Society, or the kingdom of God on earth, with Messiah/Christ at its head. However, many other souls who have entered the covenant and are candidates for celestial glory, but who are not yet perfect or completely pure and other souls who believe in Him will be caught up to meet Messiah/Christ; souls who are living the equivalent of a terrestrial law, who have lived much of His teachings without having entered the covenant through baptism and/or having received the Holy Ghost.

Able to abide the laws of a terrestrial glory to which the earth is upgraded, during the Millennium, these and their posterity born during that period will be subject to the same conditions as those in the covenant on earth. They will have opportunity to exercise their agency, deciding for themselves if they wish to enter the covenant.

However, as the final judgment approaches at the end of the thousand years, and the second upgrade of planet earth is at hand, only those who have entered the covenant and are living the provisions of the celestial law will be able to live on the newly celestialized earth. It has been likened to a giant Urim and Thummim, a crystal or a sea of glass.

It appears another purpose of the Millennium, then, is to ready this globe and its people for a celestial glory, where all of earth's resurrected inhabitants are being taught to live a celestial law and are being made worthy to live in the presence of the Father, and are being readied to receive their inheritance as heirs and joint heirs with Messiah/Christ.

Those caught up to meet him and their posterity born during the Millennium will not be subject to death as we know it, but will be changed in the twinkling of an eye in time, never tasting death.

Mingling together on this upgraded earth will be four kinds of personages: [1] those who are caught up to meet him; [2] those of Enoch's city, now returned, [3] those born during the Millennium, and [4] those who have been resurrected to date. No further change is needed in those who have been resurrected, but those caught up to meet him, those of Enoch's city and those born during the Millennium will be changed in the twinkling of an eye, after having lived a full life or more by today's standards.

In the meantime, the process of resurrecting all those made in the express image of God, begun at His Second Coming, will continue. Those found ready and worthy to come forth in the morning of the first resurrection are brought forth, followed by those worthy and ready to come forth in the first general resurrection. The first to come forth are those already living a celestial law in the world of disembodied spirits, or those candidates for celestial glory who have been so ordained for such glory and have been judged worthy to now come forth in the morning of the first resurrection, even though they still may be less than perfect and are not yet completely pure, including those who entered the covenant and lived its provisions during their mortal lives; and those who were introduced to, accepted the provisions of the covenant and conformed their lives to them, after their mortality, during their stay in the world of disembodied spirits. These, whose ordinance work was done vicariously by family and friends in the Lord's temples on earth who are ready and worthy to come forth in the morning of the first resurrection, will also come forth at that time.

Those sufficiently living a celestial law who come forth in the first resurrection will be followed by those ready and worthy of a terrestrial glory, followed by those ready and worthy of a telestial glory, until all have been resurrected by the end of the thousand years, except for a few known as the sons of perdition.

Missionaries will likely continue to work among those living on the upgraded terrestrialized earth during the thousand years until all have had an opportunity to accept Messiah/Christ's atonement and partake of His sacred ordinances, including baptism, receipt of the Holy Ghost, and the ordinances of the temple essential to living a celestial law. Those who accept and enter the covenant and keep its provisions become heirs and joint heirs with Jesus Christ as the Apostle Paul declared.

Missionaries will also continue to work among those who are awaiting resurrection and as they accept the atonement and keep the provisions of the covenant, and as their temple ordinance work is done by family and friends living on the upgraded earth, these individuals are then readied and when found sufficiently worthy, will be resurrected.

Not only are the saving ordinances of the temple to be performed for all whoever lived, a welding link, that is, a sealing of all generations from the present day back to father Adam, must be performed, worthy of all acceptation.

This means that, in addition to perfecting our individual lives to the point we are worthy of a celestial glory, another major effort of the Millennium will be family history research, oral and written, enabling families to be welded together via temple ordinances and sealings, for the billions upon billions who once lived on earth. They will be given the opportunity to choose whether they enter the covenant. Each has agency to accept or reject what has been done for them. To those who accept these ordinances and covenant to abide by its provisions, said ordinances become binding, and they are put into effect as if the recipient received them personally while on earth.

Commingling of mortal and resurrected personages, those caught up to meet Him, and those born during the Millennium will take place on this upgraded earth. The ability of resurrected persons living the celestial law to visit lesser kingdoms including the world of disembodied spirits, facilitates the process of identifying forebears in the spirit world, who need to be taught the gospel, for whom no record of their lives was kept, or for whom any previous record had disintegrated.

Organizationally it appears the Lord will return to the structure as at the beginning, which is patriarchal in nature. There will be 144,000 high priests 12,000 from each of the twelve tribes of Israel playing important roles, but the father or patriarch of each family will continue to play an important role for his immediate family, both for his children and for his forebears. There is some indication that a worthy father and mother in the covenant will be resurrected together, or near simultaneously, and will receive all the blessings of Abraham, Isaac and Israel and their wives.

There is no mention of the ecclesiastical offices of the Church being in governing roles during the Millennium, but a father in the covenant is a patriarch, and a king and a priest in his family. He holds that office forever, and will have the birthright, kingly and priesthood blessings Abraham, Isaac, and Jacob once had, before the sin of Reuben.

After Reuben's sin the Lord through the voice of father Israel, distributed these three blessings to three of his sons and their posterity; the birthright went to Joseph and his posterity through Ephraim and Manasseh; the right of kings went to Judah and his posterity; and the offices of the temporal priesthood went to Levi and his posterity.

With the gospel's restoration in our day, however, these three blessings are being conferred upon all males who enter the higher ordinances connected with the Lord's temples, regardless of lineage, personal righteousness being the soul criterion. These blessings and living worthy of their continuation are essential to being ready for the final judgment, at least for those who aspire to a celestial glory, eternal life and returning to the presence of God the Father.

From our review of the scriptures we see that all the families of the earth are being blessed and will continue to be blessed through the Lord's covenant people Israel, the true believers in Messiah/Christ. These blessings come to all families of the earth who accept the invitation to come unto Messiah/Christ and be perfected in Him. All those who hear the messages of those already in the covenant and act upon them by being born of the water and of the Spirit, are no longer strangers or foreigners, but fellow citizens with the Saints and of the household of God; and after they have partaken of the ordinances of the temple they become candidates for a celestial glory and a return to the presence of God the Father.

Whether they be of literal lineage of Abraham and Israel or adopted into their families by entering the covenant, they position themselves to be recipients of the redemptive powers of Messiah/Christ, patterning their lives after Him, and perfecting their lives step by step, principle by principle, under the canopy of a Zion Society.

As the gospel floods the earth and its messages permeate nations, kindreds, tongues and peoples, those attracted to its light will continue to be gathered spiritually and geographically, becoming part of the Zion Society which will become the new world order, and such will it be when the Savior or Messiah/Christ appears again on earth.

But what kind of organization will be in place after he comes? Will it be an extension of the current structure including Bishoprics, Stake Presidencies and Area Presidencies etc, or will it continue to shift to the patriarchal order, the priesthood order of the days of Abraham, Isaac and Israel until there is no further need for these administrative offices?

What transition steps organizationally lie ahead preparatory to the final judgment after the Millennium? And what will be the roles of the various tribes of Israel in this effort?

Transitional steps to return the established Zion Society's organizational structure to that of a patriarchal order likened to that of the days of Abraham, Isaac and Israel have not yet been revealed, but some outlines indicating such changes are now dimly seen.

To better understand them, we look to the blessings given by father Israel to his twelve sons and their posterity shortly before his death, as he prophesied what would befall them in the last days.

We do know that large numbers of the lost ten tribes of Israel must return, and the lineage of each person of each tribe is to be determined by record or by revelation. We do know that 144,000 high priests will be called by the Lord, 12,000 from each of the twelve tribes of Israel, and these high priests will have particular spiritual and temporal roles to play in helping the Lord bring to pass the eternal life of all who choose to enter the covenant and keep its provisions.

As mentioned in Chapter IV, just as resurrection or being saved from mortal death is a free gift, and we don't have to do any earthly thing to obtain it, because our Savior ransomed us by paying the price for Adam's transgression; so certain blessings accrue to the posterity of Abraham, Isaac and Israel because these three obeyed the voice of God, and their posterity do not have to do any earthly thing to obtain these blessings.

However, being saved from spiritual death is a different matter. The Savior, in addition to paying the price for Adam's transgression, paid the price of our sins also, but He did so on condition of our repentance and our compliance with His stipulation that we must be born of the water and of the spirit, else we cannot enter the kingdom of God. Lineage, no matter how illustriously, cannot save us from spiritual death, but repentance, personal righteousness, compliance with requirements of the covenant and the approval of Lord, can.

Because some of the Lord's blessings accrued to Israel's posterity, literal and adopted, they have important roles to play, responsibilities to meet, and work to perform in these last days and on into the Millennium. Twelve thousand high priests from each of the tribes of Israel are part of that organizational structure. From an examination of the blessings Israel gave his twelve sons just prior to his death recorded in Genesis, we gain some insight concerning the roles each of these tribes will play in these last days.

Since a spiritual and a geographical gathering of Israel is underway, it would appear that the spiritual gathering will continue to be led by the posterity of Joseph to whom the birthright blessing was given, and through his two sons Ephraim and Manasseh.

The greater blessing was given to Ephraim by Israel, but Manasseh was also given his blessing at the same time, when Israel placed his right hand upon Ephraim's head and his left hand upon Manasseh.

Manasseh and his posterity were made one of the twelve tribes Israel along with Ephraim; Ephraim having replaced Joseph and Manasseh replaced Levi. Levi's posterity did not receive a land blessing, but were distributed among all the other tribes with responsibilities to perform priestly duties of a temporal nature. By replacing Joseph in this manner with Ephraim and Manasseh, the Lord's promise to give Joseph a double portion for saving Israel's house from death was fulfilled.

As the kingdom of Judah was about to fall the Lord led selected persons of the lineage of Manasseh and Ephraim out of Jerusalem and to the land of America. They brought with them the writings of the house of Judah and added their own scriptures as an another testament of Messiah/Christ. Later they buried that record

527

which was found with the Lord's help generations later. Thus, just as the posterity of Judah kept the record we know as the Bible's Old Testament and gave it to the world, which foretold the coming of Messiah, the posterity of Joseph through Ephraim and Manasseh kept another testament of Messiah or Christ on the American continent and gave it to the world. These tribes are now blessed with the major responsibility and opportunity of preparing the two Jerusalems one in the Holy land and the New Jerusalem in America for the return of Messiah/Christ; thereby returning to the structure after the united kingdom under Solomon was divided: the southern kingdom under the leadership of Judah's posterity and the northern kingdom of Israel under the leadership of Ephraim's posterity. These two kingdom's will then be united as one kingdom again, under the leadership of the Messiah/Christ.

Just prior to Israel's joint blessing of Ephraim and Manasseh, he gave a blessing to Joseph in which he said Joseph's posterity [through Ephraim and Manasseh] would become a multitude of people, and they would receive lands of inheritance.

It was Joseph who preserved the spiritual blessings of Israel's family, in addition to saving them from mortal death because of the famine. Joseph's saving the family of Israel from spiritual and temporal death was a type and a shadow of things to come through the Savior who would save all mankind from spiritual and temporal death. It is Joseph's posterity that has been given the assignment to bring the Zion Society into fruition in these last days, as part of the birthright blessing.

But what are the assignments of the other tribes and what is the nature of the work they are to do in these final days just prior to and after the ushering in of the Millennium?

Much work of a spiritual and temporal nature must be accomplished to ready the earth and its people for the scheduled upgrade of both. Mankind is still under command of God, not only to multiply, and replenish the earth, but to subdue it, or bring it under control, probably by using priesthood powers of a high order, including sealing powers like those that Elijah the prophet possessed and used, enabling him to control the elements. Elijah was able to call down fire from heaven, to seal the heavens with no rain for three and a half years until he called for it, was able to bless a widow's meal and a cruse oil in a miraculous way, and was able to raise a boy from the dead.

These sealing powers and others of the Melchizedek Priesthood, including the power to move mountains, to turn waters out of their course, and to hold off armies, are vested in righteous holders of this priesthood. These powers, which transcend the powers of man on this earth, will likely be used to subdue it, bring it under control and return it to a paradise like unto Eden before the Fall.

With the consumption of all corrupted things in the course of the events surrounding the Saviors' return, it would appear that whatever infrastructure for the Zion Society on earth in its upgraded state is needed will be put in place. The intelligence, knowledge, skills and priesthood powers of the members of these tribes ,coupled with their natures, as prophesied, will likely be pressed into service. There will likely be a structure in place to govern both temporal and spiritual matters, so that the people have places to live, and things to do in both areas and are governed in an orderly manner.

The temporal priesthood including the offices of deacon, teacher and priest, and bishop rightly belong to the tribe of Levi and they once again will perform them, particularly the role of a bishop as it pertains to tithes and offerings, houses of worship and care of the poor and needy.

It would appear that a huge building program will be undertaken during the Millennium. This program is likely be headed by the sons of Levi with resources provided by all. The house of Judah will likely provide a disproportionate share. The sons of Levi will once again offer an offering unto the Lord in righteousness, probably in tithes and other offerings, and in all temporal affairs.

The right of kings was conferred upon Judah and it would appear that his posterity will have important governing roles to play within the Zion Society, fulfilling father Israel's blessing that, "thou art he whom thy brethren shall praise ...thy father's children shall bow down before thee ... the scepter shall not depart from Judah, nor a lawgiver from between his feet, until Shiloh [Messiah] come and unto him shall the gathering of the people be."

From apocryphal writings we learn that both Reuben and Simeon married Canaanite women. Among their descendants will be 12,000 high priests from each tribe. It would seem that given that Canaan was descended from Ham that Reuben and Simeon's posterity led by their respective 12,000 high priests will play important roles in the gathering, perfection and redemption of Ham's posterity.

Father Israel's blessing of Zebulun indicates his posterity were to dwell near the sea, and that they were sailors and fishers. From other sources we learn that Zebulun indeed earned his living from the sea during the summer and kept sheep with his brethren in the winter. He gave food and clothing generously to neighbors and friends in need, explaining "even as a man doeth to his neighbor, even so will the Lord do to him."

He counseled his children not to hesitate in showing compassion and mercy to all men. No doubt Zebulun's posterity will play important roles in seeing to it that there are no poor and needy in Zion, and perhaps will set up the distribution of food and other temporal resources via the ships of the sea.

Zebulun married Merushah, daughter of Molad, the son of Abida, the son of Midian, the son of Abraham, through Keturah. It would seem that the 12,000 high priests of Zebulun and his posterity might well be assigned to help gather, perfect and redeem Abraham's posterity through Midian and the other sons of Abraham through Keturah.

Issachar was faithful, strong and a good follower. He stuck to the tasks at hand and did not seek power or glory, or the vain things of life. He counseled his children to shun envy, evil, maliciousness, and to walk in guilelessness, to love the Lord and their neighbors, and to have compassion upon the poor and the weak.

Issachar, accompanied his brother Levi to the land of the east and took a wife, a daughter of Jobah, the son of Yoktan, the son of Eber and her name was Aridah. It would seem therefore, the 12,000 high priests of Issachar and his posterity's assignment might well include working with Eber's posterity who had settled in the far east.

Dan had married a Moabite named Aphlaleth, daughter of Chamudan. He had seen in vision the return of his posterity after their dispersion and that they would settle in the New Jerusalem where the righteous rejoice, and that the Lord would come and dwell among them in a place like unto Eden. Dan, wise as a serpent, shall judge his people, as father Israel prophesied he would. It appears likely the 12,000 high priests of Dan may well help gather, perfect and redeem the posterity of Abraham's father Terah through his brother Haran and nephew Lot.

Gad had also married the daughter of Amuram, the son of Uz, the son of Nahor, Abraham's brother. Her name was Urith. Though Gad's posterity was initially overcome and over powered by others, they will overcome at the last and be redeemed of the Lord. Gad was overcome with a hatred that he had for his brother Joseph, because he felt Joseph had given a false report to father Israel about a lamb he and his brothers Dan and Naphtali had slain. But through the course of his life he overcame this hatred and forgave Joseph for his alleged trespasses and taught his posterity to replace hatred with love, and to be forgiving of those who transgress against them. It appears the 12,000 high priests of Gad may play an important role in the gathering, perfection and redemption of the posterity of Abraham's brother, Nahor.

Naphtali also went to Haran with Gad to obtain a wife, and brought back with him Merimah, daughter of Amuram, the son of Uz, the son of Nahor Abraham's brother. Naphtali was swift as a deer and served his father as a runner, while young carrying messages on several important journeys. Naphtali said that the Lord made the physical body of man, after the likeness of the body of man's spirit, one perfectly fitting the other, and that God created every man after his own image, but each man and woman is a unique person. He knew the writings of Enoch and encouraged his posterity to unite with the posterity of Levi and Judah, declaring through them salvation shall arise upon Israel, that Messiah would come through their loins. It appears that the 12,000 high priests of Naphtali will also help gather, perfect, and redeem the posterity of Abraham's father Terah, through his brother Nahor.

Asher had initially married a descendant of Ishmael, son of Abraham through Hagar, but she died without offspring, so he married a widow, a daughter of Abimael, a descendant of Eber and Shem. He and his posterity had been assured they would always have plenty to eat. Asher had prophesied that the Most High God would come Himself as a man, eating and drinking, and would have power greater than Satan. He was and is to save all Israel and the Gentiles as well. Asher's 12,000 high priests will likely help gather, perfect and redeem the posterity of Eber and Shem, their forebears.

Israel had sent to Haran to obtain a wife for Benjamin. Her name was Mechalia, the daughter of Aram, the son of Zoba, the son of Terah, Abraham's father. Benjamin's posterity in large measure merged with the posterity of Judah. As his life came to a close Benjamin recalled the words of father Israel and declared that though his brother was scorned and rejected and sold into Egypt by his brethren, Joseph had compassion on them, forgave them and saved them from a famine of bread. Drawing a parallel to this experience, Benjamin declared a blameless one, a Lamb of God, would be sent to save all Israel and all the world from the sins of its people.

Benjamin implored his children to walk in holiness according to the commandments of the Lord, promising them they would again dwell securely and all Israel shall be gathered unto the Lord. In that day, he, Benjamin, would no longer be called a ravening wolf on account of his posterity's ravages, but rather would be called a worker of the Lord, apparently in reference to father Israel's blessing.

Given the posterity of Benjamin's close identification with Judah's posterity their 12,000 high priests may well do work similarly to those of Judah, but also helping to gather, perfect and redeem the posterity of Abraham's father Terah.

The priesthood held by Abraham, conferred upon him by Melchizedek, came down from the fathers from Shem, son of Noah through whom the covenant blessings had been continued. We see from the intermarriages of the sons of Israel the lineage of Ham's posterity is represented through Reuben, Simeon and to some extent Judah. If would seem therefore, that these tribes will have a major role to play in helping to gather, perfect and redeem all of this lineage. Helping to gather, perfect and redeem the posterity of Shem will likely rest with several of the tribes indicated above.

Given Japheth, the third son of Noah, was enlarged by the Lord, and many believe they settled early in the Far East, such enlargement may account for the great populations of Asia. Genesis indicates Japhath shall also dwell in the tents of Shem, implying receptivity to the messages of the covenant, and a responsibility on the part of all of covenant Israel and their tribes to help gather, perfect and redeem the posterity of Japheth.

Much of the above is speculation, and should be treated as such. It is presented here, simply to stimulate the reader's thinking about the great work of redemption which lies ahead and who will do it. All of the Lord's covenant people will be of the lineage of these tribes of Israel, by assignment in the premortal world, or by adoption through entrance into the covenant while on earth.

While we do not yet see the outlines clearly as to what our respective assignments during the Millennium will be, we do know that we will be actively engaged in the gathering, perfection and redemption of all the world's people who elect to enter the covenant, and we will not be idle, whatever our efforts may be there.

The work of the Millennium prepares the earth for a celestial glory and prepares its people for the final judgment.Those found worthy will inherit the celestialized earth, will enter into the presence of God the Father and become heirs and joint heirs with Jesus Christ.

But much is to be done before the arrival of the Millennium. The work will be done and the prophecies by the Lord's authorized servants will be fulfilled. For in the words of Joseph Smith:

"the standard of truth has been erected; no unhallowed hand can stop the work from progressing; persecutions may rage, mobs may combine, armies may assemble, calumny may defame, but the truth of God will go forth boldly, nobly, and independent, till it has penetrated every continent, visited every clime, swept every country, and sounded in every ear, till the purposes of God shall be accomplished, and the Great Jehovah shall say the work is done." (Wentworth Letter)

The work to which he refers is the work and glory of God, which is to bring to pass the immortality and eternal life of all who come unto Christ, are perfected in Him, redeemed through His atonement, and are returned to the presence of God the Eternal Father in a perfected, glorified and exalted state.

Bibliography

1. The Holy Bible, Authorized King James Version, Old and New Testaments, The Church of Jesus Christ of Latter-day Saints, Salt Lake City 1979.

2. The Holy Scriptures Containing the Old and New Testaments, Board of Publication of the Reorganized Church of Jesus Christ of Latter Day Saints, Independence, 1964.

3. Smith, Joseph Jr., Translator, The Book of Mormon, The Church of Jesus Christ of Latter-day Saints, Salt Lake City, 1981.

4. Smith, Joseph Jr., The Pearl of Great Price, A Selection from the Revelations, translations and Narrations of Joseph, The Church of Jesus Christ of Latter-day Saints, Salt Lake City, 1981.

5. Smith, Joseph Jr., Prophet, The Doctrine and Covenants, The Church of Jesus Christ of Latter-day Saints, Salt Lake City, 1981.

6. Heap, Norman L., Adam, Enoch and Noah, Adam, Family History Publications, Walnut Creek, CA. 1992.

7. Heap, Norman L., The Twelve Sons of Israel, Family History Publications, Walnut Creek, CA. 1988.

8. Heap, Norman L., Moses, Aaron and Joshua, Family History Publications, Walnut Creek, CA. 1990.

9. Heap, Norman L., Redeemer of Israel, Family History Publications, Walnut Creek, CA. 1995.

10. Heap, Norman L., Abraham, Isaac and Jacob, Vantage Press, New York, 1986.

11. The Lost Books of the Bible and the Forgotten Books of Eden, including the Testament of the Twelve Patriarchs, World Publishing Company, Cleveland, 1926.